LATIN AMERICAN SOCIAL MOVEMENTS IN THE TWENTY-FIRST CENTURY

Latin American Perspectives in the Classroom
Series Editor: Ronald H. Chilcote

LATIN AMERICAN SOCIAL MOVEMENTS IN THE TWENTY-FIRST CENTURY

Resistance, Power, and Democracy

Edited by
Richard Stahler-Sholk, Harry E. Vanden,
and Glen David Kuecker

ROWMAN & LITTLEFIELD PUBLISHERS, INC.
Lanham • Boulder • New York • Toronto • Plymouth, UK

ROWMAN & LITTLEFIELD PUBLISHERS, INC.

Published in the United States of America
by Rowman & Littlefield Publishers, Inc.
A wholly owned subsidiary of The Rowman & Littlefield Publishing Group, Inc.
4501 Forbes Boulevard, Suite 200, Lanham, Maryland 20706
www.rowmanlittlefield.com

Estover Road, Plymouth PL6 7PY, United Kingdom

British Library Cataloguing in Publication Information Available

Library of Congress Cataloging-in-Publication Data

Latin American social movements in the twenty-first century : resistance, power, and
democracy / edited by Richard Stahler-Sholk, Harry E. Vanden, and Glen David Kuecker.
    p. cm. — (Latin American perspectives in the classroom)
  Includes bibliographical references and index.
  ISBN-13: 978-0-7425-5646-1 (cloth : alk. paper)
  ISBN-10: 0-7425-5646-8 (cloth : alk. paper)
  ISBN-13: 978-0-7425-5647-8 (pbk. : alk. paper)
  ISBN-10: 0-7425-5647-6 (pbk. : alk. paper)
  1. Social movements—Latin America. I. Stahler-Sholk, Richard. II. Kuecker, Glen David.
III. Vanden, Harry E.
  HN110.5.A8L398 2008
  303.48'4098—dc22

                                                                            2007043056

Printed in the United States of America

♾™ The paper used in this publication meets the minimum requirements of American
National Standard for Information Sciences—Permanence of Paper for Printed Library
Materials, ANSI/NISO Z39.48-1992.

Contents

Foreword

THE LATIN AMERICAN PERSPECTIVES in the Classroom series evolved from themes emanating from the bimonthly journal *Latin American Perspectives* (*LAP*), which since its inception has desired to make its material available for classroom use. The goal of this series is to introduce curious readers and students to important themes and issues about Latin America that have appeared in the journal and to integrate these themes and new material into coherent readers for classroom use. Pedagogically, we trim articles to their essential content, reorganize them into teachable clusters, add contextualized commentary, and prepare introductory essays. With this consistency and organization, we intend that our series be different from the often abortive efforts of other publishers to develop textbook anthologies. We also want these volumes to be relevant to a broad range of interests in the social sciences and humanities, with particular attention to Latin America.

Latin American Social Movements in the Twenty-first Century delves into the roots, evolution, and implications of social movements and their resistance to neoliberal and global capitalism. Case studies illustrate aspects of the current upsurge in social movements and activism and their political impact. This volume intends to transcend and confront mainstream literature that has focused on "transitions to democracy" and that has envisaged social movements first as a temporary resistance to bureaucratic-authoritarian regimes and, later, as secondary to the electoral politics, formal democracy, and political parties that supplanted the repressive regimes. The recent resurgence of social movements and mobilization of masses is thus seen as response and resistance to the advance of global capitalism.

The editors of this volume have worked hard through several phases to bring this material together and make it accessible. Initially, there was a lengthy process of review and revision of material submitted for the March 2007 issue of the journal, followed by a close look at and revision of additional essays intended to fill gaps and to delve into essential issues around social movements. Additionally, some writings on social movements from past *LAP* issues were integrated along with introductory material intended to provide guidance and open up discussion of key issues.

All this effort has led to a coherent volume carefully organized and intelligently presented in easily readable form. This accomplishment would not have been possible without the substantial contribution of editors Richard Stahler-Sholk, Harry E. Vanden, and Glen Kuecker and of the *LAP* journal editors who evaluated each manuscript and worked closely with authors to revise and shape their material into publishable form.

Ronald H. Chilcote
Series Editor

1

Introduction

Richard Stahler-Sholk, Harry E. Vanden,
and Glen David Kuecker

THE PAST TWO DECADES have seen an upsurge of Latin American social movements, challenging the neoliberal paradigm and the governments that would impose it. In 1994, *Latin American Perspectives* published two special issues on social movements. Edited by David Slater (1994b, 1994c), these issues focused on the significant increase in research and theory concerning the intersections of politics, economics, society, and culture in social movements. The case studies presented in them pointed to the emergence of Latin America's new social movements as important actors. The growth of these movements has been the subject of intense study ever since. In today's context, such phenomena include the indigenous mobilizations led by the *Confederación de Nacionalidades Indígenas del Ecuador* (Confederation of Indigenous Nationalities of Ecuador—CONAIE), the *cocaleros* and mobilizations against water privatizations and gas pipeline investments in Bolivia, the Zapatista movement in Mexico, the *Movimento dos Trabalhadores Rurais Sem Terra* (Landless Rural Workers' Movement—MST) in Brazil, Afro-Colombians resisting displacement in a region coveted by investors, the *piquetero* eruptions of workers and the urban poor in the wake of Argentina's financial crisis, and the incipient cross-border and migrant movements and mobilizations against "free-trade" agreements. These new formulations of activism contest the region's political and economic systems and challenge traditional definitions of citizenship, democracy, and participation. As they contest power and policy, these mobilizations challenge traditional rule by the dominant economic classes and the politicians who enable it (see Vanden, 2003).

These phenomena transcend the expectations of the mainstream "transitions-to-democracy" literature, which interpreted social movements as a temporary outgrowth of the suppression of conventional politics by bureaucratic-authoritarian regimes of the 1960s to early 1980s, a trend that would fade again with the return of electoral democracy. But some of the early "redemocratization" literature did not stand up well under critical scrutiny (Nef, 1988; Petras and Morley, 1992). The intensification of social movements appears to be not only a continuation of historical resistance and mobilization of the masses, but also a specific response to the advance of neoliberal globalization within processes of nominal democratization that often mean competition among elites without significant participation or substantive social justice (Johnston and Almeida, 2006; Veltmeyer, 2007). Although it flows most strongly from the laboring classes, this resistance is, however, by no means exclusively manifested in class-based organizing. And while the global spread of free-trade market forces involves a rollback of the state, the neoliberal state has developed new functions of structuring and policing the new conditions for global capital accumulation. In this era of increasing globalization, pressure to become integrated into global markets threatens a heterogeneous group of social subjects who, in turn, are generating new resistance movements.

These new movements seek to define a novel relation to the formal political realm by fundamentally reworking relations of power. Unlike traditional guerrilla movements or electoral expressions of the Left, they are not fundamentally organized to seize state power. Yet they have contributed to destabilizing and in some cases ousting governments in, for example, Bolivia, Argentina, Ecuador, and, arguably, Mexico, while coexisting in awkward relationships with left-leaning parties such as Brazil's *Partido dos Trabalhadores* (Workers' Party—PT) and Mexico's *Partido de la Revolución Democrática* (Party of the Democratic Revolution—PRD), and guerrilla movements such as Mexico's *Ejército Popular Revolucionario* (Popular Revolutionary Army—EPR). And they have forced policy to the left in places like Argentina. Parallel to the increase in social protest movements is the development of movement-based politics of a populist variety such as Lavalas in Haiti, *chavismo* in Venezuela, the Evo Morales phenomenon in Bolivia, and Rafael Correa in Ecuador.

Mainstream observers have focused on the apparent ascendance of the electoral Left (in its domesticated or demonized variants) across the region as the twenty-first century begins. But perhaps significant for lasting change is the grassroots mobilization that gave those "left" parties an opening and continues to hold them accountable to their base. The new movements' ability to influence and articulate policy suggests that—to some extent—they actually can rule from below. There are parallels here to the tension between the mobilized base of the Unidad Popular coalition in Chile from 1970 to 1973 and the Allende government's effort to effect change from within the existing liberal-democratic institutions, and to the "radical moderation" of the Sandinista government in Nicaragua from 1979 to 1990 (Winn, 1986; Vanden and Prevost, 1993). From the Argentine cry of "*¡Que se vayan todos!*" ("Throw them all out!") to the Zapatista concept of *mandar obedeciendo* (rule by obeying), these movements are struggling for a radical redefinition of politics.

In 2007 we edited an issue of *Latin American Perspectives* (*LAP*) on the topic of social movements as resistance to globalization (Stahler-Sholk, Vanden, and Kuecker, 2007). It built upon the 1994 special issues on social movements and political change, which highlighted the early appearance of new forms of social protest in Latin America and illustrated exciting new developments in social theory applied by scholars attempting to understand the new movements. Our 2007 special issue explored new developments in social movement practice as well as theory. This book furthers the effort to understand Latin America's social movements by deepening empirical evidence from a variety of case studies and pushing theoretical frameworks. It includes a few classic articles from the 1994 issue to further illustrate how scholars' empirical and theoretical understandings of complex social realities have developed. Articles from the 2007 *LAP* special issue combine with several new case studies in exploration of these developments. Three sets of issues unite the collection: the *origin* and context of the upsurge of social movements, the *strategies* and dynamics of their struggles, and the *outcomes* and implications of the movements.

Origins of Contemporary Movements

It is hard to take the measure of a historical trend that is still happening. Rather than simply assuming the existence of the phenomenon in question, it is worth posing the basic question, what is really new about the Latin American social movements of recent decades (Kuecker, 2004)? The phrase "new social movements" (NSMs) has been in vogue since at least the early 1980s (Melucci, 1980; Tarrow, 1998). The early invocations of that phrase focused on the advanced industrialized capitalist societies, whose emerging "postmaterialist" values and redefinitions of equality and citizenship had supposedly shifted the locus of organizing from traditional unions and parties to new, amorphous groupings around values such as civil rights, environmentalism, gay rights, feminism, and planetary survival in the nuclear age (see, e.g., Laclau and Mouffe, 1985). Yet this analysis was questioned by Latin Americanists who noted a somewhat parallel phenomenon in a very different regional context (Foweraker, 1995; Slater, 1985, 1994a). The Latin American–enriched analysis of social movements added important comparative analyses, particularly the influential compilations by Eckstein and Alvarez (1992) and Alvarez, Dagnino, and Escobar (1998a). Some usefully questioned the dichotomous terminology of "old" and "new" movements (Fuentes and Frank, 1989), suggesting a more dynamic and interactive process of movements adapting to changing forms of the state and market. The new forms of global capitalism and the challenges of its reregulation—a transition in the "world system" for some—are part of the common context for changing responses of popular mobilization in both the center and the periphery of that system (Foran, 2003). Neoliberal restructuring or reregulation of global capitalism is caused by the breakdown of the Fordist system in the capitalist center and the emergence of flexible regimes of accumulation (D. Harvey, 1989). The devastating social impacts in Latin America are part of the context of the current wave of popular mobilization (Green, 2003; Prashad and Ballvé, 2006). Indeed, there is a strong argument to be made that the region is witnessing a sea change in politics and participation and that these new movements have taken full advantage of postcolonial definitions of agency and citizenship, the Internet and other globalized communication, transnational networks of resistance, and the political space that democratization has provided to create repertoires of resistance and action that are indeed new and subversive of traditional politics and traditional political culture (Gills, 2000c; Vanden, 2004, 2006). Social movements are in some senses "new" by definition in that they eschew the conventional political institutions of the day in favor of heterogeneous collections of groups and individuals, employing impolite ("contentious") tactics and organizing challenges to old social values. Without overdrawing the old/new discontinuity, analysts of social movements since the 1980s have noted their (1) tendency to seek *autonomy* from conventional/hierarchical political institutions, (2) attention to horizontal and participatory *process* in decision making, and (3) quest for *solidarity* derived from notions of social justice linked to shared subjective identities such as race/ethnicity or gender (Hellman, 1995).

Several things are noteworthy about the changing context for social-movement organizing since the 1980s. One is clearly the framework of globalization and the neoliberal free-market project, signaled by the 1982 debt crisis that began with the Mexican crash and inaugurated a wave of "structural adjustment programs" supervised by international financial institutions. These were actually predated by the monetarist orthodoxy of the "Chicago boys," reflecting the ultra-free-market ideology purveyed by University of Chicago economists Milton Friedman and Arnold Harberger and ushered into the halls of power by the 1973 coup in Chile (the "other September 11"). The standard economic formulas that were tellingly labeled the "Washington Consensus" revolved around public-sector cutbacks (austerity), privatization, and market-oriented realignment (economic liberalization) of trade and finance (Rosen and McFadyen, 1995).

More than simply a shrinking of the state, the neoliberal project called for a reconceptualization of the state and its interaction with civil society (Robinson, 2004; Hardt and Negri, 2000). The new globalized regime of capital accumulation converted states into brokers for a transnationalized capitalist class (Sklair, 2000). The resulting destabilization of the established citizenship compact (of nation-states) has been accompanied by a new sense of outrage (Vilas, 1996; Eckstein and Wickham-Crowley, 2003; Hershberg and Rosen, 2006). An example of this visceral response can be seen in Argentina's *escraches*, the graffiti/street theater that came in the wake of the country's financial meltdown in December 2000. Their art exposed politicians who were widely seen as betraying the public trust (i.e., the state-society pact). Neoliberal market reforms make the poor invisible by redefining citizenship as market participation. Today's social movements are battles to redefine citizenship, in effect constructing a broader and more inclusionary meaning (Kuecker, 2004; Vilas, 1997). In what Yashar (2005) calls the "postliberal challenge," Latin America's poor and marginalized are demanding collective citizenship rights, not just the individualism and formal equality promised by the marketplace that in practice leaves so many destitute and disempowered. Ironically, the liberal, U.S.-style market-linked version of democratization and the concomitant emphasis on procedural democratic guarantees has helped the popular struggle to open greater political space in which mobilizations and new forms of resistance can challenge the neoliberal model and the very capitalist conception of formal, representative democracy that underpins it.

The changing political context has also included a wave of regional transitions from various forms of authoritarianism to "low-intensity democracy" (Gills, 2000a). The transitions-to-democracy literature analyzing the demise of bureaucratic authoritarianism in South America noted the emergence of social movements where traditional political organizing had been thoroughly suppressed by the military regimes of the mid-1960s to mid-1980s. The Mexican case of soft authoritarianism was somewhat distinct, with a series of mobilizations and political crises (1968 Tlatelolco massacre, 1982 debt crisis, 1985 earthquake and political aftershocks, 1988 electoral fraud, 1994 Zapatista rebellion and peso crash) highlighting the failure of the state to address the needs of the people, leading to a partial political liberalization in 2000 that had stalled by 2006 (Rus and Tinker-Salas, 2006). In all these cases, many mainstream political pundits and practitioners assumed (hoped?) they would quietly go away, Rosie-the-Riveter-like, when normal politics returned. They have not.

In seeking to explain the spaces being occupied by these movements, some have argued that formal democracy in the sense of "choice" of leaders, devoid of much substantive content or direct participation—polyarchy—is the logical political complement of neoliberalism (Robinson, 1996). Parties and other traditional institutions become vehicles for technocrats and marketing specialists, and people lose interest and trust. The larger scale of global market structures and the shift of power to distant international institutions results in what mainstream political scientists call a "democratic deficit," a globalization from above that critics insist can be challenged from below by those who believe that "another world is possible," to use the slogan popularized by the World Social Forum and the global justice, or *altermundista*, movement (Brecher, Costello, and Smith, 2000). This shift, however, has ambiguous implications for the relation between social movements and formal political parties. In that gray area, some parties have tried to repackage themselves as movements, and parallel to the rise of social movements is the rise of populist formulas on both the left and the right, capitalizing on widespread cynicism about the political class.

The universal condemnation of authoritarian regimes and the atrocities they committed has thoroughly delegitimized and discredited the repressive mechanisms that were required to stop the popular mobilizations and revolutionary movements of the 1960s, 1970s, 1980s, and early 1990s. In accordance with the U.S democratic model, elitist control is increasingly being exercised by hegemonic control of the media and culture, as well as attempts to define democracy procedurally (democracy exists so long as there is freedom of press and assembly and bourgeois elections), regardless of whether it really is by, of, and for "the people"—a construct defined by the impoverished majority in Latin America. As new popular movements have broken this hegemony and insisted on real, effective, and participatory democracy, they have developed and refined mechanisms of power that promote liberation and invoke visions of a new society (see Vanden, 2006). What is still unclear is whether, even if they delegitimize, discredit, and disregard neoliberal policies and traditional forms of rule and control, they will be able to implement new policies and alternative conceptions of power, rule, and the state. The fundamental question is how much liberation can be achieved with mechanisms of power that endeavor to rule from below without actually taking power and utilizing state control to achieve their objectives. Some of the same issues that Slater's (1994a) essay posed fourteen years ago remain relevant in assessing where social movements have taken us today. While they pushed formal politics toward more procedural democracy and stretched the cultural boundaries of extra-institutional forms of political activism, do they have the revolutionary potential to fundamentally alter power relations and change the regional reality of exploitation and repression?

Finally, the changing context must also include the end of the cold war, formally symbolized by the 1989 fall of the Berlin Wall but perhaps under way in slow motion throughout the late Brezhnev-Reagan years. This change may have freed some of the Latin American Left from the weight of vanguard and centralizing political models, as Castañeda (1994) has rather smugly observed. The end of the cold war generated new debates about left strategies in Latin America (Ellner, 2004, 2006; Castañeda et al., 2005). The declining appeal of state socialism and of seizing state power from above also creates space for a different model of organizing from below (Holloway, 2002).

Movement Strategies and Dynamics

In studying what is new about the current wave of social movements, it is important not to romanticize social-movement cycles of protest or assume that the strategies will necessarily be effective just because they are noble or creative. Bearing in mind the historical context, it is useful to recall that whereas revolution was a prominent feature of the Latin American agenda from the 1960s through the 1980s, now we speak the different language of social movements, civil society, and contentious politics. Some of the current social movements are also not necessarily against capitalism but more narrowly oppose the particular form of capitalism that is neoliberalism, making at least some of them reformist rather than revolutionary. Indeed, we may need to rethink the very definition of *revolution* in an era of globalization, when the overthrow of the state is not necessarily the key to radical transformation of social relations (Stahler-Sholk, 2001b). Clearly it is not just the forms of popular struggle that have adapted but also the forms of organization of the state and market in dynamic interaction with each other. The essays in this book invite the reader to consider what strategies will work in the context of global capital and a downsized state.

Revolutionary movements and organizations of the past were excessively hierarchical and centralized, which proved problematical for horizontal democracy and empowerment of the mass base. Those that still cling to their vanguard models have lost momentum. An important question to consider is whether contemporary social movements are necessarily more internally democratic or progressive than other forms of organizing and whether they necessarily lead to higher levels of empowerment. Informal networks of power can be just as stultifying as more institutionalized hierarchies and perhaps harder to change. The old revolutionary movements often found that seizing state power was hard enough, but social and ideological transformations were even more difficult. It is not yet clear that contemporary social movements solve these problems by skipping straight to the transformation phase without a foothold in state power. Before celebrating the separation from parties and other traditional organizations—the "fetishism of autonomy," as Hellman (1992) calls it—we need to ask whether that autonomy yields more horizontal participatory and transparent processes, and whether it is an effective organizing strategy. A cautionary example is the caudillo model of populists, who claim to be above politics yet mobilize from above for their own purposes. At the same time, the bottom-up emphasis of new left social movements may come at the expense of organizational focus and ideological coherence.

Another strategic challenge facing social movements is how to generate and sustain a subjective sense of solidarity in the face of the atomizing effect of the neoliberal policies applied across the region for over two decades. The new movements are defining agents of social change in ways that cut across old categories—for example, the Brazilian MST recruiting among landless peasants and urban favela dwellers; the Argentine piqueteros bringing together elements of the middle class, the workers, the unemployed, and other urban poor; and Mexico's Zapatistas issuing appeals to all those "on the left and at the bottom." The effectiveness of these attempts to construct new social subjects depends on whether they build community and collective consciousness so that the perceived commonalities of interest are transformed into durable alliances.

A related issue is the strategy of organizing around identities such as race, ethnicity, and gender. The "old Left" often suffered from blindness to any identity besides class, a category derived from material relations of production. But nonmaterial identities, woven around economic relations, influence people's willingness to act. The challenge for social movements is to connect the dots of identity-based forms of resistance that are very localized, making it very hard for geographically dispersed pockets of mobilization to communicate, interact, and do what is necessary to form a collective consciousness around an identity issue. The organizing challenge is, for example, for Afro-Colombians in the Chocó and indigenous people in Mesoamerica to see that they are being displaced from ancestral lands in the interest of mega-investment schemes such as dams and canals, and for targets of femicide in Ciudad Juárez to see the structures of transnational capital that produce the maquiladoras and drug cartels that interact with patriarchal ideologies in a murderous brew. Identity politics are problematical in terms of forming the larger collective consciousness that may be necessary for a revolutionary agenda. Lacking that agenda, being fragmented leaves identity-based movements vulnerable to co-optation, as in what Charles R. Hale (2004) calls "managed neoliberal multiculturalism" or the "*indio* permitido." Identity does not have to be a narrow and exclusionary basis for mobilization, but connecting such identity to broader struggles against neoliberalism is a strategic challenge.

The relation between social movements and allegedly progressive parties and governments is another challenge. The dilemmas can be seen in the various positions reflected, for example, in the Brazilian MST's critical distance from the ruling PT, the Zapatistas' avoidance of the PRD electoral sideshow, and the Ecuadorian indigenous movement's ambivalence toward the Pachacutik option of morphing from movement into party. The Argentine piqueteros divided over responses to reformist concessions by the Kirchner administration. Left-leaning governments face the discipline of global financial markets, as illustrated by "Lula Lite" in Brazil and by the market-friendly platform of the 2006 presidential candidate Andrés Manuel López Obrador in Mexico. The Chávez administration in Venezuela, with its oil resources, may be the exception that proves the rule, but the government's autonomy from international finance does not necessarily mean social-movement independence from the government (Ellner and Tinker-Salas, 2005). It remains to be seen how Bolivian President Evo Morales will fare in facing the dual pressures of grassroots mobilization and international constraints.

Similarly, the strategy of forming transnational social movement networks is a double-edged sword. They may be a necessary response to the organizing advantages of increasingly mobile global capital, but old colonial patterns may be replicated in the relation between northern-dominated nongovernmental organizations (NGOs) and local grassroots organizations in the South. Not every component of civil-society organizing is a social movement, and not all social movements are progressive. Institutions such as the Inter-American Development Bank or corporate-sponsored outfits like Conservation International have learned the advantages of funding workshops for well-behaved local groups to undercut the initiative of more radical bottom-up mobilizing.

By the early twenty-first century, it was clear that a quarter century of neoliberal policies had failed to improve economic growth or income distribution (Sunkel, 2005; Reygadas, 2006). Yet the neoliberal agenda evolved beyond its original formulation as a specific set of economic policy prescriptions, leaving a cultural and political legacy of a shrinking concept of the public realm. States and international organizations retooled their discourse to endorse and fund "civil society participation," creating an ongoing danger that social movements might lose their autonomy as they become institutionalized and transformed into NGOs (Foweraker, 2005), and that in filling in the gaps where the state has withdrawn as guarantor of rights, social movement organizations could end up reinforcing the neoliberal reconfiguration of citizenship based on the market and individual responsibility (Dagnino, 2006).

What Now? Assessing Social Movement Outcomes

If contemporary social movements aim to bring about fundamental change without taking state power, they nevertheless have to have some effect on the state. Their lasting impact may depend on their ability to bring about change in political institutions to consolidate their gains. Civic mass protest movements have demonstrated a capacity to bring down governments, but if they are not going to enter the new governments themselves they need to devise another way to affect policy beyond the yes-or-no referendum of the street. Revolutionary movements of the past that had the goal of taking state power (and sometimes succeeded) faced problems of how a movement organized for insurrection might become one that governs (Selbin, 1998); or, in the Sandinista case in Nicaragua, how to go back to being a movement that might "govern from below," in the language of Daniel Ortega's unfulfilled promise of 1990. Contemporary social movements that do not seek state power nevertheless have to deal with issues of internal power relations in their organizations and parallel governance in their territorial spaces. The challenges can be seen in the Zapatistas' bold and creative solution of *Juntas de Buen Gobierno* (Good Governance Councils) and "leading by obeying," an experiment that appears promising but does not entirely avoid the issue of how to transform the state—a challenge that they have taken up since late 2005 with the national outreach known as "the Other Campaign" (N. Harvey, 2005).

If we think of social movements that are concentrating on organizing civil society rather than taking state power in terms of a Gramscian war of position, we also need to be aware that changing power relations through resistance leads to countermeasures by the state, including sophisticated strategies of low-intensity conflict and low-intensity democracy. As social movements are experimenting with new strategies, there are also adaptations in the "Washington consensus" on neoliberal economics and in the politics of counterinsurgency (Kuecker, 2004). With the Free Trade Area of the Americas (FTAA) stalled in its original formulation, the package is being broken into little bits, as bilateral agreements negotiated between the United States and individual Latin American countries, and pushed through piecemeal. Riding the wave of social movements, international financial institutions and "development" agencies are co-opting the language of civil-society participation and sustainability, with PowerPoint-ready workshops to train their preferred domesticated intermediaries.

The outcomes of today's social movements will not be apparent until after a few more rounds of these dynamic struggles. Some of the keys will include the ability of the movements to create local self-sufficient economies that represent viable alternatives to global capitalism and regional social movement solidarity such as the Latin American women's movement, Vía Campesina, or the Mesoamerican coalitions against the Central American Free Trade Agreement (CAFTA) and Plan Puebla-Panamá (PPP). In raising the unanswered question of social movement outcomes, an issue that remains to be explored is whether the resistance can survive if it does not put forward a coherent anticapitalist alternative. In an era of globalization and mobile capital, creating local political and economic autonomy without transforming larger structures (i.e., revolutionary change) may mean that the problems caused by those structures are simply displaced to other places in the world that are not organized in local resistance. Alternative models that seem locally promising (such as fair-trade, organic shade-grown coffee) do not necessarily translate into a globally sustainable model of alternative development.

New Ideas, New Praxis

The essays in this collection include several classic pieces from the 1994 issue of *Latin American Perspectives*, plus a body of work that brings new research and new perspectives to bear on these questions of origin, strategy, and outcomes of social movements in Latin America today.

Part I of this volume traces the historical evolution of Latin American social movement practice and theorizing, beginning with Slater's 1994 essay. He marks an important departure from orthodox, class-driven Marxist approaches to social movements by acknowledging the diversity between and within social movements. Informed by feminist scholarship, Slater embraces difference and thus opens explorations of multiple points and forms of resistance and reconsiderations of power. Multiple subjectivities of social actors raised new political questions for Slater, leading him to explore how Latin American social movements pursued more radical meanings of democracy. Slater's analysis also puts on the table the difficult question of the transformative promise and limitations of identity-driven social movements. While the new wave of social movements offers a radical political imaginary, Slater cautions that the imaginary might not necessarily be revolutionary in practice. After fourteen years, this caution remains a valid observation. In the following chapter, Vanden frames the current wave of social movements in historical context. He uses the examples of the Brazilian MST and Bolivian indigenous movements to reflect on historical continuities and discontinuities, highlighting new repertoires of collective action including national mobilizations that have altered or toppled governments.

Part II focuses on the political economy of neoliberalism, examining how the global free-market paradigm influences conditions for popular organizing. Hellman's 1994 article draws on the Mexican experience since the 1982 debt crisis, arguing that the downsizing of the state disrupted the traditional clientelist patterns of state-society interaction that had sustained the one-party dominance of the *Partido Revolucionario Institucional* (Institutional Revolutionary Party—PRI). The analysis not only helps understand the rise of Mexican independent organizing and the PRI's 2000 electoral defeat, it also suggests that the market-driven breakdown of old citizenship compacts throughout Latin America can create a space for new democratizing demands from below, so that the political implications of neoliberalism are far from predetermined. Spronk and Webber take a structuralist approach to the origins and context for emergence of social movements, comparing the Bolivian mobilizations over control of natural gas and water. Drawing on David Harvey's (2003) concept of "accumulation by dispossession" (which updates Marx's concept of primitive accumulation for the postcolonial/neoliberal era), they emphasize differences between these movements stemming from the different strategic places of the two resources in today's global capitalist system. Spronk and Webber are attuned to questions of agency and issue framing that shaped each movement. Both of these chapters, in contrast to the old "resource mobilization" approach to comparing the economic and political resources of power contenders and their "political opportunity structures" (Tilly, 1978; McAdam, McCarthy, and Zald, 1996), specifically address the changing macro context of neoliberal capitalism and the social movements embedded within.

The essays in part III explore movement strategies and dynamics, examining in particular the importance of subjective consciousness in the process of constructing new social subjects. Kuecker takes us into the life experiences of communities in the Ecuadorian mountains confronting transnational mining. The essay offers a close-up portrait of a movement, highlighting the centrality of community-building strategies in forging the collective consciousness and motivation of participants. His study also raises a critical larger strategic question of whether local victories are sufficient to challenge mobile capital in a global system. Stahler-Sholk's piece on the Zapatista autonomy movement examines some of the ambiguities and pitfalls of the concept of "autonomy" in the era of globalization. The Zapatista movement, while deeply rooted in the local through the construction of alternative models of community in Chiapas, is also struggling to find a strategy of wider mobilization that will help bring about macro changes in Mexican national politics and in the articulation to the global economy. Issa's article on the Brazilian MST, Latin America's largest social movement, adds new perspective on the ideological dimension of organizing. Focusing on the concept of *mística*, she explores the processes that built a subjective sense of solidarity among the social subjects of rural struggles in Brazil, a key factor in MST's growth and longevity.

Ethnicity and race are the focus of the chapters in part IV. Mora, writing on the Zapatistas, focuses on indigenous identity. She illustrates how the movement's formulation of indigenous collective rights destabilizes the neoliberal paradigm but also poses challenges for an old-left vision still wedded narrowly to class analysis. Becker's study of the indigenous Pachacutik movement in Ecuador highlights the intersection of ethnicity and class, focusing on the dilemmas and compromises involved in the movement's decisions about joining with a broader array of social forces in entering the party/electoral arena. Becker demonstrates why the movement had more success in ousting a government than in creating a replacement. Dixon's study of Afro-Colombians reminds us that race has long been an overlooked dimension of popular organizing in Latin America. He shows how Afro-Colombians recast their struggles in the framework of human rights as part of a strategy of black movements throughout Latin America to leverage transnational support networks. This argument is an example of how mobilizing around identities that transcend national borders (such as race) constitutes a new strategy for confronting neoliberal policies, which in the Colombian case contribute to violent displacement that disproportionately affects black and indigenous communities. Perry's article on black women's neighborhood movements in Brazil takes an ethnographic look at the intersection of race with gender and class, exposing the global invisibility of the movement. She examines how black women domestic workers strategically use their knowledge as "outsiders-within," choosing to organize within the gendered domain of their neighborhoods for the collective benefit of their communities. Like Dixon, Perry illustrates how social actors creatively redefine sites of contention in confronting the neoliberal model.

The essays in part V focus on gender and women's movements. Schild's 1994 article broke new ground, questioning whether women's movements would return to invisibility with the return of electoral democracy to Chile and elsewhere or whether they had effectively redefined the political. She argues for engendering the analysis of social movements rather than simply adding on women as another set of cases (assigned to women social scientists in a gendered division of labor). Swanger's contribution brings us the feel and the voices of emerging solidarity among women organizing in the alienating Mexico-U.S. border environment of Ciudad Juárez, where women struggle in the twilight zone of maquiladora sweatshop labor and gendered violence. Her close examination of the internal dynamics of organizing conveys a sense that the consciousness-raising is more important for the long term than the specific organizational forms and outcomes in the short term.

Part VI highlights some of the complexities of social movement "repertoires of contention" and alliance strategies, with two analyses of the movements of Argentine workers and neighborhoods arising out of the financial crisis of the 1990s. Villalón's contribution on the Argentine piqueteros illustrates not only the diverse social origins of movement participants who largely left their old party and union ties behind, but also the richly creative range of strategies and tactics they deployed. Echoing Slater's warning, Villalón's analysis carries a cautionary note about outcomes, as the breadth of the coalitions proves a source of strain and the electoral Left co-opts a layer of leadership from the movement with a modicum of social compensation. Alcañiz and Scheier focus on a specific radical group within the piquetero movement that adopted a creative strategy, building on Communist Party networks and cooperative economic projects to gain financial and organizational autonomy from the state while resisting party control. These case studies illustrate the dilemmas of movement strategy and the complexities of sustainability.

Finally, part VII examines transnational dimensions of social movement organizing. Swords's article recasts the scope of the Zapatista case by examining social movement "networks," specifically groups inspired to organize in parallel to the Zapatista initiative. She shows how the movement has altered political discourse about democracy and development, suggesting that transnational issue framing is part of the changing movement response to neoliberal globalization. Martínez and Rosset examine a network that links peasant movements beyond the geographical confines of Latin America. *La Vía Campesina* (the Peasant Way) represents a transnational social movement that grew out of Latin American agrarian struggles. They document how the movement used collective and rotating leadership, internal political training, and autonomy of member organizations to build a coalition that reinforces an identity of peasant internationalism and shapes global discourse on issues such as people's food sovereignty. Spalding's chapter focuses on Mesoamerican mobilizing against neoliberal trade and investment schemes, specifically PPP and CAFTA. Her analysis of this transnational resistance network points to the challenges of organizing against globalization processes that continually shift the locus of decision making, requiring tremendous agility in adapting between insider/outsider and national/international modes of organizing. While the movement was not immediately successful in stopping either initiative, it did build important consciousness about corporate trade and development agendas in ways that affected the political landscape.

In the editors' concluding essay, we highlight some trends and raise some critical questions for further reflection and action. There are still gaps in the research agenda on Latin American social movements. There have been significant advances in understanding the movements' origins and dynamics, but more theoretical work is needed on their outcomes. The region's political shift to the electoral Left at the beginning of the twenty-first century calls for academic and activist analysis of the opportunities and problems posed for social movements. The essays in this volume should help stimulate debate on the possibilities and pitfalls of contemporary social movement organizing in Latin America. Critical thinking and collective action are intertwined components of making a better world possible.

I

HISTORICAL CONTINUITIES
AND NEW TRENDS

Vía Campesina and CLOC (Coordinadora Latinoamericana de Organizaciones del Campo) protest, October 2002 in Quito, Ecuador, against the proposed Free Trade Area of the Americas (FTAA). Photo courtesy of Peter M. Rosset.

IN THIS FIRST SECTION of the compilation, two overviews of Latin American social movements—one written in 1994 and one in 2007—frame the movements and their theorizing in historical context. These two vantage points in time highlight the regional dynamics and trends, helping to explain the origins, dynamics, and outcomes of these movements, which will be explored in detail in the rest of this volume.

David Slater's 1994 essay captures the essence of the distinctive features of the movements, providing a valuable reference point for assessing where they are heading in the twenty-first century. Slater emphasizes three aspects of scholarship about Latin American social movements. First, he notes growing attention to agency and subjectivity in the constitution of social subjects, reflecting a more nuanced interpretation than an older generation of formulaic class analysis. This notion has clearly been validated as movements have continued to define and assert new and multiple identities in the course of their struggles, such as the dramatic rise of indigenous movements in Ecuador, Bolivia, and Mexico, or the locally rooted struggles of black women domestic workers in Brazilian neighborhood organizations. Indeed, such flexibility and even spontaneity in the formation of social subjects—arising, for example, out of the streets and factories of Argentina in the midst of financial crisis—have proven to be adaptive responses to the atomizing effects of neoliberal economics and shallow procedural democracy.

Slater's second observation relates to controversy among scholars about the political relevance of social movements regarding differences over the meaning of democracy. This too has remained a relevant theme. Social movement practice has continued to push the boundaries in experimenting with radical, participatory democracy, such as the Zapatista autonomy movement in Mexico and the sense of community among land occupiers in rural Brazil, both of which still struggle to effect change in their national political systems. Movements in Bolivia, Ecuador, and Argentina have proven they can bring down governments, but this raises new questions about whether they then need to organize in a different way to usher in alternative forms of governance. A different set of questions comes to mind about the democratic nature of a movement such as the one mobilized by Venezuelan president Hugo Chávez, seemingly harnessed to the fortunes of a specific government.

The third theme Slater identifies is a sense of hope. At the time of his essay, hope was an important counterweight to the "end-of-history" discourse accompanying the end of the cold war, which portrayed unchallenged U.S. hegemony and unfettered free markets as inexorable developments. Today it is clearer that the U.S.-championed neoliberal paradigm is widely questioned. It is also clearer that hope is no longer pinned on a final revolutionary moment, but is rather unleashed in the joyful cry of "Another world is possible" and expressed in a willingness to model alternatives without claiming vanguard correctness or waiting for authorization from parties or governments. Women's groups on the U.S.-Mexican border, Mesoamerican regional mobilizations against free trade agreements, and the international peasant alliance Vía Campesina all represent new forms of organizing that reject the constraints of national borders or traditional ways of defining politics. Slater also warns against Euro-American ethnocentrism in our analysis, emphasizing the importance of both the historical specificity and the intellectual perspectives of the global South.

Harry Vanden's contemporary overview dovetails with Slater's analysis. Vanden reminds us that the struggles of marginalized groups are always open-ended, redefining the rules of doing politics as those rules are defined (by elites) at the time, and that we can really only fully recognize protest cycles after they have succeeded; for example, who would have thought at the time that slavery could ever be ended in Haiti, that landowner domination could be challenged in Brazil, that military rule might be ended in Chile and Argentina? While specific social mobilizations adapt to changing historical contexts, popular struggles in and of themselves certainly are not new.

Vanden provides another important update to social movement analysis in Latin America. He notes that these movements can no longer be attributed just to the undermining of the bureaucratic-authoritarian regimes that held sway in much of the region from the mid-1960s through the 1980s. The last twenty years have seen land takeovers and road blockages in Ecuador as part of an indigenous revival; the chain of events following the Caracas "IMF riots" of 1989 leading up to the "Bolivarian" mobilization of Venezuela's poor; the Zapatista rebellion of 1994 that inspired networks of supporters throughout Mexico and beyond; and the Bolivian mass mobilizations of 2003 and 2005—all of which, Vanden suggests, points to a "political sea change" in the region. He focuses on the cases of Brazil and Bolivia to illustrate the robustness of the movements, their innovative forms of struggle, and their significant impact on politics.

Together these two essays offer historical context for identifying the continuities and novel features of Latin American social movements going into the twenty-first century. If there is an upsurge and renewed vibrancy in these movements, it remains to be seen which will survive, which will prosper, and which will fade away. Indeed, the more detailed examination of specific social movements in the chapters following this section underscores the considerable complexity, dynamics, and dilemmas of counterhegemonic struggles as they are developing in Latin America.

2

Power and Social Movements in the Other Occident

Latin America in an International Context

David Slater

ACROSS A BROAD RANGE OF SOCIAL and political enquiry, the analysis and conceptual location of social movements continue to evoke controversy and engender new spheres of reflection. In exploring the emergence of social movements and especially what have come to be termed "new social movements" as a significant presence in much contemporary debate, three main factors can be mentioned. First, there has been a growth of interest in questions of agency and subjectivity. In the wake of growing disillusionment with traditional class analysis, the issue of the constitution of social subjects and their potential relation to collective action and political change has become increasingly pivotal. Second, the controversies surrounding the potential political relevance of social movements, especially in connection with the differential meanings of democracy, have tended to flow into and reinforce the importance of discussions of the state-society nexus. Finally, in an era sometimes characterized in terms of a posited "end of history" and one in which the precepts of neoliberalism and possessive individualism have gained greater currency (Connolly, 1991: 172) the widespread occurrence of movements of protest has engendered a sense of hope. Social movements have, however tenuously or indeterminately, held open the possibility of another horizon; optimism of the will, in a time of disenchantment, has been given a new dynamic.

The original version of this essay appeared in *Latin American Perspectives* 21(2), Spring 1994: 11–37.

Interpreting Social Movements: Moving Beyond the Centrality of Class

The incorporation of agency, subjectivity, and action into the realm of class analysis has been and remains a hallmark of much mainstream Marxism, especially in relation to development studies. The problems associated with attempting to explain contemporary social movements within the established frame of class analysis have not gone unnoticed. Melucci (1992: 44), for example, comments that researchers have often found themselves in the uncomfortable position of a hiker on unfamiliar ground without a map and in this situation "turned back to consult old maps trying to get their vague recollections of the new terrain to strike a chord with the familiar outlines of the map worn out by habitual use." But, precisely what are the essential shortcomings of class analysis, as embedded in the Marxist tradition?

In the first place, it has been customarily assumed that classes have "interests" that result from the overall structure of class relations and therefore function, *a priori*, as the necessary basis for the mobilization of actors, divorced from any analysis of the varied constitution of the social subject or the dynamic of collective wills. The failure of classes to become conscious of their "interests" gives rise to the notion of "false consciousness." It is further presupposed that a class in struggle, for example, the proletariat, has a consciousness that emanates from or is rooted at the point of production. Such a position has led feminist writers such as Barrett (1988: xiv) to refer to "classical Marxism's obsessional focus on production and the world of wage labour." Moreover, the working class has been conceptualized as the preordained and central revolutionary social subject, thus dispensing with the need to explain the processes whereby varying forms of political subjectivity are constituted and through which the propensity to act collectively may emerge in certain specific circumstances.

Overall, the major problem with Marxist class analysis, as well as with the related ways in which class is employed in much of the radical development literature, concerns the failure to theorize subjectivity and identity. This failure is in turn conditioned by the belief that what classes do is spelled out by their situation in the relations of production, which precedes them causally as well as logically. In Marxism, classes, as Castoriadis (1987: 29) reminds us, "are the agents of the historical process, but its unconscious agents"; "it is not men's consciousness that determines their being but their social being which determines their consciousness." However, the reproduction of material existence, as well as the constitution of social being, must presuppose thought; they are not prior to it.

In an increasing proportion of the contemporary literature that deals with issues of democracy and power, many of the more obviously reductionist aspects of Marxist class analysis have been or are fast being abandoned. Nun (1991: 16–17), for instance, writes:

> I am vindicating the importance of a perspective which raises the contradictory relations between capitalism, the state, and democracy, but in no way the antiquated canonic definitions of the class struggle, whose economic reductionism, voluntarism, and rationalism have often been exposed. What is more, class dynamics should be analyzed and specified in distinct concrete situations and neither exhausts the reality of these situations nor excludes the other forms of domination and antagonism expressed by the "new social movements." Having said this, it is from a class perspective that exploitation and the capitalist aspect of the state emerge as topics; and it seems to me that neither one nor the other can be liquidated today by theoretical fiat and even less, by change in intellectual fashion.

In an interesting footnote, Nun adds that the danger of the "nonclass" fashion is that by fixing its gaze too much elsewhere it may end up "throwing the baby out with the bathwater." In other well-tuned social analyses, class is also retained as an important variable in the explanation of social movements, for example, the connection between the rise of a so-called new middle class and the emergence of new social movements. In these examples, I suggest, in the attempt to link a class category with a social phenomenon or a particular kind of identity the analysis is sometimes short-circuited. Hence, while it might be possible, after an analysis of the formation and development of a particular kind of collective consciousness, to use the class category as a "point of arrival," not infrequently class is used as a predetermined "point of departure." What, then, are the alternatives?

Space of the Subject/Territory of Movements

Evers (1985), in his discussion of identity and subjectivity, has suggested that "in the process of creating new patterns of socio-cultural practice and of reconstructing fragments of an autonomous identity, the individuals involved as well as the group as a whole constitute themselves as the subjects of this process . . . ; to be more precise, they develop the corresponding fragments of a new subjectivity within themselves" (1985: 59). He argues that if the process of emancipation is bereft of a definite terminus, so is the process of the constitution of its subjects; hence, "no individual and no collective entity can . . . ever be regarded as being wholly subject; . . . they are bearers of *fragments* of subjectivity, in so far as they have succeeded in overcoming *some aspects* of alienation and in constructing *some first traits* of an autonomous identity"

(1985: 60). This emphasis on fragmentation and on the interweaving of individual and collective subjectivities and identities gives Evers the context for arguing that "our monolithic concepts of social subjectivity have exploded, and we find that the aggregate state of subjectivity is not solid, but liquid or even gaseous, penetrating—and blending with—the most varied elements within the social texture" (1985: 67). Evers is calling our attention not only to the well-recognized heterogeneity of social movements and of collective actors but also the complex constitution of individual identities. In this sense, the concept of "multiple identities," which can be used in relation to categories of "class," "gender," "ethnicity," "locality," etc., touches only part of the complexity and often departs from an implicit notion of a unified subject.

Nowhere has the critique of such a notion and its embodiment in androcentric approaches to social life and explanation been so effectively developed as in feminist theory. Mouffe (1988) provides one opening. Her thesis is that in each individual there are multiple subject positions corresponding both to the different social relations in which the individual participates and to the discourses that constitute these relations. For example, each social agent is inscribed in a range of social relations connected to gender, race, nationality, production, locality, and so on. All these relations are the basis of subject positions, and every social agent is thus the site of many subject positions and cannot realistically be reduced to one. Moreover, each subject position is itself "the locus of multiple possible constructions, according to the different discourses that can construct that position" (Mouffe, 1988: 90). From this it follows that the subjectivity of a given social agent can never be finally fixed; it is provisionally and often precariously constituted at the intersection of various discourses.

This kind of analysis gives us the possibility of interpreting the space of the subject in terms of a series of positions that of course acquire meaning within a matrix of discursive practices. The development of a democratic struggle can be seen as not only the articulation of the differential struggles of several subaltern groups but also the struggle for the democratization of the multiple subject positions of each agent in the struggle. For example, within the ecological movement there would also be a continuous struggle against racist/ethnocentric and sexist/patriarchal positions and not solely against positions causing environmental devastation/degradation. And, naturally, such struggles take place on a contested political terrain where the new right is deploying a discourse that seeks to articulate visions of freedom, democracy, and progress to ideas of authority, hierarchy, and possessive individualism.

The notion of fragmented identity and subjectivity finds echoes in the feminist literature, where there has been a concern to move away from the rationalist assumption of a self-present and unitary subject. This tendency has been paralleled by the orientations of postmodern politics. However, it has another source in psychoanalysis. As Flax (1991: 60–61) reminds us, in Freud's later work "the mind's structure and processes become increasingly fragmented, fluid, and subject to complex and often unconscious alterations . . . the equation of the mind and conscious thought or reason or the psychical and conscious becomes untenable." The distinction between inner and outer determinants of experience breaks down, and each aspect of the mind—ego, id, and superego—is seen as constituted in and through inner and outer experiences. In a similar vein, Fuss (1989: 33), in her examination of feminism and difference, stresses the importance of interpreting the notion of the "I" as a "complicated field of multiple subjectivities and competing identities."

In the general context of feminism and poststructuralism, subjectivity is customarily seen as a process. There is a continual deferral of fixed meaning, and conscious subjectivity, acquired in language, is viewed as inherently unstable. Meaning can have no such external guarantee as, for example, it has in the case of mainstream Marxism, where meaning flows from the laws of history or the logic of world capitalist development. The fixing of meaning in society, or as according to Weedon (1987: 97), "the realization of the implications of particular versions of meaning in forms of social organization and the distribution of social power, rely on the discursive constitution of subject positions from which individuals actively interpret the world and by which they are themselves governed." In this argument, "it is the structures of discourses which determine the discursive constitution of individuals as subjects." Weedon goes on to suggest that

> discourses, located as they are in social institutions and processes, are continually competing with each other for the allegiance of individual agents. . . . The political interests and social implications of any discourse will not be realized without the agency of individuals who are subjectively motivated to reproduce or transform social practices and the social power which underpins them. . . . In this way, "individuals are both the *site* and *subjects* of discursive struggle for their identity."

As a consequence, it can be argued that the interpellation of individuals as subjects within particular discourses is never final; it is always open to challenge and destabilization so that in the case of some social movements, for instance, opposition to the sedimentation of established meanings requires the articulation and coalition of different subject positions and political ideas. When this occurs, we have an example of what Foucault (1980a) referred to as "reverse discourses." The emergence of "challenge and destabilization" relates to the idea of "points of resistance" within the network of power. For Foucault there is no single locus of "great refusal," "no soul of revolt, source of all rebellions." "Instead," he writes, "there is a plurality of resistances, each of them a special case: resistances that are possible, necessary, improbable; others that are spontaneous, savage, solitary, concerted, rampant, or violent; still others that are quick to compromise." Although there may occasionally be "massive binary divisions," "great radical ruptures," more often one is dealing with "mobile and transitory points of resistance, producing cleavages in a society that shift about, fracturing unities and effecting regroupings, furrowing across individuals themselves, cutting them up and remolding them." Resistances, for Foucault, are the odd term in relations of power; they are "inscribed in the latter as an irreducible opposite" and distributed in irregular fashion: "the points, knots, or focuses of resistance are spread over time and space at varying densities, at times mobilizing groups or individuals in a definite way." When these points of resistance can be strategically codified, a revolution becomes possible, in somewhat the same way that the "state relies on the institutional integration of power relationships" (1980a: 95–96).

The multiple points of identity within the space of the subject remind us of the impossibility of one fixed center for subjectivity. An iconoclastic question arising out of some postmodern treatments of political subjectivity—What do a trade unionist, a racist, a Christian, a wife-beater, and a consumer have in common?—produces an answer that effectively undermines any facile view of "the politics of identity": they may all be the same person. In a similar vein, the following question has been posed: If a white male worker is a militant in his factory, organizing against the capitalist, but returns home and is a sexist and goes out onto the street and is a racist, in what sense is such a worker "revolutionary"? A further feature of the complexity of "identity politics" is that an oppressed subject can also, simultaneously, be an oppressing subject. The struggle against racism and ethnocentrism within the feminist movement is one example (L. González, 1987; Mohanty, 1988); another is the emergence in one of London's neighborhoods of an "unthinkable" alliance between black people and the National Front when homophobia overshadowed racism in a campaign against gays (Mercer, 1990: 49).

The indeterminate, unexpected, unfixed aspect of subjectivity and the politics of identity are deeply inscribed in the post-Marxist understanding of movements. Žižek (1990: 250), in his commentary on Laclau and Mouffe's (1985) text, argues with reference to the series feminism–democracy–peace movement–ecologism as follows:

> insofar as the participant in the struggle for democracy "finds out by experience" that there is no real democracy without the emancipation of women, insofar as the participant in the ecological struggle "finds out by experience" that there is no real reconciliation with nature without abandoning the aggressive-masculine

attitude towards nature, insofar as the participant in the peace movement "finds out by experience" that there is no real peace without radical democratization, etc., . . . we can say that something like a unified subject-position is being constructed: to be a democrat means at the same time to be a feminist, etc.

But, of course, such a potential unity is not an expression of some kind of internal necessity but rather the possible result of a "symbolic condensation" that is radically contingent; it is one possible political construction among several. It is possible to think of movements in terms of the social construction of what Melucci (1992) calls collective identity. Thus, actors or social agents produce an interactive and shared definition of the goals of their action and the terrain on which it is to take place. For Melucci, such a definition is an "active relational process," and collective identity is a "definition constructed and negotiated through an activation of the social relationships connecting the members of a group or movement." Here, "cognitive frames, dense interactions and emotional and affective exchanges" (1992: 49) are implicitly present. But how do we conceive the political in such a construction, and how is this "active relational process," with its emotional exchanges and modes of social learning, brought into being?

Fuss (1989: 36), considering some related aspects of these questions, suggests that the possibility of coalition and affinity among women depends on politics; that is, for Fuss, politics grounds affinity and coalition and not the other way around. Such a starting point, of course, is present in Mouffe's (1988) use of the concept of political antagonism. The formation of antagonisms does not necessarily lead to democratic struggles and the emergence of oppositional social movements. How resistance and contestation are articulated will depend on the relation of political forces and the power of competing discourses. For example, the curtailment of civil rights may be legitimated through the invocation of a national security doctrine, in the sense that some social subjects will tolerate limitation and even loss of their rights when interpellated within this doctrine.

The democratic struggles and oppositional social movements that have emerged can be seen as taking on the character of a politics of contestation. At the same time, however, there is always, as Melucci (1992: 50) expresses it, "an opaque, hidden part of collective action," since actors cannot simultaneously act and be their own analysts. This opaque, submerged side of action is to be traced to the impossibility of a transparent and totally self-knowing subject. What Freud once referred to as the abyss of the unconscious can have a subversive and destabilizing effect on collective practices when previously unfathomed feelings and tensions break the surface of a movement's interpersonal structure.

In the above passage there are two central themes that require far more elaboration: the differential meaning of democracy in relation to struggles and movements and the shifting nature of the "political." These two themes come firmly together in the following sections, but before bringing this first one to a close there is a further feature of the interpretation of social movements that needs to be put on the agenda: the issue of ethnocentric universalism or "Euro-Americanism" and the connection between difference and otherness.

The Other Moves In: Subverting the Center

Elsewhere I have argued that Euro-Americanism has at least three defining features: (1) the persistence of absence, (2) assumptions of universality, and (3) the problem of "worlding" (Slater, 1992). With reference to the social movements literature, the South is very often present through its absence. For example, Eyerman and Jamison (1991), in their general overview of the international significance of social movements, develop their argument as if the West were a self-contained entity, as if somehow it could be apprehended and comprehended of and by itself; neither "social movements of the third kind" nor the intellectual contribution of Third World social scientists appear on the horizon. Along such a trajectory, intellectual confinement and Euro-American introspection retard any genuine global expansion of meaning.

Second, the peculiarity and specificity of the Euro-American "universal" remain invisible, submerged beneath the assumptions of generality. In our case of social movements, analysis and theoretical reflection carried out by many First World social scientists create the frames for ongoing conceptual debates and research agendas. These structures of thought, which come to life in relation to the historically concrete experiences of the West, are projected out and implicitly inscribed with universal significance. Thus, as, for example, Third World women have argued, it is important to be aware of the various facets of ethnocentric universalism present in Western feminist discourse (Mohanty, 1988).

Third, it is possible to talk of the double bind of ethnocentric universalism. Thus there is not only the supposition that the West acts as the primary referent for theory and philosophical reflection, but also the frequent inclination to express an interest in the periphery in the context of information retrieval, the incorporation of token, often stereotyped themes such as "the culture of tradition" or "violence," and above all the simplification of the heterogeneity of the periphery. Within this persuasion, there is no interrogation of the bases on which the principle of "worlding" unfolded, no appraisal of the discursive construction of the "First World" as contrasted to its others.

The Western literature on social movements is sometimes unexpectedly punctuated by stereotyped and caricatured images of the Third World. Otto Wolf (1986: 37), for example, writes of Third World peoples that "they cannot achieve a decisive advance in handling the 'new' questions of women's liberation and ecology, since they are confronted with the still potent fetters of traditional custom—often of a quite patriarchal kind—and with pressing problems of quantitative need that make it very tempting to neglect qualitative long-term concerns such as the reproduction of ecological systems." Melucci (1989: 189) in a passing reference, connects the Third World, or his image of it, with grandiose political programs that have in practice resulted in "violence and totalitarianism." The overall point here is that while the purpose is *not* to engage in a politics of simple reversal whereby (paraphrasing Stuart Hall) we would replace "the essential, bad, white (First World) social subject" with the "essential, good, black (Third World) social subject," it is essential to recognize diversity, openness, and the plurality of agency and subjectivity (Julien and Mercer, 1988). While we may wish to examine the meanings of revolutionary ruptures in the periphery, the changing dynamic of violence in specific situations, or the particularity of cultural traditions in given instances, *equally* we may wish to analyze the content of democratic struggles, the complex constitution of popular imaginaries, or the transcendence of cynicism in forms of community. In all cases there will be heterogeneity and difference that break open the "othering" caricatures of Western discourse and grant to those "intellectual prisoners of the West" the opportunity to learn rather than to "other."

Sometimes discussions in the center will be mounted around the theme "democracy and the Third World," conveying the image of a separation between the democratic West and the nondemocratic Rest. What can democracy mean in the South, and in particular in Latin America, and how might this connect with social movements, power, and the political?

The Diverse Ambits of Democracy

Democracy can be thought of as a floating signifier *par excellence*. While the Reagan administration launched "Project Democracy" and the "Democracy Program" to promote, as Huntington (1984: 193) put it, "democratic institutions in other societies," the Sandinista government of the 1980s attempted to develop its own combination of representative democracy with popular or direct democracy. Whereas a Huntington, following Schumpeter's (1987) definition of the "democratic method," would sign up behind the United States government as the carrier of democracy to Third World countries, a Chomsky (1989) would argue that this diffusion of democracy was a cover for imperialist domination and the policing of development. Theoretically, if we speak about "democracy" in the context of, say, Central America in the 1980s, the ambiguity and unfixity of the term stems from the context itself, which is constituted to a certain extent by the coexistence of Marxist and anti-Marxist discourses. Since these discourses are antagonistic but operate largely in the same argumentative context, there is a destabilization of the relations that give the term "democracy" its identity. In this sense democracy becomes a floating signifier, ambiguity subverting any possibility of fixing its meaning (Laclau, 1989).

In Latin America, by the middle of the 1980s democratization had become as crucial as revolution had been halfway through the 1960s. In the 1990s, writers such as Moisés (1991) refer to a certain Latin American paradox: that while the 1980s was characterized by a general eclipse of authoritarian rule and the reemergence of democratic regimes, the new decade has ushered in a dramatic worsening of the social and economic problems endemic to the region. Weffort (1991), whose article on modernity and democracy provides much of the stimulus for Moisés, couples the old problems of the Latin American region—polarization, marginalization, underemployment and unemployment, poverty, and social deterioration—with the new problems of emigration and drugs. Weffort talks of social decadence and disintegration, of the dangerous prospects of a "generalized anomie," of a broadening and deepening of violence, of a "social apartheid," of a loss of a future, and of a sense of internal and external disintegration combined. Against this dystopia is pitted a belief in democracy; for Weffort (1991: 93, my translation), "confronting the possibility of national disintegration, for the countries of Latin America, the force of democracy is the force of hope." And this democracy refers not only to the kind of political regime but also to the extraordinary increase in the organizational capacity of civil society. This increase as well as a growth in political participation signifies a strengthening of the bases for democracy and therefore, according to Weffort, an impulse for modernization; at the same time, an increase in the bases for democracy is accompanied by an intensification of social corporativism.

Weffort is not alone in many of his illuminations. In times of "desborde sin revolución" (Touraine, 1989: 38), crisis might be defined not just in socioeconomic terms but by a broader collapse of the existing order or system of values. Lechner (1991), in his brief consideration of democratization in the context of postmodern culture, emphasizes the absence of a horizon, the sense of a loss of a future, the crisis of political identity. Taking an example from the Chilean experience, he contends that neither the development policies of Frei nor the socialist reforms of Allende nor the neoliberal measures of Pinochet have crystallized in a process of sustainable and stable social transformation. Lechner sees time in this context as a sequence of events, of conjunctures, rather than as a structured period of past, present, and future: "we live in a continuous present" (1991: 68). And perhaps in this kind of time zone social movements are, following Melucci, only "nomads," with no fixed position on the terrain of civil society.

Located in a Mexican context, Zermeño (1989) is more explicit and more empirical. In his interpretive arena of the "dynamics of disorder," he rightly draws our attention to the "return of the leader" and to the highly precarious presence of social movements in urban Mexico. Contrary to the sometimes complacent description given by researchers and militants, marginality in the barrio must also be seen in terms of the universe of egoism, the war of all against all, envy, and the law of the survival of the fittest. For Zermeño, there is a proliferation of the excluded without the rise of a popular subject. He talks of a "delinquent conformism," of an anonymous atomization, the absence of both tradition and project, of violence, of the ridicule of suffering, of resentment, negation, withdrawal, and of an individualistic imaginary nourished by the media. Here we have, in Zermeño's words, the extreme situation of marginal youth. Moreover, in the Mexican case it is argued that the bases for social struggle are frequently atomized by repression, division, and co-optation, whereby the leaders move into the *buropolítica*. In this study, the emancipatory potential of social movements is seen as being suffocated by a deeply entrenched system of political clientelism.

Other writers are more optimistic, although the examples tend not to come from Mexico. Rowe and Schelling (1991: 186) write that "perhaps one of the most significant contributions of the new social movements has been the creation of a new political culture manifested in a broader concept of democracy and new methods of political resistance, entailing novel forms of organization and of cultural action." Oporto (1991: 24) expresses the view that in Bolivia civic and regional movements have effectively put on the agenda the democratization and decentralization of the state. Rafael De la Cruz (1989) argues that in Venezuela social movements are society's response to the crisis of socio-cultural and political relations, as well as the prevailing model of development; they represent the emergence of an alternative social project. Arditi and Rodríguez (1987) point to the significance of new themes and practices being brought to the political surface in Paraguay "in spite of the state." In particular, they refer to values of social equality, the right to participate directly in decision making, the reconstruction of the self-esteem and dignity of the popular sectors, and the validation of autonomy from the state and solidarity within and between the various sectors in struggle—peasants, workers, students.

When the question of the connection between social movements and democracy is raised, it is useful to suggest that there is a possibility of a "double democratization," the interdependent transformation of both state and civil society. For Held (1991: 231) this transformation can be viewed in terms of the enshrinement of the principle of autonomy in a constitution and bill of rights, the reform of state power to maximize accountability (within the terms of a constitution) to elected representatives and ultimately to the citizen body, and experimentation with different democratic mechanisms and procedures in civil society. Such an approach finds an echo in Bobbio's (1989) distinction between political and social democracy. For Bobbio, current forms of democratic development ought to be understood as the occupation of new spaces in the arena of civil society. The process of the democratization of society (democratization being defined as the "institution and exercise of procedures which allow the participation of those affected in the deliberations of a collective body" [1989: 155]) goes beyond the boundaries of political democracy. In Bobbio's words, it is quite possible to have a democratic state in a society in which most institutions, from the family to the school and from private enterprise to public services, are not governed democratically.

The approaches developed by Held and Bobbio give us some useful normative handles to hold onto when thinking about the possible meanings of democracy. However, they bring us back to the difficulty of thinking the political—the problem of rights and ethics within the procedures of democratic practice—and to the question of the differential imaginations within which the content of democratization acquires meaning. As Nun argues, there is a tendency in Latin America, as elsewhere, toward the dissemination of idealized versions of modernization. The *continuity* of this process, with respect to what Sunkel refers to as transnational integration with national disintegration and Nun calls the growth of a marginal mass, is forgotten. Instead we are presented with imaginary discontinuities, as if Latin America had never experienced capitalist penetration, as if its economies had never been open to the world market, as if the early-1960s doctrine of modernization had never existed. There is also a tendency toward the inversion of the relationship with democracy; now political democratization is viewed as an obligatory and preliminary step to economic and social modernization. But how meaningful, or even secure, is that democracy when—in societies already severely eroded by earlier waves of capitalist development—the new wave of capitalist modernization is accompanied by pervasive privatization and the withering away of the social and economic functions of the peripheral state?

Nun suggests a "spiral of delegitimation" with the following shape: (1) the rise to power of politicians who have won electoral majorities through abundant and attractive promises, (2) as a result of the magnitude of the crisis they then confront, strong centralization of decision making at the executive level, to the detriment of parliament and the political parties, (3) in the absence of improvements, decline in the government's popularity, leading to (4) extensive disillusionment of large sectors of the population and a concomitant loss of credibility of most political leaders, and (5) a "defensive withdrawal into the private sphere, citizen's apathy, and rapid widening of the gap between legality and legitimacy" (1991: 23).

Faced with this scenario, Nun makes the following important proposition: In the precarious context discussed in relation to the "spiral of delegitimation" and the persistence of gross social and economic inequalities, "the defense of public liberties and the very consolidation of a representative government depend on a rapid development of multiple forms of participatory democracy" (Nun, 1991: 26). He refers to the need for a democratization of political parties, trade unions, and corporations, "full accountability of the representatives, financial transparency of the organizations, etc." This call for an extension of the principles of democracy to the economy and for a reemphasis on participation is an example of an "oppositional" use of the term "democracy" not unlike the vision of combining ideas of a "governed democracy" (representative institutions) with a program of "governing democracy" (popular democracy) (Barros, 1986: 68).

In any consideration of the ambits of democracy, the increasingly important dimension of territoriality, especially in relation to popular mobilization and social struggles, needs to be taken into account. The concept of territorial democracy—the idea that when we discuss the different features of the democratization process or the connections between political and social democracy there is also a need to think of democracy as being instituted or developed in and across space—underlines the inadequacy of interpreting democracy as evolving on the head of a pin. In the Peruvian case the eruption of regional and local social movements from the mid- to the late 1970s helped to put on the political agenda the institutionalization of regional government. From the 1979 Constitution through subsequent legislative innovations, the bases were established for the holding of regional elections and the installation of regional governments; a new political space for radical democratic struggles was brought into being (Slater, 1991b). Similarly, in Bolivia and Colombia [see Dixon chapter in this volume], struggles at the local and regional level have helped to generate a trend toward some degree of political decentralization and the territorialization of democracy. In Chile the political debate on the possible composition, structure, and functions of regional government, originally put on the administrative agenda during the Pinochet era, has reemphasized the polysemic and radically ambiguous nature of democracy.

Although it is certainly feasible to trace the connections between the actions of local and regional movements and the opening up of new spaces for democracy, to what extent do these actions, mobilizations, and pressures lead to a change in power relations? Further, if democracy can be seen as polysemic and ambiguous, surely the social movements can as well?

Power and Rethinking the Political

In an important sense power can be seen as having two faces; power is not expressed as one-way traffic. The duality consists in the ability to have "power over" and the "power to." In this frame, the "power to" is conceptually prior to the "power over," but not infrequently power is conceived as only the latter, the power to dominate (Patton, 1989). Toward the end of his life Foucault clarified the difference as he saw it between power relations and relations of domination, suggesting that "there is a whole network of relationships of power, which can operate between individuals, in the bosom of the family, in an educational relationship, in the political body, etc," and that this very complex field sometimes meets "what we can call facts or states of domination, in which the relations of power, instead of being variable and allowing different partners a strategy which alters them, find themselves firmly set and congealed." He goes on: "When an individual or a social group manages to block a field of relations of power, to render them impassive and invariable and to prevent all reversibility of movement—by means of instruments which can be economic as well as political or military—we are facing what can be called a state of domination" (Foucault, 1988: 3).

How, then, does the capacity to act, the "power to," find a way of unfreezing this state of domination—of reversing this impassive, invariable state? How do other relationships of power subvert and turn back this kind of fix? Traditionally, one answer would have come from an almost automatic reference to the necessity of revolution. Power had to be seized, taken hold of, wrenched away from repressive apparatuses and exploiting classes. In the violent climax of revolutionary insurrection, the steely instruments of the new society would be forged and put to immediate use. But if revolution, as a violent rupture, is in historical eclipse, does this mean that radical democratic transformations are foreclosed?

On another occasion Foucault suggested that there were three kinds of struggle: against ethnic, social, and religious domination, against exploitation that separated individuals from what they produced, and against submission and subjection. For struggles of this third type, which Foucault saw as becoming increasingly significant, he suggested a number of new or original features: (1) questioning the status of the individual—on the one hand, "they assert the right to be different" and, on the other, "they attack everything which separates the individual, breaks his links with others, splits up community life, forces the individual back on himself and ties him to his own identity in a constraining way"; (2) opposition to the privileges of knowledge, to secrecy and disinformation—calling into question the relation of knowledge to power; and (3) rejection of "economic and ideological state violence which ignore who we are individually, and also a refusal of a scientific or administrative inquisition which determines who one is" (Foucault, 1986: 211–212).

These novel features, which are relevant to any discussion of the new social movements, represent part of the "reverse discourse" alluded to earlier; these new oppositions challenge domination as a particular "congealed" structure of power relations. Foucault stressed the connection between the state ("this new political structure" that combined individualization with totalization) and the individual. He summarized: "the political, ethical, social, philosophical problem of our days is not to try to liberate the individual from the state, and from the state's institutions, but to liberate us both from the state and from the type of individualization which is linked to the state; . . . we have to promote new forms of subjectivity through the refusal of this kind of individuality which has been imposed on us for several centuries" (1986: 216).

These new forms of subjectivity will vary in content as well as context. Writing specifically about the United States, Connolly (1991: 85) argues that the most ominous form nihilism assumes today is a "nonpolitics of nihilistic consent to the everyday extension of discipline and normalization." The regulated operation of a political economy of productivity within a society of growing surveillance and normalization freezes democracy at the level of electoral politics. In the example of the United States, which is often projected as a kind of "gold standard" for global democracy, electoral politics, in Connolly's revealing words, "contains powerful pressures to become a closed circuit for the dogmatism of identity through the translation of difference into threat and threat into energy for the dogmatization of identity" (1991: 209–210). Against these trends and realities, social movements have the potential to contest and bring into question normalizing conceptions of possessive individualism; they can oppose the "nonpolitics of nihilistic consent" and the spread of political autism.

Latin America offers multiple examples of new subjectivities in formation. Colombia, a country characterized by intensified violence, what Connolly has referred to as the "nontheistic reverence for life" has become a crucial element of many civic movements—the struggle for the sanctity of life is part of a new subjectivity. In Peru, the *rondas campesinas* (village patrols) held back the spread of *Sendero Luminoso* in certain northern areas of the sierra; this was achieved through the development of communal and collective forms of social organization that acted as an effective dike against infiltration (Starn, 1991). Through the strength of communal and collective forms of defense the rondas campesinas nurtured a space, no matter how precarious, within which the difference of individuality was protected against Sendero's violent "normalization" of dogma. In Bolivia, the *comités cívicos*, as an organizational expression of regional social movements, provided a space for the maintenance of forms of democratic association in times of military dictatorship. In the contemporary discussion of national identity and the modernization of the state, these committees carried onto the national agenda ideas and proposals for decentralization and the territorialization of democracy that combined older demands and claims with newer forms of collective identity (Slater, 1991a). In Brazil, where there are reported to be approximately 100,000 church base communities (CEBs, inspired by Liberation Theology), with over 2 million participants, Levine and Mainwaring (1989: 214) suggest that "because the normal practice of CEBs encourages critical discourse, egalitarianism, and experiments in self-governance within the groups, even the most 'apolitical' CEBs can have long-term political consequences."

These examples illustrate not only the existence of points of resistance but also the emergence of "reverse discourses" and, through the power to oppose and struggle, the possibility of unfreezing some of the structures of domination. But perhaps it can be countered that many of these struggles are basically defensive in nature and of no significant threat to state power, expressing only an "artificial negativity" to established order. In an essentially First World context, Peterson (1989) argues, in his critique of Melucci, that the alternatives of the social movement activists, rather than being subversive, help to oil the machinery of the existing societal order. For Peterson, Melucci's perspective results in a conception of today's social movements as "emancipating the state in its relationship to civil society, rather than emancipating civil society in its relationship with the state"; at the end of the day, the social changes generated by the social movements are functional to the continued existence of present-day society— "their 'explosive' or transcendental power is non-existent" (1989: 426). Similarly although less dramatically, Howard (1988: xi) writes, "the practical difficulty which social movements pose is the translation of their social challenge to the existing system into a political practice that transcends it." Perhaps, after all the words, all one can say is that the movements *are* there, and they *move*. On the brink of banality let us pause and retrace our steps to the phrase Howard employs, "political practice," and the idea expressed above by Levine and Mainwaring in relation to the CEBs, "long-term political consequences." How are we thinking the "political"? In what ways are the social movements "political"?

It ought to be clear that there can be no single fixed function for the political. The political is not a "level" split off and granted relative autonomy from other "levels" the constitution of which is itself a political act. Sometimes the political is delimited as the domain of state power, against which civil society must organize its institutional and interactive mechanisms of defense. Often a binary distinction is drawn between the realm of the political, bounded within the state, and political parties and the space of the social, framed around the family, the school, religion, the individual, movements, and so on. However, dissolving this binary split, just as the post-Marxist would transcend the base-superstructure division, or the post-structuralist would subvert any idea of a presupposed separation between "institutions" and "discourse," we can argue that the very genesis of society is itself political. Expressed differently, the political dimension has a certain dual nature in the sense that it is both inscribed within the different spheres of the social whole and constitutive of the terrain on which the fabric and fate of the social whole is decided. What is and is not political at any moment changes with the emergence of new questions posed by new modes of subjectivity, for example, "the personal is political," and different kinds of social relations. But, also, the "political" does not eliminate the social conditions from which its question was born; gender, sexuality, religious belief, the "milieu," regionalism, and so on, may become political, but they are not *only* political.

A crucial element in the erosion of the contours of certainty concerns the questioning of the given, of what appears to be the socially obvious. When "the given" is not accepted as such but referred back to the initial act that led to its installation, the unstable sense of it is revealed, reactivated. As Laclau (1990: 212) puts it, "it is through the desedimentation of all identity that its prospective being is fully revealed." The desedimentation of the social means laying bare its political content. Since it is also important to accept the plurality of the social, this then means that the desedimentation of the socially given, in its plurality, entails revealing the protean nature of the political.

It has been remarked of social movements that they challenge and/or redraw the boundaries of the political. What this can mean, certainly in the context of the above remarks, is that these movements can subvert the traditional "given" of the "political"—state power, political parties, and so forth. But their role has also been revealing the political essence of the social. Social struggles can be seen as "wars of interpretations" within which the meaning of their demands and historic claims is constructed through their practice. Instead of talking of the necessity of one unified global emancipation based on the universalist dogma of the Enlightenment, we are now in an era of emancipations, of the plurality of emancipations.

Movements of resistance, collective wills, social struggles do not have to be emancipatory in any predetermined, unitary manner. Struggles for a decolonization of the imagination take place in the same time and same space as attempts to eliminate the other; attempts to learn from the other coexist with attempts to banish the other. While there is a "crisis of representations of the future," a dissolution of fixed horizons, an evaporation of old markers, at the same time there is now the possibility of the development of a new political imaginary. Instead of being subsumed under the universalist sign of the class struggle, the old driving force of historical progress, demands that have previously belonged to separate discursive terrains can be brought together.

Traditionally, it might have been possible to suggest a division between an ethics of conviction and an ethics of responsibility. Carried inside some of today's reverse discourses of emancipation is an ethics of conviction *in* responsibility—for the environment, for human rights, for difference, for emancipation from oppression, exploitation, and subjection. In and outside these movements, the academic also has a responsibility—to break the silence that often accompanies the spread of neoliberalism, the extension of surveillance, and the production of "normal individuals." Revealing the political in the social of the institution is accepting that responsibility—becoming an opposing fragment rather than just a thinking fragment.

3

Social Movements, Hegemony, and New Forms of Resistance

Harry E. Vanden

The history of subaltern social groups is necessarily fragmented and episodic. There undoubtedly does exist a tendency to (at least in provisional stages) unification in the historical activity of these groups. . . . It therefore can only be demonstrated when an historical cycle is completed and this cycle culminates in a success.

—Antonio Gramsci, *Prison Notebooks*

The emergence of new political and alternative movements despite their scant participation in [traditional] political life marks the start of a new way of conducting politics which responds to the legitimate demands of the marginalized majorities.

—Juan del Grando, mayor of La Paz, greeting the rise of the new political movement MAS and its then leader and Coca Growers Federation head, Evo Morales

THE MASSES have resisted elitist rule in Latin America in a variety of ways. Since the initial rebellions by the native peoples against imposed European rule there have been innumerable uprisings and other forms of resistance led by the exploited masses themselves in Latin America. With the notable exception of the slave uprising in Haiti led by Toussaint L'Ouverture, most were brutally and successfully suppressed and the particular offending segment of the masses repressed and returned to their subaltern position. But

The original version of this essay appeared in *Latin American Perspectives* 34(2), March 2007: 17–30.

even these outbreaks were rare, and it was more commonly vanguard movements or political parties dominated by elements of the urban elite that led the revolutions that enjoyed some success in Latin America (Bolivia, Cuba, Chile, and Nicaragua). The daily hegemony exercised by the ruling classes generally managed to avoid such unseemly eruptions of popular anger. With the growth in literacy and the widening of the franchise, the national media, elite opinion makers, and globalized communication networks like CNN and CNN en Español exercise more subtle—but no less pernicious—forms of hegemonic control over the Latin American masses.

Seen against this background, the backlash against economic neoliberalism and the globalization process is all the more interesting. As has been the case in the U.S., the national and international economic elites have used all the mechanisms of intellectual and cultural domination at their disposal to exercise hegemony and convince all classes of Latin Americans of the virtues of globalized neoliberalism. Despite their best efforts, there has, however, been a genuine change in Latin American politics. Indeed, the progression of events suggests that that there is a more profound realignment afoot—one that may well represent a political sea change in the region.

The origins of what we now term new social movements could be traced to mobilizations like the Peasant Leagues in Brazil's Northeast in the fifties and early sixties, or the mobilizations by mass organizations in El Salvador in 1979 and the very early 1980s. These and other movements were repressed before they could fully develop a praxis that would challenge traditional decision makers and traditional elitist decision making practices. Yet, even while under brutal military governments in the seventies and eighties, new forms of organization began to develop in neighborhood and women's organizations in Chile and Argentina, and in the countryside in Brazil where the Landless Rural Workers' Movement (MST) was forged in the early eighties (see Slater, 1994b, 1994c; Jelin, 1994; Schild, 1994; and Vanden, 2005). But even in those countries that did not fall victim to bureaucratic authoritarian rule in the seventies and eighties, the masses began to stir and assert themselves in new forms of contentious actions, like land takeovers and the blocking of roads in Ecuador in the late eighties and early nineties. In Venezuela the urban masses exploded against the imposition of neoliberal austerity measures by the government and in Argentina similar looting erupted (for Argentina, see Serulnikov, 1994). The Caracazo in 1989 saw the mass mobilization of thousands of mostly poor, mostly urban, mostly marginalized Venezuelans who thrust themselves into the streets and forced their way into the political process. Their contention was so effective that the Venezuelan elite was forced to do what their Dominican counterparts had felt obliged to do when confronted with a similar situation in1984—call on the armed forces to repress the popular mobilizations. By forcing the less politicized Venezuelan armed forces into a repressive role to sustain very unpopular neoliberal policies, a series of events was put in motion that led to the formation of a Bolivarian movement in the armed forces, coup attempts in 1992, and the eventual popular mobilizations that gave Hugo Chávez and the Fifth Republic Movement (Movimiento V República) victories in the elections of 1998 and 2000, the support to overthrow the coup attempt against him in 2002, and the votes to defeat the referendum in 2004.

There have been other manifestations of popular protest against austerity measures and elements of the conservative economic policies that came to be called neoliberalism in Latin America. These have been manifest in diverse forms: the Zapatista rebellion in Mexico in 1994, the national indigenous movement led by the Confederación Nacional de Indígenas del Ecuador (CONAIE) in Ecuador, the regime-changing popular mobilizations in Argentina, the Movement of Landless Rural Laborers (MST) in Brazil, and the massive mobilizations in Bolivia in 2003 and 2005.

The nature of these protests suggests a political sea change that is sweeping Latin America. It should be noted, however, that although the forms of mobilization and the decision making processes within them represent new repertoires of action, such movements are also a recent and vociferous manifestation of the specter of mass popular mobilization against the governing elite that has haunted Latin America since colonial—if not precolonial—times. In recent years, a great many of the masses—and some of the middle class—seem to feel that the much touted return to democracy, celebration of civil society and incorporation in the globalization process has left them marginalized economically if not politically as well. The reactions in Mexico, Brazil, Bolivia, Ecuador, Venezuela, Argentina, and even Uruguay have been strong and significant and, in varying ways, make one wonder if indeed the political project of the international financial elite and their national allies is working for the common people.

In Latin America, democracy and effective government have evolved slowly. All too often, traditional forms of bourgeois democracy and limited citizen participation have not served the people. The mechanisms that were designed to ostensibly transmit the popular will to the decision makers so that they could govern in accordance with popular desires and needs have been weak historically at best. From the eighties on, the processes of U.S.-inspired democratization and economic neoliberalism were offered as the preferred ways to remedy these weaknesses if not as the only alternative to follow. Neoliberalism (in the context of a democratized government based on Western liberalism) was pushed by international financial institutions like the International Monetary Fund (IMF), and by the U.S. government. The acceptance of these doctrines was sold as a prerequisite for a golden age for democracy and economic development patterned on the United States, and as such was being held out to Latin America and much of the rest of the world as the model to follow.

Yet, as the linked models of Western, capitalist style democratization and neoliberal economics have taken hold throughout the hemisphere, their suitability as a form of governance and viable economic system is being called into question. Throughout Latin America there is growing skepticism that neoliberal economic policies will remedy the residual poverty and maldistribution of income and wealth that have plagued Latin America. Referring to income distribution, Brazil, for instance, had a Gini coefficient of 0.59 at the end of the nineties, reflecting some of the greatest inequality in the world (Franko, 2003: 357). Indeed, despite growth and macroeconomic stability during the nineties, no Latin American country experienced a decrease in income inequality, and many, including Argentina, Bolivia, and Nicaragua, saw income inequality increase (Franko, 2003: 355). This pattern has continued in the years that followed. Worse yet, statistics from the World Bank indicate that economic performance was disastrous in 2002, with overall negative growth of 1.1% (Shifter, 2003: 52). Even though economic growth has improved in 2003, 2004, and 2005, countries like Peru, Bolivia, and Ecuador are still in severe crisis. Poverty is persistent throughout the region and has risen in many countries. A large segment of the population seems left out of what growth has taken place. As the masses and segments of the middle classes have expressed their frustration, the last few years have seen popular uprisings, aborted presidential terms, economic chaos, attempted coups d'état and the continued impoverishment of the masses if not segments of the middle class. This in turn calls into question the legitimacy of the governments—if not the political system—and the ability to govern. The progression of events suggests that there is a realignment that is profound and that may well represent a radical change in politics in the region. The ascendancy of new, progressive political parties like the Workers Party (PT) in Brazil, the Movement toward Socialism (MAS) in Bolivia and the election of Tabaré Vásquez in Uruguay underline this trend. Further, it can be suggested that it is the democratization and celebration of civil society that have created the political space in which the masses can maneuver and mobilize, and in which political movements can grow.

Dissatisfaction with elite rule or an exclusionary political project, or with policies that cause or perpetuate the economic or ethnic marginalization of the masses is certainly not new in Latin America. It has engendered rebellions like those led by Túpac Amaru in the 1780s, Toussaint L'Ouverture in Haiti in 1791, and Hidalgo and Morelos in Mexico in 1810. There have been many other uprisings like that led by Farabundo Martí in El Salvador in 1932. Indeed it was the generalized dissatisfaction with Porfirio Díaz's political ruling class in *fin de siglo* México that induced *los de abajo* (the underdogs or those on the bottom) to enroll in the various armies—and thus the revolutionary project—of the Mexican revolution. Such dissatisfaction and its focus on the failure of the political elite, have led to other less successful political rebellions as well. The Bogotazo and the ensuing *violencia* in Colombia from 1948 to 1956, and the Bolivian revolution in 1952 are cases in point.

Focusing on the last few decades, the economic slowdown during the "lost decade" of the 1980s combined with greater mobilization as political repression fell prey to the end of authoritarian rule and the expansion of democratization, to create a new political dynamic in many of the Latin American nations. Civil society became the locus of action and new forms of political action followed. The projection of an elitist armed vanguard as the spearhead of necessary change, began to fade in the face of unarmed political and social mobilizations. The assertion of popular power that had been seen in popular mobilizations like the pre-coup peasant leagues in Brazil's Northeast, began to bubble up in new and different forms. By the time neoliberal economic policy became more widespread in the 1990s, there was a growing realization that the extant political systems in much of Latin America were proving unable to meet the needs of the vast majorities. Indeed, there is a growing consensus that the traditional politicians' political enterprise is leaving behind the great majorities, and effectively further marginalizing specific groups within those majorities. Such groups include indigenous people and peasants in southern Mexico, Ecuador, and Bolivia, rural laborers and the poor in Brazil, and those who live in the slums and who have been left out of the diffusion of oil wealth in Venezuela as well as large segments of the lower and middle classes in Argentina and Uruguay. Changing attitudes have often led to the abandonment of established political parties for new, more amorphous, ad hoc parties like Chávez's Fifth Republic Movement in Venezuela (MVR), or the Frente Amplio in Uruguay, to the upsurge of new political/social movements and mass organizations, and a plethora of national strikes, demonstrations, and protests such as those that washed across Argentina at the end of 2001 and the beginning of 2002, or that swept across Bolivia in 2003 and 2005.

As has been the case all too often in Latin America, the political systems have been unable to provide basic security in food, housing, education, employment, or monetary value and banking to wide sectors of the population. That is, large segments of the population have been marginalized from the nation project, and the governing institutions have been unwilling or unable to provide solutions for their situations. Indeed, in the eyes of most of the Latin American popular sectors, the structural adjustments and neoliberal reforms representing the Washington Consensus (common positive perspective on neoliberal economic policies and liberal democratization shared by international financial institutions and the U.S. Government) have threatened their security and well being. The insecurity and dissatisfaction felt by the popular sectors and segments of the middle class thus drive them to new forms of protest—to expand their repertoire of contentious actions as Sidney Tarrow (1998) might suggest—and to seek new and different political structures that might better respond to their needs. Old style parties and governments dominated by the elites are increasingly seen as unable to respond.

These current mobilizations seem to be different from the popular uprisings that preceded them. The systems of mass communication and related communication technology, and easy, low cost access to the internet have combined with higher levels of literacy, widened access to higher education and much greater political freedom under the democratization process (see UNDP, 1999: 3–9). This has occurred when ideas of grassroots democracy, popular participation and even elements of liberation theology and Christian Base Community organization have been widely disseminated. However, unlike radical revolutionary movements of the last few decades, these new movements do not employ or advocate the radical, revolutionary restructuring of the state through violent revolution. Rather, their primary focus is to work within civil society, and push government and society to the limits to achieve needed and necessary change and restructuring. As the nineties progressed, dissatisfaction with traditional political leaders and traditional political parties became more widespread as did a growing trend to doubt the legitimacy of the political system itself, and calls for a return to democracy and honest government (see Vanden, 2004). Traditional personalism, clientelism, corruption, and personal, class and group avarice became subjects of ridicule and anger if not rage. The effects of neoliberalism and continued classism and racism amidst ever stronger calls for equality began to be felt.

The dissonance was great. Thus one might conclude that the traditional political institutions seemed too far removed from the masses spatially, politically, class wise and in regard to political culture. Though not always well or precisely articulated, new demands were registered. They were not, however, always addressed to the political system per se, but to society more generally, since there were growing questions about the system's relevancy and legitimacy. Something different was being sought. Different groups were looking for new political structures that allowed for, if not encouraged their participation. Specific segments of the population sought forms of political organization that they could call their own, new structures that would respond to the perceived—and not always clearly articulated—demands being formulated by the popular sectors. Further, the widespread dissatisfaction and varied protests and mobilizations were shattering the cultural and political hegemony historically exercised by the dominant classes and transnational capitalism. Nonetheless, it remains to be seen if such forms of contention can force sufficient changes in the national economic and political power configurations to achieve greater economic equality and ensure effective political participation. Some even wonder if these new forms of contention will ultimately fail to force the restructuring of Latin American society and ultimately prove ineffective in generating the change that is so sorely needed. In the meantime, these movements represent an intense challenge to the extant neoliberal capitalist systems and the established parties and politicians—if not the forms of governance themselves—and are extremely subversive of the status quo.

Bolivia

Events in Bolivia are illustrative. In October of 2003, U.S.-educated Bolivian President Gonzalo "Goni" Sánchez de Lozada was forced out of office by massive displays of popular power by social movements, community organizations, unions and students. A staunch advocate of globalization and neoliberal policies prescribed by international financial institutions like the I.M.F. and World Bank, Sánchez de Lozada was also symbolic of the upper class Western-oriented political elites that have governed Latin America autocratically since the Spanish conquest in the early 1500s. His tormentors were equally symbolic of those the political class had long ruled and repressed. They were small farmers, indigenous peoples, miners, workers, students, and intellectuals who dared to challenge the status quo. Historically, the masses have been continually usurped by various political elites and rarely permitted to rule in their own right. This established a traditional pattern of rule and governance in the region that was more authoritarian than democratic and always elitist. Rarely were the masses allowed to rule or decide policy on their own at the national level. Indeed, in Latin America people of popular extraction and of color have been few in the rarified halls of national government. (The example of Mexico's great national hero, Zapotec Indian Benito Juárez, is one of the notable exceptions.) And even when people of color or those from the popular sectors were in the governing circles, it remains to be seen how often they ruled in favor of the masses.

So it was all the more amazing that the departure of Sánchez de Lozada was effected by "los de abajo"—those on the bottom (see Azuela's classic novel, 2002). He had been forced from office by those who had most often been powerless in Bolivian history. The groups that converged on the Bolivian capital of La Paz and other large cities were predominantly lower class miners and agricultural workers and peasants, people who were mostly indigenous and the poor generally. Theirs was a struggle that had been going at least since the indigenous and peasant uprisings led by Tupac Amaru and Tupac Katari in the 1780s. However, this time it was coordinated, effective, and most importantly, successful. Long before such national mobilization occurred, local communities often formed their own organizations to fight some aspect of colonial rule, exploitation or, more recently, globalization that was impacting them at the most local level. This reaction can, for instance, be seen in the strong grassroots movement against the privatization of the public water supply in the mostly indigenous community of Cochabamba, Bolivia in 2000. There, The Coordinating Committee to Defend Water and Life (Coordinadora de Defensa del Agua y de la Vida), remained locally rooted (see Shultz, 2003: 34–37). Yet—unlike previous local actions—this struggle was always framed in an international and national context. The protesters championed their cause through the internet and sent delegations to international meetings like the World Social Forums in Porto Alegre, Brazil. Further, they were not only very aware of the international dimensions of their struggle and of its globalized causes, but were equally aware of the possibilities of international links with similar struggles and the international anti-globalization movement generally. This awareness, and their electronic and personal links to other movements in Bolivia and outside, later facilitated their integration into the broad national coalition that set forth a national agenda through support for Evo Morales and his MAS Party in the 2002 and 2005 presidential elections. This awareness and extensive networking with other new social movements allowed this and other local or regional movements to become part of a near unstoppable national mobilization that toppled the Sánchez de Lozada government and would eventually carry Evo Morales and his MAS party to power. By linking the local effects of the neoliberal privatization of the water supply in Cochabamba to global policies and national politics, they linked their struggle to a growing regional and international consensus, and to a national movement with concrete, achievable objectives.

Social Movements and the Bolivian Crisis

The intensity of the politicization of this and other social movements in Bolivia was demonstrated by the massive protests and the popular mobilizations that rocked the nation in 2003 and again in 2005. As had occurred in Ecuador in 2000 with CONAIE and allied groups, the popular mobilizations of indigenous peoples and rural peasants were through a newly formed mostly peasant indigenous federation that called for the blockading of roads and popular mobilizations. This indigenous group, the Union of Bolivian Rural Workers and its leader Felipe Quispe were quickly joined by those who grew the coca leaves the Sánchez de Lozada government was eradicating under the direction of the U.S. government. This had been resisted vigorously by the cocaleros (Coca Growers) of the now famous Coca Growers Federation and its indigenous leader, Evo Morales (who had finished barely a percentage point behind President Gonzalo Sánchez de Lozada in the 2002 elections). Other groups like the above-mentioned Cochabamba Coordinating Committee to Defend Water and Life also joined. An ongoing economic crisis and a crisis in traditional politics combined with strong U.S. pressure to open Bolivian markets and virtually eliminate the centuries-old cultivation of coca leaves, to stimulate the masses to meet and mobilize at the local, community level and to heed the calls of the social movements for action. The development of communal organization was also strong and had increased since the 1952 Revolution distributed land to the indigenous peasants. There were peasant unions and local community organizations throughout the Andean region of the country (interview, Gonzalo Muñoz, MAS alternate delegate to Bolivian Chamber of Deputies, La Paz, July 5, 2005). A strong Landless Movement had also developed in the non-Andean Santa Cruz region and became an instrument of peasant mobilization there. As indigenous groups had met in congresses and assemblies—often termed "Assemblies to Take Sovereignty"—in the late eighties and early nineties they had reached the clear realization that they needed instruments to achieve political power. As their consciousness developed, they began to speak explicitly of the "Sovereignty of the People" and the need to create "Political Instruments for the Sovereignty of the People" (interviews, Antonio Paredo, head of MAS bench in Bolivian Congress, La Paz, July 4, 2005; Silvestre Saisari, past president, landless movement in Bolivia, Tampa, Fla., February 17, 2005). As their thinking evolved, they constructed affiliated peasant unions, social movements and political movements like Pacakutic and MAS.

Yet even in what might be termed one of Latin America's most organized societies (Ballvé, 2005), the precipitating event was a U.S.-backed plan to sell Bolivian natural gas through a Chilean port that landlocked Bolivia had lost to its southern neighbor in the ill fated War of the Pacific (1879–1881). The disastrous failure of the neoliberal model that President Sánchez de Lozada had so strongly advocated added to the widely shared perception that this new trade deal was but one more ruse, to extract wealth from the nation and leave the indigenous masses even more poverty ridden and totally subject to the influence of outside forces (Rother, 2003). Historically, most peasant and indigenous uprisings and even many strikes by the tin miners had been characterized by their local nature and lack of linkages to national movements and international conditions. As suggested by comments from the protesters themselves, this uprising against Sánchez de Lozada and his policies was quite different. The voices of the people could be heard in the growing demonstrations:

> He has governed the country for the benefit of the gringos and the multinational companies and the Chileans, not for the Bolivian people. (R. Clavijo, cited in Rother, 2003)

> Globalization is just another name for submission and domination. We've had to live with that here for 500 years and now we want to be our own masters. (N. Apaza, cited in Anti-Trade Message, 2003)

The Union of Rural Workers and the Cocaleros were soon joined by other social movements, urban unions, and students as they mobilized in massive demonstrations in La Paz and other cities. The government futilely tried to repress the demonstrators, causing the loss of 80 lives. This enraged the opposition even more and increased the president's isolation. Meeting in their villages and union headquarters many more decided to join the uprising. Bolivian miners and others across the country also joined the protests and decided to march on the capital. As his political backers dropped away in the face of the mass mobilization Sánchez de Lozada was forced to resign and leave the country.

By the beginning of 2005 there was a growing popular perception that the essential rights of the people were not being honored by the successor government of Carlos Mesa and that the natural gas reserves—symbolic of national patrimony—were once again being looted by foreign interests. This occasioned popular mobilizations by the same popular movements that had driven Sánchez de Lozada from office. Indeed, as the government of former vice president Mesa was beset by similar massive mobilizations in May and June of 2005, the extent of the political power of the mobilized masses once again became manifest. With Evo Morales and his MAS party taking a prominent leadership position, the coalition of new social movements and labor unions pushed even harder. They were unwilling to allow the president of the senate—as the next in line constitutionally—to assume power when Mesa left. Nor was the head of the Chamber of Deputies acceptable. Both were seen as old line politicians who would betray the indigenous people and other mobilized popular sectors once in office. Further, the mobilized movements made it clear that a constituent assembly was necessary to draft a new constitution that would restructure the state to make it more responsive to popular interests and new elections for the national legislature were necessary to get more legislators who were from the common people and were linked to their interests. Only when these conditions were met and the President of the Supreme Court assumed power until new elections could be held, did MAS and the mobilized movements accept a settlement. This ongoing struggle culminated in the formation of a new government after elections were held in which Evo Morales was elected with an outright majority in the first round of voting.

This represented a substantial change in politics, as the mayor of La Paz observed in the quote at the beginning of this chapter. Indeed, these events seemed to well represent the unification of subaltern groups and culmination of an historic cycle that Gramsci foresaw in the quote that opens this chapter. The new social movements in Bolivia had been able to take politics out of the presidential palace and halls of congress where elitist politics—and the traditional political class—dominated and into their space—the villages, neighborhoods, popular councils, and the streets and rural highways that they could control. They had taken the initiative themselves and had been able to forge a broad, national coalition that cemented the two presidents' downfall and established the viability of their social movements as key political actors whose demands had to be heeded. Unlike Ecuador in 2000 and the Bolivian revolution of 1952, they had done so without seizing power themselves, but had demonstrated just how effectively they could use and mobilize massive political power on a national scale. They had done so *from below*, through a broad coalition of social movements with strong identities and deep, democratic ties to their constituencies. They had initiated a form of participatory governance that would radically alter decision making practices in their Andean nation and that suggested that government must indeed serve the people if it was to endure.

Morales and his Movement Toward Socialism (MAS) were able to ride this wave of protest and mobilization as he was elected as the first indigenous president of Bolivia and MAS secured substantial representation in the national legislature (12 of 27 in the Senate and 73 of 130 in the Chamber of Deputies) in the new elections of December 2005. Indeed, Morales seems to have well captured the dynamic essence of the combined movements that brought him to power. As he said in his inaugural address on January 22, 2006,

> We can continue to speak of our history, we can continue to remember how those who came before us struggled: Tupac Katari to restore the Tuantinsuyo, Simón Bolívar who fought for this larger nation (*patria grande*), Ché Guevara who fought for a new more equal world. This democratic cultural struggle, this cultural democratic revolution, is part of the struggle of our ancestors, it is the continuity from Tupac Katari; this struggle and these results are Ché Guevara's continuity. We are here, Bolivian and Latin American sisters and brothers; we are going to continue until we achieve equality in this country. (www.Bolivia-usa.org, accessed June 20, 2006)

Brazil and the Movement of Landless Rural Workers, the MST

Politics in Brazil have also been altered by the insertion of the largest Latin American social movement into the national political arena. The MST (Movimento dos Trabalhadores Rurais Sem Terra) was formed as a response to long-standing economic, social and political conditions in Brazil. Land, wealth and power were allocated in very unequal ways in Brazil since the conquest in the early 1500s. Land has remained highly concentrated and as late as 1996, 1% of the landowners owned 45% of the land (Petras, 2000: 35). Conversely, as of 2001 there were some 4.5 million landless rural workers in Brazil. Wealth has remained equally concentrated. In 2001 the Brazilian Institute of Government Statistics reported that the upper 10% of the population averaged an income that was nineteen times greater than the lowest 40% (Brazilian Institute of Statistics, 2001). The plantation agriculture that dominated the colonial period and the early republic became the standard for Brazilian society. The wealthy few owned the land, reaped the profits, and decided the political destiny of the many. Slavery was the institution that provided most of the labor on the early plantation system and thus set the nature of the relationship between the wealthy landowning elite and the disenfranchised toiling masses who labored in the fields. Land has stayed in relatively few hands in Brazil, and the agricultural laborers continued to be poorly paid and poorly treated. Further, after the commercialization and mechanization of agriculture that began in the 1970s, much of the existing rural labor force became superfluous. As this process continued and became more tightly linked to the increasing globalization of production, not only were rural laborers let go, sharecroppers were expelled from the land they had farmed and small farmers lost their land to larger family or commercial estates. This resulted in growing rural unemployment and the growth of rural landless families with few prospects. Many were forced to migrate to the cities to swell the numbers of the urban poor while others opted for the government sponsored Amazon colonization program whereby they were transported to the Amazon region to cut down the rainforest and begin to cultivate the land. Few found decent jobs in the city and the poor soil of the former rainforest would allow for little sustained agriculture. Thus their plights worsened.

The immediate origins of the Landless go back to the bitter struggle to survive under the agricultural policies implemented by the military government that ruled Brazil from 1964 to 1985. The landless rural workers in the southern Brazilian state of Rio Grande do Sul began to organize to demand land in the early eighties. Other landless people soon picked up their cry in the neighboring states of Paraná, and Santa Catarina. These were the beginning of the MST (see Stedile and Fernandes, 1999; A. Wright and Wolford, 2003; and

Bradford and Rocha, 2002). They built on a long tradition of rural resistance and rebellion that extends back to the establishments of *quilombos* or large inland settlements of run-away slaves and to the famous rebellion by the poor rural peasants of Canudos in the 1890s. In more recent times it included the famous Peasant Leagues of Brazil's impoverished Northeast in the 1950s and early 1960s and the Grass War and peasant struggles in São Paulo State in the 1950s (see Welch, 1999 and 2001). When the MST was founded in southern Brazil in 1984 as a response to rural poverty and lack of access to land, wealth and power, similar conditions existed in many states in Brazil. Indeed, there were landless workers and peasants throughout the nation. Thus the MST soon spread from Rio Grande do Sul and Paraná in the South to states like Pernambuco in the Northeast and Pará in the Amazon region. It rapidly became a national organization with coordinated policies and strong local participatory organization and decision making, and frequent state and national meetings based on direct representation.

By 2001 there were active MST organizations in 23 of the 26 states (interview, Geraldo Fontes, MST national leadership, São Paulo, September 17, 2003). Today the MST is a vital, vigorous and often militant national organization that is arguably the largest and most powerful social movement in Brazil and Latin America. The ranks of those associated with it number over a million (Fernandes, 2005). It has a high mobilization capacity at the local, state and even national level. In 1997, for instance, the organization was able to mobilize one hundred thousand people for a march on Brasilia. Their views are well articulated. They have a clear understanding of the increased commercialization of agriculture and its consequences for the way in which production is organized, if not rural life more generally. Similarly, they are fully conscious of how globalization is strengthening these trends and threatening their livelihood. In small classes, meetings and assemblies and through their newspaper, *Jornal Dos Trabalhadores Sem Terra*, magazine, *Revista Sem Terra*, and numerous pamphlets, they carefully educate their base through a well planned program of political education. They even establish schools in their encampments, settlements and cooperatives to make sure the next generation has a clear idea of the politics in play. In this way, they effectively challenged the cultural hegemony exercised by the dominant national classes and the international capitalist system.

The Landless also facilitate the organic development of highly participatory grass roots organization, beginning with groups of ten families organized as a Base Nucleus in each neighborhood. Local general assemblies are used frequently and all members of the family units are encouraged to participate. Regional, state and even national assemblies are also held on a regular basis, with representatives of the lower level units attending. Leadership is collective at all levels, including the national where some 102 militants make up the National Coordinating Council (Coordinacão Nacional).

Their political culture and decision making processes break from the authoritarian tradition and are subversive of the dominant political culture. The movement has been heavily influenced by Liberation Theology and the participatory democratic culture that is generated by the use and study of Paulo Freire's approach to self-taught, critical education. Indeed, the strongly participatory nature of the organization and the collective nature of leadership and decision making have made for a dynamic new democratic, participatory political culture that challenges traditional authoritarian notions and vertical decision making structures (see MST, 2000, and Rodrigues Brandão, 2001). One of the characteristics of new social movements like the MST is their broad national vision. Thus the Landless envision a thoroughgoing land reform and complete restructuring of agrarian production in all of Brazil. The MST believes that is impossible to develop the nation, to construct a democratic society or eliminate poverty or social inequality in the countryside without eliminating the latifundio. But they go on to say that agrarian reform is only viable if it is part of a popular project that would transform Brazil's economic and social structures (MST, 2000).

Like many of the new social and political movements in Latin America, the *Sem Terra* are well aware of how their struggle is linked to international conditions. Thus they begin by challenging the positive vision of neoliberalism presented by the globalized media and the attempt at hegemonic control that it exercises. In a draft document on the "Fundamental Principles for the Social and Economic Transformation of Rural Brazil," they note that "the political unity of the Brazilian dominant classes under Fernando Henrique Cardoso's administration (1994–2000) has consolidated the implementation of neoliberalism [in Brazil]," and that these neoliberal policies led to the increased concentration of land and wealth in the hands of the few and the impoverishment of Brazilian society. The document goes on to say that "Popular movements must challenge this neoliberal conceptualization of our economy and society" (see MST, 2001a).

Mass political mobilization is another fundamental organizational principle as seen in their massive mobilizations for land takeovers and demonstrations. This vision is widely disseminated to those affiliated with the organization. A pamphlet disseminated by the organization, "Brazil Needs a Popular Project," calls for popular mobilizations, noting that "All the changes in the history of humanity only happened when the people were mobilized." And that in Brazil, "all the social and political changes that happened were won when the people mobilized and struggled" (MST, 2001b).

This type of national organization had not been the case in prior local or regional movements. Previously, identity was much more locally rooted. As had been the case in other Latin American countries, traditional elite dominated politics and bourgeois political parties had proven unable and unwilling to address the deteriorating economic conditions of the marginalized groups who were suffering the negative effects of economic globalization. The response by the new movements was grassroots organization and the development of a new repertoire of actions that broke with old forms of political activity. Developing organization and group actions began to tie individual members together in a strongly forged group identity. They were sometimes assisted in this task by progressive organizations concerned with economic and social justice. In the case of Brazil and the Landless, this role was played by the Lutheran church and especially the Pastoral Land Commission of the Catholic Church. Although these organizations assisted the Landless as did some segments of the Workers Party (PT), the organization never lost its autonomy. It was decided from the onset that this was to be an organization *for* the Landless Workers that would be run *by* the Landless Workers *for their benefit as they defined it*. They engaged in direct actions such as land takeovers from large estates and public lands, the construction of black plastic covered encampments along the side of the road to call attention to their demands for land, and marches and confrontations when necessary. They even occupied the family farm of President Fernando Henrique Cardoso shortly before the 2002 election to draw attention to his landowning interests and the consequent bias they attributed to him. They were at times brutally repressed, assassinated and imprisoned, but they persevered, forcing land distribution to their people and others without land. Their ability to mobilize as many as 12,000 people for a single land takeover or 100,000 for a national march suggested just how strong their organizational abilities were and how well they could communicate and coordinate at the national level. They also created a great deal of national support and helped to create a national consensus that there was a national problem with land distribution and that some substantial reform was necessary.

The Landless have been well attuned to the international globalization struggle and consider themselves part of it, helping to organize and participating in the World Social Forums in Porto Alegre and sending their representatives to demonstrations and protests throughout the world. Indeed, at least one recent work suggests that this was part of a developing global backlash against economic globalization (see Broad, 2002). Struggles that were once local and isolated are now international and linked (see della Porta and Tarrow, 2005). The news media and growing international communications links like cellular phones and especially electronic mail greatly facilitated the globalization of struggle and the globalization of awareness of local struggles and support and solidarity for them. This and the dramatic actions like massive land takeovers by the MST also generated considerable support at the national level and international level and help to define what might be considered a local problem as a national problem that requires national attention and national resources to remedy it.

The interaction between the MST and the Workers Party (PT) is also instructive. Although relations between the two organizations are generally excellent at the local level, with overlapping affiliations, the national leaderships have remained separate and not always as cordial. The MST has maintained a militant line in regard to the need to take over unused land and assert their agenda, whereas much of the PT leadership has wanted to be more conciliatory. Thus the Landless backed and supported Lula (Luiz Inácio "Lula" da Silva) and the Workers Party in most local campaigns and the national campaigns for the presidency. In this way they helped to achieve significant regime change in Brazil, where Lula was elected with 61.27% of the vote in the second round of voting in 2002. Indeed, realizing the PT's historic challenge to neoliberal policies and elitist rule, the Landless turned out heavily in the election to join some 80% of the registered voters who participated in the voting in both rounds. Once the election was over, the Landless did not press to be part of the government. Rather, they continued to press the government for a comprehensive land reform program and a redistribution of the land and wealth. There would be no return to politics as usual. The PT would press its "0 Hunger" program and other ameliorative social and economic initiatives and the MST would press the PT government for the structural reforms (e.g., comprehensive agrarian reform and economic restructuring) that it considered necessary. Indeed, this pattern was similar to the strained relationship that the Zapatistas had had with progressive parties in Mexico. Beginning in 2004 the MST displayed considerable dissatisfaction with what they considered the relative inaction of the PT government in regard to land reform and was threatening to once again engage in massive land takeovers, even though such actions were often portrayed quite negatively by much of the media. The Lula government was facing increasing pressure from international financial institutions and national economic interests to moderate its policies and was further beset by scandals in 2005. By functioning in civil society and not becoming part of the government, the MST was, however, free to pursue its original demands for land reform and socio-economic transformation, offer some critical support to the besieged PT government, but continue to push for real change from below.

Conclusion

As suggested by the examples of Bolivia and the MST, as new social movements grow and are politicized, they come to represent a clear response to the neoliberal economic policies that are being foisted on Latin American nations by international financial institutions, the U.S. government and national economic elites. They have become bulwarks in the resistance to the process of neoliberal globalization advocated by the Washington Consensus and have aggressively resisted the implementation of neoliberal policies. Unlike the governments and ruling parties like the PT, the MST and other new social movements are embedded in civil society and can take advantage of the considerable political space that has opened up as nominal democratization becomes more institutionalized.

As they engage in grassroots organization and massive local and national mobilizations, the diverse groups in Bolivia, the MST and social movements elsewhere have challenged how politics are conducted in their countries and the region. Their growth and militancy have generated whole new repertoires of actions that include national mobilizations so massive that they can topple governments (Bolivia, Ecuador, and Argentina) and/or force them to change their policies. Indeed, they pose the possibility of at least some form of "rule from below." They have left the traditional parties far behind as they forge new political horizons and create a non-authoritarian, participatory political culture. Such movements are also using existing political space to maximum effect. In the process they are strengthening participatory democratic practice substantially and altering the way politics are conducted in Latin America. What remains to be seen is if such actions—no matter how concerted—are sufficient to achieve the long needed structural reforms in the elite dominated internationalized capitalist systems that dominate in Latin America. If indeed such mobilizations are—as Gramsci might conclude—coming together in a new cycle of subaltern actions culminating in successes that are breaking the historic hegemony exercised by the ruling classes in Latin America, we are still left to ponder if this in itself will lead to a new historic stage of popular empowerment, or if this is just a giant leap along that road.

II

NEOLIBERAL GLOBALIZATION AND DEMOCRACY LITE

The Changing Political/Economic Context of Social Movements

Opponents of neoliberalism march in Quito, Ecuador, on October 31, 2002, against Seventh Ministerial Summit of the Free Trade Area of the Americas (FTAA, or ALCA in Spanish). Photo courtesy of Marc Becker.

O NE OF THE BASIC QUESTIONS running throughout the essays in this volume is the relationship between economics and politics. The answers provide much of the framework used for analysis of social movements. All of the authors in this book place considerable emphasis on the emergence of neoliberal economic policies for understanding social movements, and they also see those policies as directly connected to politics (in contrast to the neutral/automatic image that free marketeers themselves like to promote). Starting in the early 1980s, neoliberals implemented policies to limit the role of the state in economy and society. This rollback happened right when large segments of the population needed state services the most because they were adversely affected by economic restructuring, due to the removal of subsidies and protections that were associated with the "import-substitution industrialization" (ISI) development strategies of the postwar period. Social movement organizations frequently filled the void by organizing community-based services, but they could not equal the state's former capacity to foster the public sector. The state quickly became the promoter and defender of narrow, elite political and economic interests, often to the neglect of the people. Privatization, deregulation, and state rollback decreased accountability, shifting many decisions to closed corporate boardrooms. While many observers want us to think neoliberal globalization has generated an era of democracy, analysis of social movements clearly demonstrates that the combined impact of free market and a shrunken state can be highly undemocratic. Although the formalities of elections generate the appearance of democracy, the gap between formal procedure and substantive reality created rising anger directed against the political class by a wide spectrum of civil society, as well as grassroots pressure.

While each of the essays in this collection explores the economy-state question, the two selected for this section highlight important points for thinking about the question. Both illustrate the undemocratic nature of neoliberalism, but do so from very different analytical perspectives.

Judith Adler Hellman's article, which first appeared in 1994, examines the dynamic interaction of neoliberal policies and political struggles in Mexico. This study makes clear that the political complement to neoliberalism was already undergoing adaptation by the 1990s. The Salinas administration's National Solidarity Program (PRONASOL) aimed to reconstruct a more selective form of clientelistic control over society. This is an example of the "targeted social compensation programs" that many governments used to implement unpopular austerity measures with dwindling state resources available for co-optation. Hellman shows that even new popular organizations not linked to the ruling Partido Revolucionario Institucional (PRI) party could be captured by these repackaged clientelist structures, suggesting it was premature to assume that new social movements would necessarily lead to democratization. As it later turned out, the combination of shrinking state funding and expanding independent organizing did destabilize Mexico's dominant-party system, but Hellman's larger point remains important: the neoliberal economic reconfiguration of state-society relations creates new spaces for political contest, and it is by no means predetermined whether that space will be effectively organized by hegemonic forces from above or democratizing initiatives from below.

Susan Spronk and Jeffery Webber compare the social struggles over the privatization of water and natural gas resources in Bolivia between 2000 and 2005. They apply David Harvey's concept of "accumulation by dispossession" to argue that in contrast to primitive accumulation in an earlier stage of capitalism, the neoliberal era accumulates capital by transforming public resources into global commodities, generating forms of social struggle that differ from old working-class mobilizations. They distinguish between the structural significance of gas versus water at the macro level in the global economy, examining the ways in which such differences may affect the framing of issues for social movements. The strategic importance of hydrocarbons for global capital meant that the "gas war" mobilizations had to be framed in macro terms of protecting the resources of the nation, whereas the "water wars" could be framed as reclaiming the commons and protecting local/communal property rights. Spronk and Webber also point out that issue framing alone does not guarantee successful outcomes, as the state responded with massive violence when a globally strategic commodity was at stake; and even the movement's success in ousting President Gonzalo "Goni" Sánchez de Lozada did not immediately derail the neoliberal project.

The two chapters in this section together illustrate the importance of establishing the relation between economics and politics in analysis of social movements. The core questions of origins, dynamics, and outcomes are highlighted by analysis of the link between economics and politics. Neoliberal restructuring since the 1980s has played a role in the origins of a new wave of social protest, but the trimmed-down states also have adjusted their political strategies for neutralizing popular mobilization. Movement strategies therefore must adapt to this changing political context, also recognizing the background role of global capital in shaping state responses. The increasing intensity of social mobilization does not necessarily guarantee successful outcomes.

4

Mexican Popular Movements, Clientelism, and the Process of Democratization

Judith Adler Hellman

T HE STUDY OF NEW SOCIAL MOVEMENTS in Latin America has proven irre-
sistibly attractive to many scholars. Examining these movements allows us
to explore the formation of new identities, the emergence of new political and
social actors, the creation of new political spaces, and the overall expansion of
civil society. While all or any of these phenomena seem sufficiently intriguing
to claim our attention in their own right, the most common rationale offered
for the study of new movements is their apparent link to the democratization
process. Through the last decade, in books, articles, and, above all, in doctoral
dissertations produced around the globe, scholars have justified their interest
in new social movements in terms of the presumed importance of these organizations in the consolidation of democratic institutions. Most theorists
writing in this field would agree with Alvarez and Escobar (1991) that these
movements have "a democratizing impact on political culture and daily life,"
and "contribute to the democratization process." The problem for most analysts is that we do not know enough about *how* this takes place, that is, the way
in which "grassroots democratic practices [are] transferred into the realm of
political institutions and the state."

When I look at the gap between the broader theoretical discussions of the
question and the specific Mexican reality, I am tempted to attribute the faith
in the democratizing powers of new movements displayed by other analysts to
the fact that they are, perhaps, generalizing on the basis of South American
cases. And yet, it turns out that not only students of the transition process in

The original version of this essay appeared in *Latin American Perspectives* 21(2), Spring 1994: 124–142.

the Southern Cone or Brazil are claiming that new social movements have this potential. On the contrary, a number of contributors to the most important recent collection on social movements in Mexico (Foweraker and Craig, 1990) depart—albeit with a bit more caution—from the very same premise: that the growth of a social movement sector is part and parcel of the march toward democracy. Munck (1990: 29), for example, argues that

> the demands of social movements . . . necessarily spill over into the political arena, because access to power, or at least influence on power, given economic conditions, is needed to satisfy their demand for tangible benefits. . . . From here springs the great potential that the actions of social movements can form a part of a wider democratic project.

Foweraker (1990: 3) writes,

> The breadth and impetus of these movements have come to present a strong challenge to the existing system of political representation and control; recent events (and especially the elections of July 1988) have suggested that popular movements might be the wedge that will force an authentically democratic opening within the political system overall.

What, precisely is this "wider democratic project"? What would a "democratic opening within the political system" look like? Is there any evidence that Mexican movements observed by these scholars in the late 1980s subsequently contributed to the institutionalization of democratic expression? Before we can address these questions, or search for evidence of a direct link between the development of new social movements and democratization in Mexico we need to examine the evidence that Mexico is in the process of democratization.

Mexican Exceptionalism

While I am in complete sympathy with virtually any effort to develop a framework for understanding Latin American politics on a broad comparative level, the attempt to shoe-horn the Mexican case into models designed principally to explain the military domination or the democratization of the Southern Cone and Brazil has frequently brought Mexicanists to grief. Mexico was never as authoritarian as the countries that this model was originally formulated to analyze (see Middlebrook, 1986). And the framework currently in fashion for the study of the democratization process does not provide us with a very comfortable fit for the Mexican case. This is because Mexico is not democratizing as rapidly as the slowest South American case, if indeed, it is even limping along in that direction.

Why, then, the confusion? Evidence that a "democratic transition" is underway in Mexico rests largely on a series of political and, above all, electoral reforms that began with Luis Echeverría's (1970–1976) response to the 1968 student movement: an *apertura democrática*, a "democratic opening" that loosened state censorship of the press, gave more space to democratic tendencies within the state-controlled labor movement, permitted parallel, autonomous peasant and labor movements unaffiliated with the official party sectors to organize and strike, and strengthened ties between the PRI (Partido Revolucionario Institucional) and the Socialist International (Shapira, 1977).

Echeverría's efforts to open the political system and reinvest it with legitimacy culminated in the political reform he initiated in 1976 that came into effect under his successor, José López Portillo (1976–1982). While the Federal Law on Political Organizations and Electoral Processes reinforced PRI hegemony by guaranteeing the continued numerical superiority of the official party in all governing bodies, local, state, and federal, it gave new impetus to the formation of a formal, parliamentary opposition. The 1977 law facilitated the registration of new opposition parties, gave "minority parties" the right to sit on the supervisory committees at the polls, provided these parties with electoral commission grants for the payment of campaign expenses, and guaranteed all registered parties access to television and radio time and financial support for their parliamentary staff and their party press. The legislation also increased the size of the Chamber of Deputies and reserved a quarter of the seats in the Chamber to be distributed among minor parties according to the proportion they receive of the total vote.

Notwithstanding all of these encouraging changes, as the right-wing opposition National Action Party (PAN) gained strength between 1977 and 1988, the clean-up of the electoral process that many analysts anticipated would be likely to take place in a more competitive and mature electoral system did not occur. On the contrary, electoral fraud continued to be as prevalent as ever with the PRI-controlled Federal Electoral Commission disallowing on technicalities what were in fact clear PAN victories at the state and local level in the PAN's area of support, the northern border states. Despite a new level of interest and media scrutiny from the United States (prompted by the Reagan regime's obsessive focus on elections as the single indicator of democracy and political health in Central America), the PRI continued through the 1980s to steal elections, although it began to employ more sophisticated methods to do so (Gómez Tagle, 1987: 208–210). Manipulation of computer data largely replaced out-and-out ballot box theft and strong arm tactics at the polls, although the latter also took place. And, after the

1988 elections in which the center-left coalition that formed around the populist candidacy of Cuauhtémoc Cárdenas in all probability won a plurality of votes in the Republic and unquestionably a majority of votes in the Valle de Mexico, the crudest forms of pre-electoral intimidation and violence and postelectoral tampering resumed.

What does the election of 1988 tell us about the prospect for democracy in Mexico? As one analyst of Mexican politics has noted, the election shows that the PRI is clearly disposed to negotiate with the opposition on the rules of the political game, but not on the results (Gómez Tagle, 1989: 1). The appropriation by the ruling party of what was most likely an opposition victory makes clear that the official party is not prepared to cede presidential power under any circumstances. And, in the elections held since 1988, evidence of electoral fraud continues to be, if anything, more incontrovertible than ever. In short, since coming to power, the Salinas regime has employed harassment, intimidation, manipulation, and outright fraud to guarantee that the PRI would regain lost ground.

I have reviewed the evidence on democratization because we cannot analyze the possible role of popular movements in this process without first determining whether Mexico is, in fact, moving toward a more open, democratic or a more closed, authoritarian system. I would argue that the system is neither more democratic nor more repressive, but more Mexican than ever. By this I mean that the manipulative interplay of persuasion and coercion that long characterized the Mexican system—distinguishing it from other Latin American regimes—continues to operate today (Hellman, 1980). However, in the early 1990s, the brutal face of the system is more often displayed. This is because the emergence of the Cárdenas candidacy provided an alternative reference point to the kinds of popular movements which, in the past, might have thrown in their lot with the reformist wing of the PRI. To the extent that these movements remain outside of the cooptive grip of the official party, repression has been used more often than co-optation to impose social control.

Under these largely unfavorable circumstances what, conceivably, could be the democratizing impact of the popular movements? The cases I will examine indicate that the democratizing influence of the popular movements on the Mexican political system has turned out to be very modest indeed. A number of different reasons could be offered to explain why this is so. We might look at the nature of the political reform process itself, or the economic crisis, or the regime's control over the means of communication, or the undiminished capacity of the regime to play off elements of the left against one another. However, the phenomenon on which I will focus in this chapter is the tendency of the new movements to fall squarely into the logic of clientelism that has always guided the political strategies and tactics not only of the official party organizations, but of Mexican opposition movements as well.

Clientelism

Running through the writings on popular movements in Mexico is the insistence that the emergence of these organizations seriously undermines the clientelist structures that have been the pillars on which PRI dominance has rested, particularly in the most backward areas of the country. Foweraker (1990: 16–17), for example, asserts that

> popular movements automatically mount a challenge to these traditional mechanisms of political control. . . . urban popular movements have resisted the clientelistic and patrimonial controls of the PRI government, rejecting the political culture of petitions and concessions in favor of popular projects and political confrontation.

Moreover, he goes on to claim that "the strategic initiatives of the popular movements . . . have rendered increasingly ineffective the use of clientelistic forms of control."

What I will attempt to show, citing the cases of several contemporary urban popular movements, is that the development of popular movements represents a less dramatic and significant departure from clientelism than other analysts have appreciated. I see these movements as deeply enmeshed in clientelistic patterns from which they escape only very rarely. Although the emergence of a new movement may challenge the old PRI-linked networks based on local caciques, it undermines the control of the caciques *only* by replacing the old networks with alternative channels that, generally speaking, are also clientelistic in their mode of operation (J. Fox, 1992: 7–8). A look at the history of independent organizations in Mexico may help us to better understand the mechanics of this process.

The "New Social Movements" of Old

Decades before Mexicanists had ever dreamed of "new social movements," pondered the thought of Antonio Gramsci, or pored over the writings of Touraine (1975), Melucci (1977), or other social movement theorists (see Tarrow, 1985), researchers used to poke around trying to understand the workings of the independent movements that regularly arose in the cities and, particularly, in the countryside. For example, in the late 1960s I studied two independent peasant movements in the Laguna region of north-central Mexico (Adler, 1970; Hellman, 1988). One was the Communist Party–linked Central Union, which grew out of the agrarian struggles and the land distribution of the 1930s. The other was the Agrarian Union, tied to Carlos Madrazo and other dissident *priístas* (forerunners of the "democratic current" that would emerge decades later under Cárdenas and Muñoz Ledo). Together with the local committees of the CNC, these organizations competed for peasant adherents in a sometimes violent contest for control over the Laguna peasantry and the influence and spoils that accompanied this control.

Perhaps because the two independent organizations referred to themselves as peasant unions rather than movements, or more likely because the issue was not yet on the agenda, no one expected these groups to promote "democratization" (Landsberger and Hewitt, 1970; Huizer, 1968; Martínez Saldeña, 1980; Hellman, 1978). Analysts of these movements, like the peasant members themselves, seemed happy enough if the leaders occasionally consulted (or at least briefed) the membership, capably represented the group's interests before bureaucrats and cotton merchants in Mexico City, resisted incorporation into the PRI, and did not stuff their pockets with *all* of the proceeds of *ejidal* (collective land) cotton sales.

When students of modern movements assess the impact of these new organizations, many express optimism about the capacity of such groups "to influence public policy," promote alternative political visions, and thus contribute to the "erosion of the ideological hegemony so long a basic characteristic of the regime" (Haber, 1990: 6, 20, 37; and also Ramírez Saiz, 1990: 243). Therefore, in drawing a comparison between old and new, it is important to note that the Agrarian Union led by Pedro Gallardo, was little more than an alternate patronage network in which Gallardo utilized his clientelistic links to Madrazo to win credits to open a cooperatively owned cotton gin and to float his impoverished *ejidatario* constituents through the current season (Hellman, 1983). In contrast, however, the Central Union could be properly described as articulating an alternative vision for the *ejidatarios* it represented and for the Laguna region as a whole. Bringing his own battery of experts into the zone (veterans of the famous League of Socialist Agronomists who had surveyed the Laguna haciendas prior to the distribution of land in 1937), Arturo Orona, the leader of the Central Union, promoted crop diversification, modernization of the irrigation network to double the land available for agriculture, and the semi-elaboration of agricultural products grown in the region (that is, a program of industrialization intended to absorb the surplus agricultural population).

All of the Central Union's campaigns to transform the economic base of the Laguna eventually found their way into public policy—an accomplishment that analysts of today's popular movements would likely take as evidence of the Central Union's impact on the system. Ironically, probably the greatest effect of Orona's decades of struggle was to inject new life into lagunero capitalism, reinforcing the agro-industrial bourgeoisie of the region who now turned from the production of cotton to wine and dairy products. To be sure, at least some of the peasant members of the Central Union also benefited directly from these changes although—as is inevitably the case when independent organizations win concessions from the state—most of the peasants who received new land and other benefits were loyal *priístas*. Innumerable cases could be used to demonstrate the pattern in which independent, opposition organizations sow the seeds for change through years of determined struggle, while quiescent PRI-affiliated peasants or urban poor reap the rewards (see Hellman, 1988: 144 and 291, fn 51).

Given this record, we can see the Central Union as an independent peasant movement whose activities ultimately transformed a key region in Mexico. In this sense, the mobilization and struggles of this group of independently organized *ejidatarios* had a significant economic and social impact (Hellman, 1981). The Central Union was also relatively more democratically structured in its internal workings than the CNC or Gallardo's highly personalistic following. But for all the changes it stimulated in the region, and notwithstanding its more democratic, responsible leadership, no one, to my knowledge, has argued that any of the Central Union's activities should or could have functioned to democratize the Mexican political system. That was not its job.

The independent organizations of old, as the new popular movements of today, arose in response to dissatisfaction with the representational structures provided by the PRI and the disinclination of the state to deliver services to poor Mexicans, be they *ejidatarios* in need of credit or agricultural inputs, or slum dwellers who lack water, electricity and public transport. The goals of the old organizations were straightforward: to establish themselves as a force with which to be reckoned on the local and, eventually, the national scene, and thus to wrest concessions from the state. The techniques applied in the olden days (i.e., before the generally agreed upon watershed of 1968) were not so different from the mobilizational and pressure tactics used by movements today— although to hear all the excited talk about "new practices," a student of movements could be forgiven for feeling some confusion on this point. Demonstrations, hunger marches to the capital, petitions, and letter writing campaigns were the tactics the old movements employed. Then as now, group members were assembled, marched or trucked (banners flying) to the Zócalo, Los Pinos (the president's residence), or the appropriate government agency.

Here they would remain—a public embarrassment to the regime—until they were received by some government functionary who promised to address, if not redress, their grievances. Peasant mobilizations, demonstrations, land invasions, hunger marches, and occupations of government offices were a constant feature of rural politics employed throughout the 1940s, 1950s, and 1960s (Hellman, 1988: 143–163).

When we examine the historical record we find organizations like the Central Union engaged in tireless, often heroic efforts to gain benefits for their constituents: sometimes demanding material concessions and, other times, fighting for more popular control over the administration of the state agencies (e.g., *ejidatario* control over the ejidal bank). Moreover, a large part of the energies of such groups was typically directed to exposing inefficiency and malfeasance of government officials and agencies, and occasionally—when a favored opposition candidate had been denied office—denouncing electoral fraud.

Ramírez Saiz (1990: 235) has argued that the new urban popular movements are distinguished by the fact that "they no longer plead for favors so much as demand their rights." But a careful look at the past reveals that the tactics of an independent movement like the Central Union typically shifted back and forth over the years, according to the strategic requirements of the moment, at times demanding, at other times pleading for the concessions it was trying to extract from the system. As I have noted, an independent organization of this sort was thought to be successful if it managed to win at least some of the benefits it sought for its members. And, while the activities of these earlier movements could be said, in some instances, to have challenged the corruption and inequality that characterized the Mexican system, their achievements were generally measured by members and leaders alike, in the material concessions they could squeeze out of the regime in power.

The New Social Movements of the 1990s

A lack of historical perspective has led some analysts of the modern movements to see the challenges facing these groups as quite new. In fact, the techniques employed by Salinas in his effort to control the development of independent movements are as old as the one-party system itself. Attempting to co-opt both leaders and whole organizations, the President incorporated popular movement leaders directly into his administration. And he offered the independent organizations funding for their most cherished projects in return for their signatures on *convenios de concertación*, accords in which popular movements agree to support Salinas's national project, "modernization," in return for a variety of favors from the administration.

In the case of the Comité de Defensa Popular (CDP), an urban popular movement based in the northern state of Durango, the rewards for joining the President's *concertación* were substantial. Funding for small business projects, support for the organization in its conflicts with a hostile state governor, and, eventually, Salinas's personal weight behind the CDP's attempts to gain registration as a political party constituted the pay-off this group received for its willingness to support the President (Haber, 1990: 24, 26–27, 31, 36).

Examining Salinas's response to the challenge of the CDP's independence, Haber (1990: 30) notes that the President saw this as an opportunity for the PRI to regain lost ground by encouraging working relationships with opposition leaders who are not affiliated with the CNOP, the official party's "popular sector." "By signing *convenios* with the CDP, Salinas may also be able to put effective pressure on the CNOP to 'modernize,' and thereby to become more politically effective."

This move to invigorate the official party organizations by encouraging the competition of independent groups seems to Haber (1990: 40) to be one of the perplexing qualities of the new regime. "Could it be," he writes,

> that, at least in some instances, the State is willing to alter its relationship with the PRI and instead of treating the official party as a State agency makes some progress in distancing itself from the party apparatus and forcing the PRI to compete with the opposition?

In fact, the practice of encouraging the growth of independent groups that operate outside of the official party channels is but another long standing technique of control utilized by the Salinas administration. Traditionally this particular maneuver serves two purposes. The development of a rival organization may stimulate corrupt or ineffectual PRI-linked organizations to mend their ways. And support thrown by the president to some independent group may undercut the attraction of independent organizations that are more genuinely threatening to the regime than the one that is receiving official encouragement.

Historical examples of this particularly sleazy form of social control abound, although no period in recent Mexican history, to my knowledge, was more fecund in the creation of state-supported "independent" organizations than the regime of Luis Echeverría. The especially nasty twist practiced by the Echeverría administration was the invention of peasant and workers' organizations that carried the names of *existing* militant peasant organizations but were headed by people passionately loyal to Echeverría (Hellman, 1988: 158–159). This period witnessed the birth of numerous state-sponsored peasant organizations that sported the name, style, and rhetoric of genuinely

militant opposition groups, but reported to the CNC (or the president himself) at the national level. As a result, the Echeverría period was marked by
profound ideological confusion as the oppressed peasant (or bewildered researcher!) who may have made his or her way to Mexico City to seek help
from the Independent Peasant Central (CCI) of Danzos Palomino or the
General Union of Workers and Peasants of Mexico (UGOCM) of Jacinto
López was now confronted with no fewer than *two* CCIs and *two* UGOCMs,
one genuinely autonomous and *muy luchador* (very combative), and the
other co-opted by the regime.

Thus we can see that today's opposition movements face the same challenges as independent groups of the past. They are inevitably faced with the
choice between two uninviting alternatives. They may fall in with the regime
(i.e., sign *convenios* or solidarity pacts) that guarantee the kinds of material
concessions that their supporters need. In so doing, however, they will compromise their independence and foreclose the possibility of articulating a critique of the regime and its policies toward the poor. On the other hand, they
may maintain a staunch independence from the regime, but risk the loss of
the popular support they command. This is because members desperately
need the material benefits and concessions for which the organization is
struggling and may not be able to afford the luxury of striking a more militant, oppositionist stance.

Democratization from Within?

But even if the new movements run the same danger of co-optation as the old
movements, and even if we acknowledge that their activities do not democratize the *system* as such, might it not be the case that the new movements are
more intrinsically democratic and therefore constitute a school for democracy
for people with little acquaintance with genuine participation? Here, unfortunately, the record is mixed, but generally not encouraging. Haber's study of
the CDP has exposed a structure that is as hierarchical as virtually any other
Mexican organization.

> Like most other popular movements in Mexico, the CDP does not foster collab-
> orative decision-making processes as much as it counts on rank-and-file support
> for leadership decisions it sends down through the organization for consultation
> and ratification. . . . The lack of participation is most noticeable around key
> strategic decisions—such as political alliances. (1990: 14–15)

In what is surely the most perceptive part of a very insightful analysis,
Haber (1990: 18) points out that the value of internal democracy is, in fact, a

matter of dispute among independent popular organizations, and that "there are pluses and minuses associated with different degrees of internal pluralism at different points in a movement's history." Most important, he notes that "internal democracy is not of paramount importance among the CDP rank-and-file" who are far more concerned with the organization's ability to deliver goods and extract concessions from the state, than they are with questions of internal equality and participatory democracy. In a passage that would serve as well to describe the long, successful leadership of Arturo Orona in the Central Union as the movements of today, Haber (1990: 19) writes,

> The ability to deliver goods and extract concessions from the state, combined with inspirational ideological positions articulated by a competent and ideally charismatic leadership, is the winning combination for most, if not all Mexican [urban popular movements]. Many CDP members are first or second generation immigrants from rural Durango and most have very low incomes and little or no formal education. Within the political culture of the CDP, as is true elsewhere in low-income urban barrios throughout Mexico, [the opportunity for] participation in decision-making is simply not valued as much as the demonstrated ability [of the organization's leaders] to extract governmental concessions and services.

These observations go a long way toward explaining the disappointing picture that meets the eye when we look more closely at the much vaunted role of women in these organizations. Although female participants outnumber male in all of the urban popular movements, women are not merely under-represented but sometimes totally absent from leadership ranks. In the CDP, for example, where women constitute the overwhelming majority of participants, Haber (1990: 19) reports that the efforts to effect changes in the status of women either in the CDP-dominated neighborhoods or in the organization's power structure have largely proven futile. And Stephen's (1992: 86) work on rural movements provides a similarly discouraging view. She notes that "the few discussions that exist of women's participation" in the peasant unions that struggle for survival outside of the official party system, "create a picture of women doing a great deal of work but receiving no formal recognition." Carbajal Ríos (1988: 426–427), an activist in the Coordinadora Nacional "Plan de Ayala" (CNPA) notes,

> When the struggle is most intense, women occupy land and government offices, attend marches, meetings and sit-ins carrying their children along. They confront the police, the caciques, and the armed guards . . . and, as a consequence, are beaten and mistreated. They are always involved in the "domestic" labor of the organization, like the preparation of food and fund raising . . . [but] rarely are they recognized. . . . Women are absent in decision making in

local and regional assemblies and training and educational meetings. These activities are intended for men.

Thus, notwithstanding the elaborate rhetoric on the question, Haber (1990: 19) can observe that "real changes have been slow in coming and limited in outcome." If only for this reason, the experiences of women in the formation of the garment workers union and the cooperative movement of seamstresses is important for us to study because it represents a unique case of a movement run by and for women (Carrillo, 1990).

Ironically, Haber (1990: 20) believes that the "internal democratization of the CDP and other popular movements, parties, political institutions and Mexican political life in general is associated with the degree to which Mexico experiences a significant political, economic and social democratization process." Thus, turning the expectations of many new social movement theorists on their head, Haber anticipates that the CDP may be expected to become more democratic in its internal workings if and when the Mexican system as a whole becomes more democratic! Clearly, this prospect does not give much cause for optimism.

If the system is not growing more democratic under the pressure of movement demands, and if the movements themselves are far from paragons of participatory democracy and, indeed, only *appear* somewhat democratic when compared with either the strict hierarchical patterns of the PRI or the most Leninist parties of the left, to what extent can we see the new movements as promoting democracy either in the life of their supporters or the life of the country? In fact, the assumption that new movements are automatically more democratic seems as ill-founded as the assumption that they inevitably promote democratization, simply because they make demands on the system. I think that the lesson offered by a close scrutiny and comparison of past and contemporary independent movements is that rather than assume, we need to *inquire* how democratic such movements are either in their internal practices or their impact on the system.

The Iron Law of Incorporation

In his influential writings on urban movements, Ramírez Saiz (1986: 208) weighs and then dismisses the possibility that the movements will be absorbed into the PRI. "It is not viable," he asserts, "to speak of absorption by the system." Indeed, it is not, if by absorption we mean incorporation directly into the PRI, or its "popular" sector, the CNOP.

But we have already seen that absorption into the official party or one of its sectors is by no means the only way that militant organizations are demobilized. Even as they retain their "autonomous" identity and status, independent organizations may also be coopted: curtailing their criticism of the regime and their pressure on the system in return for hand-outs and favors from the government in power. This is precisely what Haber suggests may happen to the CDP as a consequence of the trade-offs it has worked out with Salinas. And it is also what many observers find is occurring in the case of the national coordinating body of the urban popular movements, CONAMUP. In fact, Ramírez Saiz's optimism that urban popular movements would resist the lure of cooptive offers may well be due to the fact that he was writing during the de la Madrid years (1986: 195). In this period, the official response to popular movements was to ignore them completely or repress their activities. Ramírez Saiz, along with many others, did not anticipate the slick forms of manipulation that Salinas chose to apply. For, notwithstanding the economic crisis, through PRONASOL, the "national solidarity program" the regime assigned very substantial material rewards to those popular groups willing to sign pacts and *convenios*. Using funds accrued from the sale of state-owned enterprises to private capital, Salinas channeled food, electricity, potable water, clinics, schools, and other social services to organized groups of rural and urban poor people willing to express their "solidarity" with the regime.

Of course not every popular movement responded to Salinas's overtures in the same way. Interviews that I carried out in the summer of 1990 with leaders and members of the *Asamblea de Barrios* (neighborhood assemblies) revealed a conscious effort on the part of that organization to escape the logic of clientelistic politics that governed the behavior of other movements. Like CONAMUP, the Asamblea de Barrios is a popular urban movement that grew out of the mobilization following the earthquakes that struck Mexico City in 1985. Initially formed by those left homeless in the disaster, the Asamblea outlived the emergency, expanded its membership and began to organize poor urban people around the demand for affordable housing for slum dwellers in the center city and the extension of urban services—potable water, sewer lines, electricity, schools, clinics, and bus lines—to people living on the periphery of the Federal District. Comparing the approach of his organization with that of CONAMUP, Asamblea leader Francisco Saucedo noted,

> We have, in fact, a problem with movements that are similar to ours but from which we are now trying to distance ourselves. For example, we went to the Ministry of Urban Development of the Federal District in 1987 to request the expropriation of properties that were abandoned. . . .

But, at the same time that we are pressing the authorities to expropriate these holdings as provided for in the law, other popular organizations show up at the Ministry of Urban Development saying, "what we want is a milk store for our *colonia*." In this way they make it easy for the authorities to respond by saying, "since an urban expropriation is very difficult, we will give you a *lechería* instead."

We say to these *compañeros*: "you, yourselves are demobilizing the movement because the expropriation of the speculators' holdings is the key." But these other groups are ready to settle for a *lechería* or a *tortillería* which is a benefit to be sure, but one that never gets to the heart of the housing problem.

Thus you can see that we have a different way of operating than other urban popular movements. And, as a result, we cannot be manipulated by disinformation or by anyone who comes along and says to us, "look, I have some land that I can get for you and all you have to do is lend me your support and back me." This is the way that some politicians will try to buy your loyalty.

Looking at the contradictions faced by those who want to alter the system to which they must apply for benefits, Saucedo notes,

If we go to the very authorities that we characterize as illegitimate and ask for housing, we end up reinforcing the present structures. We give the government the opportunity to resolve our problem with housing, but we reinforce its position. But if we go with other proposals and alternatives and if we pose global issues that are likely to modify the structure of government, at least we are calling these structures into question. And this is why we are struggling to have a democratically elected government in the Federal District rather than an appointed regent. (Interview, Mexico City, June 1990)

Conclusions

If the growth of new social movements in Mexico—and, perhaps, in other settings—does not necessarily correlate with democratization, why the insistence on linking the two? Perhaps it reflects the intellectual dominance of the democratization model developed by O'Donnell (1997) in the 1980s, which replaced his bureaucratic-authoritarian paradigm that commanded so much attention in the previous decade.

I am not arguing that a democratization process is not underway in the Southern Cone, in Eastern Europe, or—one might hope—elsewhere in the world. Much less am I proposing that we ought not to study this process and its *possible* link to the growth of grassroots movements. What I am suggesting is that popular movements, when they arise, constitute a phenomenon that is significant in itself. As the Mexican case indicates, popular movements do not necessarily bring about an opening of the political system. But we do not need to justify our study of these movements with the claim that they promote institutional responses that reinforce democracy. The formation of new identities, the expansion of civil society, the search for new ways of doing politics, the mobilization of new sectors of society are all important developments in themselves and we do not need to see the movements as necessarily fostering the institutionalization of democratic practices in order to legitimize our concern with these organizations.

The most compelling reason to look at popular movements in some light *other* than that of democratization is that even by the most optimistic reading, this process is not underway in Mexico. On the contrary, Mexico was a less democratic country in the early 1990s than at any time in the recent past. The 1988 elections were stolen from the rightful winners. Electoral violence and suppression of opposition victories have, if anything, increased since 1988. And perhaps the clearest sign that Mexico is moving away from rather than toward a more democratic, open system is the implementation of the decision by the de la Madrid and Salinas regimes first to open the economy, and later to cut a free trade deal with the United States. These policies, destined to totally transform the Mexican economy and culture—if not, ironically, the political system—were made without *any* democratic consultation whatsoever. As I have learned in the process of my recent research into the electronics and textile industries, these policies were conceptualized and implemented with absolutely no prior consultation of the economic elites whose interests would be affected—not to speak of the economic have-nots who would find themselves out of work and on the street.

The regime's implementation of neoliberal economic policies that are so damaging to the popular masses underscores the continued success of the mechanisms of social control that have long functioned in Mexico. The popular movements that signed *convenios* (agreements) lost the opportunity to protest the effects of Salinas's program on the poor, let alone articulate an alternative model.

Of course, it could be argued that it is not the role of a mass popular movement to formulate and promote an alternative vision of society, but rather that this is the role of a political party. I believe that here, precisely, lies the source of much of the confusion, disillusionment, and unhappiness about the place of the new urban movements in the process of democratization (Hellman, 1992). In light of the much longer-term failure of a fragmented left to effectively press for a program of democratic transformation, observers somehow expect the social movements to get the job done where the parties could not. And the movements do, to some extent, try to do just this. As Francisco Saucedo told me in the 1990 interview,

> The Asamblea de Barrios has a political as well as an economic, revindicative [demand-making] side. Among other things it is calling for the Federal District to become a state so that the Regent, who is now appointed by the president, would be replaced with an elected governor. We are also demanding popular participation at the level of *colonia, barrio* and *delegación*. We denounce repression and corruption and call for popular representation. But the central thrust of our activities has been the demand for housing, for urban services, for land, and for schools, clinics, transportation, water, sewers, and electricity.

A more realistic conception of the role and potential of urban movements would take into account the difference between a group dedicated to day-to-day struggles for life's basic necessities, and a political party that bears the burden of theorizing and organizing to promote broad societal change—and the expansion of institutionalized forms of democratic expression.

Postscript

The analysis presented above was first written for a workshop at CEDLA in Amsterdam in 1991 which was two years before civil society activists organized the non-partisan *Alianza Cívica* that mobilized millions of Mexicans to push for clean elections, three years before the reorganization of the Federal Electoral Institute (IFE) as an organism independent of state and official party control, and six years before the 22 million residents of the Mexican capital gained the right to elect the person who would govern the Federal District, replacing the "regent" historically appointed by the Mexican president. Indeed, it was written almost ten years before alternation in office at the national level became a reality when the election of the *panista* candidate, Vicente Fox, ended some 70 years of uninterrupted control by the PRI.

Nonetheless, the historical, cultural, and economic factors that push Mexicans toward clientelistic resolutions of their problems in many respects remain as strong today as the period covered in this analysis. How and why clientelism has survived the collapse of the PRI's political control and outlived the co-optive one-party system would be the subject of another essay. But it is clear that the many, if halting, steps toward full democracy that Mexicans have taken over the last two decades have not gone far enough to loosen the hold that patron-client relations have over Mexican political actors, above all the poor.

5

Struggles against Accumulation by Dispossession in Bolivia

The Political Economy of Natural Resource Contention

Susan Spronk and Jeffery R. Webber

O N JUNE 6, 2005, BOLIVIA'S GAS WAR came to an end. After months of steady road blockades and protests demanding the nationalization of the country's natural gas reserves, President Carlos Mesa offered his resignation to Congress, explaining that he was incapable of presiding over such a tumultuous country. This was one of many climactic points in a series of popular uprisings that have posed a fundamental challenge to the neoliberal model. Since the Cochabamba water war of 2000, Bolivia has seen the emergence of some of the most powerful social movements on the continent. While social movements are by no means new in Bolivia, a country with a long history of revolution and struggle, the latest protest cycle marks a renewal of militancy and growing success on the part of these movements in putting their demands on the political agenda that has potentially revolutionary implications (Thomson and Hylton, 2005).

Building on David Harvey's (2003) concept of struggles against "accumulation by dispossession," this chapter compares and contrasts the movements that erupted during key moments of this protest cycle—the water wars of Cochabamba in 2000 and La Paz–El Alto in 2005 and the gas wars of October 2003 and May–June 2005. During these events, diverse sectors of the population were mobilized in massive actions against the government, concentrating their attention on foreign investment projects that were perceived to transfer the economic benefits brought by natural resources to transnational corporations. In contrast to the anti-International Monetary

---

The original version of this essay appeared in *Latin American Perspectives* 34(2), March 2007: 31–47.

Fund (IMF) movements of the mid-1980s, these movements articulated a clear link between accumulated popular grievances and an identifiable set of government policies that was able to sustain coalitions of indigenous movements, workers, peasants, and the urban poor around a unitary national project (see Nash, 1992; Perreault, 2006). While the struggles are intimately connected and even involve many of the same participants, we argue that the fight for the nationalization of natural gas poses a more fundamental challenge to neoliberalism than the struggles around water because of the political-economic importance of the resource.

Privatization and Accumulation by Dispossession

The struggles against the privatization of the hydrocarbons and water sectors of the Bolivian economy provide exemplary demonstrations of the kinds of movements that have emerged in the neoliberal era to contest what Harvey calls "accumulation by dispossession." For Harvey, Marx rightly highlights processes of capital accumulation "based upon predation, fraud, and violence" but incorrectly imagines them to be exclusively features of a "primitive" or "original" stage of capitalism (2003: 144). In the neoliberal era, privatization has become a fundamental strategy of accumulation by dispossession, which Harvey argues is a veritable "enclosure of the commons." Privatization entails the release "at very low (and in some instances zero) cost" of a set of assets formerly owned by the state that can then be seized by private capital and used for profit (149). This latest phase of accumulation by dispossession was set in motion on an international scale largely under the tutelage of the U.S. imperial state and a neoliberal ideology that sought to redefine the role of all states, and was implemented through international financial institutions such as the World Bank and the IMF. Accumulation by dispossession is not merely privatization of formerly state or public resources, but their acquisition by transnational capital in the U.S. and other core economies.

Harvey (2003: 162–169) further argues that accumulation by dispossession gave rise to a multifaceted array of struggles that display some new characteristics. These struggles—ranging from the Ogoni people's struggle against Shell Oil to campaigns for preserving biodiversity to the thousands of anti-IMF austerity riots of the 1980s—do not take place under a working-class or trade-union banner or with working-class leadership identified as such, but rather draw from a broad spectrum of civil society. Given the wide range of social interests that participate in these struggles, he posits that they produce "a less focused political dynamic of social action" (168) than for example, that of the revolutionary socialist movements that emerged throughout the developing world after World War II. He argues that, although these movements draw strength from their embeddedness in daily life, a "danger lurks that a politics of nostalgia for that which has been lost will supersede the search for ways to better meet the material needs of impoverished and repressed populations" (177). He nonetheless sees revolutionary potential in contemporary struggles to "reclaim the commons." For Harvey, "it is often relatively easy to effect some level of reconciliation" between traditional socialist concerns and the latest wave of struggles against accumulation by dispossession when the connections are cultivated through "struggles within expanded reproduction" (177–179).

Harvey's contribution to our understanding of the dynamics of contemporary resistance injects a much-needed focus on political economy into analyses of the social-movement struggles against neoliberalism in Bolivia. Existing studies of the gas and water wars have tended to focus on the strategies of the social movements, emphasizing questions related to the subjective self-understanding and self-representation of movement actors during these moments of popular struggle. Insufficient attention has been paid to the way in which structural factors shape collective action. In what follows, we aim to analyze the context in which the social movements struggling against the privatization of water and gas in Bolivia emerged and framed their demands, in terms of the particular roles these resources played in the political economy.

A "frame" is an interpretive schema "that simplifies and condenses the 'world out there' by selectively punctuating and encoding objects, situations, events, experiences, and sequences of actions within one's present or past environment" (Snow and Benford, 1992: 137).

We argue that in the gas wars the social movements produced a macro frame and politics based on the fact that natural gas is what Jan Selby (2005) has described as a "structurally significant" resource: an important input in industrial capitalist economies, unevenly and scarcely distributed in the world, relatively easy to establish oligopolistic control over, and a central source of revenue for economic development and state building. When social movements and the state negotiate over natural gas, they are effectively struggling over the future trajectory of the state. Resources that are not structurally important—such as water—are fundamentally important to the sustenance of human life but do not have the same economic importance in the contemporary capitalist system, measured in terms of their contribution to Gross National Income (GNI). Therefore, the micro frame and politics developed by the movements struggling over water focus on local democratic control rather than on national development and the construction of a different, distinctly non-neoliberal state. (For in-depth analyses of these struggles, see Albro, 2005; Assies, 2003; Crespo Flores, Fernández Quiroga, and Peredo, 2004;

Gómez, 2004; Hylton and Thomson, 2004; Laurie, 2005; Laurie, Andolina, and Radcliffe, 2002; Mamani Ramírez, 2004b; Postero, 2005.)

Natural Gas Accumulation by Dispossession

In the Bolivian context, natural gas is clearly a natural resource of structural significance, and its privatization in the 1990s is a clear illustration of accumulation by dispossession. The importance of natural gas in Bolivia's economy is on a par with the significance of silver and tin historically. The hydrocarbons sector of Bolivia's economy generates between US$1.4 and US$1.5 billion annually. Of this sum, US$860 million stems from the exploitation of natural gas, US$106 million from liquid petroleum gas, and US$460 million from condensed petroleum and gasoline (*Le Monde Diplomatique*, April 2–3, 2005: 3). To put these numbers in perspective, Bolivia's GNI was US$8.3 billion in 2000, US$8.1 billion in 2003, and US$8.7 billion in 2004 (World Bank, 2005). New discoveries since 1997 put the country's gas reserves at the second-largest in Latin America. Demand for natural gas in the neighboring countries of Argentina, Brazil, Chile, and Uruguay has experienced sustained growth in the past 10 years and is projected to continue. The combination of substantial reserves and growing regional demand places Bolivia in the enviable position of being the only Southern Cone country with the capacity to meet this demand (Villegas Quiroga, 2004: 35–39). Natural gas exploitation is a defining component of Bolivia's political economy, and therefore subject to very high stakes in the struggles over accumulation by dispossession.

With the Law of Capitalization and the Hydrocarbons Law of 1996, the Bolivian state, then under the first administration of Gonzalo Sánchez de Lozada (1993–1997), privatized the hydrocarbons sector, returning it to a type of management not seen since the 1920s (Miranda Pacheco, 1999: 242). For more than 60 years prior to 1996, "the oil industry was owned and controlled by the government. Foreign companies participated in petroleum exploration and production, splitting the benefits with the Bolivian government 50/50" (Shultz, 2005: 16). Capitalization in the case of hydrocarbons split the industry into activities of exploration and exploitation (production) and transportation with the goal of facilitating the entry of more foreign firms. Furthermore, through this legislation, wellhead royalties owed to the state by the transnationals were reduced from 50 percent to 18 percent in all "new" discovery sites.

Two specific facets of the hydrocarbons privatizing process deserve special mention because they match so perfectly Harvey's accumulation by dispossession. First, immediately prior to its capitalization, the state company

Yacimientos Petrolíferos Fiscales de Bolivia (YPFB) had been "on the verge of completing a contract to build a pipeline to connect Bolivian gasfields to Brazilian markets," which would have increased its profits "by at least $50 million a year for 40 years. These earnings, instead, were largely transferred to private firms that borrowed capital from the same international institutions that had previously offered loans to YPFB" (Kohl, 2004: 904). Second, Sánchez de Lozada's Hydrocarbons Law No. 1731, promulgated on June 26, 1996, manipulated the previous Hydrocarbons Law No. 1689—implemented just short of two months earlier, on April 30, 1996—to redefine "new" and "extant" fields of natural gas. Production defined as new under both versions of the law would be subject to 18 percent wellhead royalties as compared with 50 percent in the existing fields. The 1996 law affected principally the major natural gas camps of San Alberto and San Antonio. Each was effectively moved from "extant" (both camps previously so defined because in each case the deposits were "proven," not simply "probable") to "new" and therefore subject to the lesser royalty (Villegas Quiroga, 2004: 84–85). In Kohl's estimation, this constitutes "a giveaway that could cost the nation hundreds of millions, if not billions, of dollars over the next 40 years" (2004: 904).

The effect on the budget was catastrophic (Kohl, 2003: 346). From 1997 to 2002, Bolivia's budget borrowing increased from 3.3 to 8.6 percent of its GNI (Shultz, 2005: 16–17). As Shultz (2005) points out, privatization of the hydrocarbons sector was a key component in the World Bank's and IMF's overall plan for Bolivia. The IMF demanded that the budget shortfall be made up through cuts in social spending and increases in regressive taxes that hit poor Bolivians the hardest. Such a pathological economic model could not be sustained, and it would be yet another IMF demand to increase taxes against the poor—to reduce the deficit dramatically—that set off the massive confrontations of Bolivia's Febrero Negro (Black February) of 2003 (APDHB/ASOFAMD/CBDHDD/DIAKONA/FUNSOLON/RED-ADA, 2004; Shultz, 2005). Thirty-four people were killed in two days, setting the stage for the gas war of October 2003.

Natural Gas: Resistance

Recognizing the strength of the reactionary forces with interests in gas, Oscar Olivera argues, "[I]f six hundred thousand people had participated in the water war just to recover [the former public water company] SEMAPA and to preserve our traditional customs and practices, then all eight million of us Bolivians would have to mobilize to get back control of our hydrocarbons" (O. Olivera and Lewis, 2004: 179). Olivera's statement is a clear reflection of the significance of the differing political economies of natural gas and water and their impacts on popular struggles.

For some, the gas war of September–October 2003 represents the culmination of a rising indigenous radicalism and the ultimate exposure of the racist cleavage that most fundamentally defines Bolivian social reality (Gómez interview, 2005; Gómez, 2004; Mamani Ramírez, 2004a). For others, it signifies a convergence of the older "national-popular" traditions of the miner- and political-party-driven left and the new indigenous radical sectors (Hylton and Thomson, 2004). Finally, some see as its cause the social failure of the neoliberal model (Arze and Kruse, 2004; Escobar de Pabón, 2003). Virtually no one, however, contests that the future of natural gas in Bolivia was at the heart of the matter.

During Hugo Bánzer's administration (1997–2001) a deal to export gas through a Chilean port to Mexico and the United States was initiated with Pacific LNG, a Spanish-British-U.S. energy consortium. In 2002 Sánchez de Lozada assumed the presidency, and, as Hylton and Thomson note, "His attempt to close the gas deal in 2003 sparked massive opposition to which he responded with blunt force" (2004:18). The first major social force in the September–October insurrection was the largely Aymara indigenous peasantry in the altiplano and Lake Titicaca regions, which set up major road blockades (García Linera, 2004; Gómez, 2004; Mamani Ramírez, 2004a). These actions were met with the brute force of the state in a series of massacres in September, spawning outrage in the urban shantytown of El Alto, a city of close to 650,000 people 81 percent of whom identify themselves as indigenous (INE, 2001). These residents maintain strong familial and cultural connections to the countryside. The shantytown mobilized in a powerful, united fashion from October 8 to 17 and was met by fierce state violence. Miners from Huanuni marched to El Alto and joined in the popular struggle. The central mobilizing organizations in El Alto during this period were the Federación de Juntas Vecinales de El Alto (Federation of Neighborhood Associations of El Alto—FEJUVE-El Alto) and the Central Obrera Regional (Regional Workers' Central of El Alto—COR-El Alto).

The struggle descended from El Alto to La Paz, with the popular neighborhoods of the latter joining forcefully in the revolt. Eventually, even middle-class residents of La Paz engaged in hunger strikes against the government. With an estimated 500,000 people in the streets (Hylton, 2003), Sánchez de Lozada and his closest supporters fled the country for exile in the United States on October 17. This left the vice president, Carlos Mesa, who had distanced himself publicly from the violence of the regime, to assume office following constitutionally defined procedures. Under Sánchez de Lozada, according to the highest figures, more than 80 people were killed in September–October 2003 and more than 400 were injured by bullets (O. Olivera and Lewis, 2004: 176). While its epicenter was clearly El Alto, the protest originated in the altiplano and around Lake Titicaca and radiated out to countrywide solidarity mobilizations and marches in a host of cities—Oruro, Cochabamba, Sucre, Potosí, and Santa Cruz.

A fundamental frame during the insurrectional episode of October 2003 was the call to nationalize gas. As Álvaro García Linera (then a prominent sociologist and TV personality who became vice-president of the country after the MAS (Movimiento al Socialismo—Movement toward Socialism) electoral victory on December 18, 2005) put it, "There is a sort of collective intuition that the debates over hydrocarbons are gambling with the destiny of this country, a country accustomed to having a lot of natural resources but always being poor, always seeing natural resources serve to enrich others" (interview, April 10, 2005). The "injustice" of the frame is clearly delineated: being poor in a resource-rich land. The "us" included the popular classes and indigenous peoples struggling for a socially just developmental model with a more equitable distribution of wealth. The structural significance of natural gas made the strategic frame materially plausible and accounted in large part for its wide resonance throughout the country. The macro characteristics of the frame and the politics it advocated are also salient. Comparing the uneven geographies of the Cochabamba water war in 2000 and the gas war of 2003, Perreault points out that the gas war was a more "national, and nationalist, uprising," involving the central site of El Alto and the rural altiplano but fanning out across much of the country (2006: 165). The "them" identified included the transnational gas corporations that formed part of the transnational gas consortium Pacific LNG (Repsol YPF, British Gas, and Pan-American Energy), the neoliberal model personified in the presidency of Sánchez de Lozada, and American imperialism writ large. Finally, the pathways of change advocated by the frame to overcome the injustice it evoked involved the ousting of the neoliberal president and, literally, the nationalization of gas.

The gas war in October 2003 did not lead to a revolutionary break with neoliberal capitalism. Indeed, Carlos Mesa adopted a neoliberal reformist style of governance with the support of the MAS, the largest left-indigenous party, for the first year and four months following the event. However, the issue of natural gas would not disappear. Mesa faced ongoing mobilizations and road blockades in January, February, March, May, and June of 2005, many focused on formulating a new hydrocarbons law that would wrestle more control and profit from the transnational petroleum companies and confer them on the Bolivian state. With Mesa unable to respond to popular discontent with repression—given the popular indignation that answered Sánchez de Lozada's violence—the most reactionary elements of the Bolivian internationalized bourgeoisie, rooted in the petroleum and natural gas industry based in Santa Cruz, took matters into their own hands.

The main organization representing these interests was the Comité pro Santa Cruz (Pro Santa Cruz Committee). For weeks in January 2005 they mobilized hundreds of thousands of people—at their peak 300,000—under a right-wing populist set of demands called the "January Agenda," which was pitted against what had by then become widely known as the popular "October Agenda" (Webber, 2005). Complementing the Comité pro Santa Cruz, the key organizations pressing for the January Agenda included the Cámara Agropecuaria del Oriente (Agricultural Chamber of Eastern Bolivia), the Federación de Ganaderos de Santa Cruz (Federation of Ranchers of Santa Cruz), and, most important, the Cámara de Industria, Comercio, Servicios y Turismo de Santa Cruz (Chamber of Commerce, Industry, Service and Tourism of Santa Cruz—CAINCO). The Spanish oil giant Repsol-YPF, Brazilian state-owned Petrobras, and Enron are members of CAINCO's board of directors (Ballvé, 2004).

In the heat of a new state crisis, Mesa offered his revocable "resignation" to Congress on March 7, 2005. In his televised speech he made extensive use of imperial threats to support his new openly reactionary politics and to discredit the popular movements. For example, in response to MAS's proposed hydrocarbons law, he complained, "Brazil has told us, Spain has told us, the World Bank, the United States, the International Monetary Fund, Great Britain, and all of the European Union: Bolivians, approve a law that is viable and acceptable to the international community." He argued bluntly, "If the mechanisms of [international] cooperation with our country are cut, we cannot function." Congress refused to accept his resignation (a fact that it seems he had counted on), and he abandoned his unofficial alliance with the MAS and moved decidedly toward the right. The reaction on the left was a brief but important nationwide union of various popular forces, primarily around issues of who would control natural gas and to what ends and therefore whose interests would predominate in the future political economy of the Bolivian state (Spronk and Webber, 2005). The short-lived "antioligarchic" social pact was signed by Evo Morales (leader of the MAS), and numerous other labor and campesino leaders.

The popular struggles against accumulation by dispossession in the natural gas sector clearly played a large part in spawning a social rebellion with a macro frame and politics: in October 2003, 500,000 people assembled in the capital, and there were countrywide solidarity mobilizations culminating in the ousting of the president. The second gas war saw similar numbers in the streets to oust president Mesa in June 2005. Both moments represented serious ideological challenges to neoliberalism, even if thus far it has not yet been defeated. The October 2003 gas war generated a vicious state response, followed by Mesa's use of imperial threats and the right-wing mobilization of Santa Cruz. It demonstrated that when social movements are able to aggregate their demands around a natural resource of structural significance, the struggle becomes intense, national, ideological, and political, even if it does not guarantee victory. The local and international capitalists with interests in gas recognize its value and respond with a corresponding viciousness, employing the repressive tools of the state.

Water: Accumulation by Dispossession

Water companies tend to be among the last to be dispossessed because it takes a long time, if ever, to make profits selling water. Throughout the post–World War II period, water was considered a public good to be provided by public utilities, since the private sector was considered incapable of providing adequate services. The World Bank extended major infrastructure loans for development of public water resources because it believed that investment in public utilities and infrastructure would lead to developmental "takeoff." With the neoliberal revolution of the past quarter-century, however, the World Bank began making loans to governments conditioned on privatization of public water utilities in an effort to improve management of "scarce" water resources (Public Citizen, 2004; World Bank, 1993). Increasingly, it has been argued that water should be treated as an economic good and priced so as to recover the full costs of production directly from its users (Budds and McGranahan, 2003). According to neoliberal arguments, consumers will waste water if they do not have to pay its true cost. In a twist of logic, privatization has become a quick-fix solution to what is depicted as an impending ecological crisis—the global scarcity of freshwater. As water pollution and the specter of climate change have brought the issue of water scarcity to center stage, large transnational corporations have increasingly seen water as a resource worth possessing.

The cases of water privatization in Cochabamba and La Paz-El Alto are exemplars of accumulation by dispossession, but they demonstrate that not all accumulation strategies work as planned. Despite fears that water will be the "blue gold" of the 21st century, the growing number of failed experiments with water privatization suggest that selling water for a profit to poor people in the Third World is much more difficult than originally predicted.

The World Bank was clearly the driving force behind the privatization of water utilities in Bolivia. In the mid-1990s it extended a US$4.5 million loan intended to improve the efficiency of the public water and sanitation utilities in the main cities of Bolivia and thus make them more attractive to private investors. The municipal water utility that served the neighboring cities of La Paz and El Alto was granted in a 1997 concession to Aguas del Illimani, a consortium controlled by the French multinational Suez. In 1999 another concession transferred control over Cochabamba's municipal utility to Aguas del Tunari, a consortium controlled by the San Francisco-based construction giant Bechtel.

The privatization of the water utility Servicio Autónomo Municipal de Agua Potable y Alcantarillado (SAMAPA) in La Paz-El Alto can be counted as a modest success from a business point of view. The water system in La Paz-El Alto was a fairly attractive investment at the time of its privatization. Water was available for about 19 hours a day, and fairly high coverage rates had been achieved. Tariff increases of approximately 35 percent introduced a year before privatization doubled the utility's income and were expected to bring in US$27 million per year, greatly improving the utility's financial prospects (Guillermo Arroyo Rodríguez, personal communication, May 20, 2005). The central government further sweetened the deal by assuming SAMAPA's US$50 million debt and guaranteeing a 13 percent rate of return. Thanks in part to the role played by the state in facilitating capital accumulation, during the first seven years of the concession the company made around US$12 million (in current dollars) in profits.

Compared with the water utility in La Paz-El Alto, the public utility in Cochabamba was in poor shape. Citizens received water for an average of four hours per day, and the system served only about 57 percent of city residents. The contract awarded to Aguas del Tunari included commitments to expand water production through the construction of Misicuni, a dam and tunnel project estimated to cost over US$300 million (Assies, 2003). Recognizing the risks involved, the contract guaranteed Aguas del Tunari a real return rate between 15 and 17 percent for the 40 years of the contract. Since the World Bank (1999) "recommended" that none of this money come from the public purse, the most immediate source was the users themselves. The company hiked users' water tariffs, and this triggered the water war of 2000.

Water: Resistance

Given the negligible role that water plays in the regional political economy, the social movements that emerged during the water wars involved a more micro frame and politics than the gas wars. This micro character is reflected in the geography of the protests, the pathway to change identified by the participants, and the protests' lesser impact on neoliberalism.

In the first water war, residents of Cochabamba, frustrated over government neglect and drastically increased water bills, protested peacefully in the streets, shutting down the city with roadblocks, marches, and demonstrations. Protests became increasingly violent, with the Bolivian government dispatching riot police to control the movement. A bullet from a sniper claimed the life of a young man, which radicalized the protests and brought 100,000 people into the streets. The social base of the mobilizations demonstrated that the water war was not about tariffs alone. Coca growers, peasant farmers, and periurban residents joined the protests even though they were not customers of Aguas del Tunari and thus were not directly affected by the tariff increase. Their primary concern was the new Water Law 2029 approved a month and a half after the privatization contract was signed, which granted exclusive property rights over water to the private operator for the duration of the concession contract. The monopoly provision meant that residents were prevented from drilling their own wells, which has long been the privileged practice of some large commercial users and wealthy residents of Cochabamba and the survival strategy of periurban residents, who had formed small water committees and cooperatives that served between 15–20 percent of urban residents (Crespo Flores, 2002: 107). The law also threatened the water supplies of irrigating small farmers in the Cochabamba Valley who have managed water resources according to communal principles (*usos y costumbres*) that date back to pre-Inca times (Assies, 2003; Crespo Flores, Fernández Quiroga, and Peredo, 2004; Laurie, Andolina, and Radcliffe, 2002). Social movement leaders thus framed the struggle as one to "reclaim the commons" and defend water users against an attack on communal property rights.

The blossoming academic and popular commentary on the event has emphasized that the Cochabamba water war was the first symbolic break with neoliberalism in 15 years in Bolivia (Assies, 2003; Ceceña, 2004; Crespo Flores, 2000; García Linera et al., 2001; García Orellana, García Yapur, and Quitón Herbas, 2003; O. Olivera and Lewis, 2004). While it resulted in some important political changes—the amendment of national water legislation, the rescission of the contract, and the return of water to public management—there were limits to what it could accomplish. The many obstacles subsequently faced by the deprivatized utility demonstrate that while the battle to expel the transnational corporation was won, the war that was required to reverse neoliberal policies was not.

After the "final battle" of April 2000, the government rescinded the contract with Aguas del Tunari and signed an agreement with the Coordinadora (the network of organizations that emerged to coordinate the protests, originally called la Coordinadora de Defensa del Agua y de la Vida). Responsibility for operations immediately returned to the former municipal company Servicio Municipal de Agua Potable y Alcantarillado de Cochabamba (SEMAPA), under the control of the Coordinadora (Assies, 2003; Crespo Flores, 2002; O. Olivera and Lewis, 2004). In December 2000 the Coordinadora proposed to disband SEMAPA and form a new type of democratic water utility owned by its users, but the government refused, arguing that such forms of "social property" were not recognized under the law (Gutiérrez Aguilar, 2001: 202–203). Instead the government allowed the local water authority to be restructured to grant more "social control" over its operations. The board of directors, formerly constituted only by professionals and municipal politicians, now has three elected members from the different districts of Cochabamba (Sánchez Gómez and Terhorst, 2005).

The serious problems that SEMAPA had before its privatization could not be solved by merely inserting a limited degree of social control. Service to existing customers has not improved substantially since 2000, and attempts to expand the water network to residents in the poor southern zone of the city have been delayed because of lack of capital (Nickson and Vargas, 2002; Sánchez Gómez, 2004). The largest obstacle is the utility's enormous debt, which was transferred from the central government. Because of the public utility's poor credit rating, several plans to expand the network have been stalled because the public company had difficulty securing new loans (Pozo, 2005; Sánchez Gómez and Terhorst, 2005). Over time, the local water activists have learned that expelling a foreign company and changing the national water legislation—two central demands of the water war—were only small steps in a longer struggle to exert social control over the local water system, which remains difficult in a context in which local politicians and international lenders continue to favor private over public companies in the water sector. Despite the lobbying by water activists, it has been impossible to change national legislation to ban profits from water, since Suez still has its contract in La Paz and El Alto.

Problems with tariffs and the Aguas del Illimani contract eventually led to Bolivia's second water war in January 2005. As a struggle against neoliberalism and privatization, this one produced an even more ambiguous victory than the first. Pressured by a general strike organized by residents of El Alto that lasted three days, the Bolivian government announced on January 12 that it would terminate the contract held by the private consortium. It could be argued that the state had learned from previous mistakes in the water war and the gas war and chose not to escalate the situation with violence. It is more likely, however, that the private company actually wanted to leave, and therefore it was not necessary to defend its interests against the protestors.

Over the life of the concession, the company continually complained that it could not make enough money selling water to poor people in El Alto to recuperate its investment at an agreeable rate of return (*Le Monde Diploma-*

tique, May 28–29, 2002). In 2002 Suez, which owned 55 percent of Aguas del Illimani's shares, announced a policy of pulling investments from "risky markets" like Bolivia. Dissatisfied with the return on its investments in La Paz and El Alto, the company lobbied the government regulator to approve increases in the costs of its services. Having learned from Aguas del Tunari's experience in Cochabamba, it decided to increase the costs of services for new connections rather than offend existing customers with tariff hikes. In 2001, the cost of a new water connection increased from US$155 to US$196 and the cost for sewerage from US$180 to US$249. This price hike was still not enough, and Aguas del Illimani reopened negotiations of its contract with the government a few years later. In June 2003 it managed to reduce the amount of new connections that it was obliged to make from 15,000 to 8,000. In March 2004 this number was reduced to zero. This decision left 200,000 people who lacked household water connections with little hope of receiving services within the life of the 30-year concession, a figure that was publicized by neighborhood leaders to symbolize the corporation's disregard for the population's needs.

Similar to the ongoing struggle to exert social control over water in Cochabamba, the struggle to return water to public control in El Alto has been framed as a struggle for local democracy. The main protagonist in the conflict, the FEJUVE-El Alto, building on the new political legitimacy it had gained from the gas war, elaborated a proposal to establish a new water company controlled by a board of representatives democratically elected from all the districts in La Paz and El Alto. The hope was that guaranteeing popular participation would enable citizens to ensure transparency and efficiency in management through social control. In response to the proposal, the major financiers of the water sector in Bolivia—the World Bank, Inter-American Development Bank, and the German embassy—told President Carlos Mesa that should a public water company replace Aguas del Illimani they would refuse to extend loans.

Compared with those regarding gas, the struggles against the privatization of water in Bolivia were organized around a micro frame and politics. The protestors shared a frame that pitted the needs of the local communities of water users against the abuses of two transnational corporations, Bechtel and Suez. Both struggles involved the populations most directly affected by the exploitation of water resources either as agricultural producers or consumers. In contrast to the gas protests, the mobilizations involved people primarily from the regions affected: the residents of Cochabamba and the surrounding valley and the urban residents of the shantytown of El Alto. The urban residents who participated in the protests in Cochabamba and El Alto were disgruntled about the company's billing practices and disregard for community needs. Despite promises that privatization would bring the financing and expertise needed to expand and improve services, residents felt that they were being asked to pay the full cost of network expansion. The increased cost of services heightened the perception that water was being turned into a "commodity," a perception reinforced by the fact that the revenues went to private foreign companies whose aim was to make profit. Therefore, the protestors in both cases demanded that the new water companies be publicly owned and operated on a not-for-profit basis. The protestors' demand for social control thus reflected a struggle to democratize the management of local water supplies. The slogan of the Cochabamba protest, *El agua es nuestra, ¡carajo!* (The water is ours, dammit!), repeated by protestors in El Alto, referred to the water that fed these cities' thirsty residents and not, for example, the water that supplied the residents of Santa Cruz.

While the struggles against water privatization were crucially important, their impact has been smaller than that of the gas wars in terms of reversing 25 years of neoliberalism. Oscar Olivera, central spokesperson for the Coordinadora, sums up the dilemma faced by any social-movement leader when the sacrifices made in the struggle seem limited in comparison with the gains. He recalls a woman's comments as the blockades came down after the Cochabamba water war: "Compañero, now the water is going to be ours, what have we really gained? . . . My husband will still have to look for work. As a wife and mother, I will still have to go out into the street to sell things, and my children will have to drop out of school because there's just not enough money. Even if they give us the water for free, our situation still won't have gotten any better" (O. Olivera and Lewis, 2004: 48). Access to potable water is fundamental to the quality of daily life but of limited significance to the political economy of the Bolivian state. As we have argued, it is precisely because of this that struggles for public water have been more quickly resolved with considerably less bloodshed than struggles over natural gas.

Globalizing Resistance: Whose Resources Are We Fighting For?

We have demonstrated the importance of recognizing the political economy of different types of Third World struggles against accumulation by dispossession. Social movements fighting against privatization of water and natural gas in Bolivia have both made important gains in the struggle against the deepening of neoliberal capitalism. The protagonists in these movements have framed their struggles as efforts to "reclaim the commons," drawing upon the widespread perception that foreign interests plundered Bolivia's natural resources for centuries and left behind little but poverty. Yet the struggles over the "commons" of water and gas have had different political implications because of the role each resource plays in the political economy of the Bolivian state and the world market. The struggle around natural gas, as a resource that is structurally significant to the region's political economy, stands a greater chance of laying the foundations for an alternative globalization movement that looks for ways that "better meet the material needs of impoverished and repressed populations" (D. Harvey, 2003: 179).

The violence perpetrated by the state to protect private interests in the hydrocarbons sector as opposed to water reveals one of the cruel aspects of neoliberal capitalism in the era of globalization. Access to potable water arguably has a greater immediate impact on the quality of life and contributes more to public health than the benefits that may accrue from the nationalization of gas. Nonetheless, water remains an invisible input to industrial production, and therefore its exploitation does not contribute directly to GNI. In the dollar-and-cents terms of the market, water remains a much less valuable resource than natural gas, and the state is less likely to use violence to defend private property rights to it.

It may seem paradoxical that across the globe the privatization of water has been more consistently controversial than the privatization of gas. The issue of water privatization strikes an emotional chord; water has cultural and symbolic meaning as the essence of life. It also falls from the sky and does not require complex technological mediation to bring it from source to user. Therefore, it is much easier to frame arguments that it belongs to "us." The right to water is enshrined in the Universal Declaration of Human Rights. In global protests in Cancún and Genoa it is common to hear the argument that it is "immoral" to privatize water. There are numerous sessions on fighting water privatization at the World Social Forums. Despite the importance of the issue, there is no comparable global network defending the right to natural gas. No "right" can be said to exist because gas is a thoroughly commodified resource that has long had big dollar signs attached to it. Natural gas is not normally considered a "commons."

It is therefore testimony to the revolutionary potential of the Bolivian social movements that they framed one of their central demands around the nationalization of natural gas. The escalation of popular struggle over a structurally significant natural resource at the national scale may have delivered a critical blow to neoliberalism in Bolivia. Such self-organization of the popular classes to hit capital where it seriously hurts serves as an example for social movements struggling for economic and social justice throughout the Third World.

III

COMMUNITY-BUILDING STRATEGIES, CONSCIOUSNESS, AND AGENTS OF SOCIAL CHANGE

MST national congress in Brasilia, June 10–17, 2007. Photo courtesy of Douglas Mansur.

ONE OF THE THEORETICAL CHALLENGES for understanding social movements is the development of concepts to bridge the gap between structure and agency; that is, explanations that emphasize the objective structural conditions that give rise to popular mobilization and those that focus on the subjective formation of collective identities that turn actors into agents of social change. While some old-left analysis focuses on the determining influence of class structures and some new mainstream analysis concentrates on the openings created by "political opportunity structures," many of the works in this volume examine the connections between the shifting political-economic structures at the macro level and the diverse processes of collective consciousness formation shaping today's social movements.

There is a culture of protest, and the cultural practices of social groups have empowering or disempowering implications, as the feminist movement has long reminded us with the slogan, "The personal is political." To be sure, a myopic obsession with the unique internal dynamics of any group can cause it to lose sight of its connections to a larger political struggle, and some of the extreme formulations of postmodern and poststructuralist analysis can have depoliticizing implications. Yet people are motivated to act based not on abstractions, but on their immediate lived experiences. In an era when neoliberal globalization has an atomizing effect that disperses workers, devastates communities, and undermines collective definitions of rights, it is particularly important to assess counterhegemonic strategies for reconstituting communal identities in social struggles.

Glen Kuecker's chapter tells a dramatic story of a tiny Ecuadorian community's struggle against a subsidiary of a transnational mining corporation. He emphasizes the culture of scrappy survival and resistance in remote marginalized communities on the frontiers of global capital—the "*colono* mentality"—along with the ideological influences of liberation theology and ecological groups in shaping the consciousness of an agrarian-based social justice movement. At the same time, the power of giant transnationals to mobilize state institutions and elites and to strategize on a global scale raises troublesome questions about whether community consciousness is enough for social movements to prevail.

Richard Stahler-Sholk's chapter on the Zapatista movement looks at some of the dilemmas of constructing a model of autonomy in small indigenous communities of Chiapas, Mexico. Participants in the movement draw strength from multiple identities as indigenous people, poor peasant inheritors of the Mexican Revolution, and bearers of an alternative political vision of self-sufficient "resistance" and participatory decision making. Yet the state and global corporate interests have also maneuvered to isolate and divide the communities and monopolize the allocation of resources, rights, and recognition. As the movement continues to evolve, its future will depend not only on the consolidation of identity and consciousness within the autonomous communities, but also on the ability to generate effective organizational links to a wider agenda through initiatives such as the Zapatistas' "Other Campaign."

Daniela Issa's contribution examines Latin America's largest social movement, Brazil's Landless Rural Workers' Movement (MST). Its well-known red banner and highly disciplined peasant recoveries of land to "occupy, produce, resist" have made the MST a visible symbol of the region's new social movements. Issa focuses on the movement's strategies for generating *mística,* a combination of collective consciousness and a concrete pedagogy of empowerment through symbolic political action. Building on liberation theology and rural culture, these practices help explain the MST's growth and resilience in the face of fierce repression and stark social inequalities.

These three chapters not only highlight the mobilizing power of ideas in challenging the dominant ideology, but also suggest how the praxis of organizing strategies grows out of these alternative visions. Of special importance to each of these essays is the place of consciousness formation and reproduction as a process internal to communities of resistance, and how the process influences movement strategies and potential outcomes.

6

Fighting for the Forests Revisited

Grassroots Resistance to Mining in Northern Ecuador

Glen David Kuecker

JOSÉ ENRÍQUEZ HAD AN EVENTFUL START to his day on May 12, 1997. José was the caretaker of a copper mining exploration camp near the Andean mountain community of Junín, which is located in the Intag region of Imbabura Province, northern Ecuador. He was alone at the camp, which normally hosted a group of mining engineers from Bishi Metals, a subsidiary of Mitsubishi Corporation. The previous evening all of Junín's 50 families had met with representatives from Acción Ecológica (Ecology in Action), a nongovernmental organization (NGO) based in Quito, and *Defensa y Conservación Ecológica de Intag* (Ecological Defense and Conservation of Intag—DECOIN), a grassroots ecological organization formed to resist mining in the region. The meeting had concluded with the community determined to take dramatic action against the company. Next morning, 87 people from Junín hiked up the 6.5 km mountain trail to the camp, where they collected all of the property at the camp, inventoried it, and packed it for the trip back down the mountain. They had José sign the inventory, which included things like cups, plates, geological equipment, rolls of wire, an electrical generator. José went to García Moreno, the first town of significance on the road to Apuela to notify the company and the government. A day passed as people from Junín, now numbering 200, moved the property down the mountain and awaited a response. The next day, not having heard anything and according to plan, they burned the mining camp to the ground. Before leaving, they nailed a simple wooden sign to a post. It read, "Not Another Step Forward for the Miners." It was a prophetic slogan: to date the people of Junín have proven victorious in keeping mining out of their community (*El Comercio*, May 27, 1997).

According to Carlos Zorrilla, a 30-year Intag resident and DECOIN's president in 1997, "the case of Junín is a clear wake-up call to governments all over the world, and to big mining companies in particular, that local populations must not be ignored, and that their rights to decide their own future must never be overlooked" (*Drillbits and Tailings*, 1997: 1). A decision by 200 people to confront one of the largest corporations in the world is a story that attracts our attention. The people of Junín, however, challenged more than Mitsubishi; they also frustrated the plans of the Ecuadorian government and the World Bank. When 200 people stop the neoliberal project in their corner of the world, we might expect people to take notice. Their story of resistance, however, remains widely unknown.

Junín's story is a case study of grassroots resistance to neoliberalism, and it highlights three main themes. First, it illustrates the core issue of who has the power to decide. In this case, the people of Junín determined that it was their right and not that of the World Bank, state technocrats, or corporations to decide the fate of the forests. Second, it highlights the distinction between what John Holloway (2002: 22) calls "power over" and "power to" that is central to an understanding of today's social movements. In Junín, similar to places like Chiapas, highly marginalized communities seek empowerment, the ability "to do" instead of seeking dominion over others. Third, it provides an example of how today's social movements construct alternatives to neoliberalism. Confronted with the prospect of mining, the people of Junín were challenged to devise a replacement for it, an alternative development project that was ecologically feasible and met the criteria of community empowerment. Their resistance to mining has fostered an agrarian-based environmental ethic that constitutes a radical challenge to neoliberalism, placing the idea of community above profit, production, and consumption. Taken together, these themes show that community ultimately proves the key to resistance because it is not reducible to the logic of free-market capitalism. The irreducibility of community is the Achilles' heel of today's capitalism, because the neoliberal paradigm fails to factor the power of community into the cost of production. This essay first places the Junín case in the political and economic context of mining in Ecuador and then explains how the community organized its resistance. It concludes with an analysis of Junín as a social movement.

When asked why Ecuador needs mining, Ecuador's under-secretary of energy and mining (interview, summer 2003) replied, "Ecuador has the moral obligation to conduct mining. . . . The world needs minerals. Ecuador has minerals. Ecuador has the obligation to provide them." It was a perfect statement of the neoliberal project for Ecuador: it has the obligation to destroy its greatest asset, biodiversity, in order to pay off its greatest liability, an unpayable foreign debt. The under-secretary's statement reflects policy makers'

thinking about Ecuador's economic problems. They are immense and potentially impossible to resolve. Despite a high rate of growth in the gross domestic product (GDP) during the 1970s, when it peaked at 9.1 percent per year,
Ecuador has faced steep declines ever since. Average GDP growth dropped to
2.1 percent in the 1980s and 1.6 percent in the 1990s (World Bank, 2003: 1).
In 1990, a decade before an economic meltdown, the total payment made by
Ecuador on its foreign debt was 10.5 percent of GDP, a figure that fell to 9 percent in 2002 through vigorous austerity programs. Ecuador is unquestionably
a primary-product exporter; in 2000 these products made up 90 percent of
exports (UNDP, 2002: 199). Export-dependent, Ecuador is highly vulnerable
to fluctuations in global supply and demand and experiences severe limits on
keeping capital within the country that make it dependent upon borrowing
from the developed world. A chronic inability to meet debt payments shapes
the political economy (Gerlach, 2003).

When addressing Ecuador's intractable economic problems, World Bank
analysts explicitly view mining as one path of development. They think pri-
vate-sector development of mineral resources will stimulate economic
growth, and they call for legal and administrative reforms to encourage private investment (P. Fox, Onorato, and Strongman, 1998). This thinking mir-
rors the logic of the austerity programs promoted throughout Latin America
by the World Bank and the International Monetary Fund (IMF), in which
loans were made conditional upon a drastic reduction of state spending (Gerlach, 2003; Green, 2003). In Ecuador, the World Bank advised downsizing government by "transferring to the private sector many of the responsibilities
currently under public sector purview" (World Bank, 1994). These policies,
however, failed miserably, and Ecuador faced total economic collapse in 1999.
In August, it failed to make the interest payments on US$ 6.5 billion in Brady
Bonds and then defaulted on them. To save itself, in January 2000, Ecuador
dollarized its economy and undertook ever more extreme austerity measures
(World Bank, 2000; 2004). With dollarization, Ecuador became directly linked
to the U.S. economy. Moreover, it now has only two options available for getting U. S. dollars: borrowing and exporting at higher levels than before. Borrowing is possible only under strict IMF conditions, and therefore policymakers prefer increasing exports of primary products. The Ecuadorian state
has consequently been very keen on pushing mining into new areas. Such
places, unfortunately, are often ecologically vulnerable rain and cloud forests.

A tiny group of Ecuadorians has power over the nation's mining policy. It
determines policy to the exclusion of the communities in which mining
takes place, and without input from Ecuador's 12 million people. Under
Minister of Energy and Mines Pablo Terán's direction, Ecuador encouraged
rapid and apparently unrestricted foreign development of the mining sector.

In one interview (in *Northern Miner*, November 5, 2001) Terán boasted, "This is a very deregulated system, very hands-off on the part of the state. The Ecuadorian government has turned into a facilitator rather than a policeman, as we used to be." Mining promotion features legal reforms friendly to foreign capital and a slick advertising campaign. According to the Ministry's promotional material, "the Ecuadorian government has made substantial efforts to improve the investment climate for both domestic and foreign companies," including "a complete overhaul of Ecuador's minerals administration system" (Ministry of Energy and Mining [Ecuador], 2001a).

The reforms featured the "single title," which replaced a system requiring the holder to renew the title for each stage of the mining process. This measure undermined the state's ability to regulate mining and hold title owners accountable, and eliminated community input into the process. The single title is valid for 30 years and can be revoked only for failure to pay fees. The reforms also included "the complete abolition of royalties from mineral production." There is a US $100 application fee for a title and a fee of US $1 per hectare (2.5 acres) until production starts; then the fee increases to US $16. According to Terán, "You can now obtain a mining title in any region of Ecuador in about two weeks—there's no hassle, no red tape, nothing like that. And soon you will be able to apply for a title over the Internet." He continues, "Once you have your title, you don't have to report what you are doing, and it is up to you what you do." Lacking reporting mechanisms, a review process, and community input, the new mining law was an excellent way for mining companies to externalize the costs of development and production. Profoundly undemocratic, these reforms provide an example of the way neoliberalism steals the power to decide from communities and gives it to corporations.

Ecuadorian policymakers maintain that mining will bring prosperity to the nation. "We also realize," explains Terán, "the value that a successful mining project will bring to Ecuador's development." He continues, "We would rather that the company made a success of bringing a mine into production, and benefit the communities in the area concerned" (Ministry of Energy and Mining [Ecuador], 2001a). Such prosperity is only the short-term boom of an export sector. Unlike agricultural export production, the mineral export sector is finite. The potential short-term gains are offset by long-term costs that Minister Terán does not mention. The destruction of Intag's biodiversity must be weighed against the temporary jobs and infrastructure promised by mining. His "development-at-any-cost" approach overlooks the externalized costs of pollution, environmental destruction, community displacement, health problems, and social ills such as prostitution and alcoholism (Evans, Goodman, and Lansbury, 2001: xiii; Sampat, 2003).

The concept of comparative advantage drives the thinking of neoliberals like Terán. Countries are expected to develop economic specialization where they enjoy an "advantage." Ecuador's advantage is abundant natural resources and ecological diversity. According to the neoliberal model, it should specialize in raw-material export in exchange for commodities it does not produce. For many, this approach is the sum of all logic, a beautiful paradigm that justifies free market economics. Comparative advantage, however, falsely assumes that all countries are equal when exchanging their advantages. Obviously, equality between Ecuador and the U.S. is an absurdity. Trading bananas, a commodity with minimal value added, for automobiles, a commodity with considerable value added, eventually results in trade deficit and chronic underdevelopment of capital. In the case of mining, as Peter Colley (2001: 25–26) argues, high technology and existing infrastructure encourage companies to invest in the exploitation of existing mines, often in developed countries, instead of launching new mines in places like Ecuador, where low technology, poor or nonexistent infrastructure, unskilled labor, corruption, and political instability significantly increase costs. Ecuador's comparative advantage is not so much raw materials as the ability to offer highly favorable terms to foreign investors. Ecuador's reformed mining laws allow multinational companies to operate in ways that are often illegal in their own countries. Ecuador's comparative advantage is in allowing multinationals to externalize the costs of production in Ecuador—costs that are absorbed by Ecuadorian society while remaining out of sight to First World consumers. Ecuadorians carry the expense while corporations profit; that is the reality of comparative advantage.

One company that took comparative advantage of Ecuador's reformed mining laws was Mitsubishi. It arrived in Ecuador in July 1991, when the Ecuadorian government reached an agreement with Japan to collaborate on mining exploration. Japan turned to Bishi Metals to undertake exploration along with the state-owned Corporación de Desarrollo e Investigación Geológico-Minero-Metalúrgica (Metallurgical Mining Geological Development and Research Corporation—CODIGEM). Junín's selection was made possible by the government Proyecto de Desarrollo Minero y Control Ambiental (Ecuadorian Mining Development and Environmental Control Technical Assistance Project—PRODEMINCA). Funding for PRODEMINCA came from a US$ 14 million World Bank loan, a US$ 8.7 million loan from the governments of Britain and Sweden, and from the Japanese government as part of the Bishi Metals agreement. According to the Ministry of Energy and Mining (2001a: 1), PRODEMINCA's main objective was to provide a detailed geological survey of the entire country, the first ever conducted. The survey was done between 1990 and 1992 and identified 20 percent of Ecuador's surface as containing mineral resources (interview, David Kneas, April 2002). With an estimated 72 million tons of copper, Junín showed immediate promise, but to extract this mineral bonanza companies like Bishi Metals would need to build an ecologically destructive open-pit mine (*Drillbits and Tailings*, 1997: 1).

When the neoliberal project arrived in Intag, it came in the form of the geologists and engineers who conducted the PRODEMINCA surveys. Prior to their arrival, neoliberalism had been defined by the near total absence of the state and its services, which compounded Intag's marginalization within Ecuador. Deep within the Andes, Intag is a very difficult place to reach. It is quicker to fly from Quito to Houston than to travel from Quito to Junín. It is exceptionally difficult to build the basic infrastructure—roads, bridges, telephone, and electricity—needed to integrate Intag and communities like Junín with the rest of Ecuador. In addition, the heavy and prolonged rains reduce roads to quagmires passable only on foot or, preferably, mule. Intag is still recovering infrastructure destroyed during the last El Niño year (1997–1998), whose rains left 20,000 Ecuadorians homeless and destroyed 1,300 miles of roads (Gerlach, 2003: 160). The historic weakness of the Ecuadorian state augments geographic marginalization; the long arm of the state has yet to reach Intag, leaving its population to a rustic existence that fosters strong community bonds for self-preservation. The majority of the region's inhabitants are *colonos* (colonists), both *mestizos* (persons of indigenous and European ancestry) and Afro-Ecuadorians. They migrated to Intag seeking the independence and security of land acquired either by squatting or by purchase. With the earliest colonists having settled no more than 100 years ago, Intag's distant relationship to the nation-state is also a consequence of the relative newness of its communities.

Like other Latin American social movements, Junín's struggle against mining is embedded in the political economy of the neoliberal state. As shown by William Robinson (2004), the role of the nation-state has recently undergone profound change. This change includes the disarticulation of the state from society in its subservience to transnational elites, institutions, and corporations. In Ecuador an already weak and ineffective state became more so with neoliberal economic reforms that reduced government spending by cutting public-sector funding. These policies had the harmful impact of increasing Ecuador's need for social services precisely at a time when the state's ability to provide them was drastically restricted. Unable to address the deepening social problems caused by its economic reforms, the neoliberal state failed to help Ecuadorians as they descended ever deeper into poverty. Poverty has increased from 34 percent in 1995 to 46 percent in 1998 and an alarming 69 percent in 2000. The World Bank estimates that 88 percent of the rural population lives in poverty, up from 54 percent in 1995 (World Bank, 2003: 19). In 1998, the poorest 10 percent had only 0.9 percent of the national income while the richest 10 percent enjoyed 41.6 percent. In 2000, 17.7 percent of Ecuadorians earned US$ 1 a day or less, while 40.8 percent existed on less than US$ 2. With a per capita GDP at US$ 1,897, in 2002 Ecuador is one of the poorest Latin American countries (UNDP, 2004). Communities already marginalized such as Junín were pushed to the edge. Evidence of the precipice can be found in migration statistics: of a population of 12 million, at least 1 million have migrated to either Spain or the United States. Remittances rank as the second-largest item in the gross national product, making Ecuador's truest comparative advantage the export of humans (De la Vega, 2004). In 2001 remittances reached US$ 1.5 billion (World Bank, 2004: 13). Visitors to Intag will find males in their twenties and thirties who have done their tour of duty in Spain or the United States, who recount a harsh and bitter experience of racism, exploitation, and alienation. Migration is an age-old survival tactic for communities throughout Latin America. When faced with the brutal realities of impoverishment and a debilitated state apparatus unable to deliver basic services, communities organize for self-preservation. In the case of Junín, marginalization was the political and economic context that stimulated the consciousness-formation necessary for organizing against mining.

Prior to the arrival of the mining company, a powerful social process was under way. It combined the lived experiences and worldviews of the region's colonos with the empowering and politicized doctrine of liberation theology. Together they created the core of the community's resistance to mining. When I asked community members to describe the colono mentality, the consistent reply was "independent," "hardworking," and "honest." They emphasized the centrality of land ownership, being one's own boss, having a strong family, and counting on members of the community. These are people who know struggle. Many have literally carved a life out of the forests, which can be unforgiving to human inhabitants. One community member, 56-year-old Viktor Calvache (interview, Junín, August 12, 2004), explained, "Not everyone can be a colonist. . . . It's a rough, valiant life . . . Your technology is the ax . . . your consciousness is shaped by hard work." They know the hardships of illness, child mortality, and a short life span. Diet is basic and not always secure. These realities make people from communities like Junín *bien bravo* (defiantly determined), a term often heard in Intag when people refer to the people of Junín. Hard work and sacrifice instill a fierce determination to preserve their agrarian way of life. "We love our homes and we love our land," says Calvache, and "we are organized to protect our community." There is, of course, a variant to the *bien bravo* colono identity. It is the colono who seeks quick riches— the age-old dream of El Dorado. Colonos of this kind are willing to sell land for profit or clear-cut trees for the market and are firmly supportive of mining (Walter Garces, interview, Apulea, August 11, 2004).

"All of us are called to be leaders, because we are all humans. If we all think this, then we can put ourselves in that position," stated Padre Giovanni Paz at a popular education meeting in Junín (June 4, 2003). His introduction of liberation theology was central to the environmental awakening throughout Intag. During the 1990s he organized communities for the resolution of problems arising from marginalization, and his efforts led to grassroots projects of environmental and economic diversification. Liberation theology laid the groundwork for grassroots resistance by educating community members to be leaders, to see themselves as humans with full rights as citizens, and to organize for the improvement of the community. In awakening the communities, liberation theology assisted the process of conscientization, in which critical self-reflection leads to analysis of the relations of power; this is an awareness that was lacking in the colono mentality, but necessary for the resistance movement to form. Early in the process, Padre Giovanni worked with Carlos Zorrilla, a Cuban national who grew up in the U.S. and arrived in Intag in the 1970s. Carlos owns an eco-preserve, La Florida, which is a model for sustainable-development alternatives to lumber production and mining (Carlos Zorrilla, interview, La Florida, August, 2004). Carlos and the padre collaborated on environmental education projects for the region's youth. Their work provided an ecological framework for the colono mentality's agrarianism, resulting in a local ethic that linked protecting the environment to agrarian life. A folk environmentalism was firmly in place when the mining company arrived.

When state and corporate engineers and geologists first appeared in Intag, they immediately raised concern among locals. People had learned to distinguish between outsiders like Paz and Zorrilla, who had lived, worked, organized, and socialized among them for years, and newly arrived outsiders, especially those who came to inspect their lands. The presence of these professionals led community members to research the implications of mining, and investigate the legacy of mining in other parts of the world. This research revealed a disturbing record of environmental destruction, deepening poverty, and social disintegration. Alarmed, they formed DECOIN in 1995, and it has been the eye of the storm ever since. DECOIN connected Intag with the emerging antiglobalization movement by establishing links with environmental organizations that provided information, training, money, and solidarity. Of special importance was Quito-based Acción Ecológica, which had experience in supporting community struggles against state and corporate raiders of the environment. Acción Ecológica helped develop international solidarity with the communities' aims. As Keck and Sikkink (1998) have shown, international advocacy networks assist grassroots groups in framing issues for campaigns. One such organization is the Sloth Club, a Japanese NGO that promotes permaculture, alternative energy sources, renewable resources, and ecotourism. It joined forces with DECOIN in 1996 in order to implement alternative development throughout Intag. It also provided DECOIN with an international connection that made possible the movement's first letter-writing campaign, designed to pressure Mitsubishi and the state to respect local anti-mining voices.

Along with the NGOs, community members made valuable contributions. Mary Ellen Fieweger (1998), for example, played a critical role in a study of mining companies that resulted in the publication of a history of mining. An organic intellectual, Fieweger offers the movement a lifetime of organizing experience, a deep knowledge of Ecuadorian history, and a special facility for empowering others. She established a community newspaper, *Periódico Intag,* to improve communication among geographically separated communities. The newspaper is a model of popular education, serving as a vehicle for teaching computer skills, the basics of journalism, and ways to think about the world. It maintains an anti-mining editorial position, reports on alternative development projects, and functions as the newspaper of record in the region, which is especially important considering the disinformation campaigns of those who favor mining (Fieweger, interview, La Florida, August 13, 2004). The newspaper's success is best measured by the attacks it endures from mining interests, especially an effort by Ascendant Exploration to sue it for libel (*Periódico Intag,* October 2004).

At first, community members were favorably impressed by the prospect of mining. This attitude resulted from mining company efforts to win their "hearts and minds." Multinational mining companies, as Al Gedicks (2001: 159–178) shows, have faced such fierce grassroots resistance that they prepare locals for mining with propaganda and services and attack the anti-mining arguments of the ecologists. Mining companies tell people they will all get jobs, share royalties, and have roads, telephones, health clinics with doctors, and schools as rewards for their support. For marginalized people, promises of streets paved with gold are very appealing, especially given the get-rich-quick mentality of some colonos.

DECOIN understood that it had to counter the mining company's community relations campaign. With Acción Ecológica it developed popular education workshops about the disadvantages and dangers of mining. The aim was to create a context for experiential learning by placing people in situations in which the convergence of reflection and experience leads to individual transformations of consciousness and action. The vehicle for praxis in this case was a jointly sponsored trip to Peru in 1996 that introduced community members to the negative ecological and community impact of an operating copper mine. As a result of these efforts, peoples' attitudes toward mining became increasingly negative. To build upon its successes, DECOIN started shade-grown organic coffee projects as an example of sustainable development alternatives to mining (Carlos Zorrilla, interview, La Florida, March 2002).

The movement's turning point came in 1997, when DECOIN's research discovered an environmental impact study for the proposed copper mine. The study had been commissioned by Bishi Metals as part of the process of gaining concessions, but it was never shared with the communities. The study presented a gloomy forecast of widespread destruction. The open-pit mine was projected to bring extensive deforestation leading to desertification. In addition, it would deposit tons of waste minerals; its heavy metals would pollute the surrounding environment. Rivers would also be contaminated with mercury and cyanide, which would pollute drinking water, threaten aquatic life, and present health risks to persons bathing or washing clothes in the water. The report outlined how Cotacachi-Cayapas National Park would be threatened by the project. More ominous, it estimated that 100 families would be displaced by the mine, which would require flooding a populated valley for waste disposal (Japan International Cooperation Agency, 1996). Community leaders went house to house sharing the findings with families, taking time for discussion and reflection on what it meant for their lives.

The environmental impact study greatly increased anti-mining sentiment. The threat of relocation was a direct attack upon the colono mentality and stimulated the *bien bravo* attitude of defending community. It was clear that state officials and mining company representatives had not been forthcoming about the negatives of mining. They had offended one of the most basic *colono* values—honor and integrity. Local values were further affronted when government officials and company representatives failed to answer repeated requests for meetings; the silence highlighted the way neoliberalism marginalizes communities like Junín. After the third snub, community members took the *bien bravo* action of torching Bishi's mining camp.

DECOIN also challenged the World Bank. The Bank had provided the funds and conceptualization for PRODEMINCA, which amounted to "a complete overhaul of the minerals sector administration system and the institutions involved" (Ministry of Energy and Mining, 2001b: 10). In 1999, however, DECOIN threw a wrench into the World Bank's plans. It initiated a claim against PRODEMINCA, using an appeals process within the Bank's mechanism for development programs, for failing to conduct an environmental impact study as the Bank required. In a victory for the local ecologists, the Bank ruled in DECOIN's favor in February 2001: "Management was in apparent violation of certain provisions of the policies and procedures on Environmental Assessment . . . relating to processing, geographical scope, baseline data, and concerning consultation during preparation" (World Bank Inspection Panel, 2001). The victory was perhaps only symbolic. As Rich (1994) demonstrates, the World Bank's appeals mechanism and policy oversight often divert attention from the shortcomings of its development programs. In this case, the Bank made the minerals survey available to interested developers, saving them the cost of doing their own surveys.

Junín's victory over Mitsubishi and the World Bank is testimony to the ability of grassroots organizations to alter structures of power. Key to shifting the terrain is building national and international networks of solidarity on which locals can depend. The struggle, however, goes deeper than driving companies like Mitsubishi out of places like Junín. It also requires implementing alternatives to corporate globalization. Groups like DECOIN understood this crucial element, working proactively to implement their vision of a world without mining. To succeed, the communities of the region had to be what David Korten (1999: 215–216) calls "cultural creatives" that "have a strong commitment to family, community, the environment, internationalism, and feminism. They have a well-developed social consciousness and are optimistic." Cultural creatives are the antithesis of corporate globalization, the concentration of wealth and power by a few individuals, companies, governments, and global institutions.

Intag's cultural creatives integrate economic activities with the environment in a sustainable fashion. Communities have developed alternative economies with subsistence farming, shade-grown coffee production, sugar collectives, fish farming, and ecotourism. These projects typically have support from NGOs, which provide funding as well as technical support. Locals have also sought financial aid to purchase land to be added to eco-preserves that are "no-go zones" for lumbering or mining. In promoting these alternatives, community members have forged a strong alliance with the indigenous mayor of Cotacatchi County, Auki Tituaña, one of the leading figures in Ecuador's indigenous political party, Pachakutik (see Becker, this volume). With 25 percent of the population, Ecuador's indigenous people have combined formal politics with deeply rooted cultural resistance in becoming strong national political actors. Although they won only 6 seats in the national election in 2002, they have been key players in displacing two presidents in the past decade. Pachakutik, known for honesty in government and strident opposition to neoliberalism, was well positioned to help Intag communities with the struggle against mining. Tituaña's formal support provided legitimacy, leverage, and national exposure to the local struggle. He worked with DECOIN in making

Cotacatchi County an *ecocantón*, in which mining is banned and alternative, environmentally sustainable projects are promoted (Sheehan, 2003: 144; Carlos Zorrilla, interview, La Florida, March 2002).

These projects are a key component of Intag's success. They demonstrate to locals that other paths are possible and that, despite what state and corporate officials say, they can live an agrarian life without mining. This foundation provides community members with the social fabric, organizational experience, consciousness, and commitment to resist mining. The popular education tactics emphasize community and horizontally extend the decision-making process. Community members who have learned about shade-grown coffee or running a newspaper become teachers and pass along their knowledge to others, extending empowerment throughout the commons. In the process people become empowered, fully actualized, and more invested in a world without mining, and they learn to work together and become skilled in consensus-driven decision making. They build momentum with each project and gain confidence in their abilities.

Mining companies, according to the chief executive officer of Rio Tinto Zinc (RTZ), one of the world's largest mining corporations, "are being naive about how easy it is to operate in someone else's back yard. We . . . see problems virtually everywhere" (Moody, 2001: vii). When RTZ evaluates potential mines, it is fully aware of how grassroots organizations like DECOIN operate. Roger Moody, founder of Minewatch, points out that multinational corporations are increasingly under attack by a global network of environmental activists (2001: vi–vii). Efforts of environmental groups like the Sloth Club and Acción Ecológica, in solidarity with local, grassroots organizations like DECOIN, have increased the cost of operations for the multinationals. Community resistance tips the balance of comparative advantage by adding negative factors to the cost of production, which includes not only having to abide by environmental regulations that may call for expensive technologies, machinery, and skilled labor, but also maintaining a favorable corporate image. Gedicks (2001) shows that corporations spend millions of dollars on pro-mining advertising, funding NGOs that disseminate propaganda, and supporting academics who advocate under- or unregulated mining. Other costs include extra staff required to handle community resistance, lawyers and lobbyists, and payments to corrupt officials or to buy off recalcitrant communities. When such costs go up, the multinationals often leave. The cost threshold for Mitsubishi was crossed with the burning of its camp.

Unfortunately for the local communities, the macro-structural factors of comparative advantage subsequently tipped against them. The world price of copper skyrocketed from US$ .82 per pound in 2000 to US$ 2.59 in 2007 because of the increased demand caused by China's construction boom (Kharas, 2005). The higher price has overwhelmed the previously prohibitive cost of mining in Junín. DECOIN and the local *bien bravos* again have their backs against the wall as they confront a new mining company, Ascendant Copper. It is a speculator in mining properties whose goal is to secure title to the lands and government concessions in Junín, and then sell them to a major mining company that has the capital to develop them. The cost for the mine is estimated at US$ 1 billion. Ascendant has to ensure that the communities to be affected are in support of mining because no major company will invest a billion dollars in a project that has a history of organized resistance. To sell, it needs to eliminate the grassroots resistance to mining, and therefore it has launched an aggressive campaign against those opposed to mining.

Ascendant's efforts have all of the features of low-intensity conflict employed by Latin American states to crush grassroots opposition. It exploits the internal divisions among colonos by attacking the environmentalists and supporting those who seek quick riches through mining. The company offers generous perks to those who work with them by providing the infrastructure and resources that the state is unable to deliver. Roads, bridges, schools, and health clinics have all been built as tools for winning local hearts and minds. The company provides free medical services in which the doctors tout the benefits of mining and plant lies about the leaders of the opposition. It distributes Christmas presents to children in a shameless effort to gain favor. In short, it exploits people's poverty to sell its project.

The campaign also includes intimidation. Upon its arrival in Intag region, Ascendant launched a million-dollar libel suit against *Periódico Intag*. A former Ecuadorian general, César Villacís, once in charge of Ecuador's secret police, was the member of Ascendant's board of directors responsible for community relations. His frequent appearances at community meetings sent a message to locals that the Ecuadorian military supports mining in Junín. During meetings in the summer and fall of 2004, pro-mining people physically confronted those in opposition, pushing some, destroying video equipment, and brandishing pistols. In December 2005 the conflict escalated when communities organized direct action, burning down Ascendant's "experimental farm." This repeat of the May 1997 burning of the Bishi Metals' mining camp was a direct statement by Inteños of their frustration with the company's presence. Ascendant responded with a legal campaign apparently aimed at jailing the resistance, which failed as Ecuadorian courts dismissed all charges against community members for lack of evidence. In September 2006, Carlos Zorrilla's home was invaded by Ecuadorian police. During the raid his office was ransacked, important documents were taken, and false evidence was planted in the house. Zorrilla, who escaped minutes before the police arrived, was forced into hiding until the courts dismissed all the charges, again for lack of evidence (Gedicks, 2007; Zorrilla, 2006).

After the 2005 fire, Ascendant dramatically increased its armed presence by contracting "security guards" and hiring the international security firm Honor and Laurel. By June 2006, its armed presence was alarming enough that Intag Solidarity Network (ISN) presented a report to the Canadian government warning that the Canadian-based company was paramilitarizing the region and was prepared to use violence to eliminate resistance (ISN, 2006). Desperately seeking to complete a legally required environmental impact study, Ascendant became very aggressive in its attempts to enter the concession zone, an area that rests within Junín's community reserve. Violent confrontations occurred in October and November, climaxing on 2 December 2006, when a company contractor used pepper spray and fired at least 40 rounds of ammunition at community members (Gedicks, 2007). Ecuador's widely respected Comisión Ecuménica de Derechos Humanos (CEDHU) formally denounced the event as a paramilitary action. The December violence led the Ecuadorian government to order Ascendant Copper to stop work, and it rejected the company's environmental impact study for failure to consult with communities. These setbacks were compounded in January 2007 with the inauguration of leftist president Rafael Correa. His administration has promised to review all mining concessions, and in apparent reference to Ascendant, it charged mining companies with causing a state of civil war in communities. In July 2007, the government issued yet another stop-work order, strongly condemning Ascendant for its actions in Intag region. Despite these actions and a strong protest to Canadian securities regulators by DECOIN, Miningwatch Canada, and Intag Solidarity Network, the company was able to raise an additional US$ 12 million on the Toronto Stock Exchange. Ascendant's days in Intag may be ending. Community members, however, are fearful of the damage the company might cause on its way out. In July, for example, one female community member was brutally assaulted by a man dressed in black and wearing a ski mask. Local leaders continue to receive death threats (Amnesty International, 2007; ISN, 2007).

The case of grassroots resistance to mining in Ecuador illustrates the importance of community in the analysis of social movements in Latin America today. Capitalism is a ruthless mechanism of social, political, and economic exclusion that destroys the social fabric and effective citizenship. People are not, however, passive recipients of this assault. They fight back. The *bien bravos* of Junín are resisters, organizers, activists, and organic intellectuals working to reconstitute community. Through their organizing they are constructing a new form of citizenship from the bottom up, as opposed to the market-based citizenship promoted by neoliberalism. These competing constructs of citizenship are central to understanding the tension between corporate globalization and new social movements throughout Latin America. While social movements defined by concepts of autonomy, empowerment, and citizenship do not aim to take state power and constitute significant departures from past revolutionary ones, they are no less revolutionary in their style, substance, and actualization. They constitute a radical challenge to the capitalist system as currently constituted, but not necessarily to capitalism itself.

One key area of debate in the social movement literature is whether today's resistance constitutes a departure from the "new social movements" of the 1980s (Kuecker, 2004). The Junín case is an agrarian-based social-justice movement of resistance to the marginalization of neoliberalism. Its environmental aspects share tendencies with the environmentalism of the new social movements, especially their "not in my backyard" feature. In defending their agrarian way of life, the people of Junín effectively relocate mining to other locations of the world where the costs of environmental destruction are lower because of lack of community resistance. Yet Junín does represent a significant break with the new social movements in seeking alternatives to mining and to the harshness of the neoliberal order. Many new social movements lack a critique of capitalism; the movement in Junín identifies a particular form of capitalism—neoliberalism—as the cause of its problems, though it is not necessarily opposed to capitalism.

What is clear from the Junín case is that neoliberalism offers a new context for social actors. It is defined by the transnationalization of sovereignty and power that concentrates them in the hands of elites, corporations, and institutions. In confronting this transnational trinity, marginalized people on the local level devise new strategies to contend with problems caused by neoliberalism. These strategies include new modes of organizing that emphasize empowerment and horizontal decision-making processes, in strong contrast to neoliberalism's authoritarianism. Similar developments throughout Latin America constitute a sharp departure from earlier "new" social movements that planted the seeds for them (Kuecker, 2004).

The more recent modes of organizing include an important role for civil society, especially NGOs. The formation of civil society was a significant byproduct of the new social movements of the 1980s, and its maturation as an important actor is a defining feature of today's resistance. In the case of Junín, the grassroots formation of DECOIN and the support of Acción Ecológica and international NGOs played crucial roles in the development of the resistance to mining. The distinction from NSMs of the 1980s rests in the way civil society changes the relations of power. The involvement of civil society in solidarity with actors at the grassroots can block or frustrate the designs of elites, corporations, nation-states, and global institutions, altering the comparative advantage formula by increasing costs.

Students of today's social movements confront the troubling issue of evaluating the effectiveness of tactics and strategies. Can these movements produce change without taking power? In Junín, constructing alternatives to neoliberalism is not criticizing capitalism and the structures of power it produces. The liberation theology effort at empowerment is not necessarily an attack on capitalism. While in radical opposition to neoliberalism, the movement in Junín is fundamentally reformist. Community consciousness is aimed at altering relations of power as against its overthrow. Yet, a Gramscian war of position, in which social actors are better off transforming structures of power when they are not in a position to take state power, is highly appropriate at this juncture in the history of the movement. It is, however, highly vulnerable to the capacity of capitalism for survival. Junín can drive out the Mitsubishis and Ascendants—a remarkable accomplishment—but that is not necessarily a victory over capitalism. As the price of copper goes up, the comparative advantage formula restores a favorable cost-benefit scenario that negates the negatives of organized community. Until it dies or is overthrown, capitalism ultimately prevails. The logic of capitalism will send yet another company to get the copper out of the mountains of Ecuador.

7

Resisting Neoliberal Homogenization

The Zapatista Autonomy Movement

Richard Stahler-Sholk

I N THE DOCUMENTARY *ZAPATISTA!* there is a scene in which the ski-masked Subcomandante Marcos tells the camera that the rebels rose up against the Mexican government in 1994 only to discover that the Mexican government didn't exist; instead, they found themselves fighting against the structures of global capital (Big Noise Films, 1998, www.bignoisefilms.com). Social movements do not literally resist neoliberalism; they resist a specific landlord's hired guns trying to drive them off the land they need for subsistence or a specific agency that privatizes their water supply and triples the rates. In Mexico they resist a golf course in Tepoztlán, an airport in San Salvador Atenco, a Costco in Cuernavaca—all local and concrete manifestations of a global logic that disempowers people who lack capital and ignores their right to establish their own priorities. A growing number of movements in Latin America are engaging in innovative organizing against the injustices of the neoliberal paradigm (Gills, 2000b), departing from the revolutionary focus on seizing state power (Foran, 2003). Privatization, fiscal austerity, and economic liberalization have resulted in the contraction and redeployment of the state, shifting the locus of political struggles away from direct contestation for state power and opening new spaces to contestation (by new movements and old) over whether they will be controlled from above or below.

The Mexican state acts increasingly as a broker for global capital as it attempts to re-regulate the conditions for accumulation on a global scale. Neoliberalism involves not simply a headlong retreat of the state but rather a renegotiation of

The original version of this essay appeared in *Latin American Perspectives* 34(2), March 2007: 48–63.

state-society relations. The attempted recomposition of capitalist hegemony included targeted social compensation programs such as the National Solidarity Program—PRONASOL. Those somewhat contradictory efforts to create a reformulated clientelism for the neoliberal era (Hellman, 1994)—more selective and flexible than the old corporatist structures had allowed—did not entirely succeed in shielding the dominant-party form of the Mexican authoritarian state from political change. The shift from state-orchestrated to market mechanisms of distribution overlapped with new forms of social-movement-based struggles, ranging from the debtors' movement El Barzón to independent unions and neighborhood associations (Williams, 2001; Otero, 2004). As the turn to the market left state authorities in control of fewer resources for co-optation, increasingly independent social sectors formulated their demands not in terms of clientelistic expectations but in terms of citizenship rights (J. Fox, 1997). This discourse of rights is characteristic of the newly constituted social subjects confronting neoliberalism throughout Latin America by simultaneously claiming indigenous and other collective rights that markets deny and the citizenship rights that the neoliberal state pretends to offer equally to all (Eckstein and Wickham-Crowley, 2003). The Zapatistas organize in newly contested spaces paradoxically created by neoliberal globalization itself (Stahler-Sholk, 2001a), joining independent peasant and Liberation Theology organizing that predated the neoliberal era (N. Harvey, 1998).

The forces of globalization that affect class relations are experienced (and resisted) through a variety of locally relevant identities, including ethnicity and gender (Nash, 2001; Yashar, 2005). In Chiapas, elaborate structures of labor control were constructed in the centuries after colonization by grafting them onto co-opted "traditional" religious/civic hierarchies in indigenous communities. Changes in the global political economy of post-1982 (oil/debt shock) Mexico were experienced locally as community power struggles that went to the core of what it meant to be part of the indigenous community (Collier, 1994; Rus, 1995). The state regularly mediated private capitalist development initiatives (e.g., logging operations in the Lacandón Jungle in the second half of the twentieth century) by reinventing indigenous identities and lines of authority in ways that facilitated the particular strategy of capital accumulation (De Vos, 2002). Resistance to neoliberalism, then, has taken the form of a movement for autonomy, with the protagonists struggling for the right to define themselves culturally, socially, and politically.

The Potential and the Pitfalls of Autonomy

Social movements by definition operate outside conventional politics, and "new" social movements are distinguished by their emphasis on autonomy, participatory process, and solidarity around perceived collective identities. The neoliberal project implies atomization and loss of control to global market forces, posing dilemmas for movements seeking to reassert community identity and grassroots empowerment. On one hand, the "fetishism of autonomy" (Hellman, 1992)—eschewing affiliation or engagement with any political structure for fear that it might absorb the newly asserted identity—can be a dead end. On the other hand, negotiating a share of power with existing political institutions runs the risk of replicating dominant hierarchies (serving global capital) and distancing the "autonomous" representatives from their social bases. Movements in Mexico and elsewhere experiment and debate over how best to conceive of autonomy (Díaz-Polanco and Sánchez, 2002). Zapatismo as a social movement consists of various layers, including the political-military structure (insurgents and militia) of the Ejército Zapatista de Liberación Nacional (Zapatista National Liberation Army—EZLN) that went public in 1994; the "networks" of national and international supporters; and the "support-base" indigenous communities in the "conflict zones" (eastern jungle, border, northern zone, and central highlands) of Chiapas. I will focus on the support-base communities to consider the sustainability of the movement, highlighting three dilemmas: (1) the limits of territorially based autonomy, (2) autonomy and curtailment of resource allocations, and (3) the neoliberal "multiculturalism trap."

One model of autonomy, drawing on the experience of the Nicaraguan Atlantic region, proposed a regionally based self-governance that would amount to a kind of territorial decentralization negotiated with the state. This model was actually under construction in parts of the jungle region prior to the 1994 Zapatista uprising, particularly in areas of predominantly Tojolabal settlement, in the form of Regiones Autónomas Pluriétnicas (Pluriethnic Autonomous Regions—RAP). This approach in effect created a new, fourth level of government (alongside the federal, state, and municipal institutions) and constructed a new "pluriethnic" indigenous identity among the various indigenous groups that had formed part of the migrant stream settling the Lacandón Jungle agricultural frontier of eastern Chiapas since the 1950s.

The RAP project of autonomy-as-decentralization was accelerated by its promoters in the space created by the Zapatista rebellion, advancing faster among its leadership than the creation of consensus within its diverse base. It therefore suffered from tendencies toward *cacicazgo* or "boss" politics as well as from the competing, more local identities of the *ejidos* reflecting the political economy of rural Mexico (Mattiace, 2003: 95–111). Critics of the RAP, including some academic advisors to the Zapatistas, argued that such territorial jurisdiction acquired at the cost of being subsumed within the existing state structures was only pseudo-autonomy (Esteva, 2003: 252–253). The Zapatistas themselves, who preferred a model of autonomy that built from the community level upward, remained open to a kind of pluralism of autonomies—"a world in which many worlds can fit"—that did not force a choice between autonomy models.

One of the pitfalls of the territorial or parochial interpretation of autonomy—whether in Chiapas, Guatemala, or Ecuador—is that it bottles up the protagonists in a spatial location precisely in an era when their subsistence and cultural identity depend on mobility (Colloredo-Mansfeld, 2002). The exploitation of indigenous communities has often revolved around elites exchanging a territorially bounded degree of local autonomy (for example, in "traditional" highland communities in Chiapas) for a controlled flow of migratory labor, historically to the Soconusco region within Chiapas (Rus, 1995) but increasingly in the past decade to the United States. Chiapas soared from 27th to 11th place among Mexican states in remittances from 1995 to 2004 (Secretaría de Gobernación/Consejo Nacional de Población CONAPO, "Remesas," http://www.conapo.gob.mx/publicaciones/nuevaera/04.pdf), reinforcing the local power of *caciques* dominating the transit and moneylending businesses. Chiapas ranked #1 in the National Population Council CONAPO's index of marginalization, while US$500 million in remittances in 2004 exceeded the value of the entire state's corn harvest (Daniel Villafuerte, cited in Pickard, 2005). This formulation of autonomy may therefore not represent a real alternative to neoliberal globalization, but rather replicate the top-down structure of existing political institutions without developing new leadership capacity at the local community level. The Zapatistas have eschewed such regionally based formulations of autonomy in favor of the community-based model—which proved to have some tactical advantages when the Mexican military attempted to encircle and close the noose around the Lacandón jungle region of Zapatista core support in December 1994, the first year of the rebellion. It was then that the Zapatistas popped up in 38 self-proclaimed "autonomous municipalities," many of them located outside the region of military encirclement.

A second dilemma relates to resource allocation. The Zapatistas have been careful to distinguish themselves from secessionist movements and insist on framing their demands as rights claimed on the basis of indigenous ethnic identity *and* Mexican national citizenship. However, the same neoliberal ideology that "frees" individuals to fend for themselves in the market can also spin off unprofitable state functions and services that used to be part of the citizenship compact. The market paradigm privatizes gains while socializing costs and risks. Thus social sectors and regions may be cut loose as newly autonomous without state resources, free to compete with each other for a share of the shrinking pie. For example, when the PRI party-controlled corporatist apparatus of resource distribution started to be slashed by the neoliberal austerity ax in the 1980s, it was partly replaced by more modest social compensation programs such as PRONASOL (and later PROCAMPO and PROGRESA, the latter reconfigured as the "Oportunidades" program by President Vicente Fox) that were more open to claimants independent of the ruling party. Yet this seeming recognition of autonomous spaces in society turned out to be a new mechanism for division and co-optation (Collier, 1994). As a wider range of groups competed for scarcer state resources, they became vulnerable to clientelistic local politicians or, for that matter, to paternalistic NGOs moving into the breach.

An example of this "autonomy without resources" pitfall can be seen in the Mexican agrarian counterreform inaugurated by the 1992 reform of Article 27 of the 1917 Constitution. Peasant rights to petition collectively for land were ended, and the existing ejido social-property sector (previously protected from the market) would now be susceptible to individual parcelization and titling under the PROCEDE program. This was touted as "freeing" individual members of ejidos to pull out their separate parcels of land and put up the titles as collateral for loans or eventually to sell the land. Of course, after decades of public infrastructural investment bestowed on private large-scale agribusiness, the 1989 dismantling of the state coffee-marketing board Instituto Mexicano del Café (Mexican Coffee Institute—INMECAFE) and post-NAFTA competition from U.S.-subsidized agribusiness products such as corn entering the market, those "free" choices of peasant producers were shaped by major structural constraints. In Chiapas, a state with 4 percent of the population but 27 percent of the backlog of unresolved land reform claims by 1992, poor peasants saw the reform of Article 27 not as rural modernization but rather as the removal of their last hope for subsistence security, leading many to shift from other independent peasant organizations to the ranks of the Zapatista rebellion (N. Harvey, 1998).

In developing an autonomy model entailing separation from government programs, the Zapatistas, in order to sustain a social movement, faced the challenge of offering resources (land, social programs) to their support-base communities. This was complicated by the fact that it was often non-Zapatistas who benefitted materially from the opening created by the rebellion, for example, in the surge of land invasions/recoveries after 1994. Rejecting official aid in order to expose government hypocrisy implied short-term sacrifice for a longer-term political strategy—resistance in the Gramscian sense of developing counterhegemonic ideology in a war of position. This effort was in practice often ambiguous, as Zapatistas and non-Zapatistas were interspersed territorially and even within villages (Pérez Ruiz, 2004). The boundaries of Zapatismo as a social movement "in resistance" were also blurred by the fact that many non-Zapatistas also resisted programs like PROCEDE that undermined ejidos and indigenous communities, viewing them as a threat to an important source of community and social capital. In a conversation on the Zapatista caravan from Chiapas to Mexico City in March 2001 with a long-time activist from the Organización Campesina Emiliano Zapata (OCEZ), he worried that individuals pulling their parcels out of the ejido would drain the communally managed social investment fund, undermining the collective process of deciding on priorities for the community's well-being. An elderly Purépecha woman on another leg of the caravan expressed analogous concerns about PROCAMPO (the temporary per-hectare compensation for the elimination of crop subsidies). She suspected that signing up for a payment associated with a particular plot of land was a little bit like selling rights to the land. This kind of struggle for community control against the atomizing force of the market is the basis for the Zapatista notions of autonomy. Ironically, the Article 27 reforms were coupled with reforms to Article 4 of the Constitution for the first time explicitly recognizing the multiethnic character of the Mexican nation. Both were criticized by independent peasant and indigenous rights organizations as top-down, nonparticipatory initiatives. Their juxtaposition illustrates the way the neoliberal model recognizes the pluralism of indigenous identities as long as those identities do not become the basis for collective organization around substantive rights.

This leads to the third observation about the dilemmas of autonomous movements confronting neoliberalism. The neoliberal project in Latin America is being tweaked to include "managed neoliberal multiculturalism" (C. R. Hale, 2002). The same states that oversee economic liberalization and privatization are establishing themselves as arbiters of the boundary between individual and group rights, carefully circumscribing the latter to exclude challenges to class-based inequalities. In the case of Chiapas, the only topic area in the peace talks following the 1994 Zapatista rebellion that led to a signed agreement was the negotiation over indigenous rights and culture, which led to the San Andrés Accords of 1996. The accords conceded state recognition of *usos y costumbres*, the normative system of decision-making authority through which indigenous communities traditionally governed themselves. For the Zapatistas, this was a fundamental victory for community-based autonomy. Yet it soon became clear that the Mexican government regarded the systems of community assemblies and assignments of duties as merely a quaint vestigial practice frozen in time, unrelated to contemporary struggles over land and resources. The implementing legislation for the San Andrés Accords bogged down in five years of government delays and redrafting, until finally the multiparty Congressional Commission for Concord and Pacification (Comisión de Concordia y Pacificación—COCOPA) put forward a compromise, watered-down text. When the Zapatistas reluctantly accepted the

COCOPA draft indigenous law, the federal government backed away from that too, returning with a new version that totally stripped the substantive rights components from the San Andrés agreement. This was the backdrop for the Zapatistas' March 2001 caravan from Chiapas to Mexico City, culminating in Comandante Esther's historic address to the Congress. When they had returned home, however, the government introduced its gutted version of the "indigenous rights law" which passed despite being denounced by every major indigenous and human rights organization and voted down in all the states with large indigenous populations (Stahler-Sholk, 2005). At the same time, the administrations of President Vicente Fox and Chiapas Governor Pablo Salazar promoted an ostentatious brand of *neoindigenismo* that included co-opting prominent indigenous professionals into new bureaucratic structures, sponsoring community-development-cum-counterinsurgency, unilaterally creating new municipalities in indigenous areas, launching "intercultural universities," and rhetorically celebrating multicultural "inclusion" without letting indigenous people define their own identities (A. Hernández, Paz, and Sierra, 2004).

In the process of this debate between the top-down and bottom-up versions of indigenous rights, the Zapatistas sponsored participatory forums and *consultas* in an effort to link the struggle for autonomy in Chiapas to a broader social movement. This mobilization of support included the Congreso Nacional Indígena (National Indigenous Congress—CNI), part of a new national indigenous movement awakened in part by the Zapatista rebellion. The CNI rejected the officialist indigenous rights law, as did the United Nations special rapporteur for human rights and indigenous questions, the Mexican anthropologist Rodolfo Stavenhagen, who noted that the law violated Convention 169 of the International Labor Organization (ILO) on indigenous rights (which Mexico had signed in 1990) by bypassing popular consultation. He also reiterated the critique by the Mexican Academy of Human Rights that the law empowered state legislatures to supercede anything enacted by indigenous communities.

A further example of this neoliberal multiculturalism trap can be seen in President Fox's Plan Puebla Panamá (PPP), a multibillion-dollar scheme of proposed massive infrastructural investment in southern Mexico to incorporate the region into the global market. In contrast to previous development schemes, the PPP ostensibly acknowledges the marginalization of indigenous populations of the Mexican South, using the language of sustainable development (Nash, 2003: 81–87) to promote what local communities denounce as biopiracy—commodifying and commercializing the biodiversity and other resources of this region. Even the multiculturalism of the indigenous populations is identified as a marketable asset for ecotourism. Yet indigenous communities that practice self-sufficient production and resist being converted into a Disneyfied, homogenized "Maya region" are accused of inefficiency, or worse yet, of sabotaging the development rights of other indigenous groups (i.e., of not being multicultural enough).

The Zapatistas, rather than bargaining for a limited version of territorially based autonomy within a federal model, have insisted on the rights of each community to develop its own network of relations. Rather than accepting the state's power to define the boundaries between individual and collective rights, they have insisted on a concept of ethnic citizenship (N. Harvey, 1998; Nash, 2001) that claims rights of Mexican citizenship *and* indigenous social identity, consistent with the broader hemispheric resurgence of indigenous movements (Yashar, 2005). This diverse interpretation of autonomy defies easy classification, and the Zapatistas have had limited success in generating a national political movement. Yet the resiliency of the Zapatista resistance in the face of massive counterinsurgency and "development" policies has made it a powerful symbol and an invitation to develop alternatives to the logic of global capital.

Struggles for Autonomy in the Zapatista Communities

The Zapatista autonomy movement has developed in several phases, following the changing political dynamic of the rebellion. Burguete (2003) identifies the first three phases: The first began in December 1994 in response to the government's attempted military encirclement of what they assumed to be the Zapatista stronghold, the Cañadas (canyons) that spread through the Lacandón Jungle in the eastern part of the state (the agricultural frontier which had experienced swelling colonization by mainly indigenous poor peasants since the 1950s). Defying the encirclement, the Zapatistas announced their organized presence in 38 municipalities that included a good part of the central highlands, formalizing this proclamation of autonomy with the EZLN's January 1995 "Third Declaration from the Lacandón Jungle" (http://www.ezln .org/documentos/1995/199501xx.en.htm). A second phase, following the February 1996 signing of the San Andrés Accords, began in October 1996 when Zapatistas boycotted municipal elections and refused to recognize the officially elected authorities, instead following indigenous *usos y costumbres* to choose leaders in open community assemblies. This created in effect parallel structures of local government. In a third phase after 1997, when it became clear that the government was reneging on the essential content of the San Andrés Accords, the Zapatistas further institutionalized their de facto autonomous municipal governments and in many cases expelled the official governments. It was in this period that the federal government launched joint police-military raids in April–May 1998 to dismantle the autonomous municipalities of Ricardo Flores Magón and Tierra y Libertad and the State Government of Chiapas approved a remunicipalization creating seven new municipalities designed to undermine the Zapatista autonomy claims. This was followed by a long period of accumulation of forces that the Zapatistas called "strategic silence," rebuilding local organizational networks under the noses of the occupying military forces—including new headquarters for the raided municipalities. Yet this was also a period of strained economic viability as coffee prices fell and government projects lured away supporters. In August 2003, a fourth phase began when the Zapatistas formed regional representative *Juntas de Buen Gobierno* (Good Government Councils) based in centers called *Caracoles* (literally "conch shells," a Mayan symbol) (Stahler-Sholk, 2005). These replaced the former Aguascalientes, regional multiservice centers for clusters of autonomous municipalities.

One of the challenges for the Zapatista project of community-based autonomy has been dealing with issues of pluralism and factionalism among the communities. A variety of independent credit, marketing, and land rights organizations had been organizing in the predominantly indigenous areas of Chiapas since the 1970s, becoming increasingly radicalized in response to the ravages of neoliberalism (N. Harvey, 1998). Zapatista clandestine organizing efforts in this era intertwined with those of groups such as the Asociación Rural de Interés Colectivo (Rural Collective Interest Association—ARIC), Unión de Uniones de Ejidos (Union of Ejido Unions—UU), religious catechists mobilizing under the Liberation Theology-inspired Bishop Samuel Ruiz, and a rather elaborate local sociopolitical structure (the *común*, or communal assembly) that had emerged in the no-man's-land of the Cañadas settlements which were essentially beyond the reach of the state (Leyva Solano, 2003).

In some cases, Zapatista affiliation became one more potential division that community members had to negotiate. Where parallel autonomous and official government structures coexisted, conflicts between members of divided communities sometimes produced jurisdictional disputes that escalated into clashes between the competing authorities, which served as pretexts for coercive state intervention against the Zapatistas (Burguete, 2003: 211). Yet in other divided communities, the specter of state intervention was enough to motivate direct negotiation of conflicts between the factionalized local governments (Stahler-Sholk, 1998: 69–71), creating an incipient autonomy from the state that went beyond Zapatista affiliation. In one autonomous municipality, authorities reported in 2005 that most of the disputes heard by their "Honor and Justice Commission" were actually brought by non-Zapatistas, including two paramilitaries after a drunken machete fight (interview,

August 18, 2005). Religion has also been a potential source of division that the Zapatista autonomy movement has had to negotiate carefully. Religious divisions had long reflected local political conflicts, as both Catholic Liberation Theology and Protestant denominations represented markers of separation from the "traditionalist" Catholic/cacique/Partido Revolucionario Institucional (PRI) local power structures in indigenous communities in Chiapas. The EZLN appealed to these escapees through a new unifying identity that cut across lines of religious affiliation, validating class, and indigenous collective identities (Eber, 2003).

The Zapatista rebellion also placed indigenous communities in the position of having to define their relation with the PRI, often an awkward choice in the pre-2000 days when the party monopolized the state institutions and treasury. The PRI's famous patronage machinery was reinforced by the Mexican army's civic action (*labor social*) and later government programs in the conflict zones, reinforcing divisions by offering handouts (*despensas*) of food and other basic supplies only to PRI supporters. Even electricity was individually doled out in some areas, with family-sized solar panel units for each thatched hut that declared its officialist loyalties. In areas more distant from the military occupation in Chiapas such as the neighboring state of Oaxaca, such tactics reinforced a populist image of the PRI that allowed some peasant communities to construct an identity for themselves in which they were both pro-PRI and pro-Zapatista (Stephen, 1997). But in the conflict zones of Chiapas, where the lines were sharper, the Zapatistas demanded a degree of sacrifice from communities who wanted to consider themselves "in resistance," in that they were expected to reject government aid.

In practice, the community responses were mixed. One Cañadas community, returning from a month of refuge in the hills following the military's illegal February 1995 offensive that broke the ceasefire, had scarcely begun to clean up from the army's looting and pillage when a helicopter appeared carrying Mexican Congresspersons offering aid (see Stahler-Sholk, 1998: 68). After an open-air assembly while the busy legislators waited impatiently, the members of the demolished community came back with the response that they would refuse aid from the government that had just sent the army after them. Instead they requested a withdrawal of the troops who were still camped nearby. In another community in the Che Guevara Autonomous Municipality, when a government health inspector arrived uninvited to check for malaria cases, suddenly no one could speak Spanish. Afterward villages expressed their suspicion that an earlier visit by a government vaccination team had left women sterilized, a view that reflected their deep distrust of "help" from the state. In the contested Montes Azules Biosphere Reserve near the Guatemalan border—coveted by global capital for its biodiversity and hydroelectric resources—government agencies launched an aggressive campaign beginning in 2002 to divide and evict communities, combining threats with offers of resettlement land and resources. Settlements of Zapatista sympathizers that were newer (often displaced from other regions) and/or on the political or geographic fringes of integration into the movement (e.g., the geographically overextended Libertad de los Pueblos Maya Autonomous Municipality), lacked a viable resistance strategy, and the Zapatistas preemptively relocated seven of them in 2004.

Self-reliant, sustainable development is an important challenge for the Zapatista communities. Since 1994, they have developed a variety of self-sufficient production, exchange, and social service projects: collective garden patches, rabbit raising, beekeeping, candle making, agroecology experimentation, locally controlled schools, networks of health promoters trained in combinations of traditional and modern healing, etc. Most of these started on a small scale, but the development of the five Aguascalientes centers allowed some coordination and planning beyond individual communities, including boot-making and textile-weaving cooperatives (problematical in terms of gender segregation, as the Zapatistas sought to draw on traditional identity but reinvent more egalitarian and less hierarchical traditions) and the regional autonomous secondary school in the highlands center of Oventik. These projects also built on indigenous traditions of a community labor tax, a pool of person-days of labor to which each family contributed. These nonmarket alternatives to the neoliberal model were an effort to create material conditions for the support-base communities to hold out while inspiring a broader movement capable of changing state policies. The government sought to break that independence by depriving communities of land (Nash, 2003: 80) and otherwise isolating them.

Economic "autonomy" from the state and from the global market entailed other tradeoffs. The Zapatistas had to improvise a mode of relations with nongovernmental organizations (NGOs) to preserve community control. Since the 2003 creation of Juntas de Buen Gobierno headquartered in five Caracoles, the regional Juntas and municipal autonomous councils review NGO projects to decide whether and on what terms they can proceed (Earle and Simonelli, 2005)—instead of letting NGOs drive the development process, which could be just as divisive as the government's deliberate counterinsurgency aid. This has reinforced the autonomous authorities' legitimacy and participatory experience in self-government. As the Zapatistas explained (Marcos, 2003: pt. 2):

> It was a matter of time before people came to understand that the Zapatista indigenous people had dignity and were not looking for alms, but rather respect.

. . . There is a more sophisticated kind of handout which is practiced by some NGOs and international organizations. It consists more or less in their deciding what the communities need and, without even consulting them, imposing not just particular projects, but also the timing and form of their execution. Imagine the desperation of a community that needs potable water and instead is given a library, or needs a school for children and is given a course in herbiculture.

Where projects were established in specific communities, the Juntas sometimes charged a 10 percent tax for the region. The collective fund would create a counterbalance to the uneven development that reflected the convenience and preferences of NGO funders, reaffirming the concept of community empowerment. The Zapatistas would now have some modest revenues to respond to needs and proposals emanating from the communities, an escape from the "autonomy without resources" trap, though it meant defining self-sufficiency in terms of wider networks of fair trade and solidarity. It also meant tightening the criteria for Zapatista-affiliated communities "in resistance" (i.e., rejecting government aid), a tradeoff that sacrificed some pluralism and flexibility in pushing communities to define themselves as "in or out." The new structure of the Caracoles—extending the parameters of the movement into statelike functions—posed broader questions of whether a social movement/rebellion/revolution must eventually institutionalize and in the process lose some of its mobilizational impetus. The Juntas included a governing council of two representatives from each of the autonomous municipalities composing the region, who rotated every 10–15 days. This new dynamic logically entailed some tradeoffs. The frequent rotation of representatives fostered grassroots participation and accountability but perhaps at some cost of efficient continuity. The new task of regional representation also required travel and extended shifts outside the community, which in light of gender roles in the indigenous communities might reduce women's participation in governance structures within a movement that sought to simultaneously advance class, gender and ethnic demands (Speed, Hernández Castillo, and Stephen, 2006).

In reformulating the structure of community representation at the regional level, the Zapatistas were explicitly cutting out the intermediary roles of both the political-military apparatus of the EZLN itself and self-appointed leaders and organizations of civil society (Marcos, 2003: pt. 6):

The military structure of the EZLN "contaminated" in some ways a democratic and self-governing tradition. The EZLN was, shall we say, one of the "anti-democratic" elements in a relation of direct community democracy. . . . Since the EZLN, on principle, is not fighting to take power, none of the military leadership or members of the Clandestine Revolutionary Indigenous Committee can occupy positions of authority in the community or in the autonomous municipalities. . . .

Often dishonest people deceive national and international civil society by presenting themselves in the cities as "Zapatistas.". . . Now it will just be a matter of contacting one of the *Juntas de Buen Gobierno* . . . and in a matter of minutes one can find out if it is true or not, and if he is a Zapatista or not.

This reaffirmation of the authority of the communities fit the Zapatista commitment to *mandar obedeciendo* (lead by obeying), reflecting the attention to process that characterizes new social movements. Yet it left unclear the role of the EZLN leaders (or of the civic Zapatista National Liberation Front, FZLN) in connecting to a national movement, particularly during periods of "strategic silence" when there was no dialogue with the government.

It was this dilemma of potential isolation within their autonomous regions—containment within a space that could be ignored, the "*indio permitido*" (C. R. Hale, 2004)—that the Zapatistas sought to address with their June 2005 "Sixth Declaration of the Lacandón Jungle." They broke a four-year silence to hold a series of encounters/forums with civil society, inaugurating "The Other Campaign," in which Zapatista leaders would visit other movements throughout the country from January–July 2006 to refocus the national agenda away from election-year politicking (N. Harvey, 2005). In November 2005 the Zapatistas dissolved the FZLN and curtailed the role of Enlace Civil (an organization that had served as a clearinghouse for NGOs working in autonomous territories), reflecting the new emphasis on direct decision making by Zapatista community-based civil authorities.

Zapatista communities struggled to develop self-sufficient production and exchange without dependence on resources (capital, land) controlled by others, to avoid being uprooted and dispersed by market forces that threatened to "free" the community members as individuals at the expense of their collective right to preserve a different system. The Zapatistas understood this resistance as "sustainable development," but within the larger context of the crisis of Mexican peasant agriculture it was not clear that the survival strategies of the autonomous communities—including sporadic "fair trade" and other solidarity support, some collective production (mostly limited to newly settled land "recovered" from ranchers), and wage labor when necessary to make up for low market prices for corn/beans/coffee—amounted to an alternative to capitalism. The state and transnational corporations (as well as corporate-funded NGOs such as Conservation International) also used the term "sustainability" to argue that small-scale peasant agriculture is an inefficient throwback, unsustainable in the era of corporate-dominated globalization. The same government that expels indigenous settlers from the Montes Azules region in the name of protecting the environment also plans ecologically destructive mega-investment schemes such as agroindustrial African palm and eucalyptus plantations under the framework of Plan Puebla Panamá. That corporate model appears "sustainable" only if it is subsidized by infrastructural investments and, for that matter, by military (and paramilitary) coercion that structures the market by clearing resistant communities from the area to be "developed." The Mexican army blamed jungle colonists for the devastating fires that swept the Lacandón region in 1998, when in fact this had never occurred in 30 years of settlement prior to military incursions and road building in the region (Nash, 2003: 86–87). Like members of the movement led by Chico Mendes in the Brazilian Amazon, Zapatista communities in the Lacandón realize that poor peasant land colonists can be scapegoated for their subsistence efforts unless they explicitly practice agroecology. Yet the autonomy that comes from sustainable agriculture is precisely the reason these communities are targeted for dismantling to make way for capitalist "development."

In the Montes Azules region, in the crosshairs of global capital and Plan Puebla Panamá, corporate-backed bioprospecting and dam projects clashed with peasant cultivation. In one community I visited in June/July 2003, a group of Ch'ol families newly displaced by paramilitary violence in the northern part of the state was planting crops and building houses with only hand tools and the wood, palm fronds, and vines found in the jungle. The group's arrival was met with threatening visits by armed "Lacandones" (actually Maya Caribes), a tiny indigenous group that had been co-opted by the government since 1972, when a newly imagined "Lacandón Community" was granted rights to over 600,000 hectares of forest in exchange for lumbering concessions to corporate interests (De Vos, 2002). That suspect concession ignored settlements by other indigenous groups, many of which had legal rights to their lands through the agrarian reform. The government further muddled the issue in 1978 by establishing the Montes Azules Biosphere Reserve, overlapping much of the territory of the previously defined Lacandón Community. In 2000, with bioprospecting operations under way in the area, the corporate-funded NGOs Conservation International and World Wildlife Fund launched a "conservationist" campaign, demanding eviction of settlers from Montes Azules on environmental grounds. The government then began evicting Zapatista communities, using combinations of Lacandones (pitted against other ethnicities), agents of the Federal Prosecutor for Environmental Protection (PROFEPA), and federal military units.

These evictions, rationalized by a discourse of governmental protection of indigenous (Lacandón) rights and (corporate-defined) environmentalism, served the combined purposes of anti-Zapatista counterinsurgency and clearing the way for global capital (CIEPAC, *Chiapas al Día* Bulletins 393,

February 3, 2004; 347, June 10, 2003; and 378, October 15, 2003; http://www.ciepac.org/bulletins). In the particular community I visited, the newly arrived Ch'ol settlers had quickly petitioned for incorporation into the Zapatista autonomous municipality of Libertad de los Pueblos Maya. Their survival strategy also included designating a community member as "agricultural technician" to receive training in agroecology from an NGO in the distant city of San Cristóbal, inviting another NGO to send trainers to the community for follow-up workshops on techniques of sustainable agriculture, negotiating with a young community member who was finishing his secondary schooling in the northern zone to return to the new settlement to establish an autonomous primary school, inviting the San Cristóbal-based "Fray Bartolomé de Las Casas" Human Rights Center to maintain a rotating observer presence in the community following threatening visits from paramilitary and military forces, and preparing to send a representative to town for training to link up with the Network of Community Human Rights Defenders. For all their resourcefulness and apparent unity of purpose, however, the government managed to divide them, inducing one faction to sign a document apologizing to the "Lacandón Community" for occupying "its" land and promising to leave "voluntarily." Then in January 2004 the military and other government agencies invaded, arresting the leadership and evicting the community. This case again illustrates the complexity of the autonomy struggle. The state, serving the interests of global capital, has appropriated the language of agrarian reform, indigenous rights, and environmentalism. The community, having been violently evicted from one territory, had a shaky claim to "sustainable development" (clearing rain forest to plant corn) based on the counterfactual of how transnationals planned to use the land. Also, their tenuous historical and geographic link to the autonomous municipality made it hard to ensure "good government," the basis for the Zapatistas' legitimacy claim for the right to local self-rule.

Other important elements of the Zapatista construction of grassroots autonomy have included community-controlled education and administration of justice. In the early aftermath of the 1994 uprising, some of the government-supplied bilingual teachers who had worked in indigenous communities in Chiapas abandoned their posts, and others were expelled by Zapatista communities. Many of these teachers had been sent out through branches of the Department of Education as part of the assimilationist policies administered since the 1950s by the Instituto Nacional Indigenista (National Indigenist Institute—INI). The Zapatista communities, in rejecting the bilingual government teachers, chose to sacrifice the meager educational resources on offer in order to open new possibilities of community control and relevant curriculum emphasizing such things as agriculture and indigenous culture. Yet this meant new challenges such as negotiating for NGO assistance without losing autonomy and designing new curricula without deepening the divisions between Zapatista-affiliated and other indigenous people. In judicial administration, autonomous authorities face challenges of ambiguous lines of demarcation in areas of divided communities and dual power. Their enforcement powers in effect depend on each community's or region's acceptance of their legitimacy. Notwithstanding the rights of indigenous communities under the San Andrés Accords to implement local normative systems, the government selectively invoked human rights—privileging the individual (property) rights demanded by the neoliberal model—to undermine autonomous authorities (Speed and Collier, 2000).

Preliminary Lessons of the Zapatista Autonomy Experience

The Zapatista movement is continually evolving, reflecting the dynamic interaction between neoliberalism and the social movements that contest it. As the state brokers the reconfiguration of markets in accordance with the logic of global capital, new organizational bases and forms of organizing are emerging within civil society, attempting to build alternatives from the grassroots. This necessarily involves these movements in political struggles as they claim rights to organize autonomously from control by the state or market actors. The Zapatista example suggests that "autonomy" is not a monolithic concept or a magic bullet against neoliberalism. States implementing neoliberal projects have a variety of ways of responding to autonomy movements, trying to neutralize or divert them. Several potential dead ends for autonomy movements are identified here. One is a version of autonomy defined merely as territorial decentralization, which could convert the regional authorities into appendages of the existing power structure. A second is autonomy that cuts off local claimants from resources, "freeing" them to fend for themselves as the central state paves the way for the penetration of the global market. A third is the neoliberal multiculturalism trap, recognizing multiple (ethnic) identities while denying any substantive collective rights to the diverse groups.

In navigating between these shoals, the Zapatistas have created a space for local communities to experiment with the construction of new models of government. This pluralism and flexibility of autonomies helped the movement survive over ten years of intense state-organized counteroffensive, but the Zapatistas' future depends on their ability (limited so far) to articulate this local resistance into a national movement, as they have attempted to do with their

"Other Campaign." Community-controlled social and political institutions—schools, clinics, systems of justice, and regional planning—are part of the struggle to define collective priorities independently of the logic of the market. As global market forces reduce space for self-sufficient development, the importance of the microcosm of Zapatista autonomous communities—like the spaces occupied and transformed by Argentine *piqueteros* and Brazilian *sem terras*—is in symbolizing an alternative and inspiring new political movements that challenge the state's posture as broker for global capital.

8

Praxis of Empowerment

Mística and Mobilization in Brazil's Landless Rural Workers' Movement

Daniela Issa

> But there is another force, generally not considered in politics, which we call the act of feeling.
>
> —Ademar Bogo

O N APRIL 17, 2006, the Movimento dos Trabalhadores Rurais Sem Terra (Landless Rural Workers' Movement—MST), and its supporters gathered in São Paulo's Praça da Sé to remember the tenth anniversary of the Eldorado de Carajás Massacre by the military police in the Amazonian state of Pará, Brazil, a massacre that started as a peaceful protest by the MST and ended with the annihilation of 19 members, and the wounding of 69 others. The Carajás massacre was not only the largest massacre committed against the MST since its founding in 1984 but also the largest criminal case ever brought to trial in Brazil, with over 150 defendants, all military policemen. In contrast to the massacre committed in Corumbiara, in the state of Rondônia, a year earlier, which had outraged public opinion and forced Brazilians and the international community to face the reality of rural violence in Brazil, this massacre had national and international coverage. Five years after the massacre, in June 2001, only two defendants were sentenced to life in prison, and both await the outcome of their appeals, still free men. The MST had organized the demonstration not only to honor the dead and wounded but also to remind the community, which all too often suffers compassion fatigue, of

The original version of this essay appeared in *Latin American Perspectives* 34(2), March 2007: 124–138.

the disposability of the lives of the poor and the lack of urgency and justice on the part of the state. Under drizzling rain, politicians, union leaders, and representatives of the MST delivered their speeches as a sign of support for the movement and indignation over the violence perpetrated against the Sem Terra. As the demonstration ended, night had fallen, and 19 members of the MST wrapped in the MST's flag were solemnly carried away from the square with a song from the folk singer Chico Buarque accompanying the procession in the background:

> Essa cova em que estás com palmos medida,
> é a conta menor que tiraste em vida
> é de bom tamanho, nem largo nem fundo
> é a parte que te cabe deste latifúndio

("This grave where you find yourself, measured in palms, is the smallest concern you took from life. It is the right size, neither wide nor deep, it's your share of this *latifundio*.") Observers silently watched the bodies disappear in the darkness, and the song was replaced by occasional drumbeats as they were symbolically transported to the scene of the funeral of the massacred members. Some had tears in their eyes.

This last is an example of what is referred to in the Brazilian social science literature as a *mística*—the representation through words, art, symbolism, and music of the struggles and reality of this social movement—and is a distinctive characteristic of the Landless Movement. *Mística* is also used to refer to the more abstract, emotional element, strengthened in collectivity, which can be described as the feeling of empowerment, love, and solidarity that serves as a mobilizing force by inspiring self-sacrifice, humility, and courage. This element is clearly not unique to the MST. Its origins are found in the spiritual mysticism of liberation theology, which sees the poor as the object of love. Although most scholars agree on the meaning of the term *mística*, its translation into English varies, and it is used in different ways. This study examines the role of mística as a mobilizing element by tracing its roots and characteristics, discussing it as praxis (in its pedagogical and cultural application), and analyzing its contribution to the uniqueness and effectiveness of Latin America's largest social movement. The mística not only inspires but also serves as pedagogy of empowerment. This pedagogy relies on symbolism to convey concepts and values to a class characterized by low levels of formal education and/or literacy, and therefore is not limited to producing knowledge; it narrates history and experience, reviving the collective memory of the Brazilian peasantry and ultimately contributing to the formation of a collective Sem Terra identity. The cultural contribution of the mística as praxis is resisting the homogenization of globalization; it is the Gramscian counterhegemonic alternative. Therefore, in addition to its inspirational element mística empowers members by creating their collective identity and reviving their culture, contributing to its organization.

Though mística is the object of this study, other factors such as the role of organization, leadership, ideology, strategy and historical structures must be taken into consideration for a more comprehensive understanding of how the MST has been effectively mobilizing for over two decades. The political "opening" of dictatorial Brazil to democracy with the transition to electoral regimes in the continent since the 1980s has made the organization of social movements possible by providing the political structure for freer collective action. Yet this liberalized political framework has failed to confer citizenship rights—the right to have rights—on the subaltern members of society (Alvarez, Dagnino, and Escobar, 1998a). Moreover, the masses in Latin America have been adversely affected by free-market globalization, witnessing a continuously increasing gap in the distribution of income and an export-led orientation of their economies. Rural social movements such as the MST and the Zapatistas in Mexico have mobilized to retain or gain access to land that will ensure their subsistence and preserve their culture. The agrarian social order of Brazil is one of the most conservative in Latin America when it comes to the inequality of land distribution, debt bondage, human trafficking, practices of slave labor (as defined by people in chains or physically confined and forced to work), and landlessness (see Sutton, 1994; Comissão Pastoral da Terra, 1998; Adriance, 1996; Banford and Glock, 1985; A. Wright and Wolford, 2003). Brazil is a country that has never had a revolutionary or institutionalized break with a colonial legacy of *latifúndios*, nor has there been the will on the part of the state, much less the landed oligarchy, to carry out land reform.

Origins of the MST's Mística

The term *mística* when used in analysis of the MST has been translated into English as "mysticism" (A. Wright and Wolford, 2003), élan (Veltmeyer and Petras, 2002) "millenarianism" (Löwy, 2001), and "mystique," also used alternatively by these writers and others (Almeida and Sanchez, 2000; Harnecker, 2003). Mística in social movements is a subjective experience in collectivity, and, insofar as one is referring to the feeling and not the praxis of mística (the art, music and symbolism used to express the "feeling" and in constructing identity and culture), the above terms can be used interchangeably in the analysis of various social movements. In the context of the MST in particular, there is no English equivalent that truly reflects what mística signifies in Portuguese: one can speak of "*a força da mística*" (the power of mística) and one can say, "*Eles fizeram uma mística linda*" (They did a beautiful mística). The terms *mystique, mysticism, mystical component,* and so forth, are not applicable to the second of these uses; it would make no sense to say "I observed three 'mystiques' today." Mística in this sense is understood as a symbolic political representation and social movement frame (Johnston, 1995: Johnston and Klandermans, 1995) for the interpretation and articulation of a counterhegemonic alternative by MST participants; it is cognitive praxis (Fernandes, 1996: 232).

The MST's mística has its roots in liberation theology, which emerged in the 1960s as a result of the Second Vatican Council and the Conference of Latin American Bishops in Colombia to address the human suffering, political oppression, and material deprivation of the Majority World. This new theology adopted a preferential option for the poor and sought to liberate the oppressed through *conscientização* (conscientization) (Freire, 1967), or the process of "gaining consciousness," and participation through ecclesiastical base communities, which worked with the masses at a grassroots level by encouraging lay people to interpret Bible readings in terms of their reality. Ecclesiastical base communities played an important historical role in dictatorial Latin America by providing the space for discussion, education, and consequently mobilization of the poor when political organization was illegal. The MST as a social movement emerged from the support of this progressive theology, particularly the Comissão Pastoral da Terra (Pastoral Land Commission—CPT), an organization created in 1975 to serve the interests of the rural poor in Brazil. The CPT was directly involved in the formation of the MST as a national organization, assisting with conscientization, providing logistical support for meetings throughout the country, and adopting an ecumenical approach that avoided sectarianism (Stedile and Fernandes, 1999: 19–21; Fernandes, 2000: 75; 1996: 76–79). The MST's adaptation of liberation theology ideals and Christian mística allowed it to build on its version of mística even after liberation theology itself went into decline in the late 1980s.

The etymology of mística is traced to "mystery" and "mysticism," which the religions of the world interpret as occult to the ordinary person but revealed to a select few. The mística derived from liberation theology is precisely the opposite: it is not a doctrine, an ideology, a mystification of reality, or a secretive/selective way of looking at things but a communal religious experience (Boff, 1994b: 12; Betto, 2001b). In contrast to the traditional Judeo-Christian view of the Kingdom of God as a reward in the afterlife for the sufferings of this one, it calls for idealizing and materializing the utopia of the Kingdom of God in the here and now. As Frei Betto (2001b: 62) explains, calling on people to be the agents of their liberation, "the Kingdom of God is not up there but in front of you." The poor are central to mística, because, as the theologian Leonardo Boff explains, Christians see the passion for the poor as the passion of Jesus that continues to agonize in the incarnation of his brothers and sisters, and a parallel is drawn between the martyrdom of Jesus and the massacre of the people (Boff 1993: 16):

> Christian mística, because it is historic, is oriented toward following Jesus. This implies a commitment of solidarity with the poor, since Jesus was one of them and personally opted for the marginalized of the streets, countryside, and squares of the cities. It implies a commitment of personal and social transformation, present in the utopia preached by Jesus of the Kingdom of God that is realized in justice for the poor and, from that, [justice] for all and for all creation.

Frei Sergio Görgen (1997: 290) sees the cross as not only representing Jesus's faith, resistance, and presence among the people but also helping construct a "mística of resistance" to the suffering of life in the encampments as an analogy to that of Jesus's persecution. Liberationists recognize that the desire to transform society is not exclusively a Christian or a religious aspiration and that an attitude of mística—self-sacrifice for the collective good—is "accessible to all, without exception, as long as one is human and sensitive" (Boff, 1993: 13). The practice of humility is an integral legacy of religious mística for the MST. Boff (1994b: 13) argues that to nourish the mística one must show an openness to learning from various sources and cultural traditions, a "venerating humility toward reality." As Stedile and Fernandes (1999: 59) explain, liberationists' example of humility helped create a movement open to "all truths, not a single truth," one that learns from the experience of past struggles and heroes and recognizes its "limitations" and the "temporary nature of its participation" in the history of popular struggles as a link to future ones—features that differentiate the MST from the traditional leftist orthodoxy (Stedile and Fernandes, 1999: 58). Humility is the difference between a *militante* and a *militonto/a*, the latter being an egotistic activist who adopts a "know-it-all" attitude in leadership positions, thus losing touch with the community (Betto, 2001a). In the words of one MST member (Adão, interview April 19, 2006), "The true militant should always put the interest of others before his, should be the last one in line to eat and the first to volunteer for a difficult or dangerous task."

Catholic ritualism has been identified as another attribute of liberation theology in the mística of the MST (Löwy, 2001; Lara Junior, 2005a). While there is consensus on the ritualistic nature of mística practices in the MST as a Catholic legacy, there is a scarcity of research that accounts for the contributions of indigenous and African religiosity to mística, considering how integral they are to Brazilian culture. Boff (1994a: 94) and Betto (1994: 44) discuss the influence of non-Western, non-Christian místicas found in indigenous and Afro-Brazilian religion, such as Umbanda, as based on a relationship with

God through nature. As Betto explains, the spirituality of the poor is not institutional but animistic, incorporating belief in the sacredness of nature. Despite the ritualistic nature of Catholic mística, the "ritual" (if one can call it that) employed by the MST is not the same as that of institutionalized religion in that it lacks formal rules that *must* be followed. Místicas follow generic recommendations such as providing participants with the lyrics of a song when music is presented, but they do not have to start with any particular set of practices (poem, singing, theatre) or incorporate the use of any particular set of objects (candles, machetes, seeds) in the representation of the message every time they are practiced. Místicas can be conducted as ritual, depending upon the circumstances, but this is not always the case; they are spontaneous manifestations marking time and culture. Because death is very much a part of Brazilian peasant culture, many místicas are conducted with the solemnity of a funeral; this solemnity and the Catholic religious tradition have influenced the tone and general practice of other místicas, which consequently can be interpreted as ritualistic in character. Taylor and Whittier (1995: 176–177) identify marches, rallies, riots, and rebellions as rituals of mobilized groups and argue they are central to the study of collective actions because they represent the emotions that drive protest. To qualify místicas as ritualistic in the general sense of the word can be construed as reductionist (see Stedile and Fernandes, 1999: 130–131). Like mass protests, they are ritualistic in a broader sociological context, but above all, praxis.

Characteristics and Interpretations

It is tempting to see mística in everything, given its interrelatedness with many aspects of the Landless Movement, such as ideology, strategy, and participation. In addition to empowering subjects to continue mobilizing for the cause of land reform, mística as praxis serves a pedagogical and cultural function. The following are some general characteristics of the MST's mística: It involves the use of symbols. It is strengthened by collectivity and has a strong emotional component but is not the absence of reason. It is creative and artistic. While part of the movement, it is not institutionalized. It may be ritualistic but is not religious or denominational. Its themes center on social causes as they pertain to the MST's reality. It is experienced in the movement but also derives inspiration from outside. It fosters identity and *pertença* (belonging), which is the creation of identity by association with a group, in this case a class-based, peasant identity—the membership, partnership and inclusion of otherwise excluded subjects lacking citizenship rights.

In *O vigor da mística* (2002), produced by the MST, Bogo argues that mística has been the key element animating the MST's struggle. It is the powerful force in the fight for social causes, the "fire" based on solidarity, generosity, ethics, and morality that is embodied in the symbols of the movement. "Anytime something moves toward making a human being more humane, that is when mística manifests itself" (Bogo, 1999: 126–127). Peloso (1994: 2), who has worked with the MST through the years as a lecturer and educator, describes it as the decisive force that inspires people when they are discouraged or deceived, the "food" that reinvigorates the masses when oppression creates the perception that efforts to overcome it are pointless. Stedile, one of the founders and a national leader and spokesperson for the MST, defines mística as a "feeling directed toward an ideal" and the "social practice that makes people feel good about participating in the struggle" (Stedile and Fernandes, 1999: 129–130). The MST sees mística as important to the construction of its identity. Applying a psychosocial framework of analysis to the movement, Lara Junior (2005a) found that mística contributes to the consolidation of the MST's collective identity through its religious, cultural, and political elements. While Caldart's (2000) definition of mística is very similar to that of these writers, she is unique in arguing it necessarily occurs in collectivity. In addition to identity construction, she points out, mística is an experience that produces culture. Fernandes (1996: 232–233) sees mística as a practice which enhances the MST's organization. He defines it as "a combination of practices developed in all of the spatial dimensions of political socialization." It is the interactive space for communication, which is fundamental for the construction of knowledge and the development of relations and alliances. Consequently, this space becomes the nonmaterial territory of the movement (Bernardo Mançano Fernandes, interview, San José, Puerto Rico, 2006).

MST members describe mística as follows:

> It's not easy to explain, it's easier to live it . . . It's a source from which we feed and continue fighting, the representations of our life and what the struggle means to us . . . [Mística] comes from those who worked with the church, that's the origin. It was combining the dream with the political. Others in the left criticized us because it [mística] was viewed as idealism, ritualistic, and also because it came from the church. It was as if it had no foundation . . . Without mística we cannot be militants. We get nourished from this, and if you can't feel emotion with the *lonas pretas* [black tarps used as tents by the occupiers], the children in school, the MST's flag, then why continue? How do you face fear and stay away from your family? One of the legacies of the movement is militancy based on mística, love for the cause. (Clarice, interview, April 20, 1996)

Mística moves us, it's everything, dedication. We're not in the MST for a salary or promotion. As a militant, there's an increase in responsibility, not in salary, so it's the mística that moves us to become a militant. It moves us to cry, to joke around. The militant does not live without mística. It comes from within, your hope of a dream, of constructing . . . the objective and the cause are one; follow Che's example. (Messias, interview, April, 19, 2006)

The militants construct mística with the awareness that there is a need to change. [Mística is] when I come to the realization that I want land, food, and life for others, not just for me. That's the meaning of the militant's mística. (Gorete, interview, April 18, 2006)

To me it's this secretive thing that motivates us, it gives us impulse. It's something that you don't explain, you feel it. There's symbolism and a church legacy . . . Mística is present in our daily lives as militants, just working at the base is a moment of mística, of *pertença*. [Mística] is created in our collective way of life. We inherited a lot from theory, but in the MST it is enriched in the collectivity. Why is it that these people who live under *lona preta* live smiling, singing, and happy? It's because of mística. In school we create mística, a necessity to study more . . . Mística is a way of making the struggle happen. There's the mística of acting out the mystical act, where we remember martyrs through poetry or in the marches—and there's the mística that you live day-to-day. This mística is carried to professors, intellectuals, students, the outsiders, who also feel it. It moves you and makes you question, it's not just feeling. (Regilma, interview, April 19, 2006)

If mística didn't exist, the movement wouldn't be what it is. Every moment is difficult, and it's the mística that lifts you. When it comes time to learn, mística helps you. The MST wouldn't be what it is if it didn't have mística. It would exist, but not as it is. There are times when [mística] is uplifting, sad, or makes you think. It's not only uplifting, it teaches you, and you feel indignation. (Miltinho, interview, April 20, 2006)

The general sense of authenticity of mística is due to the fact that it has not been institutionalized; as Stedile states, "We realized that if you allow mística to become formal, it dies out. No one receives orders to be emotional; you get emotional because you are motivated as a result of something" (Stedile and Fernandes, 1999: 130). Tasks are performed in the MST through the formation of working groups or committees. If a march is organized, for example, there are committees to attend to such concerns as the participants' health, food, representation in the media, and mística. Mística committees form for organizational purposes, not to formalize the practice. Those who serve on them cannot volunteer at all times for the task; there must be rotation of participants. There is minimal documentation on guidelines for consideration in the practice of mística, and místicas are generally not documented or recorded, except when they mark important events or when outsiders are studying them. As one militant notes:

> [Mística] is extremely creative and free, and it's that liberty which makes it mystical. Sometimes we're asked: Why don't you write down the místicas? They are so beautiful! And we don't do it because it's creative; it's created in the moment. The murderers of Carajás, who [enjoy] impunity, cause us indignation, and so we represent that. Mística is not a theatrical representation with a script, it's more [a creation] in the moment, despite being prepared. (Regilma, interview, April 20, 2006)

In a letter to Bogo, Ranulfo Peloso created an outline to help orient those participating in místicas. His purpose in putting his reflections on paper was to clarify what he understood as an erroneous conception of místicas as being created to dramatize for entertainment purposes, to convey mystery, or to shock. When it acquires any of the above characteristics, místicas are no longer authentic and would fall into the category of mysticism. The following considerations have been discussed in the MST but not institutionalized (Ranulfo Peloso, personal communication, May 2006):

The celebration is beautiful when it is practiced with brevity, a certain solemnity, and simplicity. It is good to use symbols, gestures, cultural expressions, personal testimonies, but one must avoid having it become a merely theatrical representation.

A mística should not be expressed for entertainment purposes—no surprises or sensationalism. People should be involved in the process of preparing it. If a poem is used, a copy of the text should be provided so that people will have access to what is being read, and the same for music.

It is important to avoid the use of mística to adorn a meeting—("Now that the mística is over, let's get down to business"). It should not become the task of "specialists," even though some are more creative and sensitive than others. It should not occupy one's entire focus ("I couldn't attend the course, because I had to prepare the mística"). It must not turn into a competition ("Their mística was better than yours"). Something that worked in the Northeast of Brazil would be out of context and inauthentic in the South. Preparation is necessary to avoid improvisation but should not become a torment to those who are coordinating the celebration.

Místicas can be conducted at the beginning of a meeting to help get everyone's attention and recall the spirit that unites the group, but a song, poetry reading, silence or "word of order" (encouraging expression) can be presented out at any appropriate moment.

Zander Navarro (2002: 11) argues that the MST's mobilization has not emancipated the MST members and that its national leadership has become more radical and centralized over the years. This leadership has control over the intermediary militants, who display "an almost religious devotion" to the movement, but are not strong enough to control it, and this is why "indoctrinating mechanisms" such as education and mística are necessary. Navarro does not explain how mística is used for indoctrination, and while it is not central to his argument, the question may be raised whether this is the case. There is no question that the practice of místicas is centered on social themes relating to land reform, rural violence, and the cultivation of peasant identity, and in this sense they are limited in scope, as they are a reflection of the reality of the Sem Terra. Yet within such scope, the themes vary greatly in subject and from region to region, because they are interpreted subjectively and created spontaneously. The preparation of a mística can take anywhere from a few minutes to a few hours, except when it marks an important event or requires rehearsal (for mime, dance or theatrical representation). Místicas are participatory and decentralized cultural practices; there are místicas in virtually every activity undertaken by the movement, some of them created on the spur of the moment, and it would be difficult to control their creation or execution most or all of the time. In addition, místicas are often used for encouragement, where a social cause is the underlying theme, but the primary purpose is building morale, so characterizing them as merely a reflection of ideology is reductionist and incomplete. For top-down indoctrination to occur as Navarro seems to suggest, místicas would have to be institutionalized or bureaucratized and members would have to be sanctioned when they deviated from the rules dictated from above. Despite the consensus that the MST has become institutionalized as a social movement over time because of its organization (see Martins, 1997; Stedile and Fernandes, 1999; Welch, 2006), no such institutionalization or bureaucratization has occurred. While there are various ways of exercising control, from subtle psychological pressure to the "groupthink" mentality seen in cohesive organizations (Janis, 1972), future research or studies would have to answer whether the MST's mística is used to indoctrinate. Were one to argue that místicas are indoctrinating because they reflect the ideology of the movement, then practically everything in society could be considered similarly indoctrinating: the media, the schools, the universities, the corporations, and the other institutions of the established order.

Mística as Praxis: Pedagogy and Culture

Pedagogy

Associated with Freire's (1967) work and general Marxist theory, praxis is the application of theory to practice. Learned concepts acquire meaning as theory is applied to one's experience. The purpose of mística as praxis is communicating concepts and messages through symbolism that serve to educate largely unlettered people on a variety of subjects, political, cultural, and historical, while asserting their identity in the process. The pedagogical outcome of mística is therefore not only knowledge but the creation and reassertion of values and the construction of a class- and culture-based identity that leads to empowerment. Empowerment through mística takes various forms, not just inspiration to mobilize politically, as is the general perception. For example, a group may want to conduct a mística to convey the values of self-sacrifice and courage. To do so, it may choose to represent Che Guevara as a primary example of those values or recall the courage of Oziel, one of the fallen in the Carajás massacre, whom many members knew personally. While for some Che is remembered with almost saintly devotion, remembering *compan-heiros/as* in their struggles also contributes to value reinforcement and to identity construction and reformation.

On April 18, 2006, students of the Florestan Fernandes National School conducted a mística to encourage one another to finish the course through the second phase of the curriculum. Although these students were educated, highly articulate and politicized members, they carried out a mística to relay the importance of continuing to study, because a few students in their class dropped out weeks before. The classroom was adorned with the flag of the MST, a basket lying on top of it, seeds, and a number of red folders and badges with the students' names on them. Each of the folders contained course material, a notebook, and a pen. The mística started with a samba dedicated to the importance of education in Brazil. When the music finished, two students read a poem and a third passed a red folder and a badge to the person whose name was on the badge, offering that person a word of encouragement to continue studying. This person did the same to the next person, and so on, until everyone had received a folder and a word. Then they all pronounced the word of order and sang the MST's anthem. The act of passing on the folders symbolized the militants' wish to pass on to colleagues their personal desire to continue studying. The underlying theme of this mística was the importance of education, but the purpose was to encourage students to get through the course.

Use of Symbols

Místicas rely on symbolism and art to convey feelings, stories, messages, concepts, and values (see Bogo, 2002: 109–134). Given that the peasant culture has been largely based on the oral tradition, the use of symbols in the practice of místicas has great value. Symbols materialize the abstract and acquire various meanings and connotations. The cross has been a particularly strong symbol from the beginning, marking historic occupations such as that of Encruzilhada Natalino, but today it is giving way to the MST's flag (Caldart, 2000: 135). The flag is red with a map of Brazil and two rural laborers, a man and a woman, representing the family. The black plastic tarps (*lonas pretas*) used in the initial stage of an occupation have become another symbol associated with the MST as occupation became the method of struggle and access to land, the means by which agrarian reform will be brought about in Brazil (Fernandes, 2000, 2001). To many in the MST the sight of *lonas pretas* provokes mística.

Seeds have very strong symbolism, representing, among other things, family farming, subsistence, and hope. In recent years, they have also symbolized the MST's position against the use of transgenic seeds. Many *camponesas* habitually set aside seeds for future generations. The use of seeds as a symbol in místicas has also been noted in Lara Junior (2005a) as forward-looking representation of hope, dreams and utopia. Additional symbols include tools, the monthly *Jornal Sem Terra*, and others that reflect a much more local culture and subjective impressions (Stedile and Fernandes, 1999: 132). Symbols are used not only in the mística itself but also to adorn the meeting place as part of creating the atmosphere for the delivery of the message. Lastly, there are human symbols, those whose legacy influences the movement and become frames of reference such as Che and Oziel (see Stedile and Fernandes, 1999: 59–62). Symbols have been used to communicate from time immemorial, but the MST has employed them as an artistic reflection of the deeply creative nature of the Brazilian popular classes. Communicating and evoking feelings through symbols is itself an art, and in that sense the movement has operationalized symbolism as a form of speech. Lara Junior (2005b: 75) argues that artistic manifestations in general have not been recognized as a political and revolutionary force throughout history, despite being present since the emergence of the MST, at first through religious songs: "I was still in the settlement, but we had already started to mix this Christian and religious thing with other mística methods, like, for example, we started to express the mystical moment by singing, in reality songs of the struggle, of *companheiros* that wrote and spoke of the struggle, and we continued to carry the cross and all the other main symbols as well." He points to the importance of music, in particular, in inspiring members with courage to face the difficulties of their reality and mística as the stage for "spontaneous artistic manifestations and creation of the symbolic universe" of the MST. Music has acquired a "super dimension" as a part of the peasant nature and an authentic expression of the "soul of the masses" (Bogo, 2002: 149).

Collective Memory

The construction of movement identity occurs by rescuing the collective memory of past peasant struggles, reviving the contributions of proponents and martyrs of land reform and those who fought for the rights of the oppressed and repressed. It recovers a past that contradicts the myth of Brazilian passivity. In essence, it is the story that must be told to a largely unlettered class, and the use of representation, celebration, and ritual is not only a creative method but a highly effective one. The collective memory of the Brazilian peasantry is constructed from recollections of quilombos like Palmares, messianic movements like Canudos and Contestado, rural social movements like the Peasant Leagues of the 1950s—heroic moments of popular resistance to structural inequality of land distribution in Brazil (Martins, 1997; Fernandes, 2000). The MST sees itself as a continuation of these historic movements, especially the Peasant Leagues, while also incorporating the lessons and contributions of other Latin American peasant movements, revolutions, and organizations (Stedile and Fernandes, 1999: 39). This legacy of resistance is a part of the Sem Terra identity, as was its resistance to the military dictatorship's (1964–1985) modernization policies of the 1970s. The government's desire to exploit the Amazon and provide land in the region encouraged migration from all over the country. Its failure to back up its colonization plans with adequate infrastructure and to control the spread of *grilagem* (appropriation of land through fraudulent titles) in great part carried out by investors, companies and powerful individuals made the Amazon an unsafe and inhospitable place for the landless (Banford and Glock, 1985). The MST was born out of southern migrants' resistance to being uprooted to the Amazon (north) to satisfy the military's quick fix for landlessness (Stedile and Fernandes, 1999; Fernandes, 1996).

Pertença (Belonging)

The importance of mística as praxis in elitist and hierarchical Brazil is evidenced by the empowerment it brings to those who are deemed inferior subjects, stripped of identity, rights, and *pertença*. Dagnino (1998: 47–48) characterizes Latin America's elitism as a form of *social authoritarianism*, which produces a social classification by class, race, and gender that establishes distinct "places" in society; these *social places* distinguish those whose equal rights are guaranteed by the nation-state from those perceived to be inferior and therefore unworthy of being bearers of rights (as seen in the delay to bring justice in the cases of Eldorado de Carajás and Corumbiara Massacres). At the same time, members of the elite and ruling class are deemed beyond the reach of the law. It is what Baierle (1998: 121) calls *social apartheid*, arguing that the masses in Brazil do not perceive public spaces as public at all; in fact, the formal spaces of politics and government are viewed as private spaces of the educated and privileged.

In exercising collective memory, the Landless remind themselves that there is an abundance of agricultural land in Brazil and while they have historically been denied access to part of it they will only gain access through organization. They understand that their struggle should not be simply for access to land—access to credit and education must accompany it—but that as long as there are landless in Brazil they will continue mobilizing. Theirs is an identity based on a belief in change and the possibility of a better future.

Mística influences the identity of the Sem Terrinhas (children of the Sem Terra), who have been born into the collaborative and communal culture of the settlements, with the sacrifices and difficulties inherent in land occupations. According to educator Deise Arenhart (2003), their identity, based on the rural context, the working class, and the movement, is distinctive because of the collective nature of their lives. She demonstrates that a key element in creating that identity is mística as it is used in the representation of history and in passing on the memory of their parents' struggles. She reports that children see mística as a source of learning and a form of expression. "When children feel the power of an occupation, a word of order, a song that talks about them, it seems that they learn their origin, history, reasons, strength, and the value of the Sem Terra people" (2003: 6). She has also observed, however, that when children conduct místicas, they focus not so much on the content of the message as on the pleasure of representing. In one particular mística, the children represented an occupation, the violence of the police and landowners, and the care of the nurses for the wounded. At the end they invited everyone to a party and asked all the participants (landowners, police and Sem Terras) not to fight anymore. Everyone agreed, and the mística concluded with a message of peace. This example illustrates the fact that children conduct místicas with the authenticity and naivete characteristic of their age, once again displaying the freedom to create and interpret that is seen in the movement.

Conclusion

Democratization has provided the structural context for the MST's mobilization, but mística, in conjunction with organization, strategy and leadership, has transformed an otherwise amorphous and alienated mass, through identity formation, from passive to active agents as an organized social movement. This emotional component, characterized as the love for a cause, is also the praxis of pedagogy and culture that creates identity through *pertença* and revives the collective memory of the MST. Conscious of the extraordinary power of místicas, the MST has used them to educate members and rescue their culture, by promoting solidarity, self-sacrifice for the common good, and the family while insisting that the equitable distribution and proper use of land are the solution to most of Brazil's social ills. Through this praxis of empowerment, which utilizes art and symbolism, the MST reinforces the class politics that the forces of neoliberalism have fractured.

The lives of the Sem Terra are marked by great sacrifices, and the continued struggle and organization of the MST can be in part explained by mística. Without hope and the belief that the movement can effect significant change in Brazil, the struggle would be far more challenging. The praxis of mística in constructing the MST's collective identity and preserving its culture is the articulation of a counterhegemonic alternative to globalization. Paraphrasing a poet, Salete, a student at the Florestan Fernandes School, said, "To dream is detrimental to the established order, and organization is what the dominant class fears, because what they fear isn't weapons, but these two elements."

IV

ETHNICITY AND RACE IN SOCIAL AND POLITICAL MOVEMENTS

First Intercontinental Encuentro of Zapatista Communities with Peoples of the World, Oventic, Chiapas, December 30, 2006–January 2, 2007. Photo courtesy of Richard Stahler-Sholk.

E THNICITY AND RACE HAVE LONG BEEN important factors in understanding so-cial protest mobilization in Latin America. Those identities have been intertwined with class inequalities since color-caste stratification systems emerged in colonial times, creating the historical context for an ethnic/racial dimension of mobilizing for social justice. In more contemporary times, the often invisible racial dimension of oppression was made more explicit in the 1970s when Afro-Brazilians began organizing around black identity within the overall democratization struggles against military rule. The outspoken neighborhood activist Benedita da Silva brought the voice of the favelas into the "big house" when she became Brazil's first black woman senator in 1986. Indigenous movements have also seen a significant resurgence, symbolized by the 1992 mobilizations against the official quincentenary celebrations of European invasion. The Nobel Peace Prize that year went to Rigoberta Menchú, the Maya-K'iche' indigenous rights activist from Guatemala. Two years later the Zapatista rebellion in the Mexican state of Chiapas put indigenous people on the world stage again. Indigenous movements have continued to grow, shaking the political landscape in Ecuador and Bolivia.

Various factors may account for the increasing salience of ethnic and racial identities in popular mobilization. Neoliberal policies that hurt the poor disproportionately affect communities of color, given the racially unequal distribution of poverty. The atomizing impact of privatization and cutbacks in social programs also leads some to resist by reasserting communal identities and defending collective concepts of rights, as the formal equality of individual rights is belied by concentrations of market power. Yet the subjective experiences of Afro-Latin and indigenous communities are not simply reducible to class, and the social subjects of these new mobilizations are not necessarily willing to be absorbed by parties or other institutions claiming to represent their political interests.

Of the four essays in this section, two address indigenous movements and two focus on Afro-Latin groups. Mariana Mora examines the Zapatista movement, not in terms of its external projection but rather as it is experienced within the autonomous indigenous communities in Chiapas, Mexico. She contrasts the Zapatista model of autonomy—resisting government co-optation—with the neoliberal project that defines it as individual co-responsibility for government social programs. Mora offers a critique of the hidden assimilationist logic of the Mexican government's discourse of "multiculturalism." She also notes the challenge for the Zapatista movement: to recognize racial power dynamics as more than just an appendage to the anticapitalist thrust of their "Other Campaign" to build a broader left movement.

Marc Becker's chapter gives a detailed explanation of the political strategies of the indigenous movement in Ecuador, focusing particularly on the dilemma of whether to participate in party/electoral politics. The movement faced questions of how to work in plurinational popular coalitions that embraced both ethnic identities and class consciousness. As the Pachakutik movement shifted between strategies of mass mobilization and electoral competition, they often found that mass uprisings could do little more than oust governments, while electoral politics challenged internal unity. The case highlights a key problem for social movements—whether they can exercise power without taking control of the state.

Kwame Dixon examines the transnational aspect of identity-based movements. Focusing on Afro-Colombians, he argues that reasserting the rights of black communities in terms of human rights allowed the movement to recast itself within the framework of a transnational social movement. His study focuses on the struggle for legislative recognition of ancestral rights of Afro-Colombian communities in the Pacific region, which has attracted land speculation and mega-investment proposals by global capital. This case suggests that the transnationalization of racial identities can force a broadening of the definition of citizenship to include collective rights, which could challenge the ability of Latin American states to serve as brokers for neoliberal globalization.

Keisha-Khan Perry's chapter on black women's struggles against racist urban renewal policies in northeast Brazil focuses on the way social movements negotiate the complex intersections of race, gender, and class. Perry examines why and how black women assumed the leadership in the neighborhood movement. Her interviews with activists show how women seized the available (gendered) neighborhood spaces, as the regime shifted toward formal democracy while evicting the poor in the name of "development." Black women domestic workers faced multiple levels of oppression, sharpening their awareness of racial, gender, and class power dynamics. They chose neighborhood associations as their organizing vehicle because the labor movement focused too narrowly on class, to the exclusion of racial justice and the housing issues the women experienced.

These four studies together suggest that the left ignores issues of racial and ethnic identity at its peril. At the same time, identity-based social movements face the challenge of negotiating multiple identities and defining new organizing strategies that unite people around shared experiences of exploitation.

9

Zapatista Anti-Capitalist Politics and the "Other Campaign"

Learning from the Struggle for Indigenous Rights and Autonomy

Mariana Mora

IN JUNE 2005, the Ejército Zapatista de Liberación Nacional (Zapatista Army of National Liberation—EZLN) entered a new phase of its 12-year struggle against economic exploitation and for the radical recognition of ethnic-racial and gender differences in Mexico. In anticipation of the 2006 presidential campaign, the rebel army launched *La Otra Campaña* (the Other Campaign), designed to link nonpartisan anti-capitalist national liberation struggles around the country. Criticizing left political parties in Latin America, such as the Partido dos Trabalhadores (Workers' party—PT) in Brazil and the Partido de la Revolución Democrática (Party of the Democratic Revolution—PRD) of Mexico, for having abandoned their Marxist-Leninist origins, the Zapatistas are attempting to reassert their own anti-capitalist roots in a "new way of doing politics." After the 1994 uprising, the rebel army exchanged the traditional guerrilla objective of taking state power for the organic construction of alternative political processes and linked class analyses to struggles against ethnic-racial and gendered inequalities. As stated in the June 2005 Sixth Declaration of the Lacandón Jungle (EZLN, 2005), the Other Campaign now seeks to rearticulate these different elements into a "national campaign for building another way of doing politics, for a program of national struggle of the left, and for a new Constitution."

The Other Campaign surfaces after more than a decade of Zapatista struggle for the recognition of indigenous rights. A quick glance at politics in Mexico highlights the influence of this struggle on counterhegemonic practices and

---

The original version of this essay appeared in *Latin American Perspectives* 34(2), March 2007: 64–77.

state policy reforms. In 1996, the rebel army initiated a series of four rounds of peace talks with representatives of the federal government, the first of them on indigenous rights and culture. The San Andrés peace talks generated charged public debates over the terms on which to recognize the pluricultural makeup of the nation-state, debates that continue to serve as key references in the redefinition of left political practices, the transformation of state-indigenous relations, and the reconfiguration of the nation. The eventual noncompliance with the 1996 San Andrés Accords on the part of the federal government and the 2001 unilateral implementation of constitutional reforms with regard to indigenous rights by the Mexican Congress resulted in the de facto implementation by Zapatista base communities and an important sector of Mexico's indigenous population of their right to autonomy and self-determination. In fact, indigenous autonomy *en los hechos* (in practice) has become the primary way in which indigenous actors struggle to reconfigure socioeconomic and political relationships with other social actors and with the state.

The Other Campaign seeks to articulate these local autonomy practices to other struggles throughout Mexico in an effort to strengthen indigenous autonomy initiatives and ensure that they continue to tackle broader structural inequalities. At the same time, after 12 years of fighting for the recognition of indigenous rights, the campaign creates a key space for implementing a radical politics of recognition through the collective construction of a diverse national political force (i.e., not a political party). In this sense, the new phase of the Zapatista struggle represents an opportunity to draw from the multiple forms of cultural knowledge and experiences of historically marginalized political actors in constructing anti-capitalist alternatives that transform the hierarchical positioning of ethnic-racialized groups in society.

At the same time, the current political moment poses a number of challenges for an emerging left attempting to articulate different social political movements and their trajectories as part of the consolidation of a national liberation struggle. The recentering of an anti-capitalist critique and the use of the term "capitalism" (absent from Zapatista discourses since 1994) has drawn the interest and participation of political organizations using a predominantly class reductionist analysis, such as certain socialist groups and independent labor unions that had historically remained on the margins of the Zapatista movement. While representing a historically important component of the left in Mexico, these organizations approach the anticapitalist discussions of the Other Campaign in terms of economistic and determinist analyses that contrast with the political experiences of other participating groups. During the meeting with indigenous organizations, a representative of Nación Purepécha referred to these tensions by saying that "the left has not completely understood the indigenous movement; they are illiterate in terms of autonomy and that we as indigenous people are fundamental to the fight against capitalism." These historical differences surfaced during the initial phases of the Other Campaign.

The first assembly of the Other Campaign was held September 16–18, 2005, in the Zapatista civilian center of Francisco Gómez. The more than 2,000 participants represented diverse political actors, some whose political formation began with post-1994 Zapatismo, others who were participating for the first time in an event convened by the rebel army, and still others whose experiences in struggles dated back to the 1970s. Those present included representatives of urban youth forums, feminist collectives, different trade unions, nongovernmental organizations, and indigenous organizations from all regions of the republic. Reflecting this diversity, an eclectic mix of posters decorated the wooden walls of the auditorium where the meeting was held, banners of anarchist groups, political caricatures depicting pop-culture figures such as Chespirito, signs demanding the immediate release of political prisoners, and even three-meter long images of Marx, Engels, and Stalin, hung by a socialist organization that refused to take down the last of these despite numerous complaints.

Throughout the two-day plenary session, discussions centered on the organizational, structural and political makeup of the Other Campaign, with the objective of collectively establishing the content of this emerging political force. Despite a decade-long struggle for indigenous rights, only a minority of speakers directly addressed the fact that this new form of anticapitalist politics needed to ensure the equal participation of actors across gender, ethnic-racial and sexual identity lines. Rather than situating antiracist and antisexist politics as guiding principles throughout the day's agenda, discussions on the respect for differences were allocated to the agenda item labeled "A Special Place for Differences." Many indigenous, feminist, and gay and lesbian groups criticized this structure, arguing that, while a particular space for such discussions was necessary, it was essential to establish that they formed part of the transversal axes running through all the issues defining the Other Campaign. To do otherwise meant simply annexing "the recognition of differences" to those topics considered the heart of political debates. "I don't put to the side the fact that I am a woman and a lesbian when I talk about the organizational structure of the Other," said a representative of one of the participating feminist groups.

Perhaps as a response to the lack of discussion of antiracist politics, Alejandro Cruz, a representative of Organizaciones Indias por los Derechos Humanos en Oaxaca (OIDHO), an indigenous organization from Oaxaca, said,

We observe and relate to other [non indigenous] actors with caution. We are worried because all kinds of people, indigenous and non-indigenous, will participate in this Other Campaign. Our experiences have demonstrated that in spaces such as these we begin to fight amongst each other because, even though we say we're creating a new way of doing politics, politics hasn't changed entirely. But despite this fact, we are present because we want to talk to everyone. However, we need to keep in mind that a campaign doesn't triumph because of its just cause, but in the way in which it is carried out.

What insights, then, do the past 12 years of constructing indigenous autonomy offer to the creation of an anticapitalist politics that listens to, translates and transforms relationships between indigenous and nonindigenous actors? In this essay, I draw on the experiences of Zapatista support base communities that since 1996 have engaged in the creation of autonomous municipalities in EZLN territory. Through the knowledge emerging from these practices, Zapatista women and men are charting political road maps that maneuver through a complex terrain marked by a rearticulation of neoliberal hegemonic forces and a legacy of left politics of recognition positioned between mestizaje ideologies and Indianist discourses. Zapatista knowledge offers an analysis of the way in which the cultural logics of late capitalism articulate to political economic interests, in terms of both the ethnic-racialized ordering of society and the tendency of the neoliberal state to govern by encouraging people to meet their own (individual) socioeconomic needs. The meanings and practices of Zapatista autonomy offer three key contributions to the debates currently under way. The first addresses the tensions involved in generating alternatives to the cultural and economic logics of a neoliberal project. The other two reflect forms of indigenous political identity formation that potentially destabilize the racial ordering of Mexican society. Recognizing these contributions is fundamental to the construction of anticapitalist and antiracist politics in the Other Campaign.

Indigenous Autonomy and Neoliberal Governance

A central task for the political actors giving form and substance to the Other Campaign is to identify changes in late capitalist logics and their relationship to shifting Mexican state forces. This is particularly important because the current rearticulation of neoliberal hegemonic processes includes not only a reterritorialization of capital but also the domestication of dissident claims in the service of dominant interests. During the first phase of the Other, Subcomandante Marcos, referred to as Delegado Zero, traveled for six months throughout the republic listening to diverse organizations' accounts of the changing conditions affecting their lives and livelihoods. During these exchanges, groups such as the indigenous and peasant organizations from Guerrero and Oaxaca identified capital's increased interest in commodifying traditional knowledge, particularly in relation to the genetic patenting of the medicinal properties of plants and the privatization of seed banks and resources previously considered national patrimony, such as water. This analysis contributed to the reconceptualization of late-capitalist interests and served to identify new focal points of struggle.

The emphasis placed by the Other Campaign on the political economic logics of late capitalism contrasts with the mixed level of discussion and debates in terms of its cultural logics. Two cultural logics influencing processes of indigenous autonomy will be discussed here: (1) the mechanisms by which state forces govern citizen subjects in a neoliberal era and (2) the official multicultural programs adopted by the Mexican state in response to counter hegemonic struggles of past decades.

Since the 1980s, neoliberal reforms have effected a profound transformation of the Mexican state. The emphasis on deregulation and the dismantling of protectionist measures that were part of open market policies resulted in the privatization of social services and the transfer of state responsibilities to non state actors. Neoliberal state restructuring shifts government policies and discourses away from populist and clientelist relationships towards an emphasis on partnership initiatives that encourage social actors to ensure their own well-being (Rose and Barry, 1996). Rather than producing subjects dependent on the state to provide for their needs, this "enabling state" encourages citizen subjects to make choices for their own self-realization with the aim of their becoming better able to effectively participate in the market (Rose, 1999). Social programs now tend to focus on "co-responsibility" with the affected populations, usually requiring that they modify their habits and receive training that foster human-capital development.

The most important program reflecting this shift is Oportunidades (formerly Progresa), a social assistance program established in 1997 that targets those living under conditions of extreme poverty. Oportunidades benefits 21 million people, about a fifth of the Mexican population. This type of social program, which exchanges money for human-capital development, is representative of the poverty alleviation programs sponsored by international development agencies and is one of the new mechanisms for regulating individuals. Oportunidades is designed to develop the capacities of the poor through cash transfers to women, scholarships for school-age children, basic health services, and bimonthly economic support ranging from US$15 to US$150, depending on the number of children attending school (interview, Sandra Davalos, San Cristóbal, December 2005). Oportunidades, as its name suggests, is designed to transform the poor from passive recipients to active, empowered modern subjects with the freedom to make choices about their lives.

During a recent interview, a regional delegate of Oportunidades described what she considered the most important characteristic of the program (interview, Sandra Davalos, San Cristóbal, December 2005).

[The most important impact of the program] is the change in habits and in the attitude of the participating women. I see how the women who receive the bimonthly checks take their role more seriously, they have to share the responsibility to make sure that the program works. And this responsibility elevates their self-esteem as indigenous women. If they don't go to the health training sessions or if they don't send their kids to school, they are dropped from the program. ... I see that they are reaching a certain level of [civic] maturity because they can now decide over their lives. Oportunidades teaches them that they have the power to make choices. That is part of building democracy [in Mexico].

This suggests that the program is less about developing the poor through economic distribution than about socializing the poor to think about themselves in new ways, for example, as active, rational, and responsible for solving their own problems (Luccisano, 2004). The change in "attitude" includes associating human freedom with the attainment of human capital, where "autonomy" is defined in terms of the autonomy of individuals to choose among the alternatives offered to them. While great emphasis is placed on self-management and on "empowering" individuals to meet their own socioeconomic needs, these are divorced from any resource redistribution initiatives and even more so from any analysis of the persistence of structural inequalities.

The cultural politics of autonomy *en los hechos* cannot be understood in isolation from the hegemonic processes that ensure the state´s capacity to govern specific population groups. The neoliberal governing mechanisms that foster responsibility in individuals and self-governance in collectives appear, at least on the surface, to coincide with Zapatista autonomous efforts to "do things ourselves without the presence of the state." However, while reflecting the neoliberal conditions under which resistance takes place, Zapatista autonomy also represents a critique and a potential destabilizer of these conditions. Specifically, by emphasizing the relationship between struggles for cultural recognition and access to resources, Zapatista community members critique the divorce of self-management from resource distribution.

Indigenous self-determination in the region of the EZLN is enacted through the creation of autonomous rebel municipalities. In a communiqué dated December 16, 1994, the EZLN declared 38 rebel municipalities as part of insurgency tactics demonstrating territorial control. During this initial phase, local community members pronounced themselves Zapatista supporters by rejecting state institutional presence and government social programs. Two years later, in the context of the 1996 peace negotiations on indigenous rights and culture, the terms "indigenous" and "autonomous" were linked to the *rebellious* nature of these municipalities, thereby suggesting that through these spaces Zapatista members participated in the implementation of rights packed with the federal government during the San Andrés peace talks in 1996. In fact, as a Zapatista community member explained, "Autonomy and resistance are part of the same struggle; one can't exist without the other." For that reason, she continued, "we cannot expect anything from the government. We don't accept Oportunidades or government teachers or [agricultural] programs. That is why we have our own education, health and other commissions, so we can resolve our own needs ourselves."

After the 2001 unilateral approval of constitutional reforms on indigenous rights by the Mexican Congress, the creation of Zapatista autonomous municipalities took on heightened political meaning in a context that polarized the rebel army and the federal government. In August 2003, a few months prior to the tenth anniversary of the uprising, the EZLN announced the creation of *Juntas de Buen Gobierno* (good-government councils) to govern autonomous municipalities clustered into five regional *caracoles* and coordinate activities with the health, education and agricultural commissions created to provide EZLN base communities with social programs alternative to those of the Mexican state. The practices of the *juntas* and commissions are part of multilayered sets of autonomous processes existing in a highly charged political terrain in which Zapatista communities, non-Zapatista peasant organizations, and representatives of official government institutions dispute local power. While carrying important ethical-political weight, establishing autonomy by rejecting state institutional presence has proved incredibly difficult; the search for additional resources is perhaps one of the main reasons Zapatista supporters withdraw from "the organization." This political tactic has been criticized by observers, who argue that it diminishes the capacity of poverty-stricken indigenous communities to redistribute resources.

During a series of collective interviews with Tzeltal and Tojolabal Zapatista civilian bases in the region of Caracol IV, I asked why they considered autonomy *en los hechos* to be a form of struggle and what were the main obstacles they encountered. Three men responded (names of community members have been changed to protect identities):

Teodoro: Land was what we were originally struggling for, but once we had it, we saw that we needed to decide how we were to organize ourselves, how were we to work the land, how were we going to make decisions, and how were we going to coordinate with the other communities and with other people in Mexico. We also saw that we needed to do things ourselves so as not to continue being "limosneros" [beggars] of the government. That is when we saw that what we were doing was autonomy.

Mauricio: Because autonomy means to govern ourselves. We no longer have to depend on the federal government but rather on what we think and decide amongst ourselves. . . . Before it was the government who made the decisions. He didn't ask, he just informed. However, our autonomous government impulses and promotes rather than orders.

Nicolas: But the construction of autonomy needs more resources, that is the greatest obstacle. It is the most difficult part. We have our land, we have our own government, we work and work and work and we still don't find good markets to sell our products. That is why we have the Other Campaign, for things to change here, we have to change things elsewhere.

I have placed these responses together because on one level they represent different moments of local Zapatista indigenous autonomy. A first moment surfaced in 1996, when the decision to construct the autonomous municipalities generated a reinterpretation of the movement originally conceived as primarily agrarian, as one that linked resource distribution to self-determination. A second moment is represented by almost a decade of local political practices, from 1996 to 2005, focused on building the cultural politics of autonomous governance. A third is the current attempt to link local processes to other struggles throughout the country.

On another level, these reflections offer an analysis of the tensions involved in creating alternatives to hegemonic political economic and cultural projects. The creation of autonomous governing bodies is considered inseparable from resource redistribution, in this case the rebel takeover of land previously owned by mestizo cattle ranchers. While autonomous practices are suggested to represent enabling forms of self-governance, they are clearly linked to a critique of structural inequalities represented by the understanding that the autonomy project is limited unless it is folded into a network of broader struggles for resources. The move toward self-governance emerges as a critique of populist state practices that generate dependency and passivity. This reflection is offered by indigenous subjects whose agency has for decades been negated by Mexican state institutions implementing paternalistic and assimilationist policies. The practices of autonomy seek to reposition indigenous actors in Mexican society in the context of recent state multicultural reforms and dominant definitions of cultural identity.

Unmasking Mestizo Universalism

The 2001 constitutional reforms with regard to indigenous rights and culture failed to comply with the San Andrés Accords and revealed the government's lack of commitment to new relationships with Mexico's 56 indigenous peoples. They eliminated the legal right to the collective use of natural resources and declined to recognize the indigenous community as a tier in the federal structure. The federal government recognized indigenous rights almost exclusively in culturalist terms, disassociating cultural rights from political and territorial ones.

Recent scholarship characterized the Fox administration's indigenous policies as *(neo) indigenismo* in that they continued to be founded on developmentalist ideologies in which the "indigenous problem" is defined as a matter of economic backwardness and isolation (Hernández, Paz, and Sierra, 2004). From the 1950s on, the Instituto Nacional Indigenista (INI) implemented programs for introducing what it considered isolated indigenous communities to capitalist relations and promoting cultural assimilation. However, during the Salinas administration (1988–1994) the INI was transformed from a service provider to an economic development agency as part of the restructuring of the state occurring in the light of NAFTA. The Fox administration continued this process by closing down the INI in 2000 and establishing the National Commission for the Development of Indigenous Peoples and by reproducing ethnocentric and economistic perspectives of social well-being. These *neo-indigenista* state practices and discourses exist in a tenuous relationship with the official multiculturalist programs that emerged in response to the counterhegemonic struggles of past decades.

One of the most publicized of these multiculturalist reforms is the Intercultural Universities being established throughout the republic, the first in the state of Mexico in 2004 and in San Cristóbal, Chiapas in the fall of 2005. The new universities, a unilateral state response to the San Andrés Accords, were created in order to "facilitate the egalitarian nonhierarchical integration of the diverse cultures that make up our republic" (interview, Andrés Fabregas, July, 2005). Transforming educational institutions to meet the needs of a largely indigenous population is an important component of changing the conditions under which indigenous actors participate in a predominantly mestizo society, but the creation of the Intercultural Universities is linked to broader hegemonic processes. Disassociating ethnic differences from territorial rights and the right to self-determination has the effect of re-inscribing recognition as simply a matter of egalitarian cultural participation (C. R. Hale, 2002).

The state's multiculturalist reforms are also founded on a definition of "culture" in relativist terms as a bounded entity devoid of power. This cultural relativism persists in the ways in which official reforms define "diversity." In a document circulated to new faculty members, Andrés Fabregas, the director of the Intercultural University in San Cristóbal, explained (2005), "While culture is the human capacity to create the world, socialize and symbolize it, interculturality is a relationship. The particularity of each culture is affirmed through interculturality. . . . An intercultural focus must ask, what is the context through which different cultures participate? Interculturality is possible only when cultural diversity is seen as positive and the dignity of each culture is recognized." The document maintains a functionalist definition of culture as a bounded fixed entity separate from the political-economic context in which it is embedded. According to this view, liberating each culture from unequal political-economic relations permits harmonious relationships. Separating "indigenous" from a structural context as suggested by this definition of interculturality decontextualizes identity formation and leads to solutions fixated on culture. As expressed by Teodoro, Mauricio and Nicolás, a politics of recognition that is fundamentally culturalist disregards and disguises the political and economic inequalities through which cultural differences are experienced. This engenders a pluricultural liberalism that maintains intact the state apparatus and consequently a mestizo universalism.

The other two Zapatista contributions to be discussed here are related specifically to the unmasking of this mestizo universalism. Zapatista communities demonstrate how ideologies constructing dominant mestizo and indigenous subject categories render invisible an ethnic-racialized ordering of society by hiding the link between culturally defined differences and biological attributes. In response, Zapatista women and men are developing alternative forms of indigenous identity formation that call into question this vertical structuring of society. A sense of political indigenous identity emerges in dialogue with two dominant ideologies, mestizaje assimilationist and the other essentializing Indianist. The first of these is based on ethnic definitions of indigenous identity in which cultural traits considered "backward" or "uncivilized" are progressively whitened through education and by inculcating rational conduct as part of the construction of a modern mestizo citizen.

Mestizaje as an ideology emerged during the authoritarian liberal Porfiriato period of the 1890s and eventually took on heightened meaning as part of the nation-building project of the postrevolutionary era of the 1930s. Intellectuals such as Justo Sierra and Andrés Molina Enríquez, responsible for education and land reform policies during the Porfiriato, reversed Spencerian and Social Darwinist theories of biological racism by calling instead for the improvement of races through their mixing (C. A. Hale, 1989). Creating a mestizaje ideal required separating a tolerant postindependence era from its genocidal colonial past. In order to do so, these intellectuals displaced race as a category of difference and replaced it with culture, whose signifiers, such as clothing, language and geographical location, operate along a more flexible and malleable boundary. With "indigenous" defined in terms of ethnic cultural markers, it became possible to move from an indigenous to a mestizo subject category by changing specific signifiers (Wade, 1997). Despite the replacement of biological with cultural differences, however, the latter retained many innate and embodied elements. The emphasis on education as a form of cultural improvement generated a whitening effect, thus reproducing the racially coded elements of cultural difference (de la Cadena, 2000). This masking of inherent biological traits with cultural signifiers has been formed an essential part of the intellectual and commonsense knowledge production that has fueled nation-building projects and concepts of difference in Mexico and other countries of Latin America throughout the twentieth century.

The Indianist discourses used in certain progressive mestizo and indigenous circles since the 1970s operate by infusing cultural traits with innate quasi-biological elements. In this case, indigenous actors are assumed to possess inherent cultural traits such as a spiritual connection to the earth or a holistic understanding of the universe that make them the bearers of solutions to modern national problems. While essays such as José Vasconcelos' *Raza cósmica* (1961) locate the mestizaje ideal along an evolutionary continuum, with creoles superior to indigenes, Indianist ideologies reverse the order, positioning indigenous peoples as representative of the true original Mexico (Bonfil Battalla, 1990). These discourses have played a fundamental role in creating a positive valorization of the role of indigenous peoples in the nation-state. However, this essentializing view of indigenous identity not only dehistoricizes identity formation, placing it outside of material relations, but defines cultural traits as if they were inherent, thus reproducing the masking of biological signifiers that is characteristic of the ideology of mestizaje.

Through the reinterpretations of lived experiences emerging from the current practices of autonomy, the Zapatista Tzeltal indigenous men and women I interviewed offered complex analyses of the rate of ethnic and racial signifiers in shaping indigenous identity formation. Yazmin is in her late twenties and lives in a "nuevo centro de población," a Zapatista village founded on land recovered from cattle ranchers. Her community is unique in the region because Tzeltal and Tojolabal members no longer speak their native languages. In addition, she was fortunate enough to have finished secondary school and considers herself capable of engaging in local politics. She described an experience that she interprets as demonstrating the racial ordering of local social relations:

I worked as the assistant to the municipal president's wife in the Institute for the Integral Development of the Family. They discriminated against me there because of my customs. They looked at me as if I were dirty because when it was time to eat, I ate fast and with my hands. I didn't eat the way they did. That is why I say that even though I went to school and have education and even though I no longer speak Tzeltal, I am of the Indian race. Even though the *kaxlanes* [nonindigenous people] have the same skin color as us and look like us, to them we are still Indian.

According to local standards, by no longer speaking Tzeltal and being educated Yazmin has altered the cultural markers that would place her in an indigenous category, but racial codes continue to position her as inferior to the municipal president's wife. Her analysis suggests a racial literacy according to which ethnic cultural traits are accepted only as they are whitened but the masking of racial codes continues to position her in an inherently inferior "Indian" position.

In contrast to this emphasis on whitening, the recent struggle for indigenous rights is generating processes of "Indianization" (Warren, 2001) in Zapatista communities. This includes the rescuing of cultural traditions such as dances and ceremonies, the valorization of Indian identity in the theater productions of school-age children, an emphasis on bilingual and bicultural education, and as the rejection of the humanitarian social assistance projects for the poor offered by many well-intentioned solidarity organizations. The Indianization of autonomous spaces and practices destabilizes a politics of recognition possible only by manipulating or altering specific markers and points to a shared understanding of racialized experiences. However, these processes of Indianization run the risk of reinscribing definitions of culture as bounded and historical, which would parallel hegemonic constructions of indigenous subjectivity. It is in this realm that Zapatista Tzeltal and Tojolabal women in the region play a critical role as they simultaneously emphasize the rescuing of what are considered traditional customs and critique those customs that maintain indigenous women in subservient positions. In doing so, these women link cultural production to power and destabilize fixed relativist notions of identity.

Rosana, a Tzeltal woman in her 50s and a local figure of political and religious authority, when asked if there was a contradiction in the resurgence of indigenous traditions and women's rights, explained,

> Oh, but of course men don't want to change their traditions! They say that we [as women] have to respect because that is how the elders did things. But these are excuses because they don't want to lose their power. That is why in women's meetings we discuss what are the traditions that have to change, like not letting women participate in the assembly, not encouraging the girls to go to school or when husbands beat their wives.

The political interventions of Zapatista women highlight customs not as devoid of power but as deeply embedded in oppressive relations. These women not only participate in the positive valorization of traditions but exercise their right to continually analyze, critique and change traditions so as to transform those relations. Through their participation, women such as Rosana have generated a fundamental critique of culture as embedded in unequal relations of power.

Projecting positive values onto indigenous traditions, in conjunction with a critique of those traditions, counterbalances the whitening processes of ethnic-racialization associated with the hegemonic ideology of mestizaje. At the same time, by emphasizing the power-laden content of cultural expressions, Zapatista women offer a critique of both official multiculturalist ideologies and the left Indianist politics that operates in terms of essentialized definitions of indigenous identity. In doing so they offer new political cartographies for emerging anticapitalist and antiracist struggles.

Lessons from the Other Campaign

The Mexican left intellectual Luis Hernández Navarro has argued that the Other Campaign reflects a new trend in Latin American left politics, away from an emphasis on culturalist identity claims and towards the folding of anti capitalist ideologies into struggles for the recognition of ethnic and gender differences (*La Jornada* [Mexico City], June 21, 2005). According to Hernández, this emerging trend is visible in the resurgence of socialist and anti-imperialist discourses by political figures such as Hugo Chávez and Evo Morales. Radical indigenous movements such as the EZLN and the Quintin Lamé (which operated in Colombia's Cauca region in the 1970s) and Afro-Latin anti-neoliberalist organizations such as the Comité Cívico de Organizaciones Populares e Indígenas (COPIN) in the Lenca region of Honduras demonstrate the inseparability of cultural and economic claims. However, if, as Hernández suggests, we are witnessing a recentering of radical anticapitalist discourses in social movements in Latin America, then the experiences of struggles like those of the Zapatista support-base communities offer important guidelines for ensuring the centrality of anti racist agendas under current historical conditions.

The practices of Zapatista indigenous autonomy offer new political road maps for a terrain marked by the interplay of assimilationist and multiculturalist discourses and neoliberal governing techniques. The emerging cartography locates practices of resistance to the political-economic and cultural logics of late capitalism visible in the linking of political identity claims to self-governing practices and to struggles for resource redistribution. Similarly, it critiques the ethnic-racialized ordering of society by unmasking the way biological and cultural traits work against each other in defining the indigenous. In doing so, it points to the fact that the left politics of recognition founded on cultural relativist definitions of identity and the defining indigenousness in terms of essentialized traits fall dangerously close to the official pluricultural liberalism reflected in recent state reforms.

Throughout the first twelve months of the Other Campaign, Delegado Zero met with diverse groups of people to listen to their concerns and forms of struggle. In fact, listening is a central component of the Other Campaign: the processes giving form and substance to this political proposal necessarily hinge upon the exchange of words, memories and ideas. This signifies a drastic break not only from the vanguardist politics of the past but also from the traditional political party platforms currently in force.

However, the cartography drawn by Zapatista support bases suggests that while listening is essential to the new politics of the Other Campaign, the resulting dialogues must be understood as existing in a power-laden terrain that locates indigenous and mestizo subjects in relational and hierarchical positions in which difference is experienced through political and economic inequalities. At the same time, recognition cannot be relegated exclusively to culture, because ethnically marked traits fail to account for the persistence of colonial legacies and the presence of biological signifiers producing difference in an era of globalization. This requires drawing on shared experiences of racialization that can help forge political alliances across cultural differences. Heeding the lessons emerging from 12 years of practicing indigenous autonomy in Zapatista communities responds to the concerns voiced by indigenous organizations in the plenary session of the Other Campaign and offers guidance for action in a yet-uncharted phase of the EZLN struggle.

10

Pachakutik and Indigenous Political Party Politics in Ecuador

Marc Becker

IN 1995, INDIGENOUS LEADERS in the Ecuadorian Amazon founded the *Movimiento Unidad Plurinacional Pachakutik* (Pachakutik Movement for Plurinational Unity—MUPP) to campaign for political office. This political movement emerged out of years of debate regarding the role of Indigenous peoples in electoral politics. Should Indigenous organizations put forward their own candidates and issues, or should they support existing parties that "understand and guarantee the fundamental rights of the Indigenous population" (Karakras, 1985: 48)? Pachakutik represented the emergence of a third option: forming a new political movement in which Indigenous peoples and other sectors of Ecuador's popular movements organized together as equals in a joint project to achieve common goals (Lucas, 2000: 118).

A decade later, the decision by leaders of one of the Americas' best organized social movements to enter electoral politics remained contentious, controversial, and divisive. By no means was this clearly the best decision, but in the absence of concrete alternatives, it was not immediately obvious what other course of action Indigenous militants should have taken. Indigenous communities demanded a seat at the table of political negotiations, and to take that seat required entering a realm known for its corruption, dirty dealings, and tradeoffs. Not entering would mean passing on an opportunity to have their voices heard on a national stage.

The conundrum of the inherent tensions between social movement organizing and electoral politics is by no means new, nor is it unique to Ecuador or to Indigenous movements. Academics tend to counterpoise political parties against civil society, but grassroots activists often tend to move organically from one strategy to another (armed struggles, electoral campaigns, labor strikes, street mobilizations) without making clear distinctions in what they see as a singular struggle for social justice. While sometimes social movements tend more toward autonomy (as with the Zapatistas in Mexico) and other times more toward formal political participation (as when the MST [*Movimento dos Trabalhadores Rurais Sem Terra*—Landless Workers Movement] allied with the PT [*Partido dos Trabalhadores*—Workers' Party]) to help elect Lula to the presidency of Brazil), activists are often unwilling to deny themselves access to any tools that might help them realize their goals. Activists in Bolivia supported Evo Morales's presidential campaign even while holding him at a distance. Perhaps given different strategies and goals, a certain amount of tension is not only inevitable but also healthy.

Electoral politics seem to provide as possible outcomes either victory (as with the Bolivarian Revolution in Venezuela), defeat (the Sandinistas in Nicaragua in 1990), fraud (which led to the M-19 guerrillas in Colombia), or co-optation (often the experience of populism in Latin America). The example of Pachakutik, however, provides a more complicated but also perhaps more accurate depiction of the outcome of engaging formal political processes. All social organizing strategies require certain compromises and tradeoffs, and electoral politics are of course no exception. As Karl Marx famously noted, elections are often little more than a mechanism for people to select every couple years which members of the dominant class will rule over them. But what other viable mechanisms at the dawn of the twenty-first century exist to gain power? Most activists are not content to remain permanently in opposition. They have a vision they want to become a reality. Never implementing an agenda becomes a sterile exercise that can eventually lead to a paralyzed social movement.

As neither a success nor a failure, the example of Pachakutik underscores the reality that there is no one best or correct path to struggle for social justice. What works at one time and place may be entirely wrong elsewhere. Rather than implementing dogmatic or simplistic solutions, we need to engage in continual conversations and critiques as we search for more effective strategies.

Confederación de Nacionalidades Indígenas del Ecuador

Pachakutik emerged out of a context of growing discontent with the Ecuadorian government's neoliberal economic policies that favored the wealthy elite while weighing heavily on marginalized peoples. Since the 1920s, Indigenous activists had strenuously organized against exclusionary political and economic systems (Becker, forthcoming). Granting citizenship rights to Indigenous peoples in 1979 failed to create an inclusionary environment. Instead, changing citizenship regimes challenged local autonomy that further politicized ethnic identities (Yashar, 2005). Building on decades of struggle, in 1986 activists formed the *Confederación de Nacionalidades Indígenas del Ecuador* (Confederation of Indigenous Nationalities of Ecuador—CONAIE) to press for cultural, economic, and political changes. CONAIE's most stringent demand was to rewrite the first article of the constitution to recognize Ecuador's diverse Indigenous nationalities as part of a pluri-national state. Conservative opponents condemned the move as an attempt to dismember a unified nation-state. As Leon Zamosc (2004: 131) observes, however, it was elite adherence to neoliberal policies and not these subaltern demands that made Ecuador one of the most politically unstable countries in Latin America.

A powerful Indigenous *levantamiento*, or "uprising," swept across Ecuador in June 1990, stunning the country's elite and catapulting Indigenous peoples onto the center stage of national consciousness. CONAIE forced the government to address subaltern concerns and came to be seen as a model for how civil society should organize itself to fight for its rights. Indigenous movements proved to be best positioned to stop the savageness of neoliberalism, defend national sovereignty, and implement a true democracy. CONAIE both drew on and helped foster transnational organizational strategies that gave it a highly visible profile as one of the most powerful social movements in the Americas (Brysk, 2000).

CONAIE opposed subordinating ethnic groups to a class struggle, but it also highlighted the fact that it was a mistake to embrace ethnic identities to the exclusion of a class consciousness. Rather, CONAIE (1989: 281) advocated a "third way" in which the struggle acquired a "double dimension" of organizing on a class basis together with other popular movements as well as allying with independent ethnic organizations to defend Indigenous cultures. Class and ethnicity appeared at the same time to be mutually conflictive and reinforcing. The potential strengths as well as complications of organizing along these lines also informed the creation of Pachakutik.

Movimiento Unidad Plurinacional Pachakutik

The formation of Pachakutik in 1995 was an explicit reversal of a policy that CONAIE adopted at its Third Congress in 1990: not to participate in elections because neither the political system nor political parties were functioning in a way that represented people's interests. Popular distrust of the traditional political class grew throughout Latin America as subalterns became disenchanted with the failures of empty formal democratic structures to improve their living standards (Vilas, 1996). CONAIE forbade its leaders from holding political office and boycotted the 1992 presidential elections "as a way of rejecting traditional elections, political mismanagement, and demagogic political parties" (*Hoy*, September 9, 1991). Rather, CONAIE believed that Indigenous movements could realize more profound and lasting changes as part of civil society. Many grassroots activists, however, failed to understand why they should not avail themselves of all tools at their disposal to challenge elite systems of domination. Increasingly, many local Indigenous activists believed it was time for them to make their own politics and to make good politics that would benefit everyone rather than just select individuals. This grassroots pressure forced national leaders to rethink their hesitancy to enter the electoral realm.

Pachakutik emerged directly out of social movements, and this fundamentally influenced its ideological and strategic orientations. It worked closely with CONAIE, agitating for subaltern concerns in the halls of power while civil society kept pressure on the government out on the streets. Pachakutik proposed a government based on the three traditional Andean values of *ama llulla, ama quilla, ama shua* (don't lie, don't be lazy, don't rob). Significantly, Pachakutik was not a formal political *party*, but rather organized as a political *movement* that was structured in a horizontal, democratic, and inclusionary fashion. It explicitly identified itself as part of the new Latin American Left that embraced principles of community, solidarity, unity, tolerance, and respect (Rodríguez Garavito, Barrett, and Chavez, 2005). Pachakutik opposed the government's neoliberal economic policies and favored a more inclusive and participatory political system.

Although often seen as an "Indigenous" party and the political wing of CONAIE, Pachakutik provided a shared space for all activists who envisioned a better, more humane world. Given that Indigenous peoples were a large (comprising perhaps as much as 40 percent of the population) but minority and by no means homogenous presence in Ecuador, it would be difficult for them to gain high political office without an alliance with and support from non-Indigenous sectors of the population. Intercultural alliances proved vital to its success.

Electoral Campaigns

In its first electoral contest in 1996, Pachakutik experienced moderate success on both local and national levels. It elected eight deputies (including six Indigenous peoples) to congress and two Indigenous mayors, including Auki Tituaña in the town of Cotacachi. Most significantly, longtime CONAIE leader Luis Macas won a post as a national deputy in the National Congress, becoming the first Indigenous person elected to a national office in Ecuador. Macas's victory, as journalist Kintto Lucas (2000: 5) noted, was due to his success "in combining the Indigenous vote . . . with the vote of progressive and left-wing sectors."

For the presidency, Pachakutik allied with *Nuevo País* (New Country), who ran its leader Feddy Ehlers, a white journalist, on a platform that stressed multiculturality. His campaign stops glittered with rainbow-colored *wipala* flags, a symbol from Tawantinsuyu (the pre-Spanish Inka Empire) that Indigenous movements utilized to represent the unity of women, men, Afro-Ecuadorians, Indigenous peoples, and mestizos. Ehlers placed a close third in the first round of the elections. With his defeat, the remaining political parties engaged in a *caza para el voto indígena* (hunt for the Indigenous vote) in the subsequent presidential runoff race (M. González, 1996). For its first venture into the electoral realm, Pachakutik had performed surprisingly well, which seemed to point to the ascendency of an Indigenous voice in Ecuador's public sphere.

The runoff election for the presidency pitted two of Ecuador's richest men—conservative Social Christian Party (*Partido Social Cristiano*—PSC) candidate Jaime Nebot and right-populist Abdalá Bucaram—against each other. Although most popular organizations refused to support either candidate, believing that both were equally bad, several Indigenous leaders signed letters of support for Bucaram's candidacy. These were widely viewed as opportunistic moves by individuals desiring to gain positions of political power in the new government, and perhaps foreshadowed the inevitable compromises and challenges that electoral politics would bring to a social movement.

Bucaram won the presidency largely on campaign promises of aiding the poor. Despite CONAIE's refusal to endorse his candidacy, Bucaram's populist style gained him broad support in rural Indigenous communities. Once in office, however, he implemented neoliberal reforms, including raising transportation and cooking gas prices, that hurt the poor but benefited the wealthy elite. The tactical alliances some leaders made with the Bucaram government further compromised Indigenous organizing efforts and led to splits within the movement. Several Indigenous leaders became implicated in corruption scandals, including the sale of visas. Within six months, Bucaram's economic policies alienated his popular base and a mass uprising on February 5, 1997, evicted him from power.

With Bucaram removed, CONAIE and other social movements called for a constituent assembly—a demand that eventually gained wide support. In elections for this assembly, Pachakutik won seven seats plus three more in alliances with other parties. It built a center-left minority bloc that pressed for a series of significant constitutional revisions, including recognition of

Indigenous rights. Although CONAIE/Pachakutik was not successful with all of its proposals (Ecuador was declared merely "multiethnic," stopping short of the more politically charged "pluri-national"), their actions resulted in a significant shift in the conceptualization of political institutions. The new constitution that was promulgated in August 1998 was the most progressive in Ecuador's history (Andolina, 2003).

In the subsequent 1998 elections, Pachakutik increased its electoral strength with the victory of eight candidates for the National Congress. Indigenous leader Nina Pacari gained the vice presidency of the congress, the most senior governmental position that any Indian had obtained in Ecuador's history. Perhaps more significantly, Pachakutik was solidifying its support on a local level with an increasing number of victories in municipal races. Pachakutik appeared to promise a culmination of CONAIE's drive to insert Indigenous peoples directly into debates, giving them a voice and allowing them to speak for themselves (Lucas, 2000: 118). The significant presence of Indigenous players in national politics had become undeniable.

January 21, 2000, Military-Indigenous Coup

On January 21, 2000, Ecuador experienced the last twentieth-century coup in Latin America when an alliance of lower ranking military officials and Indigenous leaders evicted president Jamil Mahuad from power. Faced with soaring inflation and a free-falling economy, Mahuad proposed a plan to replace the sucre with the U.S. dollar as legal tender. Critics denounced this sacrifice of national sovereignty, which could only undermine their standard of living. In the coup, CONAIE president Antonio Vargas, Colonel Lucio Gutiérrez, and former supreme court president Carlos Solórzano—symbolizing a union of Indians, soldiers, and the law—formed a Junta of National Salvation that briefly took power. Several hours later, defense minister General Carlos Mendoza pulled rank on Gutiérrez and replaced him in the Junta, but then resigned, collapsing the provisional government. Under pressure from the United States, Mendoza handed power over to vice president Gustavo Noboa.

With the failure of the coup, Indigenous movements began to change tactics. Activists advocated a plebiscite to recall legislators, reverse dollarization, end privatization, and grant amnesty for the coup plotters. Leaders then turned to a general strike, but when that failed Indigenous movements once again pressed for a referendum. In the midst of all these strategic shifts, Pachakutik scored its largest victory to date in the May 21, 2000, local and regional elections in which it won control of five provincial prefectures (more than any other single party) and nineteen municipal governments. Although now one of the larger parties on a local level, it had a long way to go before it could become a majority or even dominant force in national politics. Pachakutik also faced tensions between constituent calls for immediate and local concrete economic benefits that Ecuador's clientalistic political system demanded, and attempts to redesign national-level political systems to be more democratic and responsive to subaltern concerns (J. Collins, 2004: 56). Advocates commonly spoke of moving from protest to proposal, but transitioning from social movement to political party tactics was by no means an easy process.

As the 2002 electoral campaign heated up, militants within Pachakutik debated whether to forward an Indigenous person as a candidate for the presidency of the republic. At first they decided to do so and engaged in a community-based primary that finally selected Auki Tituaña, the popular mayor of Cotacachi, as their candidate. A Cuban-trained economist and a capable administrator, Tituaña was part of a very small educated Indigenous intelligentsia able to navigate both the Indigenous and white-mestizo worlds. Nevertheless, the divisions within Indigenous movements also played out in the political arena. Facing a potential rift, CONAIE decided that the time was not right to run an Indigenous person for the presidency and asked its members to withdraw their candidacies. Tituaña complied; Antonio Vargas did not.

Vargas—the now former and discredited president of CONAIE— announced that he would run for office with his own political movement, Amauta Jatari. "This is the first time that Ecuador has had an Indigenous presidential candidate," Vargas declared. "It is an historic event" (LAWR , 2002: 129). His candidacy, however, was widely viewed as an opportunistic and egotistical move, motivated more by personal ambitions than a commitment to a struggle for social justice. CONAIE condemned Vargas for running, even calling his actions treasonous. FEINE (*Consejo de Pueblos y Organizaciones Indígenas Evangélicas del Ecuador*—Council of Evangelical Indigenous Peoples and Organizations of Ecuador), the federation of evangelical Indians that supported Amauta Jatari in opposition to the more Catholic and leftist CONAIE/Pachakutik alliance, cast its support behind Vargas (Andrade, 2003). Ricardo Ulcuango, former CONAIE vice president and Pachakutik candidate for the National Congress, urged FEINE to distance "itself from the manipulation to which it has been subjected" (Saavedra, 2002: 7). Vargas faced charges of submitting falsified signatures on petitions to register as a candidate with the electoral council. Ultimately, the council allowed Vargas to remain on the ballot (some said so as to divide the Indigenous vote), but he came in last place with less than 1 percent of the vote. Perhaps significant because he was the first Indigenous person to run for the country's highest office, his actions ultimately only contributed to a fracturing of what was once seen as one of the strongest social movements in the Americas.

Meanwhile, Lucio Gutiérrez, who briefly served with Vargas in the January 2000 triumvirate, also declared that he would be a candidate. At first Pachakutik shied away from an alliance with the former coup plotter because of a learned distrust of military officials, but because of Gutiérrez's backing of social movements during the failed coup attempt, he could count on grassroots Indigenous support. When Pachakutik decided not to run its own Indigenous candidate, it chose to throw its support behind Gutiérrez. CONAIE president Leonidas Iza justified this decision on pragmatic grounds. "Going into these elections without a presidential candidate could have fragmented the Indigenous movement's captive vote, because traditional political parties take advantage of the campaign to go into Indigenous communities," he said. "So we decided to support Gutiérrez and concentrate the other candidacies on a single slate" (Saavedra, 2002: 6). This move proved to be crucial to his eventual electoral victory, as without Indigenous endorsement he barely polled in the single digits (Saavedra, 2002).

Pachakutik continued to gain strength in local races, particularly in highland and Amazonian rural communities with a dominant Indigenous presence. CONAIE leaders Salvador Quishpe and Ricardo Ulcuango led the party to victory in congressional races in the provinces of Zamora Chinchipe and Pichincha. Representing the left wing of the Indigenous movement, their victories constituted a definitive shift in political discourse. "Our presence in the National Assembly," Ulcuango stated, "is a new challenge in this long road of 500 years of searching for a more equitable pluri-national Ecuador" (*Tintají*, January 1–15, 2003). In total, Pachakutik won eleven representatives in congress and seventy-five seats on municipal governments (*Rikcharishun*, 2002a).

Luis Macas's loss in an Andean Parliament race, however, reflected the fractured regional and ethnic tensions in Ecuadorian society and seemed to drive home the point that the country was not yet ready for Indigenous peoples in national-level political offices. Early returns placed Macas in second place in this race. Late returns from the coast, where a majority of Ecuadorians but very few Indians lived, increased the vote for the conservative Social Christian Party and pushed Macas to sixth place, out of the running for the parliament. Locally, Indigenous candidates could win offices, but to gain national power they needed to move beyond their Indigenous base of support.

In a compelling study of the 2002 elections, Scott Beck and Kenneth Mijeski (2006: 167) argue "that electoral success via the creation of a voting bloc is more difficult than occasional targeted mobilizations of tens of thousands of Indian participants." While CONAIE excelled at mobilizing their grass roots in massive, cohesive uprisings, the volatile, fragmented, chaotic, and corrupt political system provided challenges that Indigenous movements had difficulties overcoming. The significant competition from political parties' established clientalistic networks meant that CONAIE could not act with a hegemonic voice in the electoral realm as it previously had as a social movement. Furthermore, neoliberalism is predicated on individualism and atomization, channeling political participation into ritualistic electoral exercises that poll citizens as individuals rather than communities (Robinson, 1996). These factors created extraordinary challenges for the expression of collective rights or the creation of a participatory democracy.

Lucio Gutiérrez

Amidst high expectations, Gutiérrez took office on January 15, 2003, just less than three years after his failed coup attempt. Privately, some Indigenous intellectuals conceded their doubts about a Gutiérrez presidency. As a career military officer, he had no political experience, and critics feared that he could become an authoritarian leader like Alberto Fujimori in neighboring Peru. Bolivian Indigenous leader Evo Morales publicly criticized him for meeting with the World Bank and the International Monetary Fund (IMF) in Washington instead of leading popular protests against neoliberalism in the streets of Quito. Leaders cautioned against giving Gutiérrez a blank check (*Rikcharishun*, 2002b).

As Gutiérrez began to form his government with little consultation with his Indigenous allies or broader social movements, it became apparent that he viewed the masses in the same light as other populists during Ecuador's long twentieth century: as a malleable force to solidify a politician's hold on power and not as an equal partner with whom to consult on policy matters or to share power. Gutiérrez would govern much like José María Velasco Ibarra and Abdalá Bucaram, who during electoral campaigns, spouted leftist rhetoric in order to appeal to the poor masses but once in office ruled in favor of the oligarchy. It is little wonder that Indigenous peoples learned to approach electoral politics with a good deal of reservation and skepticism. With so much institutionalized power stacked against them, Indigenous activists seemed positioned to make a much larger impact outside of power and on the streets as part of a well-organized and mobilized civil society. But organized protests would not result in the implementation of alternative proposals. For that, they needed to enter into the messy realm of electoral politics. Electoral politics and grassroots social movements increasingly seemed to represent diverging paths that pulled activists in two separate directions (Lucas, 2003).

After some last minute scrambling, Pachakutik walked away with four cabinet posts and several secretariats as rewards for their support of Gutiérrez's candidacy. Most significantly, Luis Macas was named agricultural minister and Nina Pacari took over foreign relations, the first Indigenous person in Latin America appointed as a foreign minister. Being named to such high positions, however, quickly proved to be a double-edged sword as powerful leaders were forced to walk a fine line between support for Gutiérrez's controversial economic policies and remaining accountable to their grassroots constituency. "Because the presence of social and Indigenous movements is what characterizes the Gutiérrez government," economist Pablo Dávalos (2003a: 4) asked, "will Indigenous peoples be willing to compromise their main project of constructing a pluri-national state in order to defend a political and economic agenda that is not theirs, and a government of which they apparently are a part but does not permit them to have control or a say in the running of the economy?" Some militants were disappointed in the failure of Pachakutik's ministers to achieve serious reforms. "The disadvantages outweigh the benefits we have obtained from power," Cotopaxi Indigenous leader José Paca stated (*AGR* 2003b: 1, 2003a: 8). Once again, involvement in electoral politics threatened to shred Indigenous movements from within.

Increasingly more activists agreed with Alejandro Moreano (*Tintají*, July 1–15, 2003) that it did not make sense for Pachakutik to remain in the government, and that "the only correct political position is to overthrow Gutiérrez." Finally, on August 6, 2003, half a year after Gutiérrez took power, CONAIE and Pachakutik removed their support, declaring that Gutiérrez "betrayed the mandate given to him by the Ecuadoran people in the last elections" (IPS/LADB, 2003: 2). Pachakutik's break with Gutiérrez left its members, including ministers Pacari and Macas, with the choice of either leaving Pachakutik and remaining in their posts, or remaining in Pachakutik and leaving the government. In the end, both resigned their posts along with almost all lesser Pachakutik functionaries. "He never listened to us," Pacari said (Saavedra, 2003: 1). "Gutiérrez is a traitor," Pachakutik coordinator Gilberto Talahua stated in what became a common charge. "I didn't trust him after the second round of elections when he changed his policies so frequently." Talahua continued, "He has become a president of the business class" (*AGR*, 2003a: 8). It is almost impossible for a minority and historically subjugated population to gain political power without entering into alliances, but coalitions with bourgeois political parties lead to inevitable class contradictions. Electoral politics threaten to be a no-win situation.

Gutiérrez excelled at exploiting divergent interests of Indigenous communities in order to weaken civil society and retain his hold on power (Saavedra, 2004a; Lucero, 2006: 31–32). Dávalos (2003b) declared that Pachakutik had become a caricature of what it was when it was founded seven years earlier. It had become ridden with sectarian divisions and a bureaucracy unaccountable to social movements. Serious divisions emerged between previously close allies CONAIE and Pachakutik, and even between CONAIE and its Amazonian and coastal affiliates CONFENIAE (*Confederación de Nacionalidades Indígenas de la Amazonia Ecuatoriana*—Confederation of Indigenous Nationalities of the Ecuadorian Amazon) and CONAICE (*Coordinadora de Organizaciones Indígenas y Negras de la Costa Ecuatoriana*—Coordinating Body of Indigenous and Black Organizations of the Ecuadorian Coast) (Saavedra, 2004b). These divisions appeared to assure the former colonel's continued hold on power. Increasingly, the conservative PSC took the lead in attacking Gutiérrez, which put both CONAIE and Pachakutik in a difficult bind of appearing to ally with a party of the oligarchy against a common enemy. From a grassroots perspective, these types of backroom dealings were what brought a good deal of disrepute to the entire political class, with discontent extending not only to the presidency but also to a hopelessly fragmented and conflictive congress (including, now, Pachakutik) that was no more popular or effective in passing legislation.

In Bolivia, social movement leader Oscar Olivera worried that electoral politics could demobilize the masses and refused an invitation to join Evo Morales's government. "If Evo fails," Olivera noted, "it will be a failure for the social movements. The gains of six years of struggles will be lost" (Dangl, 2007: 200). As if to illustrate his point, joining the Gutiérrez government had seriously weakened Ecuador's Indigenous movement. Seemingly they would have been better off had they followed Olivera, who believes that true transformations come from organizing and mobilizing people at the grass roots.

In the midst of all this, Pachakutik still managed to hold its own in local electoral contests. In October 2004 municipal elections, Pachakutik won control over eighteen mayoralties—though some observers argued it could have won more had it not been tainted by its disastrous short-term alliance with Gutiérrez (*Tintají*, November 15–30, 2004). With Pachakutik out of office, CONAIE struggled to return the Indigenous movement to its previous strength. In December 2004, CONAIE elected longtime leader Luis Macas to head the organization. Militants called on the organization to retake the initiative that it once had (*Tintají*, January 1–15, 2005). Leading the opposition as a social movement rather than as a political party, CONAIE undermined the government's attempts to sign a free trade pact with the United States and forced the government to terminate its contract with Occidental Petroleum. While Pachakutik stumbled in the electoral realm, under Macas's leadership CONAIE demonstrated that it could still occasionally marshal its Indigenous bases in street protests (Tamayo, 2006). Internal dissent fostered by entering the electoral realm, however, continued to thwart the power of the movement to forward positive alternatives.

Rebellion of the *Forajidos*

An April 20, 2005, popular uprising finally brought down the Gutiérrez government. Gutiérrez had derided the protesters as *forajidos* (outlaws), which they subsequently took up as a term of pride and honor. As had happened before with popular movements, the masses moved further and faster than the leaders. Seemingly without central coordination, thousands of people took to the streets of Quito. Unlike previous uprisings, Indigenous movements played a minor role in the mobilization, with those allied with Vargas and FEINE coming to Gutiérrez's support. Instead, this uprising was characterized by the overwhelming presence of Quito's urban mestizo middle classes. Internal fragmentation and declining confidence in leadership increasingly preoccupied with electoral politics translated into a discredited force that failed to mobilize the Indigenous masses. "If Quito threw out Gutiérrez," FENOCIN's (*Confederación Nacional de Organizaciones Campesinas, Indígenas, y Negras*— National Confederation of Peasant, Indigenous, and Black Organizations) president Pedro de la Cruz (2006: 59) lamented, pointing to strong lingering regional divisions, "the countryside voted for him." A once strong Indigenous movement appeared to have become marginalized and insignificant to the political forces sweeping the country (Merino, 2005).

2006 Elections

With the trauma of its involvement in Gutiérrez's government still echoing throughout its ranks, Pachakutik experienced a resurgence of hot debates over whom (and even whether) to support for a presidential candidate in October 2006. Should they forward an Indigenous candidate such as Luis Macas or Auki Tituaña, or should they support someone like Rafael Correa from outside the movement. Macas was well-known for his long trajectory as an Indigenous leader, but his 2002 loss in the Andean Parliament race raised questions whether he could draw support nationally. Tituaña had a reputation as an honest and capable local leader, but he lacked the national exposure for a successful presidential run. Correa was not Indigenous, but he spoke Kichwa and had gained broad popularity during a brief stint as minister of economy for his harsh criticism of neoliberal policies. Some dreamed of a Correa-Macas ticket as the best option, while others questioned whether Correa was ideologically committed to Pachakutik's center-left agenda (Lucas, 2006). Some Indigenous activists would have preferred a Macas-Correa ticket with their leader in the presidential slot, but Correa refused to entertain this proposal.

Felipe Burbano de Lara (*Hoy*, June 6, 2006) observes that the debate over electoral alliances strikes at the heart of the conceptualization of Pachakutik. Should it convert into an Indigenous party or retain its original structure as a multiethnic political movement? Pointing to the key role that Indigenous movements played in Ecuador, Barbano notes that it was very difficult to think of a renewed left without the participation of Indigenous peoples. Similarly, if Indigenous peoples did not join a broader leftist movement, they threatened to do little more than isolate themselves from wider political movements. Activists continued the dance of how to balance competing concerns and contrasting strategies in building a strong movement for social justice.

In May, Pachakutik (with strong backing from Ecuarunari) nominated Macas as its candidate with the argument that it had paid too high of a price in forming alliances outside of its own movement. For the first time, Pachakutik would run not only someone from within its own ranks but also a long-time Indigenous leader. Activists from the coast and Amazon publicly disagreed with a Macas candidacy, complaining that he had ignored them as agricultural minister. They preferred instead to support Correa, while Pachakutik's leaders pleaded with its bases to respect the movement's decisions. Ulcuango and Cholango compared Correa to Gutiérrez, contending that his actions were deeply fracturing the Indigenous movement. In reaction, Correa closed off dialogues with Pachakutik over possible alliances, even if it meant losing the support of one of the most organized sectors of civil society (*Comercio*, June 28, 2006). Running its leader for office also brought CONAIE organizing efforts to a standstill.

From the first polls, Macas ranked in last place with about 1 percent of the vote—faring about as well as Antonio Vargas did in his discredited 2002 campaign. Racial discrimination seemed to be an ongoing problem, with the media often ignoring Macas's candidacy (Macas, 2006). Nevertheless, Macas ran a serious and dedicated campaign. "Our electoral campaign is part of a national mobilization in defense of sovereignty, biodiversity, and natural resources," he declared. "To gain changes in government, it is necessary to have the backing of a strong mobilized society that will guarantee these changes" (*Rikcharishun*, 2006: 3). Despite large rallies in rural areas, Macas came in sixth place with a dismal 2 percent of the vote. Reversing earlier gains, Pachakutik also performed poorly in congressional races dropping from ten seats to only six. "When it comes to the vote, it appears that most of the Indigenous population does not trust one of their own," journalist Richard Gott (*Guardian*, October 19, 2006) wrote. "They clearly prefer to vote for a white man, who, they probably believe, may well be able to deliver the jobs and housing that they crave." One critic noted that the Indigenous vote had "gone up in smoke" (Marco Arauz, *El Comercio*, October 19, 2006).

Banana magnate and Ecuador's richest man Álvaro Noboa won the first round and faced off against Correa for the presidency. Citing the threat of Noboa's alliance with imperial and oligarchical interests, Pachakutik announced its unconditional support for Correa's candidacy. In the November 26 run-off election, Correa defeated Noboa by a wide margin, with centrists preferring Correa's leftism to Noboa's conservative policies. Ecuarunari (2006), who had opposed Correa in the first round, greeted his victory with joy. "Ecuador has begun its revolution," they declared in a press release. "The *compañero* president Rafael Correa has announced that we will recover our natural resources." Their cheer seemed to parallel that with which they greeted Gutiérrez's victory four years earlier. History seemed to be repeating itself.

In justifying support for Correa, Ecuarunari's president Humberto Cholango (2006: 34) articulated a position that merged the interests of social movements with electoral politics in a unified struggle against the oligarchy and neoliberal system. Voting was simply one more way to continue fighting "for the construction of a plurinational state and a more just intercultural society." Whether on the streets or in the voting booth, the demands were the same: nationalization of petroleum resources, a constituent assembly, and no free trade pacts. Acknowledging criticisms that writing constitutions is historically a way for elites to consolidate their control, Cholango demanded broad democratic participation of Indigenous peoples and other popular movements in the assembly. Civil society pressure would assure that a new constitution responded to the needs of the people.

A study of the election results revealed that a large part of Indigenous vote had gone to Gilmar Gutiérrez—running in place of his brother Lucio, who had been barred from the campaign—who came in with a surprisingly strong third place finish with 16 percent of the vote. In the second round, Gutiérrez initially allied with Noboa rather than Pachakutik's current ally Correa. The fragmentation resulted from an increase in clientelistic politics, more development projects that led to a depoliticalization of the population, and the growing strength of protestant churches in areas such as Chimborazo that had a high concentration of Indigenous peoples. Pachakutik's vote, nevertheless, remained high in regions such as Cayambe, with a long history of radical communist-oriented political organizing (Báez Rivera and Bretón Solo de Zaldivar, 2006). Walter Benn Michaels (2006) argues that identity-based politics are essentially reactionary because they distract from more important issues of economic inequality. Neoliberalism, Michaels contends, not racism is the problem. An apparent lesson is that in contrast to the claims of New Social Movement theory, ethnicity does not provide a strong and coherent basis for social change, but instead more traditional class struggles create better openings for political change.

In contrast to strong mobilizations against Occidental Petroleum and Free Trade Agreements (FTAs) in March 2006, the Indigenous movement's weak electoral showing seemed to underscore that it made more significant advances as a social rather than electoral movement. Sporadic mobilizations, however, could not achieve the movement's goals of participatory democracy and social justice. In order to realize more profound and permanent changes, Indigenous organizations once again called for a constituent assembly. Correa's overwhelming victory in an April 15, 2007, plebiscite to convoke such an assembly co-opted the issue from Indigenous militants. In the September 30, 2007, elections, Correa further consolidated his control by winning a majority of seats for the assembly, thereby assuring that a new constitution would be to his liking. This was a citizens' revolution, Correa declared, not one built by social movements. Pachakutik won only a couple seats in the assembly and, together with the traditional parties, was left behind as an increasingly marginalized and irrelevant political force. After a decade of struggle, CONAIE seemed to have little to show for having entered the realm of electoral politics.

How to Change the World

Referring to the popular movements that toppled Bucaram, Mahuad, and Gutiérrez, economist Pablo Dávalos notes that "three times we have won and three times we lost" (Zibechi, 2006: 1). Through these gains and reversals, it became clear that Indigenous movements were strong enough to bring governments down but not united enough to rule on their own—or even in alliance with others. Shifting from a grassroots social movement to a national-level electoral apparatus proved to be difficult and wrought with complications. When organized as part of civil society, Indigenous activists had realized the potential of a social movement. The tempting promises of political party politics, however, remained elusively beyond their grasp. In the aftermath of a failed electoral campaign, it remained to be seen whether Indigenous movements could regain on the streets what they had lost in the voting booth.

In *Change the World without Taking Power*, John Holloway (2002: 19–20) proposes that the world cannot be changed through taking control over state structures. Instead, he maintains that the revolutionary challenge facing the twenty-first century is to change the world without taking power. Petras and Veltmeyer (2005: 137, 174) similarly advise avoidance of "electoral politics, the path preferred by the 'political class' because it is predicated on limited political reforms." They condemn Pachakutik for their "serious political mistake to seek state power from within the system." Others, such as Greg Wilpert (2007) in *Changing Venezuela by Taking Power*, contend that social movements can use state structures to make positive changes. Holloway (2002: 215) concludes his book with the question, "How then do we change the world without taking power?" and then provides his answer: "We do not know." It is easy to criticize one path, but perhaps irresponsible to do so without suggesting viable alternatives.

State structures continue to play an important role in the implementation of neoliberal economic policies, and popular movements need to challenge these structures whether as part of civil society, a political party, or an armed struggle. The case of Indigenous movements in Ecuador would seem to underscore the argument that it is not possible to change the world without taking power, but neither is taking power all that it takes to change the world. As a social movement, CONAIE could disrupt the exercise of state power, but in entering government Pachakutik failed to change neoliberal economic policies. In struggling with these issues, Indigenous peoples in Ecuador are little different from activists elsewhere. Changing the world is a puzzling but pressing issue that Indigenous activists, along with the rest of us, continue to try to solve.

11

Transnational Black Social Movements in Latin America

Afro-Colombians and the Struggle for Human Rights

Kwame Dixon

THIS CHAPTER ANALYZES BLACK SOCIAL MOVEMENTS with particular emphasis on Afro-Colombians, as national, regional, and transnational actors. It examines the relations between race and citizenship in Latin America by analyzing the current struggles of Afro-Latin peoples in Latin America and the Caribbean. From Los Angeles to Rio de Janeiro, from the Bronx to Salvador Bahia—brown, black, and Indigenous peoples are challenging racial inequality, while at the same time constructing alternative models for political participation. The struggle to be full citizens, on the one hand, and the day-to-day human rights violations faced by Afro-Latin Americans, on the other, serves to reinforce the shared experiences of black peoples in the Americas. It is argued that deeply entrenched racial and social prejudices and other forms of discrimination are the foundations for the de facto disenfranchisement of the hemisphere's populations; in many black communities throughout the region, glaring poverty, widespread human rights violations, and the discriminatory impact of neoliberal agendas underscores the urgent need for constructing a common paradigm of social action in the Americas (Dzidzienyo and Oboler, 2005: 5). By analyzing and investigating the complex interactions and interrelations among culture, race, and politics, this research focuses on the cultural politics enacted by Afro-Latin social movements as they articulate and implement new visions and practices of citizenship, democracy, social relationships, and development (Alvarez, Dagnino, and Escobar, 1998b: 2).

Afro-Latin Social Movements at a Glance

Starting in the late sixties, new forms of popular protest emerged from grass-roots and popular organizations in Latin America. These new social movements reflected broad participation by groups, organizations, and associations such as squatter movements, neighborhood councils, human rights committees, indigenous organizations, various black formations, women's groups, environmental organizations, and cultural and artistic groups (Evers, 1985: 43). They are new compared to traditional political actors in that they either mobilized different people or they are the same people acting in more spontaneous, democratic, decentralized ways, or because they are introducing new participatory strategies outside of the traditional political arena. These movements may also be responding to new forms of social subordination (Hellman, 1992: 53, 167), often sharpened by neoliberal policies.

Contemporary black social movements are part of this trend, but Afro-Latin social movements in Latin America and the Caribbean have long histories. Their antecedents include maroon communities during slavery; the Haitian Revolution; the massive slave revolts in Bahia, Brazil, in 1835; and the Cuban Independent Party of Color in 1908 (Safa, 1998: 11). At times, blacks in Latin America fashioned their own independent formations such as slave runaway communities (*palenques*), black militias, religious practices, and mutual aid societies. Other times, they forged tactical alliances with whites, Indians, and mestizos to create multiracial movements that had a profound effect on the region. The independence armies, the national liberal parties of the 1800s and early 1900s, the labor unions of the same period, and the popular parties of the mid-1900s, were broad-based movements that included the core participation and support of Afro-Latin Americans (Andrews, 2004: 8). In Latin America where the two-party system was allowed to function, most politically active blacks and mulattoes identified with liberalism, contributing materially to liberalism's eventual triumph throughout the region. Liberalism brought to power most of the black and mulatto presidents who held office in Spanish America during the 1800s. The black-liberal contribution also created a tradition of anti-oligarchical political unions that would later pave the way for a major twentieth-century political movement—labor-based populism (Andrews, 2004: 93–100).

Throughout the Americas black social movement groups are now increasingly using sophisticated strategies and tactics to challenge racial and gender inequality. A new landscape has emerged as blacks are demanding more political and cultural space to advance social, cultural, and economic rights, while simultaneously articulating oppositional racial discourse. The literature on Afro-Latin social movements is sparse and focuses heavily on Afro-Brazilians, with insufficient attention to the intersection of race and gender and the cultural politics of constructing citizenship and democracy. One notable exception is Alvarez, Dagnino, and Escobar's *Culture of Politics, Politics of Culture: Re-visioning Latin American Social Movements* (1998a). In particular, the chapter on Colombia by Libia Grueso and Carlos Rosero, well-known Afro-Colombian activists/ intellectuals, and Arturo Escobar examines the constitutional reform process of 1991 and the socio-organizational activities related to collective mobilization of Afro-Colombians. It focuses on processes of black identity construction and the intersection of race, territory, biodiversity, culture, and development. The authors explore racial discrimination, collective organizing, political enfranchisement, and developmental strategies, highlighting how Afro-Colombians at a unique historical juncture responded to discursive practices related to citizenship, human rights, and democratic inclusion. Another important exception is Michael Hanchard's *Orpheus and Power: The Movimento Negro of Rio de Janeiro and São Paulo, Brazil, 1945–1988* (1994), which provides a highly critical assessment of the strengths and weaknesses of Brazil's black social movements. Hanchard argues that the process of racial hegemony (promoting racial discrimination while simultaneously denying its existence) has effectively neutralized racial identification among non-whites, making it an improbable point of mass mobilization among Afro-Brazilians in Rio de Janeiro and São Paulo. This results in the reproduction of social inequality between whites and nonwhites while promoting a false premise of racial equality between the races.

Building on these cultural insights, I focus on the way black social movements have constructed identities woven around discourses of human rights, allowing them to link to transnational networks in the era of globalization. Social movements are transnational when they involve conscious efforts to build transnational cooperation around shared goals that include social change. Through regular communication and organization, activists are able to share technical and strategic information, coordinate parallel activities, or even mount truly transnational collectives (J. Smith, Pagnucco, and Chatfield, 1997: 243). Afro social movements in the Americas like other groups (indigenous and women) in the region are transnational as many now have regional, national, and global support and connections. Additionally, many share common political or ideological views such as challenging racial and gender discrimination in education or the workplace. Along with the struggle against racial and gender discrimination, many Afro-Latin social movements have waged popular resistance to neoliberal policies of Latin American and Caribbean governments.

Black human rights activists throughout the region—including the United States—have forged common agendas around combating and denouncing racism and racial and gender discrimination. On a regional level, groups like

La Alianza Estratégica de Afro-Latinoamericanos and Organización Negra Centroamericana are working to develop common strategies to address racial and gender oppression as well as build a movement that represents the interest of their communities (which are often economically marginalized and therefore suffer disproportionately from neoliberal policies).

Throughout the region Afro-Latin groups are emerging as powerful social movement actors in various countries, like the Afro-Venezuelan Network (Venezuela); Mundo-Afro (Uruguay); Coordinadora Nacional de Organizaciones Negras Panameñas (Panamá); the Process of Black Communities in Colombia (PCN); the National Movement for the Human Rights of Black Communities of Colombia, or Cimarrón, and the Association of Internally Displaced Afro-Colombians, or AFRODES (Colombia); and Geledés, the Institute for Black Brazilian Women, and CEERT, the Center for Research on Race Relations in the Workplace (Brazil). Many of these NGOs (nongovernmental organizations) function on shoestring budgets, are often excluded from national human rights discourse and face the daunting challenge of representing communities that are often dispersed, displaced, and suffer from low levels of self-identity. Their work over the years has been quite impressive as they have developed national, regional, and transnational networks, and by doing so, have been able to more forcefully articulate their struggle from a wider lens that includes comparative and international human rights perspectives. For example, since 1998 La Alianza Estratégica de Afro-Latinoamericanos has brought together Afro groups throughout Latin America and the Caribbean, offering capacity building, leadership training, and strategic planning, as well as providing a forum for groups to address common regional strategies.

The 1990s presented new historic opportunities for Afro-Latin Americans in the transnational arena as these social movements began to effectively use transnational networks, strategies, and contacts to elevate their struggle beyond national borders. This kind of "globalization from below" was part of the new wave of social movements that responded in part to the neoliberal erasure of borders for global capital. The transnationalization of Afro-Latin social movements provided new space for black groups across the Americas to build sustained relations throughout the region and the world. It was during this time that the struggles of Afro-Latin Americans became more visible and mobile within a transnational context. Three crucial factors explain the transnationalization of Afro-Latin social movements.

First, Afro-Latin groups over the years had laid strong infrastructural foundations in their countries after many years of intensive grassroots mobilization and organization. In Brazil and Colombia, black groups fought successfully for black rights legislation and had built strong social movements. Brazil, often considered a model for other black groups in the region, spawned an impressive network of diverse groups starting in the 1970s, with progressive black formations like the *Movimento Negro Unificado* (Unified Black Movement), cultural groups like Ilê Aiyê, and newer groups like Geledés. Some of these groups were also intertwined with resistance against the market-oriented model of globalization that had produced the exclusionary "Brazilian economic miracle," and the authoritarian political model that sustained social and economic exclusion.

Second, starting in the 1990s international civil society groups such as the Ford Foundation, International Human Rights Law Group, and the Minority Rights Group began to include Afro-Latin communities in their work and reports. In particular, the Ford Foundation and the International Human Rights Law Group began to fund projects and to work directly with Afro-Brazilian groups. In 1995, the Minority Rights Group published *No Longer Invisible*, and continued to publish reports on the status of black populations throughout the region. Also during this time, universities, researchers, and policy makers started to increase their focus and dedicate more studies (beyond those focused on slavery) of blacks in the Americas. Blacks from the Americas were also being increasingly invited to the United States and Europe to discuss Afro-Latin America.

The third factor explaining the rise of transnational Afro-Latin social movements is the role of the United Nations and to a lesser extent the Inter-American Development Bank (IADB). In 1997, the United Nations decided to convene a World Conference against Racism, Racial Discrimination, and Xenophobia held in Durban, South Africa, in 2001. Leading into the main conference were a series of sessions and expert seminars held in different regions of the world in preparation for the conference in Durban. Afro groups throughout the region—for example, in Brazil, Colombia, Uruguay, Panamá, and Venezuela—would play a central and defining role in this historical conference. In preparation for the World Conference against Racism, many Afro-Latin groups began to use the strategies, tactics, and language of international human rights discourse to advance democracy in their countries. Also, many groups in the region were being trained for the Conference against Racism by the generous support provided by Gaye McDougal, then the head of the International Human Rights Law Group. The International Human Rights Law Group trained movement activists and lawyers from Brazil on the procedural and technical aspect of international human rights law in preparation for the World Conference against Racism.

Before the Conference against Racism, other events were unfolding. In 1995 (Brazil) and 1997 (Colombia), respectively, the United Nations Special Rapporteur on Racism produced two excellent reports on the status of black communities (Gele-Hanhanzo, 1995, 1997). Written squarely within the context of international law and human rights, these special reports on human rights violations brought into sharp focus issues of racial and gender discrimination, labor force exclusion, low rates of education, poor housing, and other critical factors that affect blacks in the region. At the time, these reports were seen as an objective evaluation of the black experience in Brazil and Colombia and thus became crucial organizing tools for black social movements in their struggle for human rights. Moreover, given the nonpoliticized nature of these particular reports by the United Nations Commission on Human Rights, both the Brazilian and Colombian governments reluctantly acknowledged that Afro communities in their countries were subjected to forms of discrimination rooted in race. In short, the publication of these reports was a major tactical victory for the black movements in Brazil and Colombia.

In many ways the preparatory meeting and seminars served as a motor force propelling black social movements further into the broad network of transnational actors. Afro activists from Brazil were probably the largest black delegation from Latin America, with approximately 150 to 200 attending. Additionally, the World Conference against Racism allowed the issues of Third World peoples, and the struggle of racial and ethnic minorities from advanced first world countries, to take center stage within the broader frame of the largely white-led, -controlled, and -elitist human rights movement. This reconfiguration of the struggle brought Afro-Latin Americans into the heart of what might be broadly labeled the global justice movement.

In this context, the transnationalization of Afro-Latin social movements and their strategic adoption of international human rights discourse have been key to the resurgence of black identity-based organizing, as I will illustrate by focusing on the Colombian case.

The Emergence of Black Social Movements in Colombia

Colombia has the second largest African-descended population in South America, after Brazil. It is difficult, however, to determine precisely the size of Colombia's African population: estimates range from 15 to 35 percent of the overall population of about 44 million. The largest concentration of Afro-Colombians is found on the Pacific Coast where the black population is said to be roughly 80 to 90 percent (Dixon, 2002: 82). Afro-Colombians are not homogenous—culturally, historically, or politically. There are six sociocultural regions with a strong black presence: the Caribbean Coast, the Pacific Coast (Chocó), the Magdalena, the Cauca and Patía river valleys, and the English-speaking Archipelago of San Andrés and Providencia (Alvarez, Dagnino, and Escobar, 1998a: 201). Large concentrations of blacks are also found in many of the Colombia's largest cities, and their numbers are growing because of the armed conflict that is displacing thousands of black peasants. These communities constitute a range of political visions and historical experiences and therefore possess different perspectives, strategies, and approaches on their complex political situation.

Afro-Colombians, like other black groups in the Americas, have faced institutional racism that is compounded by the ideology of racial democracy. According to the anthropologist Peter Wade, a leading scholar on Colombia, the concept of blackness and discrimination are deeply embedded in Colombian society. Drawing deeply on his extensive anthropological field research, Wade presents a composite picture of Colombian society governed by racial stereotypes and institutional discrimination against blackness and pervasive attitudes that are masked by Colombians' erroneous perception of racial equality. In Colombia, and in other parts of the black Americas, blackness is an obstacle to economic and social progress. The solution proposed by dominant racial ideologies is the process of whitening, or *blanqueamiento* (Wade, 1993).

In Colombia the historical position of Afro-Colombians in the political economy—including slavery—and the ideological construction of Afro-Colombians as nonpersons, Indians as subpersons, mestizos as half-persons, and whites as full-persons, suggest that blacks, until recently, did not have real legal standing and thus, were not considered legitimate concerns of the state. In short, Afro-Colombians were socially constructed as noncitizens and had no real legal or juridical personality before the constitutional reforms enacted in the 1990s. These changes, and the constitutional reform process, will be analyzed in the context of the Afro-Colombian struggle for human rights and democracy. It is argued that Afro-Colombians, through human rights discourse and social movements, challenged the state's narrowly constructed conception of "citizen"—read, "as white"—and reframed and expanded the concept to include Afro-Colombians, at least theoretically.

Many black social movements in Latin America fit the characteristics that define new social movements. Black-based movements are not entirely new, as black slave and maroon societies have historically challenged systems of domination. However, black social movements in the Americas are advancing an ideological reframing of Afro-Latin identity and collective rights, emphasizing the myriad ways in which race and gender, as well as other crucial factors, shape, determine, and affect the life chances of Afrodiasporic populations. Moreover, Afrodiasporic communities posit a race- and gender-centric framework along with innovative strategies to combat racist and gender violence. The various black movements throughout the Americas have drawn on their new transnational networks to develop a specific vocabulary and language to better understand the codes of racial and gender discrimination. By doing so, Afrodiasporic communities have made significant contributions to recasting social movements in Latin America, as part of the broad demand for recognition of collective rights in an era when the liberal individualistic concept of citizenship was proving unable to meet basic needs.

Starting in the 1970s and throughout the 1980s, black, urban, educated college students mainly from the Pacific Coast began to deconstruct racist practices and ideas by challenging prevailing hegemonic structures. In 1975, Juan Dios Mosqueros, along with other progressive, young student militants, founded a university student group called Soweto. These were students—with strong ties working in the burgeoning student movement in Colombia—who had become dissatisfied with traditional social movements. During this period in Colombia, left-leaning progressive groups lacked serious theoretical approaches to race and ethnicity. Moreover, they did not understand the unique historical reality of Afro-Colombians. Given these circumstances, Afro-Colombians took it upon themselves to construct a new social movement methodology, vocabulary, and language in order to better understand the multiple forms of oppression and marginalization existing in their communities (Dixon, 1994–2000 [1995]). In doing so, they had to create new frameworks in order to deconstruct patterns of racial and gender discrimination, develop new methodologies to organize their communities, and devise new strategies to defend their varied interests.

In 1975, Amir Smith Córdoba, another young black militant, founded the Center for the Investigation of Black Culture in Bogotá, which produced a newspaper called *Presencia Negra*. Many of these young progressives were influenced by the writings of Martin Luther King Jr, Malcolm X, Frantz Fanon, and Angela Davis. At the same time, a growing interest in Afro-Colombian and black culture was on the rise throughout the region. In 1977, the historic First Congress of Black Culture in the Americas was held in Cali, Colombia, which marked an important historical juncture in black organizing in the Americas. Black groups from Colombia and Ecuador and elsewhere in the Americas came together to discuss common regional problems. The founding of Soweto, the Center for the Investigation of Black Culture, and the meeting of the First Congress on Black Culture represented the beginning of a new type of social movement activity.

In the early 1980s, the left-leaning black student group Soweto was transformed into Cimarrón, or National Movement for the Human Rights of Black Communities of Colombia (*Movimiento Nacional por los Derechos Humanos de las Comunidades Negras de Colombia*). Throughout the 1980s, Cimarrón continued to build its organization and, along with other black based groups, increased its organizing efforts through grassroots mobilization and political education. By the early 1990s, the various black social movements in Colombia through grassroots education, coalition building, and wide-scale mobilization had created new institutional space for organizing around ethnic rights, which led to the black rights law known as Law 70.

Social Movements and Constitutional Changes: The Black Rights Law (Law 70)

In 1990, a unique historic movement emerged as Colombia prepared to make substantial changes to its constitution. A new Constituent Assembly began work to replace the 1886 constitution. The assembly's main task was to develop a special legal mechanism that would make indigenous peoples' rights permanent as recognized by Law 89 of 1890 (De Friedeman and Arocha, 1995: 67). Afro-Colombians as a group were totally excluded and had no representation in the assembly. The challenge for black groups, who were being excluded from this historic political process, was to seek inclusion—to get a seat at the table. Building on the organizing successes of the preceding twenty years, Afro-Colombian groups, including Cimarrón, began to organize and mobilize their constituents through grassroots mobilization, peaceful protests, and an intense lobbying campaign that targeted select indigenous leaders and politicians. Their aim was to be represented in the Constituent Assembly.

Concretely, along with wanting their interests represented in the assembly, Afro-Colombians from the Pacific Coast demanded a special article that would grant them collective titles to riverbank and jungle lands of the Pacific Coast region and other areas where they had exerted ancestral territorial domain. Their demands, however, were soundly rejected. The Colombian Institute for Agrarian Reform, which was largely responsible for analysis of the land claims, argued that there were no ethnic minorities in Colombia apart from indigenous peoples. Dismayed but not discouraged, Afro communities redoubled their grassroots mobilizations efforts by collecting signatures and peacefully seizing government buildings in the city of Quibdo, the capital of the department of Chocó. Afro-Colombians argued that their ethnic claim was linked to their ancestral ties to the lands on the Pacific Coast where they had lived for centuries.

The Colombian case illustrates some of the mixed implications of recent advances by indigenous social movements in Latin America. Collective rights gained as a result of multicultural citizenship have included the recognition of indigenous customary law as official policy, collective property rights, and official status of minority languages and guarantees of bilingual education (Hooker, 2005: 285). Juliet Hooker argues that the question of cultural and ethnic identity in Latin America is linked to a group's ability to successfully articulate multicultural constitutional demands. For indigenous groups, these demands have linked land rights (habitat) to a broad agenda of territorial self-governance and cultural rights of difference (Mattiace, 2003). In almost every case of multicultural reform in the region, indigenous groups have been much more successful in gaining collective rights from the state than Afro groups (Hooker, 2005: 286). In Colombia, for example, the legislation for Afro-Colombian communities on the Pacific Coast is in no way comparable to similar laws for indigenous peoples, whose lands, or *resguardos*, are autonomous territorial units (in contrast to Afro-Colombian collective territories).

The main difference is that the resguardos receive direct financial support from the Colombian national budget. (Without such support, the neoliberal model would have a devastating impact on indigenous subsistence communities, as in Mexico where the 1992 "reform" of Article 27 of the Constitution threatened the survival of *ejidos*.) Also, the territory apportioned to each group relative to their size is not comparable. Indigenous groups are estimated to be roughly 4 percent of the Pacific Coast population and have legal title to 1.6 million hectares. In contrast, Afro-Colombians make up 90 percent of the Pacific Coast population and have been granted legal title to only 1.5 million hectares (Oakley, 2001: 21). Hooker argues that the main criteria used to determine the recipient of collective rights in Latin America has been the possession of a distinct cultural or ethnic identity. Therefore, the question of racial framing (race, culture, and ethnicity) is crucial to understanding the struggle for black rights in Colombia

It is against this backdrop that Transitory Article 55 was established. Transitory Article 55 was presented as a compromise by the National Organization of Colombian Indigenous Peoples (*Organización Nacional Indígena de Colombia*). This article called for establishing a Special Commission for Black Communities. It is through this mechanism that Afro-Colombians would have legal standing to pursue land claim issues on the Pacific Coast as well as other civil and political rights. Article 55 would lead to the elaboration of the Black Rights Law referred to as Law 70 (Dixon, 1994–2000 [1996]).

Law 70 allows black communities in rural areas of Colombia's Pacific Coast region to apply for collective land titles, until now considered state lands or unoccupied territories (Wade, 2000: 1). This very important law also contained provisions to improve black education, training, and access to credit, and to improve living conditions for black communities nationally. It also created two seats reserved for the black communities from the Pacific Coast in the congress and a Special Ministry of Government for black community affairs. In addition, discrimination against black communities was outlawed, and Law 70 included provisions that aggravate criminal penalties for specific crimes if they are inspired by racial or ethnic intolerance or discrimination. To date, however, it is unclear if an individual or organization has been tried successfully for racial discrimination, illustrating how the neoliberal fiction of individual rights fails to protect community rights.

In this context another important group, the Process of Black Communities (*Proceso de Comunidades Negras*—PCN) was born. The PCN is a progressive network of roughly 120 black peasant organizations and, like Cimarrón, is an important player on Colombia's political scene today. Representing mainly the interests of black peasants, PCN enjoys widespread support and grassroots legitimacy, and it places a strong emphasis on black cultural identity. The regional focus of the PCN is the southwest of Colombia, concentrating on the cities of Buenaventura (the location of the PCN headquarters), Cali, Tumaco, and their surrounding rural areas. This region includes the southern half of Colombia's Pacific Coast region, predominantly rural and inhabited mainly by black people.

The PCN has worked to clarify and interpret the meaning of Law 70 by translating the legal aspects of the legislation into practical application for poor black communities who may not be able to fully comprehend its complexities, contradictions, and nuances. A major concern of the PCN has been pursuing the land title claims that rural black communities on the Pacific Coast region can make under Law 70. The PCN also has a broader sociocultural agenda as it seeks to carve out a space for black identity. And, while the PCN participates in local and regional electoral processes, they are not connected to mainstream institutional parties or traditional party politics. They focus not so much on racism but on cultural difference. Rather than working for integration, PCN sees a future of equality based on cultural difference and autonomy in which black people control territories—rather than plots of land—constructing ways of life rooted in local black cultural practices of production, kinship, and ritual (Wade, 2000: 2).

The stellar work of the PCN has not gone unnoticed by the international community. It was the recent recognition of the work of the PCN and Libia Grueso that demonstrates the transnational dimensions of the struggle for human rights in Afro-Colombia and their significance. In 2004, Libia Grueso—an Afro-Colombian human rights activist, intellectual, mother, and cofounder of PCN—was awarded a Goldman environmental prize (the largest of its kind, considered the "Nobel Prize for the Environment") for her sustainable development projects in the Colombian southwest. Like the famous case of rubber-tapper activist Chico Mendes in the Brazilian Amazon, sustainable development in Afro-Colombian regions represents a challenge to globalization and to the mega-investment projects seeking to convert natural resources into private commodities on the global market (stripping away the self-determination claims of local communities). A social worker and environmental educator, Grueso is one of the many forces behind Law 70 and is known throughout Colombia and the world for her defense of black rights. While Afro movements in Colombia and the region had already achieved international visibility, the Goldman award offered fresh opportunities to cultivate and build new allies in the transnational community.

Consequences and Implications of Law 70

Law 70 is uneven, unclear, and has been hotly contested. While the law was welcomed by broad segments of Afro-Colombian civil society, there is no common agreement regarding its significance and relevance. Some argue that Law 70 lacks real power of enforcement, while other movement leaders argue it is an effective tool for black empowerment. However, the most crucial provisions of the law (regarding collective titles) only apply to Afro-Colombians of the Pacific Coast and not to the Afro population of the Atlantic Coast, therefore leading some to conclude that the law is divisive, as it favors one group over another. This illustrates another dilemma of identity-based movements, as interests are not necessarily homogenous within any racial or ethnic group, highlighting the importance of linking identity-based struggles to their global context.

Notwithstanding these debates, the law had several significant effects on Colombia's complex sociological landscape. First, it brought the issue of black rights squarely within the parameters of mainstream discourse. Second, it increased black mobilization and organizing while simultaneously forcing "blacks" to come out of the closet and accept their blackness as a cultural and social reality. Third, it forced the Colombian state to deal with, though unevenly, growing black demands on the status and standing of Afro-Colombians as an ethnic group. Fourth, it should be interpreted as a major victory for black social groups and movements in Colombia. Lastly, it helped to propel their struggle to a regional and international level, and now as a consequence, the black struggle in Colombia has strong regional, national, and transnational links. Most importantly this law recognizes and codifies the rights of Afro-Colombians and bestows upon them rights that the state must recognize. It is the relationship between race and social citizenship that Afro-Colombians sought to address as they effectively challenged the notion of Colombia being a mainly white or mestizo nation. So with Law 70—at least in theory—Afro-Colombians became real citizens for the first time in the history of Colombia. By connecting to a transnationalized construct of human rights, black movements in Colombia inserted the collective identity of race into the concept of citizenship, challenging the neoliberal framework of rights based on individuals in a global marketplace.

With Law 70, a new level of intensity was achieved with respect to black mobilization. Small black NGOs blossomed while issues of black rights dominated the Colombian social landscape like never before. The years of black grassroots organizing had finally paid off, as Afro-Colombians now were seen as an ethnic group with a history, identity, and status, and as an official part of Colombia's national identity. In Amilcar Cabral's framework (1979), Afro-Colombians, like all peoples subject to forms of oppression, had reclaimed their past and in doing so had recaptured their culture, history, and identity.

While all aspects of the law are important, few are as problematic as the provisions of the law allowing for the issuance of titles to black communities on the Pacific Coast. Many Afro-Colombians complain that since the passage of the law, few communities have been granted titles to their properties. It is difficult, therefore, to judge the efficacy of this provision given that it is hard to determine precisely how many communities are negotiating, requesting, and receiving titles at any given time. Also, for those communities who have applied for such titles—successfully or unsuccessfully—it is not always clear on what basis such a determination was made. Moreover, since the passage of the law, land values have increased exponentially on the Pacific Coast, while at the same time, Colombia's four-decade-old armed conflict has spread to Chocó and surrounding communities, resulting in the large-scale displacement of Afro-Colombians and the loss of huge portions of their lands.

Afro-Colombian communities on the Pacific Coast occupy some of the most strategic and valuable land in the region, and the inhabitants are caught between their struggle to obtain titles for lands and a myriad of complex state and nonstate actors, including the drug traffickers, the army, the paramilitary groups—who are supported by the army—and the guerrillas. The Afro-Colombian struggle can be seen as a conflict of local communities seeking the right to define their own priorities, against powerful geopolitical and global economic interests. According to a United Nations Special Rapporteur's report on Colombia, black populations are seriously affected by violence as they are trapped in the crossfire between the drug traffickers, the army, the paramilitaries, and the guerrillas. In rural areas, where the problem of land ownership and use includes whether to grow lawful or unlawful crops or to exploit mineral resources, indigenous and black leaders are murdered by members of paramilitary organizations (armed by landowners or the military), drug traffickers, or guerrilla groups. The establishment of military bases on indigenous territories and black communities is perceived as an act of cultural aggression (Gele-Hanhanzo, 1997: 11). Moreover, each party to the conflict (the paramilitaries, formal military, drug traffickers, and the guerrillas) expects the communities to support their strategy, with total disregard for the communities' basic living conditions, and as a result the opposing party in the conflict considers them enemies and legitimate targets.

The logic of the Afro-Colombian situation is further complicated by the neoliberal reforms sweeping across the region and aggressively promoted by Colombian president Alvaro Uribe. Given the vast mineral resources and the strategic locations of Afro-Colombian communities, transnational corporations (pharmaceuticals, petroleum, and agribusiness) have taken a keen interest in the Pacific coastline. Many black Colombians are often forced to choose between staying on their lands, which means putting their lives on the line; abandoning their properties in order to save their lives; or selling their properties (at reduced values) to land speculators. Thus, the struggle to enforce Law 70, based on assertion of black identity and rights, becomes a direct challenge to the neoliberal agenda promoted by global capital seeking access to lucrative extraction and investment opportunities in Colombia. While Afro-Colombian movements have engaged with the state for purposes of passing the Black Rights Law, the slim protection offered by that legislation has obliged them to remain constituted as a social movement outside the framework of institutionalized politics.

Reports by the United Nations and other groups estimate that Afro-Colombians make up about 33 percent of internally displaced peoples (IDP). Afro-Colombians constitute a large part of the 3 million Colombians who have been forced to leave their homes since 1985 due to the gratuitous violence of the illegal armed groups and the Colombian military, as well as the U.S.-backed anti–drug fumigation campaigns. Displaced Afro-Colombians from the coastal regions now swell urban slums such as the popular neighborhood Nelson Mandela located on the edge of Cartagena de Indias (U.S. Office on Colombia, 2003: 1). Many of these displaced families are headed by women. The human rights violations committed against Afro-Colombians underscores the tensions between individual and group conceptions of human rights. Conceptually, Afro groups, like indigenous peoples, often see the group as the focal point and not necessarily the individual. Moreover, these groups focus on collective and identity issues within a human rights framework. Black and indigenous groups have broadened the conceptual, legal, and philosophical debates surrounding human rights and, in doing so, have helped to shift the discourse.

As a consequence of the war, scores of Afro-Colombian leaders have been killed or forced to seek exile. In response to the violence and displacement, Afro-Colombians have organized in their communities, and groups like AFRODES (the Association for Internally Displaced Afro-Colombians) now work with Afro-Colombians to assist them in reestablishing their lives.

AFRODES believes that communities of the southern Pacific region, and generally most Afro-Colombian communities, have suffered from the neglect of the Colombian state, racial discrimination, and social exclusion, as well as from the violation of their most fundamental rights and aggressions against their lives, culture, land, and forms of organization by armed actors.

Conclusion

Social movements in black Colombia are now transnational in scope and recognition. Like never before, the struggle of Afro-Colombians for land rights, decent housing, education, and other rights is becoming more known around the world. Afro-Colombians have established strong ties with groups in the United States, Canada, and Europe. The work of Afro-Colombians and their struggle is increasingly recognized by the international human rights community.

Like other groups in the region, in the 1970s Afro-Colombian social movements had spent a tremendous amount of time working in their communities, laying a solid infrastructural foundation and building regional and national networks. By the 1990s, Afro-Colombian social groups and networks had sprung up across the country. Also, civil society groups, U.S.-Latin American solidarity networks, and intergovernmental organizations had started to take a keen interest in Afro-Latin issues. The 2001 World Conference against Racism provided the historic opportunity for blacks and indigenous groups from the Americas to talk about their issues as well as build more networks and other forms of transnational solidarity.

By inscribing their struggles within the discourse of human rights and connecting to transnational networks, Afro-Latin movements are reconstructing identities in ways that both challenge the narrow neoliberal version of citizenship and strategically resist the disempowering impact of globalization. Their battles for legal and constitutional reform represent toeholds in the reconceptualization of citizenship to include collective identity-based rights. For Afro-Colombian communities found in strategic areas in the new process of global capital accumulation, asserting black identity in the framework of global human rights is key to survival.

12

Politics Is *Uma Coisinha de Mulher* (a Woman's Thing)

Black Women's Leadership in Neighborhood Movements in Brazil

Keisha-Khan Y. Perry

Política é coisa pra macho	Politics is a man's game
ouvi isso a vida inteira.	I heard that all my life.

—Benedita da Silva, 1997, original translation

THE ABOVE EXCERPT OF A POEM written by Afro-Brazilian politician Benedita da Silva, formerly the Brazilian minister of social action and a neighborhood and women's rights activist in Rio de Janeiro, provides a poignant critique of existing masculinist and classist definitions of political engagement. Silva's rise in Brazilian politics from a domestic worker and neighborhood activist to the federal government suggests that black women in Brazil have been able to defy social prescriptions and redefine politics not as a "man's game," but rather as a robust space for black women to occupy and lead (Silva, 1997).

This chapter analyzes black women's struggles in urban neighborhoods against the forced removal of poor black communities during urban modernization and revitalization processes in Brazilian cities. I centralize the experiences of the women of Gamboa de Baixo, a coastal community located in the center of Brazil's northeastern city of Salvador. These activists are still considered to be the unlikely leaders of the grassroots organization in their neighborhood. Black people in Brazil, particularly women, are understood to be apolitical, and their communities are thought to be easy targets for urban renewal without much challenge or organized protest (Caldwell, 2007; Johnson, 1998; Pinheiro, 2002). Although black women are rarely visible leaders in political parties or in state-level politics, my ethnographic analysis of the Gamboa de Baixo neighborhood association supports the claim that they are indeed the everyday leaders of their communities. In Brazilian cities, black women wage very real and arduous political struggles in the marginal spaces they occupy, and their exclusion from broader citywide and national politics does not negate their achievements at the neighborhood level (Silva, 1999).

State officials have heard black women's voices, and their actions demonstrate that community organizations led by black women are capable of changing public policies historically rooted in slavery and colonialism. George Reid Andrews (1991) and Kim Butler (1998) suggest that colonialism is at the core of racist ideologies and social stratification in Brazilian cities, including racial segregation and economic and racialized hierarchies. As Butler writes, urban struggles against discrimination in Salvador have emerged "to dismantle discrimination against people of African descent" (1998: 18). While Afro-Brazilians were able to prevent legalized segregation (128), they have not been able to escape widespread poverty, a legacy of plantation slavery. As is widely acknowledged, "poverty has a face in Brazil," and the color of that face is black.

Grassroots activism in Gamboa de Baixo and throughout the city of Salvador forces us to expand definitions of mass mobilization as well as to reconsider the multitude of ways in which black women's political actions draw attention to the gendered aspects of Brazilian race relations (Caldwell, 2007; Twine, 1998). Through a look at how and why women lead the neighborhood association in Gamboa de Baixo, this chapter represents a theoretical reflection on black women's key role in social movements in Brazilian cities. The ethnographic data I have collected over the past decade suggests that female leadership predominates in this case because women play important roles in social and political networks, such as organizing funerals and demanding potable water. It is not difficult to explain why the political meetings in the Gamboa de Baixo neighborhood became known as *uma coisinha de mulher*, or "a woman's little thing." Meetings are widely perceived as what women do in Gamboa de Baixo. The uniqueness of women's political mobilization and the leadership roles they have always occupied in the Gamboa de Baixo neighborhood illustrate the place of the *bairro*, "the neighborhood," particularly the social and spatial location of Gamboa de Baixo in the formation of black women's gendered antiblack racism politics focused on issues of urbanization and land rights.

This analysis incorporates the voices from activists from Gamboa de Baixo who speak from a social location that reveals the link between the politics of the neighborhood and the workplace. It supports my claim that black women's political work is deeply informed by their knowledge of an entrenched racial and gender hierarchy that provides little economic opportunity for them beyond domestic work, which continues to be one visible reminder of Brazil's neo-slavery attitudes and practices toward black women's labor. In this regard, domestic work matters greatly. While my research did not initially focus on these connections between gendered racism, labor practices, and the formation of female-led social movements, I could not ignore activists' consistent testimony of the heightened racial, gender, and class consciousness that arises from their subjugated positions as blacks, women, and workers (see also R. González, 2004). From this key insight, I draw upon black feminist, critical race, and social movement theories to explain black women's militancy against interlocking forms of oppressions, particularly at the grassroots level, and to centralize the political actions of *"quem sempre se rebelou contra a servidão* [those who always rebelled against servitude]" (Oliveira, 2000: 104). This essay provides a concrete example of the relationship between systemic racialization and feminization of poverty and the emergence of gendered class-based antiracism activism throughout the African diaspora. Moreover, social movements have become a crucial site for black women who are not generally expected to reshape policy or to engage in the global transformation of ideologies and practices of modern urban development.

History of Gamboa de Baixo's Struggle for Urban Land Rights

To explain the unique development of black women's activism and leadership in Gamboa de Baixo, it is important to outline the neighborhood's recent social and political history. In the 1960s, the technocratic and authoritarian government of the military dictatorship elaborated the Plano Diretor, an urban development plan intended to modernize all Brazilian cities. The plan forbade community participation in urban planning and considered poor communities, the majority of which in the city of Salvador were black, to be *"incapazes de ação e decisão* [incapable of taking action and making decisions]" (Associação Amigos de Gegê dos Moradores da Gamboa de Baixo, Associação dos Moradores do Nordeste de Amaralina, Conselho de Moradores do Bairro da Paz, Grupo de Mulheres do Alto das Pombas, 2001).

In 1962, this government was responsible for the construction of the Contorno Avenue (*Avenida do Contorno*) that runs along the coast of the Bay of All Saints, which demolished numerous homes and removed families, some of whom resisted displacement without much success. The road's construction separated Gamboa into two neighborhoods: *Gamboa de Cima* (Upper Gamboa) and *Gamboa de Baixo* (Lower Gamboa). That physical separation isolated the fishing colony Gamboa de Baixo, located below the Contorno Avenue, and denied the community basic services such as sanitation, electricity, and water. Isolation and abandonment exacerbated unequal social relations between working-class Gamboa de Baixo and its bourgeois neighbors above the Avenue (Campo Grande, Vítoria, Gamboa de Cima).

The *abertura democrática* (democratic opening) of the military regime in the mid-1970s and the transitional democratic government of the early 1980s promoted the political organization of poor urban communities such as Gamboa de Baixo. Neighborhood associations became a new political arena for black communities to engage in struggles for citizenship rights and make urban demands for material resources such as better schooling, housing, and working conditions. Moreover, the growth in grassroots-based political parties such as the Workers' Party (PT) established what Ruth Corrêa Leite Cardoso (1992) identifies as a set of "new relations between excluded citizens and the state apparatus" (291), which not only reinvigorated broader political participation, but also heightened class-based expectations in the developing social democracy project. Furthermore, "building autonomous associations endowed with a new role, local neighborhood groups made their demands in ways that revealed their ability to bypass traditional mechanisms of political co-optation" (292).

Benedita da Silva (1997) affirms that many women leaders in neighborhood movements emerged during these years of military rule during which the persecution of male organizers was widespread (45). For women who had previously "played a backstage role within the neighborhood associations" (45), political leadership became increasingly possible. The Women's Association in Gamboa de Baixo organized in the 1980s was one such example of black women's efforts to mobilize local residents to demand social programs for women in Salvador's impoverished neighborhoods. When the municipal government terminated the free milk programs at the end of the 1980s, the Women's Association stopped functioning as a political representative for the neighborhood. However, after the outbreak of cholera in Bahia in 1992, which caused several deaths in Gamboa de Baixo, the women began to organize themselves again. With the direct assistance of the mayoral office, they founded the organization *Associação Amigos de Gegê dos Moradores da Gamboa de Baixo* (Gamboa de Baixo Friends of Gegê Neighborhood Association). Gianpaolo Baiocchi (2005) describes this form of civic engagement as "government-induced activism" in other Brazilian cities such as Porto Alegre (51), and Willem Assies (1994) explains that the increasing numbers of middle-class left-wing militants, church activists, and nongovernmental organizations (NGOs) who understood themselves to be "at the service of the movements" and as "external agents" and "social articulators" played key roles in the formation of popular organizations (93). However, neighborhood associations have been autonomous organizations that extend from already existing political and social networks in local communities.

Led by the women of the neighborhood association, Gamboa residents went to radio stations to bring attention to the cholera outbreak and the contamination of their tap water. One important act of protest was their demand for the state to test the natural water sources and the public water pipes in the neighborhood. Testing proved that the victims of cholera had died from contaminated water provided by the city and not from the neighborhood's natural water fountains. After these actions, the community received some social service interventions such as the construction of the *chafariz*, a central water fountain in the area. During this same period, Dona Juana, an elderly Italian nun, conducted social work with women in the neighborhood focusing on sewing and adult and child literacy. From her work, she perceived the necessity of buying land and constructing a permanent space in the community for these activities, a space that was later named the Elementary School and Community Center of Gamboa de Baixo. For poor black women in Gamboa de Baixo, the training courses offered them practical skills necessary to seek employment and advance their education. More importantly, the school became a regular meeting place where the women shared knowledge of everyday happenings in the neighborhood and articulated social and political concerns about the city, the nation, and the world. The work of Dona Juana typified the work of elderly nuns such as Sister Dorothy Stang— recently killed as a result of her advocacy work in the Amazon—who have used their roles as "external agents" (Assies, 1994) to propagate ongoing local discussions of global social justice issues.

With the main issue of water resolved during the early 1990s, the neighborhood association remained politically dormant for a few years after the cholera outbreak in Gamboa de Baixo. The resurgence of the neighborhood association occurred in 1995 when news of the Contorno Avenue Revitalization Project reached Gamboa de Baixo residents. The development project involved the gentrification of the area along Contorno Avenue to promote tourism activities. The Bahian press then announced that the revitalization project involved the relocation of the families of Gamboa de Baixo to a new housing development located in the distant periphery. As the project received a lot of media attention, the Bahian state development agency started to collect demographic information on the homes in Gamboa de Baixo. The residents feared that their relocation was imminent. Hence, the community movement against expulsion started out of fear of leaving the locale most of them had known all their lives.

That fear led to anger, and residents reported to newspapers that government social workers were conducting surveys in Gamboa de Baixo without any explanations. Residents suspected that social workers were documenting the conditions of the population for probable expulsion from the urban center. At the end of 1995, the government expelled seventy-five families from a coastal community situated on Contorno Avenue, approximately one kilometer away from Gamboa de Baixo. Residents watched as the government advanced in their plans to displace all the poor black communities from along the Contorno Avenue. The city government conducted a rapid and thorough "cleansing" of the city-center and displaced all the residents from the restored historic buildings and monuments. During 1995 and 1997, community activism focused on getting detailed information about the Contorno Avenue Revitalization Project, mobilizing Gamboa de Baixo residents to participate in street protests, and developing alternative urbanization projects for the improvement of their community.

Like the Women's Association during the previous decade, the neighborhood association found its leadership and support firmly based in the women of Gamboa de Baixo. Their fear was a crucial factor in pushing forward the grassroots struggle against "black clearance" and "slum clearance" from the city-center. This stemmed from a dozen or so women who began to cause alarm, shouting, "Look what's happening." The women worked with NGOs such as the *Comissão de Justiça e Paz da Arquidiocese de Salvador* (Commission of Justice and Peace of the Archdiocese of Salvador—CJP), the *Centro de Estudos e Ação Social* (Center for Social Action Studies—CEAS), the *Movimento Negro Unificado* (United Black Movement—MNU), and the *União de Negros pela Igualdade* (Union for Black Equality—UNegro) in mobilizing the community and in discussing the global neoliberal roots of citywide revitalization projects. These organizations also contributed significantly to this intellectual and political empowerment of black women in Gamboa de Baixo and shifted class-centered debates on social inequality to include racial and gender oppression. This shift implied alterations in black women's definition of themselves as capable of being leading political actors in urban social movements and contributors to the democratization of Brazilian society. Moreover, the women maintained local autonomy while calling upon leftist NGOs and politicians as resources to decipher their rights as citizens and communities (Cardoso, 1992: 301). This relationship between neighborhood associations and NGOs and political parties was crucial for building activists' knowledge of and fight against the destructive and exclusionary practices of urbanization in Salvador.

The 1996 Habitat II conference organized by the United Nations was also crucial for Brazilian social movements organized around issues of urbanization and housing rights. Political groups like neighborhood associations, the landless movement, and the homeless movement used the Habitat Agenda as a tool for demanding national and state commitment to infrastructural improvement and fair land and housing distribution. Conference discussions centered on marginalized groups—specifically racial minorities, women, and children—and the Habitat Agenda held particular meanings for the future development of Brazilian cities. The United Nations Educational, Scientific, and Cultural Organization (UNESCO) presented a disparaging report on Brazilian cities in which they confirmed the rapid *guetização* (ghettoization) of poor neighborhoods where the majority of their residents were black and brown (*Folha de São Paulo*, August 16, 1996). The report claimed that these actions resulted in the creation of "new frontiers" in the city, reflecting the disparity between the spaces where the poor and rich, blacks and whites live. In Salvador, the government's plan to expand housing on the periphery for families like those from Gamboa de Baixo provoked debates among activists about the systemic elimination of *pretos* (blacks) and *pobres* (poor people) from the better areas of the city and generated critiques of Brazil's supposed commitment to poverty alleviation, gender justice, and housing and land reform.

Gamboa de Baixo activists used their knowledge of these international debates to advocate for the intervention of *Viver Melhor* (Better Living), a federal program of the *Projeto Habitar Brasil* (Brazil Habitat Project) designed after the Habitat II conference and responsible for the urbanization of poor communities in the state of Bahia. They were able to incorporate some of their needs into the project and guaranteed the construction of eighty new homes, the exclusion of the construction of a road within the neighborhood, the restoration of the homes that already existed, and the permanence of all families in their place of origin. Today, the Gamboa de Baixo neighborhood association continues to fight to achieve their demands for the improvement of houses that were constructed by the government less than ten years ago, the complete installation of water pipes and sewer systems, and environmental reform. Gamboa de Baixo remains intact as a community amidst the construction of luxury apartment complexes, yacht clubs, and museums.

Domestic Work, Insider Knowledge, and Grassroots Politics

As the outline of Gamboa's political history reveals, organizing and leading a grassroots movement against land expulsion and for improved living conditions represents no easy task for community leaders in the Gamboa de Baixo neighborhood association. Most meetings and protests conflict with the personal and professional responsibilities of the working women, such as thirty-three-year-old activist Rita, who works as a domestic worker from sunrise to sunset and takes care of her own household duties at night. Her dedication to the neighborhood association reflects her willingness to take on the triple-duty day of a worker, mother, and activist. Managing domestic and the political spheres simultaneously poses a tremendous challenge for this group of women activists.

In a class system that relegates black women to the bottom of the socioeconomic hierarchy, domestic workers give special insights into how gendered racism operates in Brazil and the challenges to resisting that racism. Domestic work is the number one form of employment for black women in the country (IBGE, 2004). Based on information collected from a community census designed in collaboration with the neighborhood association in 2003, more than 80 percent of working adult and adolescent females in the Gamboa de Baixo neighborhood are domestic workers. I attempt to examine how these women carve out political spaces in their everyday lives to organize a resistance movement. Theirs is a situation filled with a very stark contradiction: they carry out the least valuable and most dehumanizing forms of work on a daily basis, and yet, they are the predominant leaders of Gamboa de Baixo's community politics.

In 2003, at a board meeting of the Gamboa de Baixo neighborhood association, Rita recounted the story of the work conditions in the home of a wealthy Bahian musician who lived in the elite Rio Vermelho coastal neighborhood. At the time, it was a few days before Christmas, and Rita sadly remarked that her employer told her that he would not pay her the state-mandated thirteenth-month year-end salary bonus. Fully expecting and anticipating the extra money, she asked the other neighborhood association board members what her legal rights were as a domestic worker and if domestic workers traditionally received the extra salary. Her boss had already refused to sign her worker's card, which left her without any legal recourse, and he was paying her below the minimum wage requirement. She earned R200 per month while the national minimum salary was R240 (about US$70). As Rita claimed, there were three generations living in her employer's household and there was a lot of *hard* work. She hand washed the clothes of five adults, as well as those of two children. Like most domestic workers, she complained that she suffered acute back pains from the cleaning and ironing, and that her hands were "raw" from all the washing. "They can afford to buy a washing machine," Rita affirmed, but like most Bahians, they preferred to have their clothes washed by hand. Black women provide an available and cheap labor alternative to the expensive new technologies that make domestic work easier.

Being cheated out of a fair salary was a usual complaint of domestic workers in Bahia and led to the political organization of the *Sindicato das Empregadas Domésticas* (Domestic Workers Union of Bahia—SINDOMÉSTICO) and the *Sindicato das Lavadeiras* (Washerwomen's Union) during recent decades. A more common complaint of domestic workers is employers' refusal to pay the necessary social security taxes, obstructing workers' ability to receive retirement benefits after many years of work. After hearing Rita's story, Ana Cristina, a thirty-four-year-old resident of Gamboa de Baixo and neighborhood association board member, told of her own mother's enduring struggle to retire even though her hands were severely damaged from many years of hand washing. Ana Cristina also admitted that for several years as an adolescent and young adult, she worked as a domestic worker in her white sister's house in Gamboa de Baixo without receiving a salary. Working in that household provided her with shelter and food as well as the freedom to move about her neighborhood and to participate in community politics. However, Ana Cristina perceived her unpaid labor as a form of racial exploitation common to other black domestic workers in Gamboa de Baixo and throughout Salvador.

A discussion about what Rita should do about her exploitative working conditions erupted during the neighborhood association meeting. Ritinha, a social worker from CEAS, suggested that they contact a lawyer, and Rita said that she was already planning not to return to work with the family after the holidays. The women of the Gamboa de Baixo neighborhood association regularly confront the police fearlessly and shout in the face of state officials during meetings and group demonstrations, but they struggle with individual empowerment to overcome the oppressive conditions they deal with in other aspects of their lives. As Ana Cristina reminded Rita during the meeting, the Gamboa de Baixo struggle is not just about the empowerment and improvement of the neighborhood, but also about reinventing themselves as black women and realizing their own *projetos de vida*, their own "personal life projects." The incident with Rita raises the question of how and why black women like her have been able to mobilize on a collective basis in their communities around issues of housing and land rights, but have not been able to resist on an individual level at the workplace or even at home. In addition to tales of everyday struggles for fair salaries, accounts of employers who make sexual advances on young, attractive Gamboa girls are commonplace.

Although women tell me the various ways that they try to resist these kinds of exploitation, the vast majority continue to work under difficult circumstances, do not participate in unions, and are not registered with the Brazilian government as "formal" workers. They are oftentimes unaware that unions exist or that there are certain rights guaranteed to workers in their profession, even when working without legal documentation. To my knowledge, no woman in the Gamboa de Baixo neighborhood is affiliated with a domestic workers' union or a union that addresses their needs. These black women workers in Bahian society are oftentimes disposable and rendered invisible and are not valued as real work in Brazil. Poor women throughout the country are usually afraid to resist because domestic work is the only kind of job that they can find.

Social movement theorist Robin D. G. Kelley (1993), in his analysis of black working-class opposition in the U.S. urban South during the 1930s and 1940s, encourages us to rethink our conceptualization of black women's resistance that may privilege "mainstream politics" in the struggle against the oppressive conditions of domestic work. Kelley argues that their daily acts of black resistance and survival have a "cumulative effect on power relations" (78). This infrapolitical approach to politics refocuses our discussion on *why* (rather than *how*) people participate in social movements.

Kelley's argument helps analyze what motivates black women to lead grassroots organizations in the battle against exclusionary urban policies and aggression from the state. From this perspective, black women's political consciousness in neighborhood movements stems from the very strategies, actions, and experiences that drive Ana Cristina to work in exchange for food and shelter and Rita to abruptly leave her job. Some women from the neighborhood who work in the high-rise buildings that overlook Gamboa de Baixo explain that working in close proximity to their homes allows them to know the everyday happenings and to attend to emergencies in their homes and community.

In addition, Patricia Hill Collins, in her groundbreaking text *Black Feminist Thought: Knowledge, Consciousness, and the Politics of Empowerment* (2000), writes that "U.S. Black women's critical social theory lay in the common experiences they gained from their jobs" (10). According to Collins, forging strong "familial" ties with their white employers, black women construct "insider relationships" (10). However, these women witness and understand racism firsthand and know that while they find themselves navigating the intimate terrains of white people's lives, they "could never belong to the white 'families'" (11). In fact, Collins states that domestic workers remain "outsiders-within," socially and economically marginalized from white society. She argues that black women who work as domestics not only maintain relationships within their all-black communities but also develop complex relationships within the homes where they work. Navigating the homes of white families on a daily basis, they belong as workers, but they are permanent economic and social "outsiders-within."

In another essay, Collins (2001) emphasizes that black women are never "like one of the family," which reflects how racial and gender power operates within the private realm of domestic work. This form of social organization also indicates the "politics of containment," which for black women "marked with the status of subordinated workers," means that they are "tolerated as long as they remain in their proscribed places" (5). At the same time, domestic workers gain access to the particularities of racial ideologies and practices that they take back to their home spaces and share with each other, thereby developing a collective social critique of gendered, class-based racism.

This understanding of black women's standpoint constructed from their experiences as social outsiders in their places of work elucidates the collective action of black women in Brazilian urban communities. In Gamboa de Baixo, the knowledge black women gain as domestic workers is a source of political empowerment as well as organizing creativity. Women like Rita might not overtly resist their employers' actions, but they share their critiques with other women in their neighborhoods in spaces like an association meeting. Understanding that colonialism and racism are the root causes of their exploitation, these black women contemplate collective ways to overcome that exploitation and transform society. Still, Collins's formulation of black women's standpoint theory does not explain the relative lack of political action in the work place.

Kian Tajbakhsh's book *The Promise of the City: Space, Identity, and Politics in Contemporary Social Thought* (2001) offers a formulation of the relationship between work and political identity formation that can be applied to Gamboa de Baixo. In cities like Salvador, labor organizations rarely concern themselves with racial justice and housing rights. This absence of a class consciousness that includes the racialized poor discourages black communities from organizing around a shared class position. From this perspective, black women in Gamboa de Baixo prefer to mobilize as "*moradores*" (residents of a neighborhood) and not as "workers."

In their neighborhood organizations, black women link their class positions as poor workers to their racial and gender conditions in a structurally unequal city. They understand that they are poor because they are black women, experienced through their heightened racial and gender sensibilities at work and at home. They self-identify as residents of an urban neighborhood under siege by the police, development agencies, and private companies because Gamboa de Baixo is *preto e pobre* (black and poor). The neighborhood, unlike the workplace, is an important site of political autonomy and liberation for poor black women in Salvador urban communities. They fight to preserve the land where they have built their homes, forged social networks, and generated material resources necessary to sustain their families.

Female Leadership as a Challenge to Gendered Hegemony

Black women workers in Gamboa de Baixo continue to represent the majority of board members and primary actors in meetings and street protests. The female-centered space of the neighborhood association has not allowed for male leadership and domination to flourish, raising concerns about the way gendered racial hegemony operates and its effect on grassroots politics. Helen Davis (2004) writes that one aspect of hegemony "points to the subordinated class's willingness to collude and negotiate with the dominant power bloc"

(47). When most politicians approach neighborhood groups to garner votes, they almost always approach male residents, some of whom have bargained with the state for personal gain such as political appointments.

In contrast, black women leaders of the Gamboa de Baixo neighborhood association have been unwilling to negotiate on an individual basis because they see their community's collective interests as congruent with their own. This represents a crucial aspect of why female-led organizations tend to be relatively successful in preserving collective community rights such as access to land and improved social conditions. Patricia Hill Collins (1998) argues that these kinds of moral and ethical principles stem from women's experiences in religious institutions and underline their ideological position in black political struggles. She writes that this follows the black feminist tradition in community activism:

> This moral, ethical tradition, especially as expressed within black Christian churches, encouraged black women to relinquish their special interests as women for the greater good of the overarching community. Rejecting individualist strategies that they perceived as selfish, black women came to couch their issues as black women within the egalitarian, collectivist ideological framework of black women's community work, an approach that works well within womanist approaches to black women's politics (Matthews, 1989; Poster, 1995). Within this interpretative framework, fighting for freedom and social justice for the entire black community was, in effect, fighting for one's own personal freedom. The two could not be easily separated. (27)

Similarly, in Brazil, black women's morality informed by Christianity, and more importantly, by Afro-Brazilian religious traditions, also heavily female dominated, encourages women to abandon their special interests and fight on behalf of the entire community. Activists in Gamboa de Baixo see the collective community interests as coinciding with their own individual needs as poor black women.

Studying black women's leadership in Brazilian urban social movements requires an analysis of "how mobilization takes places in day-to-day community work" (Robnett, 1997: 15) that determines different gendered social movement experiences. Their political autonomy challenges the definitions of women's leadership that social movement theorists Karen Sacks (1988) and Belinda Robnett (1997) describe in their studies of union organizing and the U.S. civil rights movement, respectively. On the one hand, Sacks focuses on "centerwomen" or "key actors in network formation and consciousness shaping" who rarely accepted their titles as leaders and preferred to stay in the background (quoted in Robnett, 1997: 18). On the other hand, Robnett offers the term "bridge leaders" to describe the women who "were able to cross the boundaries between the public life of a movement organization and the private spheres of adherents and political constituents" (19). Gamboa de Baixo women activists embody the leadership characteristics of both *centerwomen* and *bridge leaders* because they do the groundwork necessary to mobilize community participation in the social movement, and they have also been the formal leaders who have accepted the charge of representing the collective interests in negotiations with the state and other societal organizations.

These collective interests are maintained even when black female community leaders work with the few politicians who have supported the neighborhood's cause against land expulsion. In many Brazilian urban neighborhoods, local residents tend to see politicians as *aproveitadores* (users) or as those who take advantage of the material desperation of poor communities during the electoral process to garner votes. Reflecting the general perception of black residents of Salvador's poorest neighborhoods, Gamboa de Baixo activists express that they have little confidence in the politicians who claim to represent the interests of local communities, on the one hand, but also support public policies that evict blacks from urban land, on the other. This critical relationship between the Gamboa de Baixo neighborhood and politicians provides an example of activists' rejection of class reductionism. This is particularly true with politicians who organize around class interests, but do not include race and gender in their analyses, claiming that they benefit poor black women workers and their urban neighborhoods.

Conclusion

In 2004, a group of mostly white male Swiss graduate students visited Gamboa de Baixo to learn about grassroots organizing in Salvador and throughout Brazil. After traveling to other parts of Brazil, including the Amazonian region, they were greeted by a group of female community leaders in Gamboa de Baixo. I served as the translator for the Swiss group, and many asked questions about the age and gender of the local activists. In large part, the activists were comprised of young women like Lu, a woman in her early twenties, and Ana Cristina, a then active thirty-year-old. Shocked, to say the least, the students commented that they had expected older men to be at the forefront of the movement. In fact, they had brought with them a masculine Swiss watch to present to the neighborhood association's president, who they had expected to be male.

When presenting the gift, they apologized for their assumptions and expressed that the female leadership and participation challenged their own internalized social prescriptions of women's political agency. Furthermore, they

stated that to see black women in these positions of leadership was a brave defiance of the overt racism they were surprised to have witnessed during their
trip to Brazil. With knowledge of social movements in indigenous and black
communities, their previous conceptions of Brazil's "racial democracy" had
been shattered. Moreover, one man expressed in an emotional tale that, having been previously bombarded by negative over-sexualized representations
of black women as prostitutes in Europe, female-led political mobilization in
Brazil made him face his own racism and sexism.

The preceding description of the group of European males visiting Gamboa exemplifies the global perception of black women and the lack of knowledge of black women's politics throughout the African diaspora. While it is
difficult to believe that their experiences on one day in Gamboa de Baixo
might have completely changed their individual and collective views of black
women, my understanding of this global invisibility of black women was
heightened. Though black women have always been key figures in black liberation struggles worldwide, the likes of Fannie Lou Hamer, Luiza Mahim, Lélia
Gonzales, and Amy Jacques Garvey have been ignored. Thus, sexist and racist
notions regarding black women's ability to produce political knowledge and
lead political organizations are reproduced.

Defying expectations of their roles as workers, mothers, fisherwomen, and
activists, poor black women in Gamboa de Baixo, with their unique political
assertion, have disrupted the usual social and political order in Salvador. Black
women, who represent the largest numbers in domestic work, are viewed on
a daily basis as subservient, submissive, and obedient. In fact, the only black
women that most of the elite whites who govern the city ever interact with,
often throughout their lifetimes, are the housekeepers and babysitters who
work in their homes. For black women to occupy a dominant political space
in meetings and protests as leaders of their communities challenges prevalent
disparaging stereotypes of poor black women and forces us to consider them
as important agents of social change.

The experiences in Gamboa de Baixo show that the neighborhood association represents an important political space for black women to assert their
local power and leadership. Women's everyday interactions such as removing
their neighbors' clothes from the line when it starts to rain or discussing land
disputes on each other's doorsteps provides a visible example of just how
much the personal and the political mingle at the community level. Organizing in the neighborhood enacts radical social change from the home place
where black people live, work, and play. Furthermore, as leaders of these kinds
of organizations, black women bring to the forefront their unique ideas and
methods of social protest that expand our knowledge of racial and gender
consciousness, at all levels of society. Gamboa de Baixo activists organize as

blacks, women, and poor people, leading to more expansive definitions of black womanhood and social movements on a global scale.

Moreover, the ethnographic examples from the Gamboa de Baixo neighborhood association show that black women's political actions constitute a continuation of their everyday acts of community building. The participation of black women in grassroots organizations is not an anomaly, but visible female leadership continues to be sparse in most neighborhood associations. I emphasize that domestic workers are key to the development of female leadership as a result of their knowledge gained as "outsiders-within." My argument also supports the idea that these women have common interests as workers; their work experience affects the maintenance of their home spaces. More importantly, poor black women choose to organize as residents of their neighborhoods rather than as workers because they understand that the dominance of domestic work, oppressive at its core, should not be preserved. In their social movement to improve their neighborhood, black women demand improvements in their social conditions, primarily for access to education that will prepare them for other areas of employment.

Furthermore, there are gendered differences in grassroots organizing that impact the outcome of negotiations with the state. From the experiences of the female Gamboa de Baixo activists, I conclude that their relative success is the result of the women's reluctance to deal with the state individually and their preference for collective social transformation. As black feminist theorists such as Patricia Hill Collins have argued, women activists in black liberation struggles have worked for the collective benefit of their communities. The challenge remains, however, how to negotiate between personal and communal transformation as part of their overall political projects. This challenge reflects a complex relationship of gender and racial oppression that black women experience as invisible workers, while underlining their vision for liberation from this form of enslavement.

V

GENDER AND WOMEN'S MOVEMENTS

Women delegates at the March against Neoliberalism at the Forum against Neoliberalism, Huitiupan, Chiapas, March 2004. Photo courtesy of Alicia C. S. Swords.

WOMEN'S MOVEMENTS IN LATIN AMERICA began to receive more attention when the United Nations organized the first world conference on women in Mexico City in 1975. Both the movements and the scholarship have evolved since then, and several historical developments in the region have shaped the context of those changes. One significant trend is the wave of transitions away from military-authoritarian rule that has been occurring across the region since the mid-1980s, reflecting a combination of popular mobilizations from below and pacts among the political class. Argentina's Mothers of Plaza de Mayo illustrates the power of women to challenge brutal systems of authoritarian power. Both military rule and the economic austerity programs it facilitated through coercive demobilization (pioneered under General Pinochet and the "Chicago Boys" in Chile) had a gendered impact on Latin American societies. In their wake, the continuing struggles for democracy and social justice highlight tensions between the patriarchal character of traditional modes of politics and the new gender consciousness and central role of women in social movements in the region.

Neoliberal "structural adjustment programs" have also pushed more women into the (low-) paid workforce and intensified the unremunerated household and community labors assigned disproportionately to women. Increasing labor migration in the era of globalization has affected community and family dynamics (especially in Mexico, Central America, and the Caribbean), all heightening gender consciousness and altering the organizing conditions for women in social movements. While the personal has become explicitly political (reflected in the slogan of the Chilean women's movement in the Pinochet era, "Democracy in the country and at home!"), the domestic has also become global.

Verónica Schild's 1994 article on neighborhood organizing in Chile in the 1980s and 1990s broke new ground in several ways. Her work introduced gender analysis to the study of urban popular movements and in the process challenged the invisibility of women in previous studies. Schild's research revealed the extraeconomic motivations leading women to organize as social subjects, developing a "gender-specific culture of citizenship" through the process of political learning and collective action. The study also pointed out the patriarchal mind-set in many international nongovernmental organizations and the class divide between middle-class feminists and *pobladoras* (women in poor neighborhoods), which required a negotiation of differences within the movement.

Joanna Swanger's article examines the case of Casa Amiga, a feminist organization in Ciudad Juárez on the Mexico-U.S. border. The group addresses issues of domestic violence and the wave of "femicides," or murders, of over 300 women in that city since the mid-1990s, mostly young migrants and workers in the *maquiladoras* (border assembly factories or sweatshops). Swanger's study of border life captures the alienation and violence that are part of the gendered experience of globalization. Yet she finds hope in the movement's radical creation of community, in the form of a culture of *convivio* (solidarity and mutual respect) among organized women.

The chapters in this section make clear that the models and cultures people create within their organizations, neighborhoods, and families are not just ethnographic curiosities but are in fact central to sustaining movements for fundamental social change. Movements are built by people seeking not just to resist the abstract injustice of exploitation but also to sustain community in the face of atomizing and alienating pressures in their everyday lives. These feminist insights are important for understanding not only women's participation but social movement dynamics in general.

Gendered analysis of social movements brought to the forefront the importance of the "struggle within the struggle" as a central reality in the process of consciousness raising, organizing, and resistance. As women fought for space and voice within organizations, they developed important strategies that contested gender-defined power relationships. A major outcome of these strategies is more democratic social movements. The struggle within the struggle has also highlighted another arena of contestation, one between first and third world feminisms. In this struggle, important advances in gender theory have resulted, as well as new ways of thinking about the meaning and practice of solidarity.

13

Recasting "Popular" Movements

Gender and Political Learning in Neighborhood Organizations in Chile

Verónica Schild

THE FUNDAMENTAL ROLE OF WOMEN was a key feature of neighborhood-based organizations in Chile in the 1980s–90s, raising important questions about the way popular movement organizations, and popular movements more generally, have been analyzed. Women's involvement in neighborhood-based activities is not new in Chile. During the 1960s and particularly during the early 1970s, women joined a variety of organizations in their neighborhoods or *poblaciones*. The 1980s, however, saw a veritable explosion of organizations. Moreover, the forms these organizations took were new. Groups in the urban periphery of Santiago are predominantly economic groups or handicraft workshops in which people generate some form of income. More than 90 percent of those involved in them are women (Hardy, 1987; Bustamante, 1985). Furthermore, comparative studies show that the overwhelming presence of women in neighborhood organizations is a phenomenon recurring throughout Latin America (e.g., Barrig, 1991; Corcoran-Nantes, 1990).

The newer organizations emerged in the mid-1970s with the aid of the Catholic Church as a response to the devastating effects of the economic policies and political repression of the Pinochet regime. Although the church continued to be their main supporter, these groups also received help from other sponsors—national and international nongovernmental institutions (NGOs).

In the 1990s the political context in which the neighborhood organizations emerged had changed, but the economic situation of the poorest segment of Chilean society had not significantly improved. Patricio Aylwin's center-left

The original version of this essay appeared in *Latin American Perspectives* 21(2), Spring 1994: 59–80.

coalition government (1990–94) took some steps to change this. For example, in 1991 it doubled the minimum monthly wage. However, neither unemployment nor underemployment decreased significantly immediately after the presidential elections of 1990. Increasing the minimum wage may reach some people, but does not affect those who continue to eke out a living through activities in the informal sector, as suggested by the discontent with the government's employment policies revealed by a September 1991 survey conducted in some poblaciones of Santiago's urban periphery (Vicente Espinoza, SUR Consultores, personal communication). Furthermore, the church, a key actor in fostering and supporting women's income-generating activities during the past decade, began shifting its attention and resources away from them (interview, Coti Silva, official with Servicio Nacional de la Mujer and leader of the Movimiento de Mujeres Pobladoras, Santiago, November 5, 1991). These developments made it difficult to assess the degree to which both government policies and the actions of the church affected neighborhood-based organizations. One thing is clear, however; throughout the 1980s economic groups continued to multiply in Santiago's poblaciones (Oxhorn, 1991: 86).

Women's neighborhood organizations have captured the attention of analysts searching for the ongoing institutional network buttressing a potentially new popular movement in Chile. Despite evidence of the important presence of women, these analysts have ignored the ways in which gender has shaped the character and practices of these groups. This chapter seeks to address a key problem so far left untouched in the popular movement debate—the politics of gendered participation among poor and working-class people. I aim to show how and why the newer neighborhood-based groups have made a significant cultural-political difference to women. I will first examine how the debate on the popular movement in Chile renders women invisible. I will go on to propose an alternative starting point for understanding the significance of women's recent neighborhood organizations. Beginning from the standpoint of the participants themselves, this approach places the organizations in the context of women's broader organizational life.

The Popular Movement Debate: Rendering Women Textually Invisible

Much has been written about the novelty of Latin American popular urban organizations and whether they constitute social movements, but very little has been said in this context about the women who play the predominant role in these groups. In the case of Chile, some studies have mentioned the important role of women, but they have done so in a purely descriptive manner. Others have simply dismissed the groups as apolitical. Typically, the practices of these groups have been seen as expressions of solidarity or as defensive cultural strategies limited to ensuring the survival of popular communities threatened with anomie. Eugenio Tironi's studies are a good illustration; he sought from the outset a gender-neutral popular actor—modeled, in fact, on the political culture and practices of some men—and did not find one (Tironi, 1990; 1987).

Other studies take the existence of a popular social movement for granted. Although women have been the objects of these studies—soup kitchens, handicraft workshops, and other so-called organized survival strategies have been examined—the gendered nature of these activities is rendered invisible in written accounts. These activities are typically framed in a discourse—with roots in Christian communitarianism—whose central elements are the categories *popular* and *communitarian* (Garretón, 1989; Valdes, 1987; Hardy, 1987; and Hardy and Razeto, 1984). Even Guillermo Campero, who goes farthest toward making women visible in his comprehensive study of neighborhood organizations, ultimately misses the significance of these collective activities (Campero, 1987). Relying on too narrow a conception of politics, he sees an expressive value in these activities but attributes to them no political importance.

Beyond exploring descriptively women's involvement in popular movement organizations, Campero and others have failed to associate an interest in movements with a detailed understanding of the social relations in which people involved in them are enmeshed—relations that ultimately give shape to the phenomenon. Indeed, the significance of these collective activities is abstracted from the very concrete, gendered context in which they evolve, namely, the realm of reproduction—typically, woman's realm—and is then invariably sought somewhere else (see Serrano, 1988). Questions such as the conditions under which women become involved and the character of their participation are not asked. In short, what is missing from these studies and from the Chilean debate on popular social movements more generally (see, e.g., Oxhorn, 1991; Schneider, 1991; Petras and Leiva, 1986) is an adequate representation of the phenomenon as gendered and a more complex characterization of the nature and scope of specifically poor and working-class women's own political culture and practice.

Following a pattern in the social sciences (ruled by a tacit gendered division of intellectual labor), attending to the important question of gender in relation to popular social movements in Latin America is a task so far undertaken almost exclusively by women. In fact, a growing body of literature that makes women visible in popular movement organizations has begun to elucidate the implications of *engendering* the popular movement debate (Caldeira, 1990; Alvarez, 1990; Jacquette, 1991). The following exposition aims to offer this more complex representation in the Chilean case. The subtext of my analysis is that gender as a key analytical category in the Latin American popular movement debate should be attended to by everyone and not only by women writing about other women.

The Newer Organizations: A Look from Within

Many women in Santiago's poblaciones were compelled to join neighborhood groups in the 1980s because of economic necessity. Other women, however, were motivated to join groups out of a growing need to do something, a direct response to their experience with political repression—losing a husband or a son or both—or witnessing a neighbor's loss. Still others joined groups because they felt isolated and bored at home; for them it was a natural thing to do.

Most women who joined groups for a number of different reasons ultimately found themselves in handicraft workshops. In part this was because after 1975 the Catholic Church vicariate's involvement in lending support to income-generating activities became common knowledge in the neighborhoods. Women who wanted to start or join groups simply turned to their neighbors, kin, or local priests for information. Joining a workshop often entailed immediate, tangible benefits for those in a desperate economic situation. Not only did new members receive materials and technical expertise, they also received a package of foodstuffs from the vicariate.

More generally, women's involvement in their neighborhoods illustrates how gender shaped both the policies of the authoritarian state and the opportunities for action available to women. Poor and working-class women have traditionally been responsible for the tasks of reproduction and also for supplementing inadequate family incomes (see Centro de Estudios de la Mujer, 1988; Ward, 1990; Beneria and Roldan, 1987; Beneria and Sen, 1981). The dismantling of the welfare state and restructuring of the economy forced many homemakers to supplement the dwindling or nonexistent incomes of their spouses on a permanent basis. These women turned in unprecedented numbers to government make-work programs (Cheyre and Ogrodnick, 1982; Schkolnik and Teitelboim, 1988; and Centro de Estudios de la Mujer, 1988). They also turned to the church. By sponsoring women's income-generating activities in poor neighborhoods this institution filled the void left by a retreating welfare state.

For some women, joining a handicraft workshop was a first step out of a homebound life. For others, these organizations constituted a link with the past, not a sudden break. Many older women had been active in mothers' centers, neighborhood councils, and other church-based or party-based local initiatives since the 1960s. Younger ones had been active in youth initiatives begun during the Popular Unity government and in the local cells of leftist parties. Although most groups were either suppressed or taken over by the Pinochet regime, these activists found alternative activities during the early years of the dictatorship. In addition, a new generation of activists emerged after 1973. These younger women acquired organizational experience primarily through church-sponsored youth activities such as the Girl Guides. Some of them also joined mothers' centers once they married. For many young adults the mothers' centers continued to be an important step in their activist lives.

The foregoing account suggests that the newer neighborhood organizations did not come into being *ex nihilo*. Instead, they formed part of an ongoing network of collective work sustained by women whose involvement has a distinct pattern. For example, women leaders of newer groups—and other activists who do not necessarily hold leadership positions—often share organizational skills and know-how accumulated in a variety of settings. Women may simultaneously be members of different local groups. During the dictatorship it was not uncommon to find the same women in church philanthropy or catechism groups, church-sponsored handicraft workshops, and party- or NGO-sponsored women's groups. Often women had belonged at one time or another to the Girl Guides, a catechism group, a government-controlled mothers' center, and a church group. Clearly, then, the significance of recent organizations must be understood in the context of the distinct patterning of women's organizational activity in the neighborhoods.

Women Organizing Over Time

Often women joined handicraft workshops expecting to quit as soon as their economic situation improved. For those who stayed on, cooperative work had acquired an added meaning. Women suggested an interest in learning and in personal growth as reasons for continuing to take part in handicraft workshops. They found an extraeconomic appeal in their organizations, similar to what Barrig (1991) found about similar experiences in Lima. Eugenia, a *pobladora* from the southern periphery trained as a social worker who became a member of a local women's NGO, describes the transformation that occurred with handicraft and other neighborhood-based groups sponsored by the Southern Vicariate where she previously worked:

> After a while, the church backed away from the emergency-type activities it had initiated soon after the coup and concentrated specifically on human rights

cases. By then, however, many women who had joined those groups—the majority of members were women anyway—wanted to go on participating in group activities and asked for very concrete help from the vicariate. This is how the vicariate began to develop its work with women, focusing primarily on education seminars. At first this work focused exclusively on the issue of fear, of intimidation, basically of how to face this period together. This is when a number of pobladoras like me began to join the vicariate's team. Some of us did so out of Christian convictions, others for party-political reasons because they lacked a space for action, and still others, who had been active in mothers' centers, because they refused to go on with Lucia Pinochet [Pinochet's wife] in control.

To suggest, as Campero and others do, that the noneconomic appeal of the groups and women's continued involvement in them constitutes a defensive response by *people* to their socioeconomic and political exclusion is insufficient. Pobladoras, after all, have always been excluded. The answer lies elsewhere.

Seen in the context of the ongoing *continuum of collective activities* of pobladoras, these groups are spaces in which many women acquire the elements of a gender-specific culture of citizenship (Jelin, 1990). This form of political learning involves challenging preestablished boundaries of appropriate feminine behavior and is lived by women as learning to experience themselves as confident, competent beings and acting accordingly. Practices that embody questions about who they are, what their rights are, and what fields of action are appropriately theirs are a central aspect of learning to become political agents. To use more conventional terms, developing a sense of political efficacy (see Ackelsberg, 1988: 298; Pateman, 1970: 45–66) necessarily means questioning limiting gender relations and forging alternative identities.

Linking the activities of economic-type organizations to a gender-specific process of political learning requires a notion of politics that goes beyond conventionally narrow conceptions. In this context politics is not simply about (to paraphrase Lasswell's classic formulation) who gets what, when, and how—whether individually or collectively. The "who" is not unitary and homogeneous but multiple and not equally able to participate (Pateman, 1988; Benhabib and Cornell, 1987; Young, 1989; Dietz, 1987). Politics is also about challenges to power relations that set the limits within which we define ourselves and establish our differential participation. Politics includes struggles for subjectivities—what Bowles and Gintis (1986), following Foucault (1980b, 1982), have called a "politics of becoming." Politics in this context is "also a contest over who we are to become, a contest in which identity, interests, and solidarity are as much the outcome as the starting point of political activity" (Bowles and Gintis, 1986: 8). Political learning *is* also about culture, for it involves the vocabularies and activities through which we shape our identities—what could be called the cultural-discursive resources available to us. Political learning in this context is a form of cultural production through everyday language that involves competent and creative participants, not passive receivers of preestablished discourses. It is used here to account for individuals' active relation to their subjectivities.

Challenging the boundaries of appropriate feminine behavior is a slow and uneven process that often begins with an exploration of one's own body. Eugenia describes a technique she has used in workshops on sexuality that her group has led with women since the mid-1980s:

> Women in my area have a profound lack of knowledge about their bodies. We make them draw their bodies and discover that they are not aware of certain parts. For example, many think that they urinate and have relations through the same place and are convinced, therefore, that if they run to the bathroom after having relations they can avoid getting pregnant. Few women, only the younger ones, know that they have a clitoris. Myths about sexuality are also widespread. Although the idea that in sex there are two kinds of women, married women who are "*madres de sus hijos*" (their children's mothers) and can only engage in certain forms of sex, and "others" who can engage in other forms of sex, is common in men, it is also deeply engrained in women. In one case, after one of the workshops, a woman told me that when she lived with her husband prior to marriage their sex life had been very good, but soon after marrying there had been a negative change.

Julia, a pobladora activist from a neighborhood in La Pintana who in the mid-1980s had joined a local women's group and now worked locally for an NGO organizing women in nearby poblaciones, describes another technique:

> Sometimes I bring a little box into a group and I announce, "Today we will look at the most important person in this group." We sit on the floor in a circle and I hand the box to one of them. She must open it without revealing its contents to the rest. When she does, there is a mirror that she must stare at in silence. . . . When everyone has done this we begin to describe what we saw, who we saw, and why this person is the most important . . . it is very powerful.

Workshops like the ones described by Eugenia and Julia, which illustrate the opportunities for learning that organized women refer to, have been shaped by these activists' ongoing contacts with middle-class professionals. In some cases, the professionals themselves have reached leaders of neighborhood groups directly through workshops.

Pobladoras who have participated in these workshops entered networks that could be called "symbolic" (in addition to "material") because they consist of an exchange of "knowledge" in language and because what women obtain through these networks are cultural-discursive resources. These resources make a difference not only with regard to how women act in relation to sexuality but also with regard to violence, parenting, and legal rights. Through this network women have learned to "know" differently and to act differently.

To distinguish between symbolic and material networks is, of course, somewhat artificial. One could rightly argue that the material aid that the groups receive from the church and NGOs, such as money, materials, or goods, is every bit as symbolic as the exchange of knowledge because it too is mediated by language. However, "symbolic" is used here simply to distinguish between the types of "goods" being exchanged. While in one case the goods involved are technical know-how, money, wool, foodstuffs, and the like, in the other "knowledge" about issues such as sexuality, legal rights, and parenting is exchanged. In this sense the distinction is very important because it underscores an aspect of the interactions between groups and NGOs that is too often neglected.

Through the symbolic network, ordinary members, group leaders, and pobladora activists working locally with women come in contact with popular educators, nurses, social workers, lawyers, and psychologists. This in itself is not new: historically pobladoras have been in contact with such middle-class women, for example, through the government-sanctioned mothers' centers. One could argue that their interactions with middle-class professionals are of questionable benefit because they are relations of unequal power: the latter possess "knowledge" while the former simply receive it. To do so, however, would be to misrepresent the relation between these women and to overlook the new possibilities it offers.

The professional women working for NGOs (many of whom lived until recently as exiles abroad) with whom organized pobladoras come in contact have tended to be on the left and to work for feminist goals. Defining themselves as feminists, however, has not been easy for them, especially for those who had long been leftist activists. Marcela, a nurse who joined the vicariate in the early 1980s after a period in exile and then became director of a women's NGO that works with pobladoras, describes her individual and group transformation:

> We cannot deny the fundamental role that the church played as a site where our feminist reflection began. Eventually, women's NGOs multiplied rapidly, and the innovative techniques they developed, for example, the *trabajo corporal* [body or experiential work] begun by DOMOS [an NGO that offers counseling to women], became widespread. What is clear is that professionals involved in those activities had at one time or another worked with solidarity teams of the church.
>
> We who formed this NGO began to reflect on the specifics of women's condition and gender issues when we worked in the solidarity team of the vicariate.

After all, the majority of groups with which the church worked were made up of women. However, we found it very difficult to define ourselves as feminists back then. In fact, even when we became an independent NGO we did not define ourselves as such. At that time there was a rejection of the label not only from the side of the church but also from the left. To be labeled a feminist was almost a stigma, one we wanted to avoid. Ours was, therefore, a very gradual definition as a feminist collective, privately at first and only then publicly.

The political inclinations and practices of women like Marcela shape their relations with pobladoras and translate into a commitment to work *with* them rather than *for* them, which means at the very least making resources for action available to them. More important, however, this means that for pobladora leaders the terms of their relationship with these professionals are in principle open to challenge, and this is expressed in their everyday speech as a demand to be recognized for their own worth and to be treated as equals. Organized pobladoras are not passive receivers of middle-class benevolence.

Professional women are often accountable to the foreign NGOs that fund their income-generating activities. These NGOs have had a mandate to support (and regulate through funding criteria) work with poor women. This mandate can be traced in turn to the activities generated in conjunction with the United Nations resolution on women, the Decade of Women (1975–1985), and to shifting conceptions of effective development aid in donor countries. Although the relations between donor agencies and professionals from NGOs are conflictive at times, professionals working within the church or in large male-dominated NGOs not infrequently have found support from their international sponsors for their work with women. For example, in the late 1980s the church began to redefine the scope and content of its social work. When members of the vicariate's solidarity teams—middle-class professionals and, in some cases, pobladora activists—were asked to choose between teaching the Bible and finding alternative employment, a number of them founded free-standing women's NGOs with the support of donors. In one case, the entire team of the Southern Vicariate—most of whom were pobladoras—left the church and formed a women's NGO with the support of their Swedish Christian-based donor. In addition, the fact that Julia from La Pintana is involved in organizing other pobladoras in the context of a large "mixed" NGO at all is itself an illustration of the complex relations between donor agencies, local NGOs, and their competing agendas. Professional women within the NGO, who are in the minority, were able to create an area of work with women after the elections of 1989 only with the support of the sponsoring agency, a Swedish labor union coalition.

Important elements of a feminist discourse, or rather a multiplicity of discourses, originating in these settings through the ongoing activities that bring professionals and pobladora activists and group leaders together have found their way to the poblaciones. However, the interaction between these women is not facilitated by some substratum of shared experiences. Class relations— mediated by experiences of race, ethnicity, age, and other factors—shape women's lives differently. This is important to emphasize given the temptation, implicit at least, for some feminists reflecting on the so-called Latin American women's movement to search for shared gender experiences that presumably guarantee the "real underlying unity among women" and spell out the possibility of political action. This is a form of feminist essentialism that glosses over the diversity of women's experiences and ultimately devalues the experiences of poor and working-class women. The critique of feminist essentialism within North America (Riley, 1988; Spelman, 1988) needs to be systematically extended to the Latin American case. An article describing the conflicts between middle-class and working-class feminists at regional meetings (Saporta Sternbach et al., 1992) suggests that the latter are increasingly less willing to accept their position as the subordinate "others" of Latin American feminisms.

Conflicts of needs, interests, and expectations continually arise among these women, given their very different social positions. The discourse of middle-class feminists has often been seen by pobladoras as misinformed and paternalistic because it disregards the specificities of their condition. Yet, it is this very discourse that, appropriated creatively by pobladoras, accounts for their increasing reluctance to be "spoken to." Ironically, the strong emphasis on equality and rights, a key feminist element made available to pobladoras, has encouraged these women (albeit leaders more than regular members) not only to speak differently about themselves and their place in the world but also to question their relations with middle-class feminists.

Negotiating Differences

In their accounts of what they actually do in their groups and how they position themselves vis-à-vis others, women members reveal a complex and tentative process. The process of organizing in which they take part entails negotiating differences not only with professional women but also among themselves. The tension around the choice of activities is an important way in which differences among pobladoras are manifested. As we have seen, groups typically engage in activities ranging from handicraft workshops such as knitting, sewing, or pottery to educational workshops on sexuality, leadership training, and civic education, to which their leaders—through their network—invite an instructor. Some women, often younger ones with more formal education or women who have had previous organizational experience, want the group to become an educational workshop. For these women knitting, sewing, and other handicrafts may be a necessary starting point for a group, but they are only the beginning of a process that will lead them to learn about their rights and about health and sexuality and to acquire leadership skills. The remaining women value learning handicrafts as well as other activities such as workshops on sexuality and violence.

I was able to explore this tension with leaders of organizations and group delegates during a regional meeting of women's neighborhood groups from the southern periphery of Santiago, organized by Eugenia's NGO. Nearly 200 women came together to discuss the problems they were facing in their groups. A key difficulty that group leaders identified was the lack of interest of many ordinary members in more formal educational workshops and particularly in leadership training courses. Initially, the leaders argued that sheer laziness and irresponsibility were the reason for the members' lack of interest. In a small working group and with further probing, however, leaders brought up the issue of literacy. Many members, they suggested, tended to shy away from settings where they were required to read, write, and use other associated skills. Although few of them were totally illiterate, they had simply forgotten what little they had learned in school. In addition, because they experienced this loss of skills as something shameful, many women were reluctant to bring it up in the group.

What also became clear during this meeting was that some women had been much more successful than others in negotiating time for their activities. For example, while the young and dynamic leader of one group present in the discussion announced that she had managed to negotiate house chores and childcare with her husband, the others present reminded her that her situation was rather unusual. These women had faced or were still facing the double dilemma of negotiating household responsibilities and obtaining "permission" from their husbands to participate in activities outside the home. Not everyone, as it turned out, was equally successful at exerting her rights, at freeing herself from her husband's control. A number had done so at the price of physical violence. Thus, what for some was a sign of moral fiber and liberation was for others simply a matter of luck.

Some analysts have suggested that the new economic roles pobladora women were forced to adopt during the period of acute economic crisis has led to changes in their domestic roles (e.g., Valenzuela, 1987; Cleary, 1988). Economic need, according to this view, forces women to come out of their homes and start collaborating with others. Carrying out duties competently in spheres other than the home and sharing experiences allow women to question their personal situations in a wider context; in turn, this leads them to become conscious of their class and sexual oppression and to develop a sense of solidarity based on their common identity. The lived experiences of different women suggest that this is a rather mechanical and partial account; the mediating role of ideology is not properly analyzed. As I have suggested, there is no such thing as a substratum of women's experience that, once discovered, leads to a total identification or sense of sameness. Solidarity for these women is not the outcome of discovering an identical experience or essence that lies beyond language; it is, rather, a negotiation of differences *in* language.

Beyond the organizations, women in the poblaciones share a situation of poverty that many experience on a daily basis as a struggle to make ends meet. For these women, the lived experiences of class and gender are crisscrossed by other differentiating factors. Central among these is status, though ethnic and regional origin, political and religious affiliations, and even sexual preferences may play a role. Status-based differences—long ignored in class analysis (Lockwood, 1981)—are very real for pobladoras, and, as is to be expected, women who enjoy a better economic situation and/or a higher level of formal education have a greater interest in maintaining these differences. A strong moral component and an intimate knowledge of the histories of one's neighbors come into play in establishing status. Maintaining a sense of oneself in the neighborhood entails a complex and at times very subtle strategy of distinctions. Thus, lived status differences give rise to further hierarchies among women.

The desire for self-improvement is also an important indicator of differentiation among younger women who are active in women's groups, although very often they lack homes of their own and must live as "*allegadas*" (sharing a house or a lot with relatives or with strangers). For them, having "*otras inquietudes*" (other personal aspirations or interests) figures prominently. Any number of things may be signaled by the term "inquietudes," but ultimately they all relate to a sense of being different, of being committed to, or showing a desire for, self-improvement. When these women describe the gains they have made in their groups, they very often mention the fact that they have acquired "otras inquietudes" or that it was their different aspirations that led them to join a group in the first place. Thus, leaders and activists who have come to see themselves as "*liberadas*" (liberated) use what they see as their feminist awareness as a further tool of differentiation.

Organized Women: Multiple Experiences

Depending on their level of education, their degree of involvement in organizations, and especially their past organizational experience, women appear to have benefited differently. Those who see themselves over time in a more active relation to their organizations, the doers and movers in their groups who may have come to have leading positions in them, have developed a sense of self-esteem that has translated into a strong commitment to collective work, if not to the particular organization they were involved with initially. These women have learned to question power relations and to speak in terms of their rights. They have also, to varying degrees, learned to confront recalcitrant husbands and to deal effectively with people in positions of authority, for example, doctors, social workers, or schoolteachers with whom they are in regular contact, including the professional women with whom they have worked. "*Hacerse respetar*" (eliciting respect from others) and "*pelear por sus derechos*" (fighting for one's rights) figure prominently in the speech of these pobladoras.

The label *feminism* was initially an important differentiating term for many of these women; it allowed them to distinguish between themselves and organized middle-class women. The label *feminist* is one many women refused to appropriate for themselves in the 1980s. When asked about feminism, one typical response was "Feminists are extremists, just as *machistas* are. They want everything to be done their way, just as men want things done theirs" (Eli, a member of a women's group in the southern periphery). Other women had a more subtle understanding of feminism that reflected an awareness of class-based differences. This awareness was expressed as recognition of pobladoras' limited possibilities compared with middle-class others. As Eloisa, a member of a workshop in the west side of Santiago, put it, "I say I am not a feminist because they [middle-class feminists] speak a lot about liberation but we will always be conditioned by our children. . . . If they lack food, we have to provide it for them" (quoted in Angelo, 1987: 92). Today many leaders of neighborhood organizations do not hesitate to call themselves feminists, but they invariably qualify this label. As Carmen, leader of a women's group, explains:

> We have always felt that we are different—yes, we are all women, but we live our discrimination differently. For example, it is true that the law discriminates against all women. But it affects the poor more than the rich because the rich know how to work with it, how to move around it, whereas we very often don't even know the laws exist! Thus, discrimination and the process of liberation acquire very different connotations for the two groups of women. To give you another example, bourgeois feminists talk about discrimination in the work-place, sexual harassment on the job, and so on, taking for granted that the workplace is where all women are located. . . . In the world of pobladoras, where the majority are homemakers, paid work is seen as something they still have to fight for, many don't even feel that it is a right. In fact, only recently, I remember last March 8,

many pobladoras began to talk about this right to work. These are women who either have never left their homes or have worked throughout their adult lives in sporadic jobs . . . but the idea of a formal job, the idea of the right to a salary, to work-time, this they are barely discovering.

Carmen and other pobladora activists have little doubt about the significance of middle-class feminism for poor and working-class women: "Even though women continue to be beaten at home and subjugated, they are beginning to speak about their rights and to take stands one wouldn't have dreamt of ten years ago." It is, however, Carmen's own careful distinction between women like herself and middle-class feminists that illustrates the impact of feminist discourses on the construction of subjectivities and collective identities by organized pobladoras. By claiming to speak about the reality of all women, such discourses are forcing women who do not feel identified by this representation to articulate their own sense of who they are. For example, if, as pobladora activists have often pointed out, the line initially used by some middle-class feminists about women having to liberate themselves from their families, especially from their children, is deeply offensive to them, then they are faced with the realization that their families are indeed very important to them.

In the course of acquiring a sense of personal and political efficacy, women who choose to participate in advocacy groups with men face the greatest challenge. It is one thing to develop a capacity for decision making and to acquire a public voice in a predominantly female context; it is quite another to carry these achievements into contexts in which unequal gender relations have historically appropriated for men both the public voice (with its distinct political vocabulary) and the power of decision making. The leaders of *coordinadoras* and *sectoriales* (regional or middle-level representative bodies of neighborhood organizations) have tended, with few exceptions, to be party-affiliated men (see Valdes, Weinstein, and Malinarich, 1988). Women leaders of neighborhood organizations have often complained about the authoritarian style and structure of such bodies, which in effect follow a union or party organizational model. These women have felt marginalized from decision-making. Elsa, a member of a workshop on the west side of Santiago, explains, "At the meetings of the coordinadora they try to ignore us because we complain that only three women attend. In those meetings the leader behaves like a dictator. Sitting in front of the room he tells women: 'Okay, five minutes for you, read the report,' and so on. . . . Imagine, if Pinochet is overthrown men are going to go on deciding everything" (quoted in Angelo, 1987: 82).

Women attending these meetings have often felt that politically motivated leaders ignore the needs and wishes of the grass roots and impose their own logic on grass-roots collective efforts. Feeling powerless and angered, many lose interest in these middle-level organizations. Elsa summarizes the frustration of many pobladoras with their treatment by male activists: "Women are not taken into consideration when plans and decisions are made. These are men's things. But they sure are taken advantage of when it's time to go to a demonstration or to build barricades in the streets" (quoted in Angelo, 1987: 82). However, as some pobladora leaders have pointed out, too often it is the women themselves, feeling inadequate and ill-prepared to participate in a public forum, who will choose a man to speak on their behalf. These women lack not only the power but also the skills and know-how to appropriate political spaces such as regional bodies. It is conceivable that the failure of efforts to organize the various neighborhood groups into viable regional bodies is linked in part to women's subordinate position in the wider political arena (see Campero, 1987; Oxhorn, 1991).

Politics as Struggles for Subjectivities

Neighborhood organizations are important for pobladoras as a means of becoming political agents. This does not mean that these women were passive in the past. Historically, poor and working-class women played important (if invisible) roles in urban struggles. However, most did so within the boundaries of what was considered (and they themselves lived) as appropriately feminine behavior. Castells (1984: 32, 308–309) makes a similar observation about women's mobilization for urban struggles more generally. Thus, most poor and working-class women participated on a temporary basis and in a subordinate position. The boundaries of appropriate feminine behavior are established in very real ways for pobladoras through the routines that constitute their everyday lives. Most women have been prevented from becoming significantly engaged in collective activities by structural limitations embedded in many of their day-to-day social relations. These social relations, shaped by a sex/gender system or gender subtext that legitimates sexual inequality, are limiting and actively exclude most women from the political process.

Daily social relations also shape the social meanings through which poor and working-class women make sense of themselves and their place in the world. Women's commonsense language shapes their lived senses of self, their emotions, and their conscious and unconscious thoughts, that is, their *subjectivities* (Weedon, 1987: 32; Henriques et al., 1984) in important ways. In this context, an individual's sense of self should be understood to be multiple, often contradictory, and open to redefinition. Furthermore, it is not naturally given but socially and historically constructed. However, it is important to emphasize the investment people make in their senses of self. To refer to lived subjectivities as contradictory is to speak of an intricate negotiation that often involves pain and anguish, not the effortless slipping in and out of this or that "subject position" posited by Laclau and Mouffe (1985). As Eugenia describes it,

> Exploring our identity as women, the ways we have been taught to behave like "proper women" in many areas of our lives, and learning that we can move beyond these is often very painful. Many times, in this process of personal growth we leave our husbands behind. The outcome can be very good for the couple in the long run, but more often it means the end of the marriage. For pobladoras who have little or no economic security this can be a very high price to pay.

The social meanings that constitute everyday language are not neutral but produced within social institutions, such as the family and the school, that establish proper ways of performing socially. These social meanings—with their gender subtext—regulate women's behavior by promoting some capacities and suppressing others. These organized social meanings and practices, which organize women's lives in specific ways, can be seen as discourses of correct womanhood or dominant discourses of femininity.

The way in which poor and working-class women identify themselves and their place in the world is an outcome over time of their interaction with the church, the state, the family, and other institutions. However, domination, in this case in the form of the promotion of lived experiences that suppress and marginalize a whole range of human capacities, is never totalizing. It also creates possibilities for challenges and resistances, for ultimately people are not mere cultural dupes; they are *active subjects* who engage in renegotiating their subjectivities, transforming their experiences, and shaping their collective identities. Thus, learning to speak in their own voices may very well lead—and in some cases already is leading—many organized pobladoras to new-found capacities. To paraphrase the Brazilian anthropologist Teresa Pires de Rio Caldeira, they are trading their subordinate position in political struggles for forms of participation "without masks."

14

Casa Amiga

Feminist Community-Building in Ciudad Juárez as an Alternative to the Structural Violence of Globalization

Joanna Swanger

PROPONENTS OF NEOLIBERALISM assure us that if each of us plays by the rules, then the laws of global capitalism will eventually serve to enhance the welfare of all. This process toward unfettered capitalism's promise of a world of prosperity goes by the name of "globalization," and included within this benign-sounding word are phenomena which many would rather not acknowledge: e.g., the concentration of landholdings in fewer hands; increasing rural unemployment, poverty and displacement; ecological degradation; and increased migration flows. Within the neoliberal conception of the way the world works, society is—and should be—organized around the profit-motive, for the profit-motive drives production and, according to the theory's proponents, ensures that the factors of production are organized to assure maximum efficiency and thus the benefit of the greatest good.

Globalization is both an historical phase of capitalism and the process whereby localities, regions, and nation-states, under pressure from both the transnational capitalist class as well as structural forces within capitalism, rid themselves of older cultural practices—including small-scale use-value economies and social democracy—and accept in their stead the narrow rules associated with free-market exchange-value economies. Because "globalization" also suggests the convergence of the global South and global North, Ciudad Juárez, Chihuahua, Mexico, is one of the current foci of the processes that comprise globalization.

The original version of this essay appeared in *Latin American Perspectives* 34(2), March 2007: 108–123.

Casa Amiga, located in Ciudad Juárez, was the first crisis center for women in the entire northern Mexico border zone. Its staff focuses on issues of domestic violence and "femicide" (*feminicidio*), the term that has been applied to the problem faced currently in Ciudad Juárez, the site of a wave of unsolved murders of at least 340 women over the past twelve years (O. Rodríguez, 2005). The majority of those who have been the targets of this violence share certain characteristics: most are young (teenagers or in their early twenties); nearly all have been employees in the *maquiladoras*; and many of them share indigenous features that mark them as "outsiders" to Ciudad Juárez—i.e., they are from southern Mexico or other parts of the interior.

This essay builds upon Devon Peña's (1997) analysis of popular resistance to the production strategies of the *maquiladora* industry in Mexico. Peña argues that within capitalism, people in the working class are valued solely for their work on the shopfloor and are seen in a nearly one-dimensional way—i.e., as "workers"—and also that many who sympathize with and document social movements and portray labor exploitation often fall into a similar trap of seeing people in this one-dimensional way: as exploited and as victimized. He demonstrates how a grassroots organization was able to connect shopfloor struggle with neighborhood organization and challenge a wide range of injustices; in Peña's documentation of this struggle, the creation of a political consciousness with broad radical potential becomes clear. Peña's work is an important contribution to the literature on new social movements for its attention to the less spectacular work of quotidian community organizing. This essay also draws upon the work of Verónica Schild (1994; in this volume), for although men also work at Casa Amiga, the majority of the staff consists of women. Schild emphasizes that much of the work on popular movements focuses on moments of uprising, when men have historically been far more visible than women, and thus renders the less theatrical but crucial work performed mostly by women entirely invisible. A third influence upon the analysis employed herein is that of green economist Brian Milani (2000), whose work treats the human costs of the current dominant economic structure and the ways the economy can be transformed through organization especially at the local and regional levels. He counters the orthodox left tendency to label Fordist era movements as "particularistic" by arguing that these movements "have raised fundamental questions about the nature of and content of production, the very 'why' and 'how' of our work." For Milani, this fundamental question of quality of life is central to challenging neoliberalism and to designing sustainable alternatives to it (2000: 82–83).

Informed by these perspectives, this essay explores two principal questions: (1) Does Casa Amiga see a connection between domestic violence and femicide and between them and globalization, and if so, how is this connection articulated? (2) How does Casa Amiga create small-scale, local alternatives to globalization? I argue that Casa Amiga does indeed make a connection between globalization and violence against women and children, in that both are processes of dehumanization and manifestations of alienation; and that Casa Amiga creates a local alternative to globalization through working to restore a sense of empowerment and multidimensional humanity—i.e., through community-building.

As of the fall of 2004, Casa Amiga was staffed by twenty paid workers, thirteen of whom worked at Casa Amiga itself, and seven of whom worked at the Refugio, the shelter for families in high-risk situations that opened in December 2003. In addition to the paid workers, forty people served as part- or full-time volunteers at Casa Amiga. This essay is based on a series of interviews with a small sampling of the many people who have brought Casa Amiga to life since its founding in 1999: Esther Chávez Cano, its founder and director; Eva Moreno Aguirre, head of the Prevention Program; Almendra Robles Rosales, the director of Casa Amiga's Refugio; and three people who have worked as volunteers at Casa Amiga in the summer and fall of 2003: Erick García, Aliza Frame, and Laura Norlin.

Globalization and Violence against Women: Manifestations of Alienation on the Border

All of the respondents, when asked to define "globalization," associated it with an increase in poverty; and several linked it specifically to "the feminization of poverty" and to the widening phenomenon of youth gangs. Both of these phenomena arise from changes that globalization has wrought to the concept of gender, and both have potentially negative consequences for women in particular. A familiar aspect of globalization is the phenomenon of outsourcing, corporations shifting production to "off-shore" areas to expand profits by avoiding unionization and environmental regulations and seeking out low-wage and relatively docile labor (see Cowie, 1999). In Mexico, employers justify paying women lower wages than those paid to men. Thus, women are far more likely than men to find jobs in the *maquiladora* industry, and they have gained a new importance within the family structure. In addition to the traditional gender roles that Mexican working-class and middle-class cultures have assigned to married women and their daughters— i.e., that of providing all the household labor of social reproduction— women and girls are increasingly being called upon to enter the wage-labor workforce and become primary breadwinners for their families. These jobs pay substantially higher wages than in the interior of Mexico but pay far from a living wage; thus, the emphasis upon the feminization of poverty. Many working-class women in Ciudad Juárez do not have the resources to ensure their children are being taken care of in their absence, and the rise of gangs is a growing epidemic there, where some five-hundred gangs now operate, recruiting boys as young as ten years old (interview, Chávez Cano). Chávez Cano and Eva Moreno Aguirre both made the point that the rise of gangs represents a manifestation of a loss of a traditional gender role that many women hold dear: that of being the primary caretakers and *educators* of children within the household. Thus, not only does globalization contribute to overt forms of violence, but it also represents a form of structural violence in that it can damage basic structures of family, community, and cultural integrity. Another related theme in respondents' definitions of "globalization" was that of increasing homogenization, an imposed unity that might eventually erase altogether the distinctions among cultures around the world. Esther Chávez Cano considers globalization, as it is currently happening in Ciudad Juárez, a "cultural invasion" by the United States.

The interviewees were then asked if they saw any connection between the phenomenon of violence against women and the process of globalization and if so, how they would articulate it. All of the respondents shared Erick García's reasoning that domestic violence is a consequence of socioeconomic conditions wrought by a malignant form of globalization; and several respondents expounded further upon the transformation in gender roles and elaborated on the connection between domestic violence, violence against women, and globalization as it is manifested in Ciudad Juárez. Robles Rosales stated that rapid population growth caused by *maquiladora* sector growth brought certain "cultural consequences," lifestyle changes—specifically, the arrival of 24-hour supermarkets and an active "night life"—that changed "norms of conduct." These deep changes may have proceeded faster than changes in society's conceptions of what those norms should be. Robles Rosales stated that since many women are earning their own incomes, they have far more choices about how they spend their time and that many choose to socialize more in the mushrooming nightclub scene in Ciudad Juárez. This contravenes older mores surrounding gender, especially common in the urban middle-class and in rural working-class Mexico, that hold that it is improper for women to socialize frequently outside of the home and that a woman in public should be accompanied by at least one male, who in turn is given to understand that he is to serve as guardian/protector. Much of the popular discourse in Ciudad Juárez propounds that the women who have been disappeared brought it on themselves; they were "bad women" who transgressed gender norms (on the dynamics of gender in Ciudad Juárez, see M. Wright, 1998, 2001; on a common border discourse that blames "*gente del*

Sur" for the problems the region faces, see Vila, 2000). Within this understanding that the concept of gender is changing in Ciudad Juárez faster than men as a group can tolerate—whether or not those who hold this view believe that the women bear any responsibility for being "in the wrong place at the wrong time"—there is a direct link between globalization and femicide.

For Eva Moreno Aguirre, the violence against women that globalization either causes or exacerbates is not limited to domestic violence or to the extraordinary case of femicide. She considers the very relations of production within the *maquiladora* industry itself a form of structural violence (Galtung, 1980: 67, 68): "[T]hey [the *maquiladoras*] are exploiting [the women]. That is violence." The *maquiladoras*, she states, denigrate women's capacities as humans by paying them such low wages and running them through the system as objects—instruments of production—without regard to their abilities and needs as individual subjects.

The violence that Moreno Aguirre points to in drawing the connection between the exploitation of labor and dehumanization—i.e., treating humans as means rather than as ends in themselves—is an aspect of alienation, a concept with particular salience in any border region. Marx defined "alienation" as "not being at home" (1959: 72). The word he used that has been translated as "alienation" is *Entfremdung*, which comes from the adjective *fremd*, meaning "strange" or "foreign." In its English and Spanish forms, the root of the word "alienation" comes from the French *lien*, meaning "attachment." Alienation is thus the state of being—or process of becoming—an unwelcome stranger, a rejected foreigner, one who has lost all attachments and bonds and is instead isolated and separated from community (Richards and Swanger, 2006). Two scholars who followed in Marx's footsteps by elaborating on the concept of "alienation," Bertell Ollman and Jurgen Moltmann, also emphasized the separation and isolation—i.e., the lack of community—inherent in "alienation." Ollman writes: "The whole has broken up into numerous parts whose interrelation in the whole can no longer be ascertained. This is the essence of alienation, whether the part under examination is man [sic], his activity, his product, or his ideas. The same separation and distortion is evident in each" (1971: 135). Jurgen Moltmann writes: "The ideology that 'there is never enough for everyone' makes people lonely. It isolates them and robs them of relationships" (1997: 109).

The salience for border regions of Marx's notion of alienation as being without social bonds, a permanent stranger, should be clear: border regions in general are places of constant population flux. A very small proportion of Ciudad Juárez's estimated 1.3 million inhabitants have actually lived their whole lives in this city; and nearly all of the employees in the *maquiladoras* during the economic boom of the mid-1990s through 2001 came from other parts of Mexico, especially Veracruz, Aguascalientes, Guanajuato, Jalisco, Michoacán, and Querétaro. The local sense of alienation or lack of community that arises from this simple fact of constant flux is bespoken in the discourse, mentioned above, that holds that outsiders are to blame for the femicides and related problems—both as victims and as perpetrators.

Given the presence of the *maquiladora* industry in this border region, however, the concept of alienation is even more relevant. First, *maquiladoras* are the manifestation of a production strategy that relies on breaking the production process into small parts; it is the internationalization of Taylorist assembly lines. It represents an intensification of the alienation that accompanied one of the major historical transformations in labor processes—the shift from craft labor to industrial wage-labor. For *maquiladora* workers, work is highly repetitive and physically and emotionally taxing; the wages are low; and unlike the Fordist system in which workers were partially compensated for the arduousness of their labor and the ennui that the assembly line could engender by being paid wages high enough to allow them to be the consumers of the goods they were producing, the final destination of the products made by *maquiladora* workers is a foreign consumer market. This is the aspect of alienation inherent in the exploitation of labor that Ollman highlights. Second, we return to Moltmann's statement: "the ideology that 'there is never enough for everyone.'" This ideology permeates popular discourse on both sides of the international boundary in the Ciudad Juárez/El Paso border region. Whereas many El Pasoans are quick to blame recent immigrants as "the other" who keeps unemployment relatively high, wages relatively low, and poverty levels relatively constant, many *juarenses* often do the same toward recent migrants. In both cities, where financial resources are on average quite limited, a common assumption is that there *would* be enough for everyone *if only* the process of migration could be halted (see Vila, 2000). It is this widespread belief that the best one can do in the border region is to buckle down and do whatever can be done to provide for one's family that tends to mitigate against large-scale collective actions to address some of the region's structural problems; the operative word in Spanish to express this attitude, commonly heard in the region, is "*aguantar*," meaning "to bear," "to endure." And so, throughout the region one is often struck with an unspoken sense of urgency, as individuals and households struggle to find the means to survive, somehow, on their own.

Commenting on the manifestations of globalization in the border region, poet and performance artist Guillermo Gómez-Peña writes:

> We are living in the age of pus-modernity, a blistering, festering present. And in these times, all known political systems and economic structures are dysfunctional. . . . Many see this as the era of la desmodernidad, a term that comes from the Mexican noun desmadre, which can mean either having no mother, or living

in chaos. The Great Fiction of a social order has evaporated and has left us in a state of meta-orphanhood. (1996: 25)

Gómez-Peña's characterization bespeaks the concept of "alienation." The sense of the "blistering, festering present," which, I will hazard, does not apply only to the border region but instead will be familiar to readers throughout the world, comes in part from the homogenizing aspects of globalization that result in communities looking more alike one another (e.g., in that the provision of services increasingly comes from the same corporations the world over instead of local initiatives) and our living increasingly detached from history, from sense of place, and from meaningful cultural contexts in which local communities can organize production in ways compatible with particular social and ecological environments.

Gómez-Peña's use of the term *"desmadre"* in his description of alienation brings us back to the consequences of globalization for women. The phenomena that Casa Amiga staff members have articulated with regard to the extra burdens placed upon women and upon children, who often must contribute their own labor to the household income; the loss or decline of women's roles as primary educators in the home; the exploitation and sexual harassment women face in the *maquiladoras*; and the shifting debates over gender that still punish women for contravening traditional gender norms— all of these are manifestations of the violence inherent in alienation, of fragmenting community structures. And if women are seen as the glue that holds communities and society together, as popular discourse and practice in Mexico hold them to be, then femicide is the most severe manifestation of alienation. It is all of these multifaceted forms of violence against women and children to which Casa Amiga is responding. Although it is up against a rising tide of globalization, violence, and alienation, Casa Amiga, with its small and dedicated staff, challenges this culture and creates an alternative, embodying the principle that they will be the change they want to see. They will demonstrate that another world is indeed possible.

Tearing Down the Walls Upholding the Culture of Impunity: Demanding Accountability

Esther Chávez Cano speaks of the "culture of impunity" that is Ciudad Juárez. She means that the authorities to whom the community turns in part for remedies to femicide have a tendency to look the other way or, occasionally, to offer half-hearted measures at solving the cases or punishing the perpetrators. This fact generates a wider locally held assumption that there is no penalty for the commission of such crimes and therefore might be creating the conditions for more men to become perpetrators. At the same time, the attitude of civic authorities as a whole toward organizations who take the ethical stance of advocating on behalf of women who have been victims or survivors of violence is tense at best, if not antagonistic. The staff of Casa Amiga have often endured slanderous assaults on their reputations, as payback for, in the estimation of those engaging in the slander, having damaged the city's reputation and potentially hindered tourism and foreign direct investment.

The culture of impunity's exemption from punishment for the perpetrators of bad acts that marks Ciudad Juárez is reiterated on a global scale in that the culture of capitalism rests on a set of rules that often reflexively reward unethical behavior and punish ethical behavior. The *maquiladora* industry serves as an example of the ways unethical behavior is often rewarded in capitalism: factories that moved to Ciudad Juárez from the United States were able to avoid union wages and stricter environmental protections; as a result of this outsourcing, profit margins have tended to increase, and shareholders are rewarded. However, communities that try to levy higher ethical standards upon companies will often be punished through capital flight in general and relocation of production in particular, which brings higher rates of unemployment and poverty (Lindblom, 1982; and Richards and Swanger, 2006). The philosophical and institutional underpinnings that make capitalism operate are an historical legacy handed down to the modern world from the Roman Empire, when Emperor Justinian, in 533, codified into law three principles meant to unify the many disparate communities that had been incorporated into the Empire and thereby lay the groundwork to facilitate commerce among strangers. These principles that later served as the basis for modern Western private law were as follows (Watson, 1985 and 1995; Wieacker, 1995): (1) *pacta sunt servanda* ("respect contracts"); (2) *suum cuique* ("respect property"); and (3) *honeste vivere* ("respect persons"), which has become so linked to *suum cuique* that respect for persons is defined in practice as respect for persons' rights to property and to dispose of their property in ways of their choosing, the operative definition of "freedom" as used by neoliberals.

Just as the first statement of these rules served to override the higher ethical standards of a diverse range of communities that had been incorporated into the Roman Empire, the current neoliberal insistence upon these rules as a means of ensuring good business climates the world over is a critical component of the process of cultural homogenization associated with globalization. I believe it is this aspect of globalization to which Esther Chávez Cano refers when she describes globalization as a process of "cultural invasion" by the United States. Whereas before the current phase of capitalism took hold, Mexico—and particularly its indigenous communities—still practiced a diversity of ways of life, including subsistence-based rather than exchange-oriented production, now Mexico looks nearly exclusively outward for its economic salvation, relying upon foreign direct investment and increasingly privatized export sectors.

It is strict adherence to this narrowly defined set of rules surrounding the protection of property rights that sets into motion the mechanisms of punishment and reward built into global capitalism (for without such rules, without the legal and moral climate that allows property owners to dispose of their property in whatever way they may choose, communities would not be seeing the devastating consequences of capital flight or capital strike); and if the residents of Ciudad Juárez were to launch an overt challenge to the rights of property through a large-scale collective action such as a wave of unionization and strike activity, or mass street protests, the *maquiladoras* are well equipped to shut down quickly and re-open elsewhere. Given this context, the individual survival strategies widely practiced in the border region—as opposed to large-scale collective action—make sense as globalization's complement, yet it is also precisely this fragmentation that allows the culture of impunity to flourish.

One important form of resistance that Casa Amiga presents to globalization is challenging this fragmentation, by attempting to break down the wall between civil and political society and hold the political authorities to account for femicide and other forms of violence, and by holding all members of society to account, both as individuals and as a *community*. They accomplish this by means of workshops and feminist therapy. A second form of resistance presented by Casa Amiga to the fragmentation that paradoxically complements globalization is working to supplant the culture of rampant individualism with something better and more workable, which Casa Amiga staff members term the "culture of respect" and which I term more narrowly a "culture of solidarity." Solidarity means that the burdens of one are shared and confronted collectively; constructing and encouraging the elements necessary for solidarity challenges the culture of impunity in that the grief and sorrow that one family faces when one of its members is disappeared becomes the grief and sorrow and impetus to action for a wider circle of families and, potentially, eventually the community as a whole. This strategy presents a direct challenge to alienation and an indirect challenge to the narrow rules underpinning capitalism that are much more supportive of individual rights than of the practices necessary for sustainable community.

The Radical Act of Creating Community: Feminism, *Convivio*, and the Culture of Solidarity as an Alternative to Globalization

When I asked Almendra Robles Rosales and Esther Chávez Cano what the mission of Casa Amiga was, their answers surprised me. Robles Rosales stated, "The ultimate goal is transforming social relations." Chávez Cano stated,

"[T]he mission of Casa Amiga is transforming the culture of this city." The answers were at once succinct yet vast in their implications. Casa Amiga is not merely *resisting* globalization; it is taking the radical step of, on a quotidian and small-scale basis, constructing and living out viable alternatives, a culture of solidarity. I will highlight two aspects of this culture of solidarity: feminism and *convivio*.

Not only was Casa Amiga the first women's crisis center in the entire Mexican northern border zone, but it is also one of the few organizations explicitly identifying as "feminist." This has meant an uphill struggle for Casa Amiga because in addition to the controversy that meets their advocacy work on behalf of the *desaparecidas*, the term "feminist" itself often generates suspicion and controversy. Almendra Robles Rosales made this clear in the way she prefaced a response. I had asked her to explain the nature of "feminist therapy," with which Casa Amiga assists women who have survived domestic violence. Before delving into that answer, Robles Rosales stated, "Well, there tends to be a lot of confusion surrounding the term 'feminist' . . . because people are not familiar with the term. Nevertheless . . . there are many professionals who are feminists and don't even realize it because they're not familiar with the term." As she explained, feminism for Casa Amiga means struggling for equality— "not for me to be more than he is"—but rather for the same rights regardless of sex, for equity. In this sense the feminism practiced by Casa Amiga— through feminist therapy—is a way to bring a measure of healing to this border region, a society that tends to be even more fractured, divided hierarchically along the lines of nationality, race, class, sex, and gender, than many similar-sized metropolitan areas.

The theory that underlies the practice of feminist therapy holds that the individual man is not the sole or even the most critical site of blame for acts of violence against women, nor does he avoid inflicting harm upon himself in such an act; but rather that domestic violence is part of a larger process in which society does not accord women and children the same value as adult males. This devaluation/dehumanization explains why acts of violence against women and children are damaging to men as well (interview, Robles Rosales). This is why feminist therapy and the similarly inspired workshops are often practiced in group settings, of families and of co-workers. Feminist therapy and the feminist workshops fall within the well-practiced tradition in Latin American social movements of *concientização*, consciousness-raising. Consciousness-raising itself is a form of challenging fragmentation and alienation because it depends on dialogue. Each participant speaks from her or his individual perspective, and these contributions are then examined collectively, in the hopes that together the participants will arrive at an understanding that will lend itself to better practices for the community as a whole. Almendra

Robles Rosales emphasized that these sessions do not just focus on critiquing machismo as it is commonly (narrowly) understood, but also other cultural elements that contribute to this process of devaluation/dehumanization that harms all, such as homophobia and aspects of language itself. Such critiques necessarily involve session leaders working alongside other participants to examine cultural elements they too had previously taken for granted and so is another way of dissolving hierarchies in favor of community.

Casa Amiga recognizes that the larger processes of globalization are likely to be unaffected by these small-scale actions. Nevertheless, I contend that although the actions of the members of Casa Amiga might not directly alter the course of globalization, they are planting the seeds of a workable culture that will grow up right underneath the faceless structural forces of globalization, and it is these small-scale local initiatives—each with their own unique contours—that are being cultivated all around the world which, especially by forming trading blocs, networks of cooperatives, and other forms of cross-border alliances, might be able to show the staying power necessary to supplant the cultural structures that are the driving force of neoliberalism. One of the unique contours of Casa Amiga as a small-scale local initiative is the centrality of *convivio* in building what its staff calls a "culture of respect."

Convivio, which has its root in the Spanish verb *convivir* ("to live together"), is a cultural characteristic to which many Mexicans (especially those living in the border region) point in order to distinguish ways that people from Mexico relate to one another from the stereotypically "*seco*" (dry) or "*frío*" (cold) ways in which people in the U.S. are said to relate (see Vila 2000: 61–62). It refers to rather intangible qualities that arise when people congregate with a common purpose that includes the simple enjoyment of life—qualities such as sharing, warmth, good humor, and positive energy that grows from and is strengthened by collaboration. In spite of the gravity of the situations to which Casa Amiga is responding, *convivio* infuses the work that its staff carries out. It is present in the workshops conducted in *maquiladoras*; the outreach programs for children; and the ways they manage to keep Casa Amiga a haven of warmth and calmness for receiving women and children who have suffered violence.

Convivio also sets the very context for the ways that Casa Amiga's staff members relate to one another; it is the central element in the culture of respect that they are constructing. *Convivio*, however, is such an intrinsic part Casa Amiga's culture that members of the full-time staff seem to take it for granted. It took an "outsider" to Casa Amiga, a short-term volunteer who had grown up in the United States, to see *convivio* as something so full of radical potential that it demanded to be put into words. About halfway through her internship at Casa Amiga, Aliza Frame wrote the following passage about being in the presence of *convivio* at the daily lunchtime at Casa Amiga, in which the staff members stop whatever they are doing and gather:

> I want to discuss the habits at lunchtime because I think they're important to the culture of respect that is an integral part of the way Casa Amiga not only "puts out fires" on an individual and daily basis, but it is also an example of how, by practicing a sisterhood between themselves—the people who are working to end individual and social problems—the women are legitimizing their goals and their daily actions. . . . Every day . . . people share their food and bring enough for other people to eat. Some days people cook for everyone, and other days people just bring bits and pieces that multiply into enough to feed the entire crew. It's a bit like the story of the loaves of bread and the fish when Jesus preaches to 5,000. I rarely see people walk in with food, but somehow when mealtime comes around, people pull out dishes from home of rice or *frijoles, charros* . . . or roasted chicken. The first day I worked, Eva shared her chicken with me. Carmen brings me *pomegranates* from the tree in her yard. . . . Every day I come in unprepared to get through the day without starving. . . . But these women take care of each other, and they take care of me, too. When you walk into the dining room, people get up and get you a chair, ask if you want tortillas or salsa or half of the food on their plates. I feel respected and important to them, but why? When I started working at Casa Amiga, I didn't expect people to offer me free food or even notice if I ate or not. . . . In previous jobs in the U.S., I've been mostly expected to fend for myself. . . . Even last summer when I worked at a community . . . center where the people were all very respectful and sweet, if I didn't bring lunch, I had to go out and buy something. No one thought to bring food for other people or eat potluck-style. So at Casa Amiga the routine surprised me, and I felt guilty until recently about eating their food; [but now] I have stopped feeling guilty and started participating in the lunchtime ritual of everyone bringing something small to share. . . . So now I feel like part of a community of women who respect each other, and it makes me feel so content and secure. Isn't that funny: a little thing like sharing lunch can bring women together, empower them individually and as a group, and build real commitment between them. . . . This atmosphere is very different from the one I'm used to in the U.S. (Frame, Field Study Journal Entry, October 8, 2003)

In articulating the spirit of *convivio* that takes over when members of Casa Amiga come together for the simple act of sharing a meal at lunchtime, Frame has documented certain key elements in what I am referring to as a "culture of solidarity." Frame notes how she was not expecting this kind of congregation in which people take care of one another's needs through sharing. She sees it as so very different from typical daily life in the United States. She was accustomed to the atomization that is so ingrained in U.S. culture, even at mealtimes— "people eating at their desks, going home or to a restaurant"—and to the general attitude—not exclusive to mealtimes—that one should simply "fend for oneself." The sharing and cooperation she witnessed are remarkable to her as an outsider to the microculture of Casa Amiga, and they give her a novel sense of contentment and security (on the radical implications of sharing, see also Milani, 2000: 151–154, and Richards and Swanger, 2006).

Returning to the point made by Esther Chávez Cano that globalization represents a "cultural invasion" by the United States, the U.S. is an environment conducive to the propagation of neoliberalism because elements of its mainstream culture are so well aligned to the basic rules that allow the functioning of capitalism—the sanctity granted to contracts and the unquestioned acceptance of the rights that attach to property ownership. In demanding that nation-states cut public expenditures for social services and that they privatize state sectors of the economy, neoliberal economists pave the way for others to experience atomization: these economists theorize that because reducing the safety net reduces taxes, individual families will be left with more wealth to spend in ways of their choosing. When the high spikes in unemployment that accompany privatization make it an impossibility for a majority of families to have the means to spend on necessities, let alone in ways of their choosing, the proponents of neoliberalism respond with the concept of "individual responsibility," or, in the words of Aliza Frame, "fending for oneself." James Petras delineates the conflict between the cultural values accompanying neoliberalism and those lived out by community-based organizations such as Casa Amiga in the following stark terms: "[The] cultural policy [of neoliberal political regimes] emphasizes individual outlooks over collective ones, private problems over social ones, clientelistic relations over solidarity, and mass spectacles over community-organized cultural events. They seek class cohesion at the top, fragmentation in the middle, atomization at the bottom" (1997: 85).

Not only is "individual responsibility" heralded as the cultural value most likely to make people more productive as workers, but its wide acceptance is also the key to "economic growth," for in the estimation of the proponents of neoliberalism, concepts such as "public good" and "community" are *hindrances* to economic development: the higher ethical standards the enactment of these concepts demands are likely to cut into profit margins. Neoliberalism's proponents therefore have a vested interest in the wide embrace of the notion that it is right and proper to "fend for oneself" and let one's neighbors take care of themselves as best they can. The profound sense of insecurity that is generated when there is indeed broadening acceptance of this notion brings us back to the concept of alienation as a fundamental lack of community.

It is not by happenstance that Aliza Frame experienced contentment and security in the midst of a microculture of respect and solidarity, for the intention in every small and large act undertaken in the name of Casa Amiga is to foster the creation of community. Casa Amiga encourages survivors, witnesses, and perpetrators of violence to discern the relationships between themselves as individuals and the larger structures of domination through which we have organized our economy and our societies. In posing this problematique, Casa Amiga seeks to restore a sense of balance between the concepts of "individual responsibility" and "community": in the "culture of respect" that Casa Amiga is in the process of creating, the community must come together to meet the needs of individuals, and individuals, in turn, owe certain obligations to the community as a whole. Such a notion is anathema to those for whom the sanctity of private property means that property ownership carries only rights and no obligations. Neoliberal globalization is said to promise greater welfare for all, but it is a welfare to be achieved by the individual pursuit of increasing levels of consumption and the accumulation of material wealth. By the neoliberal economists' own admission, achieving prosperity in the context of neoliberalism demands participation in the structures of domination, each individual—as *homo economicus*—looking out only for his or her own self-interest; on the way to "prosperity," security is guaranteed to no one. Through the techniques of feminist therapy and consciousness-raising workshops, the members of Casa Amiga are constructing a culture based on sharing, reciprocity, responsibility, accountability, and mutual obligation. In its own small-scale way, Casa Amiga seeks thus to enhance the welfare of all and thereby fulfill one of the broken promises of neoliberal globalization.

Conclusion

The revolution will not be televised, will not be televised, will not be televised, will not be televised.

—Gil Scott-Heron

The detrimental aspects of globalization are highly visible. Those engaged in resisting globalization understandably have the urge to make this resistance just as visible and spectacular. And while there is certainly a place for acts of visible and spectacular resistance, there is also a place for forms of resistance that are so subtle that they cannot be captured in the visual media. These forms of subtle resistance play several crucial roles within new social movements that spectacular forms of resistance do not. First, because of the contrasting natures of these two basic kinds of resistance, only the quiet and quotidian resistance can be sustained day-to-day for long stretches of years, and given that constructing viable alternatives to neoliberal globalization is to be a process measured in decades and even centuries rather than in months or in years, this patient form of struggle, which does not lose energy in the absence of cameras or other forms of public documentation, is vital. Second, this kind of resistance tends to be far less alienating of wider segments of society. Strikes, roadblocks, and other forms of spectacular resistance that are aimed either directly or indirectly at shutting down systems of production and/or distribution often have indirect and unintended consequences such as provoking shortages of goods and/or leading to spikes in unemployment; these kinds of actions can therefore antagonize segments of society that might otherwise be allied with the initiators of resistance (Barthes, 1957). Quieter forms of constructive resistance, in contrast, have a greater potential for inviting alliances across lines of race, nationality, and even of class; these are the kinds of broad cross-border alliances that will be necessary if the alternatives to globalization are to be viable. Third, because they are usually less overtly antagonistic and generally are not acts that can be captured in the visible media and therefore do not serve to stoke the fires of public imagination for good or for ill, these forms of subtle, constructive resistance tend not to occasion the kind of brutal, state-sponsored repression that is the stock and trade of neoliberalism when the public fails to be convinced of its supposed benefits.

In offering his recommendations for ways to challenge neoliberalism, James Petras writes, "The subjective factor today is the great terrain of struggle: the economic and social conditions for the overthrow of neoliberalism are being created every day in every country, workplace, and neighborhood. What is necessary is the steady creation of a new social consciousness, culture and ethics to convert those conditions into the basis for a social transformation" (1997: 91). In helping each day to bring into being a culture of respect that is part of a culture of solidarity and reaching out to others to collaborate in the mission of Casa Amiga, this is what the members of Casa Amiga are doing.

I concluded each interview by leaving it open to the respondent, asking simply, "Is there anything else you would like to say?" The final word of this essay goes to Eva Moreno Aguirre, who answered:

> Yes, I'd like to say that Casa Amiga is an important part of the change that many other organizations in the community are searching for, and not just in [this] community but in the whole world . . . which is to build a culture of respect. . . . [O]nly by raising consciousness are we able to achieve it, and in spite of all the limitations of every kind . . . we're here because . . . we are people who believe deeply in this change, although it is very small, as small perhaps as a grain of sand, [and] although we are not going to achieve it in the short term . . . Casa Amiga is present, opening a small breach, a small opening toward a new path, helping and supporting other organizations and institutions that have the same interest we have, in favor of community.

VI

REPERTOIRES AND SITES OF CONTENTION

Parties, Shop Floors, and Streets

Activists of the Movimento Sem Teto de Salvador *(Homeless Movement of Salvador) participate in the annual* Grito dos Excluídos *(Scream from the Marginalized) march (2003). Photo courtesy of Keisha-Khan Perry.*

Wнем Gertrude Stein returned to Oakland, she reportedly uttered the now-famous complaint, "There is no there, there." Social movements confronting neoliberal globalization have faced the challenge of finding new spaces and shapes of organizing against an amorphous phenomenon. Unlike manufacturers in the early period of the Industrial Revolution, the post-Fordist-period manufacturers no longer need to market their products to a local community living within a small radius of a factory where workers gather under one roof. With today's global assembly lines and global cities, the dotted lines that connect people's experiences often cross national boundaries and span vast geographic distances. Thus, the global justice movement has taken to symbolic "meeting stalking" to expose the fleeting structures of decision-making power (Seattle, Davos, Cancún), and Mexico's Zapatistas—with characteristic irony—have convened "intergalactic encounters" to bring together critical masses of countervailing power.

The two chapters in this section draw on the Argentine case to examine the shifting spaces and tactics of contentious politics. The case is significant because Argentina's financial crisis, and the 1990s Asian financial meltdown that preceded it, revealed the fragility of the contemporary model of globalization and particularly the volatility of the global "casino economy" created by the liberalization of financial flows. Since then, the "Washington Consensus" once celebrated by proponents of neoliberalism in Latin America has given way to a "Washington contentious," as U.S. efforts to promote a Free Trade Area of the Americas (FTAA) stalled and Venezuelan president Hugo Chávez began supporting an alternative South American bloc. The Argentine piquetero movement, with its factory takeovers and dynamic coalitions of workers and neighborhood activists, also seemed to represent a creative departure from old models of union and party organization.

Roberta Villalón's chapter documents the heterogenous social composition of the movement and the rich variety of tactics employed, ranging from *piquetes* and *cortes de ruta* (picketing, roadblocks) to *puebladas* (town revolts), *cacerolazos* (pot banging), *asambleas vecinales* (neighborhood assemblies), *escraches* (graffiti and flyering against corrupt officials), and *clubes de trueque* (barter clubs). The sense of solidarity and autonomy generated by these imaginative forms of protest had an empowering effect, similar to the spontaneous energy that would later erupt in what was known as the "Oaxaca commune" that occupied the downtown of that Mexican city for three months following the repression of a 2006 teachers' strike. In the Argentine case, Villalón's study also notes the tradeoff of institutionalization versus radicalism as the government co-opted some of the movement's energy by funding employment and social programs channeled through selected organizations that reined in popular mobilization.

Isabella Alcañiz and Melissa Scheier examine the dilemmas of finding new organizing spaces within existing institutional structures. As the Argentine government found ways of coopting some unions and other organizations, a more radical wing of the piqueteros—called the Movimiento Territorial de Liberación (Territorial Liberation Movement—MTL)—formed ties to the Communist Party to gain access to finance for its cooperative enterprises, giving them independence from Peronist clientelistic networks. Alcañiz and Scheier argue that this new kind of coalition with old party networks was based on the understanding that the movement would retain autonomy from party leadership. This case highlights the crucial importance of financial self-sufficiency for movements seeking to carve out new organizing spaces that are autonomous from hegemonic control by the state. At the same time, tensions remain between the horizontal organization of the social movement and the hierarchical structure and electoral aspirations of the party.

These two perspectives on the Argentine experience suggest an ongoing process of experimentation in the movement, as diverse social actors and organizations seek effective strategies and coalitions to challenge the state without replicating its power relations. While the novelty of the tactics and strategies in the Argentine case constitute a significant feature of the movement, the cautionary message about Latin America's social movements remains relevant. Governments were displaced, new social spaces created, and new political formations generated during the economic crisis. Yet, it is not yet clear to what extent these movements have transformed the larger political and economic structures of Argentina.

15

Neoliberalism, Corruption, and Legacies of Contention

Argentina's Social Movements, 1993–2006

Roberta Villalón

B EGINNING IN THE EARLY 1990S, a wave of protest spread throughout Argentina. A heterogeneous mass of unemployed and otherwise disadvantaged citizens organized alternative means of dissent. *Puebladas* (town revolts), *piquetes* or *cortes de ruta* (pickets or roadblocks), *cacerolazos* (pot-banging), *asambleas vecinales* (neighborhood assemblies), *escraches* (graffiti protests), and *clubes de trueque* (barter clubs) comprised a rupture with traditional channels of societal representation: the historically dominant unions and political parties were not only passed over but also contested by the new array of protesters' organizations.

This phenomenon illustrates what McAdam, Tarrow, and Tilly (2001: 7–8) call "transgressive political contention." They broaden the unit of analysis from social movements to "contentious politics," defined as "episodic, public, collective interaction among makers of claims and their objects when (a) at least one government is a claimant, an object of claims, or a party to the claims and (b) the claims would, if realized, affect the interests of at least one of the claimants." These authors distinguish between contained contention, where "all parties are previously established actors employing well established means of claim making," and transgressive contention where "at least some parties to the conflict are newly self-identified political actors, and/or at least some parties employ innovative collective action." Those innovative "repertoires of contention" are "culturally encoded ways such as strikes, tax rebellions, food riots, street manifestations, etc., in which people interact in

The original version of this essay appeared in *Latin American Perspectives* 34(2), March 2007: 139–156.

contentious politics" (McAdam, Tarrow, and Tilly, 2001: 16). This chapter explores the roots, characteristics, achievements and limitations of the Argentine movement, and analyzes its means of protest.

The Roots of Contention

As Auyero (2001a, 2001b), Farinetti (1999), Scribano (1999), Laufer and Spiguel (1999), and Giarraca (2001) have pointed out, deteriorating socioeconomic and political conditions related to the implementation of neoliberal reforms and the inefficiencies of a corrupt state system had a strong influence on the emergence of the 1990s social movements. Although these factors were crucial, in my view it is their combination with a long-standing crisis of the legitimacy and efficiency of conventional societal channels of representation, and a long tradition of political participation and activism (in social movement theory terms, an existing rich repertoire of contention) that explains the development of this novel wave of social upheaval.

Neoliberal Reforms

The implementation of structural reforms based on neoliberal ideals of economic management and governance, which included privatization of state-owned companies, reduction of state related employment, reform of the welfare system, administrative decentralization, deregulation of economic activities, and opening of the domestic market to foreign trade and investment, brought mixed results. In the short-term, Argentina witnessed economic growth, high investment rates, and monetary stability. But, in the medium and long-terms, the country experienced severe impoverishment, unemployment, income polarization, recession, and eventually monetary and financial instability that, combined with the rollback of the state, generated a growing heterogeneous mass of unemployed people without institutional protection from the state, the unions, or other organizations (Gerchunoff and Torre, 1996; Heymann, 2000). Moreover, initial goals of reforming the state by stripping it of perverse political practices such as corruption, clientelism, patrimonialism, and favoritism, soon proved inconsistent with government practices. While government officials, international financial institutions, and lending multilateral agencies stressed the relevance of ending corrupt practices, state negotiations with foreign investors during the privatization process and day-to-day political activities at every level of government were blatantly based on illegal deals, corruption, favoritism and clientelism (Stokes, 2003; Helmke and Levitsky, 2003; Auyero, 2000; O'Donnell, 1997). Both the increasingly damaging economic conditions and the unsatisfactory political panorama fostered citizen dissatisfaction and fed citizens' readiness to voice their demands publicly. As Auyero observed, the protest was "as much about the material living conditions as an individual and collective quest for recognition and respect" of rights (2001b: 7). Unemployment, poverty, corruption, and clientelism not only fostered popular resistance but also became objects of contention. Besides the claim for employment and welfare benefits, one of the central demands of the protesters was to bring to an end the public policies and perverse political practices that repressed them. Thus, the implementation of structural reforms in Argentina contributed to the emergence of a wave of social movements against neoliberal economics and corrupt politics. However, the adverse socioeconomic context does not fully explain why the protesters chose to create alternative organizations to express their demands.

Broken Channels of Social Representation

The traditional organizations through which that kind of demands had been normally channeled were not present: unions and political parties were not their originators or organizers. Moreover, the various types of protests constantly expressed their disagreement with partisanship and unionization, denouncing the high levels of corruption and inadequate representation of the largest unions and major political parties. Although in the later development of new protest organizations one identifies the marginal participation of certain union branches and leftist political parties, the question of why the protesters did not use these historically major channels of representation remains central. In my opinion, structural and ideological matters came into play. On the one hand, the unions lost their strength because the number of people in the labor market and those under formal labor contracts had declined dramatically after the implementation of the structural reforms in the beginning of the 1990s (Murillo, 1997; Godio, 1998; Altimir and Beccaria, 1999). Therefore, the massive number of protesters who were unemployed or worked in the informal sector, did not find organic representation or belonging in the unions. On the other hand, both unions and political parties had gone through a long crisis of legitimacy, reflected in massive accusations of their illegal political practices (such as off-the-record agreements with government authorities over financial matters), misrepresentation of social interests (such as benefiting unions' elites as opposed to the bases), and misuse of public funds (such as hidden investments of resources for non-union purposes). The alliance between the unions, the Partido Justicialista (PJ) and the working class, which had been determinant in the historical fabric of the country (Torre, 1980, 1997; Godio, 1990, 1991) was jeopardized, and both old and potential constituents were eager for new political and organizational options.

The protesters were facing major changes and found the dominant institutions unhelpful as protectors of their rights, interests and resources. The increasing level of corruption and the worsening of the socioeconomic situation brought increasing discredit to these traditional institutions and their leaders, and finally contributed to the development of alternative organizations in search of better representation and greater collective effectiveness. In particular, the protesters created unemployed associations, neighborhood commissions, ex-employees committees, and self-managed assemblies, in which they were able to express their demands and defend their interests, generally by setting up horizontal decision-making structures. In short, traditional channels of societal representation had lost their effectiveness and legitimacy, and their constituents found themselves in a position of severe economic disadvantage without any sort of institutional protection. The combination of these factors proved to be fertile ground for social mobilization.

Rich Repertoire of Contention

Previous episodes of contentious politics that occupied a central position in the fabric of Argentine society played a key role as references to the new contenders. Among them were the democratic activist civil society organizations against the military regime of the early 1980s, the proliferation of alternative political groups in the late 1960s and 1970s, the popular mobilizations in the mid-1940s for labor rights for the increasing number of low-income workers, and the radical movement at the beginning of the century to expand civil rights beyond the oligarchic elite. This history of social mobilization contributed at least indirectly to the protesters' contentious politics. As Pedro claimed, "If it were not for all the Argentines that lost their lives in their struggles for democracy and social justice, we wouldn't be out here, standing for our rights" (interview, Buenos Aires, June 9, 2002).

Moreover, these experiences provided a repertoire of tools of contention. While the protesters' methods included tactical innovations, they also had elements from previous experiences of contention. For example, the widely used street mobilizations, which were normally combined with massive strikes, included blocking streets and disturbing the normal rhythm of the town or neighborhood where the mobilization was taking place. It was the systematic use of road blocking with the purpose of interrupting the regular transportation of people and goods between towns and neighborhoods in order to gain the attention of the government and the mass media that was new. Furthermore, the protesters included both new actors—young unemployed people, women without previous political experience, and children—and old ones—former workers with a long tradition of union mobilization and ex-militants from the 1970s with a history of political activism. In the case of the neighborhood assemblies, existing methods and experienced actors were augmented by new elements such as horizontal decision-making structures and interassembly communication via new information-sharing technologies (Internet web pages, chat-rooms, virtual fora, and e-mail) in making concrete demands of local governments. In other words, if a strong contentious legacy had not existed, the wave of protests would have been less likely to emerge and, more important, to produce new organizations that were not only able to survive and expand but also to achieve concrete results.

Phases of Contention

Radical and innovative, neoliberal Argentina's social movements emerged gradually and heterogeneously. Following McAdam, Tarrow, and Tilly's (2001) proposal of identifying the dynamics of episodes of transgressive political contention, I explored the occurrence of relational mechanisms of contention (such as collective attribution of threat and opportunity, appropriation of sites of mobilization, and infringement of elite interests) in the Argentine case. The uncovering of these mechanisms allowed me to detect five phases with regard to the creation and use of diverse means of protest, organizers and participants, the level and spread of social unrest, and the achievements and limitations.

The first phase, the emergence of contention (1993–1996), was characterized by the appearance of new methods of protest, town revolts and pickets, as a response to collective attribution of threat (economic distress) and opportunity (political illegitimacy and weakness). The level of unrest was high in the cities that experienced protests, but the mobilization was still sporadic and confined to a few impoverished areas and groups. In the following phase, that of decentralized roadblocks (1997–mid-2001), there was a diffusion of picketer organizations throughout the country, raising the level of unrest and number of participants (scale shift). During this period, the use of pickets as a means of protest became increasingly regular and popular among displaced workers, unemployed, and underemployed low-income people (appropriation of sites of mobilization and certification). In the third phase, that of national picketing (July–November 2001), the level of social unrest was definitely higher and constant (scale shift and appropriation of sites of mobilization). The distinction of this stage was that certain picketer organizations became dominant at the regional and national level and organized coordinated picketing across the entire country, which changed the decentralized character of the movement without leading to homogenization or total verticalization. The fourth phase, that of the peak of contention (December 2001–2003), was characterized by the appearance of various innovations in the repertoire of contention and the engagement of other sectors of the population in the process (diffusion). Pot banging, neighborhood assemblies, barter clubs, and graffiti protests converged with picketing and multisector mobilizations, generating polarized and radical social unrest throughout Argentina fostered by arbitrary repression and state weakness. Finally, the fifth phase, pickets' resistance (2003–present), was distinguished by the persistence, increasing institutionalization and fragmentation of picketer organizations and the decline of other type of protests (Villalón, 2002). In what follows, I review the novel means of dissent.

Means of Dissent

Puebladas

The Santiagazo, a town revolt in the province of Santiago del Estero, opened the long process of transgressive political contention in 1993. Government authorities and media baptized these protests as *puebladas* (town revolts) or *estallidos sociales* (social explosions), drawing attention to the events and emphasizing their chaotic aspects. Indeed, some of the provinces that saw this kind of protest were eventually declared "provinces in an emergency situation," which made them eligible for direct economic and political assistance from the national government. After the Santiagazo there were town revolts in other provinces—in La Rioja, Salta, Chaco, Entre Ríos, and Tucumán in 1994, Jujuy in 1994–1995, San Juan, Córdoba, and Río Negro in 1995, and Corrientes in 1999.

According to the studies of Farinetti (1999), Auyero (2001a), and Laufer and Spiguel (1999), the social explosions were mostly a reaction by public-sector workers to the reduction of state employment by provincial and municipal governments under structural reform policies. The protesters were joined by other sectors of the population to various extents; Río Negro and Santiago del Estero were the provinces with the most heterogeneous group of dissenters. Basically, the protesters demanded payment of back wages, protection of jobs and recreation of employment sources, and also denounced the corrupt political class. These protests, directed at the provincial government and the local political class, were urban, local, and brief. The town revolts consisted of mobilizations and street closures accompanied by looting of "buildings of the provincial government and mansions of corrupt politicians, both those of the official party and of the opposition," and destroying "the symbols of political power" (Oviedo, 2001: 11). The police or military usually repressed these actions. While it is not completely clear whether the violence started after or before the repression and whether all the protesters supported it, it is generally argued that the violent aspect of these revolts was only a reflection of the anger that the adverse economic situation, corruption, and the unequal power structure had created.

The social unrest caused by these revolts and other kind of protests was a contributing factor to the fall of several provincial governments (Santiago del Estero, Corrientes, and Jujuy, for example), although not necessarily for the better. Finally, it is significant that despite the participation of certain dissident or new union leaders in some cases, the traditional unions (which had reached an agreement with the national government on structural reform issues) and political parties were not the promoters or organizers of the events.

Piquetes

The roadblocks or picketing started in the province of Neuquén in 1995 and spread across Argentina to the extent that in 1997, 70 percent of the provinces registered at least one mobilization of this type (*Nueva Mayoría*, 2001). These manifestations basically consisted of blocking the main roads of the cities, generally with burning tires and trucks or other motor vehicles, and completing those barriers with protesters in the road chanting and holding banners demanding jobs and denouncing corrupt governments and politicians.

> We used all the legal methods at our disposal and then waited for the government officials to give us an answer. They did not give us any solution. We are tired of promises. We have been abandoned, nobody takes care of us. We can only help ourselves. We had to go out and fight. We are going to continue blocking roads to say that we want work, even if the police, the tanks or anybody tries to kick us out of here. Such inequality should not exist! (Grupo Documental 1° de Mayo, 2001).

The participants in the roadblocks were mostly displaced workers, informal laborers, and underemployed and unemployed people—mostly low-income, nonunionized, and institutionally unprotected. In other words, they were the people who suffered the consequences of the neoliberal structural reforms, which triggered a severe increase in the unemployment rate (from an average of 6 percent in the 1980s to an average of 17 percent since the 1990s) and of the incidence of poverty (from an average of 7 percent in 1980s to an average of 17 percent in 1990s, and 36 percent in 2000s)

(INDEC, http://www.indec.mecon.gov.ar/, accessed August 25, 2005). They identified themselves and were certified by the media and the government as piquetero/as.

The dominant demands of the protests were labor and welfare issues: creation of jobs, improvement of working conditions, and implementation of social and labor policies for those outside the labor market and living in poverty. These concrete demands were generally accompanied by charges of corruption against politicians and government authorities and complaints about the increasingly unequal power structure. The roadblocks and picketer organizations replaced the dominant institutional means of protest—unions, work stoppages and strikes—with regard to these types of issues. Statistics on strikes and other union actions since the diffusion of picketing in 1997 show that, with the exception of 1998, the number of pickets was increasingly higher than the number of union actions. The decrease in the number of roadblocks in 1998 was mostly a result of the distribution of government assistance to the mobilized provinces and the labor measures taken by the Menem administration, particularly the strategic political use of the Plan Trabajar, a labor program targeted at the low-income unemployed. Less than a year later, however, the number of picketing events had quintupled (from 51 to 252 per year). It peaked at 2,336 in 2002 and has averaged 1,050 per year since then (as opposed to an average of 160 union actions) (*Nueva Mayoría*, 2004a, 2005). Since its beginnings, and despite the differences between harder and softer groups in terms of their approach to negotiations with unions and government authorities, the picketer organizations have been the driving force of Argentina's popular movements.

Cacerolazos

The cacerolazos consisted of groups of people banging pots in their houses and in the streets and plazas as an expression of their discontent with and repudiation of political and economic conditions. The first pot-banging protest took place December 19, 2001, with no previous planning or organization. It was a spontaneous reaction to a government economic policy that placed restrictions on withdrawals from banks, the so-called Corralito. In this first episode, the mass media, particularly radio and television, helped its diffusion, but then the protesters started to organize collectively. The *cacerolero/as* (pot-banging protesters) created their own organizations, using the Internet as their main means of communication. They organized and promoted their activities via email communications, posted messages on their websites (which included protest schedules, general information, and discussion fora), neighborhood newsletters, pamphlets, and friendship networks. This bypassing of the traditional channels of societal representation embraced the spirit of the picketers' protest against the political class and the most powerful economic groups of Argentina. In the words of an individual who identified himself as an "Argentine tired of being abused" (http://www.elcacerolazo.org/article.php?sid=437, January 23, 2002):

> Every day we are living through an infinite number of protests and mobilizations across the entire country. Each of them raises different demands. However, there is a point in common: we are fed up with the political class and their consecutive *dis*-governments, their abuse of the trust the citizens that voted for them, the Supreme Court of *In*-justice, the economic policies that ignored the regular citizen and supported big capital, most of it foreign. We owe ourselves a gigantic cacerolazo in the entire country, a cacerolazo that would be impossible not to hear.

The cacerolero/as were mostly middle-class and included a heterogeneous array of people, from impoverished unemployed small business managers to working professionals. All of them had recently been affected by the Corralito and the growing economic recession. Their participation in the cacerolazos helped them recognize commonalities, build a collective identity beyond their particularities, and identify the potentialities of acting together. The combination of events such as changes in the monetary system (devaluation of the currency), sudden inflation, changes in the presidency, and the declaration of policies and counterpolicies contributed to the rapid diffusion and emulation of cacerolazos throughout the country. Although the center of this type of protest was the city of Buenos Aires (9 percent of the total population held 26 percent of the cacerolazos in the period December 19, 2001–March 2002), there were cacerolazos in every province of the country. Despite the rapid diffusion, the number of cacerolazos declined over time. For example, in the last thirteen days of December 2001 there were 859 cacerolazos, but in January 2002 there were 706, in February 310, and in March only 139 (*Nueva Mayoría*, 2004b). However, this decrease did not mean that their participants had stopped protesting. A very interesting process took place: the caceroleros began to meet regularly in neighborhood assemblies.

Asambleas Vecinales

The *asambleas vecinales* (neighborhood assemblies) were derived from the cacerolazos and replicated their geographical distribution: very strong in Buenos Aires City (41 percent), followed by the Province of Buenos Aires (39 percent) and the rest of the provinces (20 percent) (*Nueva Mayoría*, 2002b). The assemblies also retained their innovative organizational character, since they were not organized by any traditional institution and remained non-partisan. As a resident of San Isidro explained, "We do not want the pure spirits of our assemblies to be distorted and corrupted with perverse politics, parties and partisans" (Chochi, interview, San Isidro, May 25, 2002). Indeed, when minority leftist parties such as the Partido Obrero (Workers' Party—PO) became involved in the meetings, the participants managed to keep them in a marginal position, particularly through the implementation of a voting system that prevented group overrepresentation. This change in the voting system was read as "a revolution inside the revolution" (Luis Gruss, interview, Buenos Aires, May 29, 2002) in that it prevented the co-optation of the movement by traditional political parties and fostered open deliberation, participation, and horizontality. The assemblies were not affiliated with any political party or other institution, but they did interact with other organizations, especially with picketer groups in coordinating their participation in multisector mobilizations.

The *asambleistas* or *vecinos* (assembly participants or neighbors) generally belonged to various sectors of the middle class and included the poor, the unemployed and underemployed, working professionals, artists, and students, female and male, old and young. Poor neighborhoods in Buenos Aires City tended not to have assemblies, while middle- and higher-income neighborhoods did. For some neighbors, the assemblies were their first direct political experience, but political party members, ex-militants of the 1970s, and active picketers were also found among the participants in this new means of protest. The assemblies were organized on the neighborhood level and, as with the cases of the picketing and pot-banging, participation was open to everybody. Generally, the assemblies were held in plazas, on street corners, and in neighborhood clubs. Decision-making was consensual. The assemblies were divided into commissions responsible for issues such as unemployment, solidarity, health, education, culture, press, and participatory budgeting (inspired by the experience of Porto Alegre, Brazil), which held meetings separately and then brought the results to a general meeting. Following the cacerolazos, the asambleas used the Internet (email and web pages) as their main means of coordination. Several assemblies also printed newsletters with information about forthcoming protests and neighbors' opinions. At the same time, the assemblies interacted with each other in regular *asambleas interbarriales* (interneighborhood assemblies) in which each assembly presented its ideas and proposals and issues were put to a vote. In the beginning, they used a "one vote per person" system, but in May 2002 switched to a "one vote per assembly" system in order to prevent the political parties from taking over by bringing people to vote for their proposals. The issues varied from presenting a popular initiative to the national government demanding a change in the management of the external debt, to participating in multisector mobilizations. The decisions were not binding but rather served to promote and coordinate activities.

In general, the more successful actions were those related to assemblies' participation in multisector protests and especially, to particular issues at the neighborhood level. For example, the Almagro neighborhood assembly (City of Buenos Aires) presented a petition to a supermarket that it offer a basic combination of food and goods at low prices, and the supermarket accepted. The assemblies in San Isidro (Buenos Aires Province) successfully petitioned a hospital to change its schedule in order to allow patients to see doctors on weekends (outside normal working hours). Assemblies in Flores, Almagro, and Colegiales neighborhoods (City of Buenos Aires) and Mar del Plata (Buenos Aires Province) organized popular trade fairs, cooperative farms, and communal shopping (to reduce costs). Finally, assemblies such as San Isidro and Almagro created solidarity dining rooms serving food that they managed to collect from individuals, businesses and official institutions. Actions directed to broader issues at the municipal, provincial or national level were not, however, so successful. One reason is that the method they used, the popular initiative, required not only a large number of supporters but also clarity and feasibility of the demands. The paradigmatic cases presented in every assembly were initiatives proposing nonpayment of the external debt, renationalization of privatized enterprises, and the removal of Supreme Court justices. In addition to the problematic character of these issues, the initiatives lacked viable goals. However, the existence of these types of petitions reflected the general spirit of the assemblies: dissatisfaction with the corrupt political class and opposition to the market-led economic development model implemented since the 1990s (Editorial, *Almagro en Asamblea* [Buenos Aires], March 2002: 1):

> We are your neighbors. We have been banging pots almost without a pause since that historical 19th of December, when we went out to the streets even though nobody had called for us. Why did we do it? To make all of them get out. All of them? Yes. But not our democracy. We say that they must all get out, so that justice can return. And to be able to build together a life with dignity in this country that has been looted and abused.

These sentiments were shared with the picketers, with whom the assemblies organized joint actions. The relationship between the assemblies and the picketers varied. Some assemblies insisted on identifying themselves as autonomous neighborhood assemblies supporting the picketers while others directly identified with picketer organizations. Thus the convergence of different groups in several manifestations did not imply a homogenization of the movement.

Escraches

The *escraches* (graffiti protests) consisted of making public accusations against persons identified as having committed serious faults that had gone unpunished. Groups of people went to the offices or homes of politicians to denounce their abuses of power and painted graffiti, held banners, and distributed flyers with the names of persons and the accusations such as "Corrupt! Thief! Assassin! Enough impunity! We want Justice!" This kind of demonstration was used in the 1970s and 1980s, especially against the military dictatorship. What was new was its use against politicians and members of the government (such as the president and the ministers of economy, labor, health and domestic security), judges (accused of being partisans rather than impartial), policemen (usually in connection with arbitrary repression of protests), businessmen (generally from big national and international firms involved in corruption cases or massive layoffs), and representatives of multilateral agencies (for example, delegations of the International Monetary Fund [IMF] and the World Bank).

Since 2001, the escraches became increasingly popular and were added to larger protests such as picketing and multisector mobilizations. On the one hand, the performance of escraches in large multisector mobilizations helped to point out those identified as responsible for the situation. On the other hand, they stressed the general spirit of contention against impunity, corruption and inefficiency and the inequalities related to the market-led development model. Certain escraches became more radical, including not only verbal but physical attacks. The violent aspect of the escraches resulted in debate about their origin. One lawyer said, "The escrache is a criminal behavior, but it is a result of another erroneous behavior: impunity and institutional malfunctioning. The escraches are an unwanted product of impunity" (*La Nación*, March 14, 2002).

Clubes de Trueque

The clubes de trueque (barter clubs) began to develop in 1995, but it was not until late December 2001 that the media and the government identified them as another means of contention. The clubs were associations in which people could exchange goods and services (from food and clothes to medical and dental checkups and training courses). Some clubs even created their own currency, so-called *créditos* (credits), to facilitate the exchange over time; one crédito was equivalent to one Argentine peso. There were two networks of barter clubs (the Red Global del Trueque [Global Barter Network] and the Red del Trueque Solidario [Solidarity Barter Network]), but not all clubs participated in them. In general, low-income people, unemployed or underemployed, used these clubs, but after December 2001 there was growing participation of middle-income people recently affected by the Corralito, devaluation, and inflation. According to some statistics, the number of clubs increased rapidly at this point: from their creation in 1995 until 2000, there were 741 clubs, but by May 2002 there were 6,800. The number of participants followed a similar pattern, increasing sixfold in 2001–mid-2002; of the 3,500,000 people who participated in the clubs, 3,100,000 got involved during 2002. The provinces of Santa Fe and Buenos Aires had the most clubs, but there were clubs all over the country (*Nueva Mayoría*, 2002a).

Although the clubs seemed to have been born of necessity, their character varied. One group of clubs emphasized the economic role and another, the social role. The "economic" clubs tended to reproduce the defects of a market with scarce resources: people started trading credits to make a profit. In contrast, the "social" clubs tended to protect the good intentions of their communal association by enforcing certain rules for membership (Diego Rosemberg, interview, Buenos Aires, May 23, 2002; *Nueva Mayoría*, 2002a). Several neighborhood assemblies organized barter fairs or associated with "social" barter clubs (*Almagro en Asamblea*, March 2002: 2–3):

> During the exchange fairs in the plaza, the residents offered goods and services according to their possibilities in a spirit of solidarity. Some people offered things without asking for anything in exchange. Other people offered the required elements for the collection (usually food) and chose something in exchange (clothes, for example). There were also cases of residents with extreme necessities that could not give anything at all.

The relevance of the barter clubs was both pragmatic and symbolic; they were not only functionally replacing formal markets but also sending a clear message to politicians, businesspeople and civil society: if the mainstream economy was rejecting them, the participants in the clubs were still resourceful subjects that could create alternative spaces for exchange of goods and services. Another phenomenon that developed along these lines was the factory takeover. In the cases of Zanon in Neuquén, and Brukman in the city of Buenos Aires, the employees took over their workplaces after they had closed down and began to produce and sell goods and services without the support or participation of the owners (see Godio, 2004).

Discussion and Conclusions

Since 1993, town revolts, picketing, pot-banging, neighborhood assemblies, escraches (graffiti protests), and barter clubs have emerged as new means of social dissent in Argentina, and they remain vibrant to this day. Their popularity resided in their innovative, alternative and radical character, their solidity derived from a rich history of political contention and social activism, and their strength increased as economic conditions worsened and the political legitimacy of traditional institutions faded. The heterogeneity of the participants in these new forms of protest—low- and middle-income citizens, the unemployed and underemployed, informal workers, professionals, artists, students, retired workers, experienced and novice, male and female, young, middle-aged, and old—gave a special meaning and value to their activism. They were able to attain a variety of goals, ranging from employment programs to the resignation of politicians. Moreover, they recreated their role as citizens by demanding that their rights be respected. The original, persistent, and successful character of the movement resulted in the recognition of the motives and actions of the protesters by fellow citizens, activists, and academics beyond national boundaries and members of the domestic and international elite and media. Despite all these achievements, the radical nature, potentialities and strengths of the movement have moderated over time.

Some have questioned the legitimacy of the picketer movement. Since the beginning, the government has reacted to the new protests in a conventional manner, promising new social and labor policies to address their demands. In particular, starting in 1997 the government implemented a labor program called Plan Trabajar (which was replaced by the Jefes y Jefas de Hogar program in 2003) that fostered the creation of new temporary employment opportunities for the unemployed poor and was funded by the national government and international loans from the Inter-American Development Bank and the World Bank. Local and provincial governments, NGOs, and community organizations (including picketer organizations), were authorized to ask for and manage resources distributed by the national government to pay Plan Trabajar employees (SIEMPRO, 1997, 1998). Although the picketer organizations did not see Plan Trabajar as a solution to their demands, they took advantage of the program because it represented a clear possibility of improving their conditions. In this way, the government fulfilled its objective of controlling social unrest but only temporarily and partially. Still, it did succeed in shifting the picketers away from their original role as defenders of the poor. The institutional strengthening of the movement had paradoxical results. As mobilization and disruption expanded, several organizations engaged in behaviors that had originally been targets of their protests, such as corruption and clientelism (Grupo Documental 1° de Mayo, 2001).

Since the number of Planes Trabajar was small, their distribution triggered political behaviors that benefited only certain picketer organizations and their members while damaging the original principle of representing and working for the poor. First, the provision of funds to provincial and municipal governments, NGOs and community organizations activated processes of political negotiations in which socioeconomic variables (such as poverty or unemployment) were generally overlooked while political variables (such as level of mobilization or political ties) were taken into consideration. Then, in the distribution of Planes by the local government or picketer organizations, assigning them to the most vulnerable was relegated to a secondary position: to obtain a Plan it was not enough to be poor and unemployed. In the case of local governments, the traditional *punteros políticos* (neighborhood political organizers) gave Planes and other resources in exchange for a commitment not to participate in the picketing (interviews in Buenos Aires with Rosendo Fraga, May 27, 2002; Julio Burdman, May 29, 2002; Hernán Brienza, May 23, 2002; and Luis Gruss, May 29, 2002). In the case of the picketer organizations, leaders gave Planes in exchange for a commitment to participate and collaborate in the promotion of roadblocks and other demonstrations. As a picketer from La Matanza reflected, "The distribution of Planes Trabajar was first based on necessity, but soon we realized that the participation of the people in the roadblocks was so important to get more plans that we decided that we will give the plans only to those who collaborated with the mobilizations and assemblies" (Grupo Documental 1° de Mayo, 2001). Therefore, several of the picketer organizations failed in their struggle against corruption and discretionary politics.

These proceedings were magnified by the media and politicians and absorbed by middle- and upper-class citizens who had not been involved in any type of protest (whether satisfied or not with the political and economic situation). Many of my field research observations and interviews revealed discriminatory attitudes against picketers; the comments of a neighbor in Neuquén illustrate this: "Mmm, those piquetero/as are black, cheap, and deceiving. They spend all day long in the streets, without looking for a job, and living off the state. They are filthy people" (Carlos, interview, July 28, 2003). The class position (low-income) of the picketers evoked long-standing racist responses that tended to associate middle- and upper-class, white, and European features with social desirability, legality and properness and lower-class, darker-skinned, and indigenous or Latin American features with social marginality and deviance. Racial stigmas influenced inter-class support of the movement.

Another limiting aspect was the temporary commitment of middle-class protesters. The movement reached its peak of social popularity and political impact when middle-class protesters joined the wave of contention in its fourth phase. However, middle-class protesters, who participated mostly in cacerolazos, neighborhood assemblies, and escraches, soon abandoned any commitment to the movement. The loss of their participation weakened the multisector coalition by reducing the pressure that government officials tend to feel when middle- and upper-class individuals express their discontent and engage in political action. Intimately related with this aspect, another limitation of the movement's radical potential was the sustainability of a heterogeneous coalition. The heterogeneity of the movement resided in the participation of local, regional and national organizations, as well as lower- and middle-class protesters, and worked both for and against its development as a unified alternative political force. Initially, the diverse interests and strategies of all the autonomous organizations were respected in order to project a homogeneous resistance, especially during national multisector protests. Yet, as the movement developed, organizational, ideological, political and socioeconomic conflicts within it eventually led to its fragmentation and polarization, jeopardizing the strength of the coalition. In this way, the limitations of the novel Argentine movement were classic ones for multiclass and/or heterogeneous coalitions. Coalitions succeed in legitimizing their demands in the eyes of authorities and outsiders and tend to achieve long-awaited goals on the basis of the diversity of their constituencies. However, as soon as the shared sentiments dissolve, each component of the coalition recovers its unique characteristics, intracoalition struggle resumes, organizational unity breaks down, decision making stalls, and finally, the coalition weakens or disappears. While there is a romantic tendency to wish for multiorigin social movements, the obstacles to organizational sustainability and success seem to be insuperable.

Finally, the potential of the movement has been both fostered and restrained by its capacity to affect the interests of the most powerful groups, which could be enhanced by a combination (again drawing on McAdam, Tarrow, and Tilly, 2001) of the following mechanisms of contention: (a) radicalization—the creation of a more extreme agenda and the use of more transgressive forms of contention; (b) scale shift and diffusion—increase in the number of protesters and the activism of other sectors of the population (in this case, sectors of the middle and upper classes, for example); (c) the polarization of the dispute—addition of new participants (either moderate or previously uncommitted) with extreme positions; (d) suddenly imposed grievances—events that heighten the political salience of movement issues, particularly when combined with extreme repression; and (e) the creation of a political force strong enough to set or influence the government's political agenda. While all of these mechanisms seemed to have occurred during the peak phase of the movement, the moderate levels of the first four in the pickets' resistance phase seem to have influenced the development of the last. Some picketer organizations, such as the one associated with the Central de Trabajadores Argentinos (Central of Argentine Workers—CTA) and the Federación Tierra y Vivienda (Land and

Housing Federation—FTV), the Corriente Clasista y Combativa (Classist and Combative Branch—CCC), and the Movimiento Independiente de Jubilados y Desocupados (Independent Movement of Retired and Unemployed People—MIJD), gradually solidified their position as legitimate representatives of diverse sectors of the population (particularly low-income citizens). This strengthened their capacity to influence particular policies (such as welfare programs and land regulations) and effectively voice citizens' discontent with governments' deeds and decisions (such as instances of police brutality, economic measures, and misuse of public funds). However, this process of institutional legitimization also increased the fragmentation and competition among the diverse organizations (Godio, 2005), which reduced the potential of the movement to embody a singular alternative governing force. This outcome is not to be considered a negative one, but it did affect the radical aspects of the struggle: unsurprisingly, government authorities have been more open to negotiating with the most moderate organizations and accepting the most moderate proposals, and this has increased the fragmentation within the movement. Here again, the dynamics of the Argentine case seem to have fallen into a classic trap for social movements: reducing their radical potential as they institutionalize and gain legitimacy in the eyes of established organizations, public and private.

Despite its limitations, Argentina's wave of transgressive political contention has become an icon of grassroots struggle in the Global South. In the midst of social, economic, and political polarization on a global scale, social movements and the creation of novel means of dissent seem crucial to the fight for social justice. All of the Latin American countries have witnessed grassroots resistance to economic and political abuses of power, particularly those related with neoliberal regimes and corporate globalization (Eckstein and Wickham-Crowley, 2003; Eckstein, 2004; Roberts and Portes, 2005). The social movements of the Global South have gathered in spaces such as the World Social Forum to frame and fortify their demands beyond national boundaries. The fear of the dissolution of the labor movement with the advance of globalization in the late 1980s has lessened with the proliferation of alternative social movements, which have not only channeled the voice of disfranchised populations but also inspired the reconfiguration of traditional labor organizations. Further analysis of the dynamics of social movements may contribute to the development of new social paradigms that is already underway.

16

New Social Movements with Old Party Politics

The MTL Piqueteros and the Communist Party in Argentina

Isabella Alcañiz and Melissa Scheier

THE MOVIMIENTO TERRITORIAL DE LIBERACIÓN (Territorial Liberation Movement—MTL), a radical piquetero (picketer) group formed by unemployed workers and activists from the Communist Party (PC) in Argentina,
emerged rapidly in the mid-1990s. By analyzing the origin and evolution of
the MTL, we hope to provide new insights into the ways in which new social
movements interact with established political parties and why they sometimes
choose more pragmatic or more radical political strategies.

Piqueteros began protesting the economic reforms of the Menem government (1989–1999) by blocking country roads and city streets and subsequently negotiating their withdrawal with political authorities. The movement has evolved into three broad factions based on their relationship with
the state: (1) groups or organizations more likely to enter into agreements
with the state are associated with the *Federación de Tierra y Vivienda* (Federation of Land and Housing—FTV) and labor confederation *Central de Trabajadores Argentinos* (Argentine Workers' Central—CTA), (2) the intermediate
Corriente Clasista y Combativa (Classist and Combatant Current—CCC), and
(3) more radical organizations such as the MTL, which have joined the *Bloque
Piquetero Nacional* (National Piquetero Bloc) (Burdman, 2002). These broad
coalitions differ in size and state-sponsored resources. The FTV-CTA has the
most affiliates and government subsidies, and even though the Bloque Piquetero Nacional has a larger membership than the CCC, it manages the
fewest state subsidies. Like other piquetero organizations in the Bloque, the

The original version of this essay appeared in *Latin American Perspectives* 34(2), March 2007: 157–171.

MTL is based on an odd alliance of unemployed workers, members of emerging social movements characterized by episodic and spontaneous social protests and horizontal ties, and political activists from one of the most rigid and hierarchical political parties of the Argentine left.

Drawing upon social movement theory (Auyero, 2003; Goodwin and Jasper, 2004; McAdams, Tarrow, and Tilly, 2001; Yashar, 2005) and our field research in Argentina, we find that while a sharp increase in unemployment and a decentralized Argentine welfare system prompted the political organization of unemployed workers, pre-existing partisan networks linking unemployed workers to institutionalized political forces determined the specific development of piquetero coalitions. These coalitions, in turn, limited the range of strategies available and determined the capacity of piquetero organizations to persist over time.

We show that access to an autonomous source of political financing, the PC's financial institution, the *Instituto Movilizador de Fondos Cooperativos* (Institute for the Mobilization of Cooperative Funds—IMFC), and prior linkages to urban and skilled worker organizations independent of Peronist clientelistic networks, explain the autonomous and radical nature of the MTL. By using the knowledge and expertise of the IMFC to access government-subsidized loans for their cooperative enterprises, the MTL is able to pursue a more radical strategy than other piquetero groups.

In examining the structural mechanisms that triggered the emergence of the piquetero movement, we concur with prior scholarship in the view that it was the decentralization of social policy initiated by President Carlos Menem that established the conditions for the emergence of new patron-client exchange networks (Delamata, 2004; Lodola, 2003; and Svampa and Pereyra, 2003). However, we challenge the preconception that there is a necessary link between state subsidies and clientelistic networks (and, by association, between piqueteros and clientelism) (Burdman, 2002; Escudé, 2005). While previous research on Argentina has highlighted the importance of clientelism in connecting city mayors, party brokers, and labor unions (Auyero, 2001c; Brusco, Nazareno, and Stokes, 2004; Calvo and Murillo, 2005; Levitsky, 2003; Stokes, 2005), we show that other mechanisms of political organization can replace the need for such links, leading to significantly different growth and mobilization strategies.

In this chapter we first provide a brief overview of the piquetero movement. Second, we outline the theoretical framework in which we will explain the emergence of new social movements in terms of preexisting political networks. Third, we explore the political and economic factors that led to the emergence of the piquetero movement. Fourth, we examine the financial and political networks that granted the MTL autonomy from the patronage networks in which other piquetero organizations were involved and show how radical mobilization is partially sustained by the human and capital resources of the IMFC. We conclude by discussing the general implications of our research for the future of the piquetero movement in Argentina.

The Piqueteros Are Coming

The official emergence of the piquetero movement can be traced to the privatization of major state owned oil industries in the southern cities of Cutral Co and Plaza Huincul, Neuquén. Created as outposts for the extraction of oil in the early 1930s, these cities were for decades the oil extraction and refining center of the state-owned company *Yacimientos Petrolíferos Fiscales* (YPF). These cities witnessed the development of a combative labor movement of petroleum workers in a southern region with a rich history of social and political organization. YPF had its headquarters in Cutral Co, a prosperous working-class city with comparatively high wages and a skilled blue-collar population. After its privatization, however, massive layoffs and a drastic fall in median income dramatically changed the economic makeup of the region. Without alternative sources of employment, in response to the news that the governor of Neuquén had canceled a contract to build a fertilizer plant in Cutral Co, recently laid-off YPF workers, union members and neighbors mobilized on June 21, 1996, to block a vital interstate road. Unable to block the entrance to the now-closed plant, the picket line moved to the highway, bringing national attention to the conflict. The piqueteros were formally born as a new social movement led by a political actor previously unknown in Argentina: the unemployed.

New picket lines on different roads of the province finally forced the governor to meet the piqueteros' demands, including calling for new bids for the construction of the fertilizer plant, restoring water and electricity to hundreds of families who had lost service because of lack of payment, and initiating new unemployment subsidies (Kohan, 2002; Young, Guagnini, and Amato, 2002). The Cutralcazo, as it was known, succeeded in putting the growing number of unemployed at the center of the national political scene (see Auyero, 2003). Moreover, in a show of political strength the new movement was able to gain significant concessions at a time when increasing unemployment made trade unions particularly vulnerable.

A second wave of picketing emerged in 2001. In contrast to the first wave, it was independent of and vocally rejected the lead of the Peronist unions. When the Alianza government collapsed in December 2001 under the pressure of violent and somewhat spontaneous street protests (following restrictive financial measures, a 300% devaluation of the peso, and the turnover of four presidents in one month), piquetero movements were significantly transformed. First, the general resentment toward conventional political leadership expressed in the popular motto *¡Que se vayan todos!* (Get them all out!) allowed leftist political parties in urban areas to gain a footing among political actors previously controlled by Peronist bosses and union leaders. Second, radical piqueteros saw December 2001 as "the vindication of all the resistance struggles and of all the acts of rebellion" (Central del Partido Comunista, 2004) and considered themselves "the heirs of 2001 . . . historic subjects in the construction of people power and counter-hegemony" (Carlos Huerta, interview Buenos Aires, August 6, 2004). The perception that the events of December 2001 constituted the beginning of a social revolutionary uprising allowed the radicalization of segments of the piquetero movement (Burdman, 2002).

Different from the Cutral Co piqueteros of 1996, the new piquetero constituency was composed of younger unemployed workers, many of whom had never held steady jobs or enjoyed worker benefits. The new leadership had deeper roots in political activism, and, while many of the early piqueteros had prior experience as labor organizers, the new mostly non-Peronist piqueteros were more closely connected to local organizations and leftist political parties. Moreover, within these left-leaning piquetero organizations, even those with prior union experience rejected the vertical organization of traditional Argentine labor institutions. The relationship between the piquetero base and its leadership therefore diverged significantly from the traditional one. The piquetero movement was characterized by horizontal and voluntary ties, with formalized mechanisms to foster collective decision making. Times and locations of road blocks, for example, are typically decided in general assemblies. Similarly, negotiations with public officials to lift the picket line after demands were granted were often carried out under the direct supervision of the rank and file. Further, these organizations are partially self-financed, with members contributing a low monthly fee (Young, Guagnini, and Amato, 2002).

The piqueteros' ability to make their demands heard rested on their form of protest: blocking heavily trafficked roads (typically vital commercial arteries in the countryside and around the city of Buenos Aires) until provincial and/or national authorities were forced to give in. Since the first picketing, the immediate objectives of this tactic have been to secure new jobs, access new government subsidies, or increase existing ones. As piquetero organizations grew to an estimated 300,000 total membership, so did the number of cash transfers to the unemployed (Savoia, Calvo, and Amato, 2004: 30–31). During the Menem administration approximately 100,000 government subsidies (Planes Trabajar) were distributed to key (electoral) areas of the counties (Ministerio de Economía, n.d.). Beginning with the Duhalde administration

(2002–2003) these subsidies increased to 2,000,000, covering close to 15% of the economically active population. The Peronist administration of Nestor Kirchner (elected in 2003) presently distributes approximately 1,700,000 (Ministerio de Trabajo, 2004).

Old Partisan Networks and New Coalitions

In order to avoid "conflating opportunities with mobilization," we analyze piquetero coalitions as the result of both contextual and actor-centered variables (Meyer, 2002: 15). The political organization of unemployed workers is explained as a response to the social costs of the Menem administration's market reforms, which became "background conditions . . . ripe for a large-scale protest" (Auyero, 2003: 39). The nature of particular political coalitions, however, is explained by preexisting social networks that shaped the way the unemployed understood their political context and developed political strategies.

Coalitions are important because they reveal not just how individuals are organized into a social movement but also how political interpretations and strategies evolve and determine the likelihood of success (Goodwin and Jasper, 2004: 167). The study of prior partisan network linkages allows us to "understand the process of putting together movements by looking at the coalitions that animate, negotiate, cooperate and compete within a social movement" (Meyer, 2002: 15). Those networks explain how coalitions and social movements can go beyond "episodes of contention" to sustained collective action (McAdams, Tarrow, and Tilly, 2001: 49).

The link between coalition formation and identity is critical for explaining how new social movements overcome problems of collective action, preventing not just against the emergence of free-riders but also co-optation, disintegration, and bureaucratization. Interpretation of the political context that cements these new groups is central to the formation of collective identities (McAdams, Tarrow, and Tilly, 2001; Meyer, Whittier, and Robnett, 2002; and Goodwin and Jasper, 2004). The ideological dimension of collective identity formation is crucial in that ideology provides continuity to social movements that have very immediate needs and relatively parochial goals. In the case of the MTL, identity was built upon programmatic strategies informed by an interpretation of the political context linked to the Communist party. The central tenets of the MTL piquetero identity were rejection of neoliberal capitalism, belief in the possibility of an alternative model for labor organization (*trabajo genuino*), distrust of the traditional institutions of interest aggregation (state, party, and union politics) dominated by Peronism, and a revolutionary interpretation of the events of December 2001.

Yet, to a great extent, the whole piquetero movement shares this ideology. Collective identity cannot explain particular piquetero coalitions. In considering the ideological dimension of the movement we see that the number of possible allies for the piqueteros is limited. The collective identity of the movement precludes the two dominant political parties (the Peronist *Partido Justicialista* [Justice Party—PJ] and the *Unión Cívica Radical/Alianza* or [Radical Civic Party/Alliance—UCR]) and the (mostly Peronist) unions from joining the piqueteros, who see them as either directly responsible for or complicit in the retrenchment of the state. One of the early piquetero leaders explained why she joined the first picketing in 1996 in Cutral Co as follows: "I was not going to the place full of politicians. . . . My reality: unemployment, poverty, injustice" (Auyero, 2003: 34). Therefore, collective identity, especially its ideological dimension, is necessary but not sufficient to explain the MTL coalition.

To explain the emergence of particular coalitions we must look at the preexisting ties: "On the whole, shared prior knowledge, connections among key individuals, and on-the-spot direction guide the flow of collective action" (McAdams, Tarrow, and Tilly, 2001: 49). The social-network approach has highlighted this connection (Goodwin and Jasper, 2004) and provides strong evidence that "the pattern of sustained networks working on several issues over time is recurrent in social movements" (Meyer, 2002: 11). Yashar (2005: 73) argues that existing networks provide social movements the capacity to organize and "the basis for generating new ones," allowing the exchange of social resources necessary to sustain collective action.

Networks are less formal and consequently less visible than institutions. Because they are actor-centered, they bridge institutions and social groups. By focusing on the political ties that underlie political parties and unions in Argentina, we can explain coalitions involving seemingly disparate institutions and groups. Further, new social movements based on existing ties tend to reinforce the fundamental attributes of the network. Thus, existing networks can be of different types and define the direction of the movement. Networks outside the clientelistic iron triangle of Argentine social politics (mayors, party brokers or *punteros*, and unions) will have difficulty gaining access to state resources. In order to sustain political mobilization without this access, the coalition will need to secure resources for its membership from some other source.

The Political Economy of the Piquetero Movement

The emergence of the piquetero social movement can be understood only against the backdrop of the failing Argentine economy. In 2001, the breakdown of the Convertibility Plan (which had pegged the peso to the dollar in 1991) and the crisis of the traditional political parties (Calvo and Escolar, 2005) triggered massive mobilizations and social protests against the government of President Fernando De la Rua (1999–2001) that led to the collapse of the economic, political and social order in December of that year. Even the traditionally lethargic Argentine urban middle class took to the streets, banging pots and pans to protest the government's financial policies. Neighbors organized local assemblies to denounce the ineffectiveness and corruption of city government. Pensioners and retiree associations, some of the first social actors to protest the pension reforms carried out earlier by president Menem and his minister of economy, Domingo Cavallo, increased their political activism. The economic crisis proved fertile ground for an increasing piquetero role in the political process. In a society in which political legitimacy was lacking, the capacity to mobilize people became an extremely powerful resource.

Social disintegration generates social protest, but the necessary conditions for the emergence of the piquetero movement were the sharp rise in unemployment in the absence of comprehensive unemployment policies and the decentralization of social protections. Both conditions resulted from the decade of structural adjustment policies by the Menem government that entailed the demise of the 50-year-old corporatist welfare state.

Rising unemployment or "hyperunemployment" with no comprehensive unemployment policy had a profound effect on the Argentine labor force (Auyero, 2003: 44). The lack of an unemployment policy was the result of 50 years of relative stability in a labor market characterized by full employment. Until the hyperinflationary crisis of 1989/1990 Argentina had never experienced an annual unemployment rate higher than 6% (Ministerio de Economía, n.d.). As a result of the privatization of state-owned enterprises and the shrinkage of the public sector under the Menem administration, the 1997 economic recession quickly grew into a full-scale depression. The country went from a national average of 7% unemployment in 1990 to 15.6% in 1999. The election of De la Rua that year did little to improve the situation. In 2000 the national unemployment rate was 16%, and in 2002 (after De la Rua's resignation) it reached an alarming 22%. Not surprisingly, the official poverty rate, which oscillated at the beginning of the Menem administration between 17% and 20%, reached 33% in 2001 and over 50% in 2002 (Ministerio de Economía, n.d.). Prior to the 1990s, full-employment policies were firmly embedded in both the public sector and the Peronist labor unions. The downsizing of the public sector and the weakening of labor organizations left vast numbers of unemployed workers with no safety net to turn to, prompting them to protest and organize.

The second structural factor that facilitated the growth of the piquetero movement was the decentralization of social policy aggressively implemented by the Menem administration beginning in the early 1990s. By "decentralization" we mean a "process of state reform composed by a set of public policies that transfer responsibilities, resources, or authority from higher to lower levels of government in the context of a specific type of state" (Falleti, 2005: 327–346). Decentralization under Menem's administration allowed local political bosses to control the growth and distribution of antipoverty and unemployment programs.

As a result of this decentralization, the national social emergency plans implemented by the administrations of presidents Menem, Duhalde (2002–2003), and Kirchner gave local governments and nonstate actors a say in the administration and distribution of the subsidies. In 1996, the Menem administration launched the *Plan Trabajar* (Plan Work); cosponsored by the World Bank. It provided a monthly wage of approximately 150 pesos (US$150 at the time) for unemployed workers in exchange for service in public-works projects. The top-down distribution of these funds involved all levels of government (central, provincial, and municipal) but gave mayors a great deal of discretion in determining beneficiaries. Furthermore, the Plan Trabajar also allowed, in some cases, the participation of nongovernmental actors (such as NGOs), which could propose social infrastructure projects that could be accomplished by public works (Lodola, 2003: 9).

In April 2002, President Eduardo Duhalde instituted a new social program, Plan Jefes y Jefas de Hogar Desocupados (Unemployed Heads of Household Plan—PJJH), by which unemployed workers with children would receive a monthly cash transfer of 150 pesos (approximately US$45 after the 2001 devaluation of the peso). In contrast to the Plan Trabajar, the PJJH does not require the beneficiary to work. Rather, the requirement was that recipients participate in job training or community service (CELS, 2003). PJJH funds were to be distributed and monitored by local administrative councils made up of political authorities, churches, NGOs, and even labor confederations such as the CTA (Vales, 2002). The current Kirchner administration continues to distribute the PJJH subsidies in much the same way as Duhalde did, although President Kirchner's first minister of social policy attempted to grant a greater role to NGOs in order to curb the power of mayors and party brokers.

The decentralization of social subsidies beginning with the Menem administration had two effects. On the one hand, as we argue here, it prompted the organization of unemployed workers, who could directly manage subsidies by formally organizing as NGOs. On the other, it encouraged the expansion of clientelistic networks among municipal leaders, party brokers (especially the majority Peronists), and potential beneficiaries (Auyero, 2001c; Calvo and

Murillo, 2005; Delamata, 2004; and Lodola, 2003). As a result, there have been numerous claims made by PJJH recipients of the misuse of subsidies for clientelistic purposes (CELS, 2003: 41; *La Nación*, August 8, 2005).

Thus, piquetero organizations have been forced to compete for funds and to develop the management skills needed to administer both Plan Trabajar and PJJH subsidies. Piquetero groups with ties to either organized labor or the government, such as the FTV and the CCC, manage the greatest number of subsidies. For example, the FTV-CTA, led by Luis D'Elía (called the "official piquetero" because of his job in the administration), with 120,000 members, is said to control approximately 75,000 subsidies (Savoia, Calvo, and Amato, 2004; Epstein, 2006). Barrios de Pie, a close piquetero ally of the FTV, with 60,000 members, is reported to manage 11,000 PJJH (Savoia, Calvo, and Amato, 2004). The CCC, with 80,000 piqueteros, controls 40,000 subsidies. Indeed, as one observer notes, "the piqueteros have functioned as one great parallel social agency" (Burdman, 2002). In contrast, the Bloque Piquetero, which includes the Polo Obrero and the MTL, has a membership of over 90,000 piqueteros but manages only 10,000 subsidies (Savoia, Calvo, and Amato, 2004). Of the 5,000 MTL piqueteros in the city of Buenos Aires only 130 receive government subsidies (Carlos Huerta, interview, Buenos Aires, August 6, 2004). Nationwide, the MTL receives 4,000 PJJH subsidies (Epstein, 2006).

Growing unemployment rates and the significant decentralization of social policy allowed piquetero organizations to distribute coveted government subsidies to organize the unemployed. At the same time, the institutionalization of the piquetero movement also gave new organizational spaces to opposition parties that could not penetrate the tightly controlled Peronist unions. Piquetero organizations belonging to the Bloque Piquetero Nacional and closely related to leftist parties such as the PC, the PO, and the MST also grew by deploying other types of organizational and financial incentives.

Piquetero Cooperatives and the Rise of the MTL

The rapid increase in unemployment and the decentralization of social welfare facilitated the organization of the unemployed and the rise of the piquetero movement, but among the piqueteros we find organizations with different levels of dependence on state resources and, consequently, varying levels of autonomy vis-à-vis the government.

After being perceived for decades as a mostly petty-bourgeois party with few links with workers, the PC returned to union politics in 1996 by taking part in the creation of the non-Peronist labor confederation CTA through the Communist Movimiento Político Sindical "Liberación" (Liberation Political Labor Movement—MPSL). This new labor confederation was founded by center-left political forces in response to the privatization of state-owned enterprises by the Menem administration and the rigid bureaucracy of the Peronist Confederación General del Trabajo (General Confederation of Labor—CGT). The CTA has a strong urban white collar composition made evident by the centrality of the state employees' union, Asociación Trabajadores del Estado (ATE).

It was through its ties with the CTA that the PC first moved toward organizing the unemployed. In 1997, D'Elía, the head of the FTV, endorsed the CTA during the high-profile nationwide protest of public school teachers (Pacheco, 2004: 17). D'Elía had been affiliated with the Frente para un País Solidario (Front for a Country in Solidarity—FREPASO), a dissident Peronist and progressive political party, and he had held several elected municipal positions in southern districts of Greater Buenos Aires (Pacheco, 2004: 17). That same year the former Communist leader and founding member of MTL, Beto Ibarra, became a member of the FTV national committee (Ibarra, 2002). In 1998, FTV formally joined the CTA (Pacheco, 2004: 17).

The alliance between PC activists and the FTV did not last long. In 2000, because of fundamental "political, methodological and socio-political differences" created by the FTV's soft-line approach to dealing with the new Alianza government, the PC abandoned D'Elía (Ibarra, 2002). PC activists led by Beto Ibarra, now with ties to mobilized unemployed workers in southern Greater Buenos Aires, joined PC activists in the city of Buenos Aires, working with the growing number of poor who were being evicted from their homes (Carlos Huerta, interview, Buenos Aires, August 6, 2004) to create the MTL in June 2001 in a popular assembly in Lomas de Zamora, a district in southern Greater Buenos Aires. The location is telling; Lomas de Zamora was the electoral district of future president Duhalde and the center of his formidable patronage apparatus (Szwarcberg, forthcoming). A founding member, Carlos "Chile" Huerta (interview, Buenos Aires, August 6, 2004), recounted the creation of the MTL as follows:

> The MTL does not appear spontaneously; rather it results from a political decision. . . . In 2001 fifty *compañeros* came together, we had been doing territorial work, but we did not have a common identity. . . . It was well-known that Peronism was well extended in the province of Buenos Aires. At the time Duhalde was there with the *manzaneras*, women in charge of social control. The idea was, let's challenge their territory, let's break the dams of containment they have built. We did well; the development of the movement was fast. We started out in Buenos Aires and now have 19 provinces.

In 2001 the new MTL broke away from the CTA, now characterized by the PC as "representing the centralist hegemony" (Central del Partido Comunista, 2004), and participated in the first National Assembly of Piqueteros on July 24. Shortly thereafter, it joined the radical Bloque Piquetero Nacional (Pacheco, 2004: 17). In 2004, rejecting the possibility of compromise for the sake of receiving more social plans, the membership expelled Ibarra for taking too conciliatory an approach towards the Kirchner administration (Carlos Huerta, interview, Buenos Aires, August 6, 2004). The expulsion of Ibarra, a central actor of the PC network, highlighted the fact that "the existence of prior networks does not equal the formation of new ones" (Yashar, 2005: 73). It also underlined the intransigence of the MTL regarding its autonomy from the state despite the fact that most of its base depended on social assistance to survive.

The issue of autonomy is a central concern of the MTL movement, even with regard to its relationship with the PC. The relationship between the PC and the MTL, albeit unofficial, is close. The leader of MTL-Buenos Aires, Carlos Huerta, noted that while it was not part of the PC, several of its members (including him) were affiliated with the PC (interview, Buenos Aires, August 6, 2004):

> There are compañeros with different thinking, who endorse socialism, and while effectively some members of the leadership are from the Communist culture and several of us are affiliated with the PC, that doesn't mean that the movement is an appendix or satellite of the PC. The movement is autonomous, within the framework of a central political project, but it has a great degree of autonomy. . . . I personally am not autonomous, but the movement is.

The MTL has grappled with its relationship to the PC. At the August 2003 meeting of its Central Committee it issued the following statement (MTL, n.d.):

> One of the debates that emerged with great force was the issue of autonomy as an attribute of the movement for the construction of popular power and the role of the [Communist] party in relation to the Movement. A party that does not impose itself on the MTL, but one that does not dissolve itself in the movement either. For this, we believe the forging of autonomy in different areas is fundamental: financial autonomy, autonomy from political parties, employers and the State and also autonomy in the sense of building consciousness and critical thought that enables each activist to become a leader.

How can the MTL remain autonomous, sustain radical mobilization, and support its deprived membership with little government assistance? How did an underdeveloped network limited mostly to the city of Buenos Aires and its southern suburbs grow into an organization with 30,000 members? The answer is that through the IMFC the PC leadership of the MTL secured self-generated employment and financial autonomy for its membership, thus minimizing their dependence on government subsidies. The IMFC constituted a buffer between the PC and the MTL, allowing the MTL to determine its own political and economic agenda.

The IMFC, the institutional backbone of the cooperative movement in Argentina, was created by the PC in 1958 and expanded to a series of multiservice cooperative banks (at one point dominating over 12% of the financial market of Argentina) (Heller, n.d.). Many MTL members credit the IMFC with making their co-op projects viable and sustainable. The IMFC lends its know-how and technical staff to help unemployed workers create and operate cooperatives. Its role in imparting the ideological position of the party to the MTL is key. The cooperative projects that it sponsors require piqueteros to be not only political but also ideological activists. It holds regular workshops and meetings in which piqueteros and *cartoneros* (cardboard scavengers) discuss the ideological goals of their movement.

Cooperative organization is an historic staple of the PC, and Argentine communists "equate [it] with socialism" (Mario Esman, interview, Buenos Aires, August 2004). However, the Argentine left has had an ambivalent attitude towards cooperatives. Even the MTL was at first wary of the PC cooperative strategy (Carlos Huerta, interview, Buenos Aires, August 6, 2004). The IMFC has advised and assisted the MTL in all of its cooperative enterprises. The two largest projects, the purchase of a mineral processing plant in the northern province of Jujuy and the construction of a workers' housing complex in the city of Buenos Ares, are very revealing of the importance of this relationship.

The Jujuy project, by the local PC, the MTL, and the IMFC, involved the reactivation of La Brava, a mineral processing plant in Tumbaya, Jujuy. The plant had been abandoned by its owners and declared bankrupt in the late 1990s (Vales, 2005). The area had a long history of PC activity: "During the dictatorship *(1976–1983)*, this town of 300 inhabitants had close to 35 activists from the party, of whom 6 are *desaparecidos* [missing]. The organization of the piquetero movement expanded on this base" (Miguel, 2005). La Brava was a processing plant of the mineral ulexite, from which boron is derived for use in such household and industrial products as Pyrex and porcelain. The reactivation of the plant "would not have been possible without the support of the IMFC," which provided legal and financial assistance (Liliana "Jujuy" Ponce, interview, Buenos Aires, August 2004). After La Brava was registered as a mining co-op in November 2004, the MTL secured a subsidy of 365,000 pesos (approximately US$12,200) from the National Ministry of Social Development for the purchase of new equipment and repair of old machinery (Miguel, 2005).

The MTL co-op already owned some mining machinery, because when the plant declared bankruptcy in 1998, unpaid workers led by the plant manager and PC activist Daniel Carreras (now the president of La Brava Co-op), "somehow collected as severance payment the machinery that remained in the plant" (Daniel Carreras, quoted on the MTL Mining Cooperative "La Brava" website, http://www.coopmineralabrava.org/historia.htm).

With the support of the Ministry of Social Development and several local politicians, the MTL attempted to have the Jujuy legislature expropriate the processing plant and turn it over to the new cooperative, but in December 2004 provincial legislators voted against it (*Diario Digital Jujuy al Día*, December 19, 2004). When the expropriation scheme failed, the MTL co-op decided to purchase the abandoned processing plant and, with money borrowed from NGOs and sympathetic social movements, managed to do so in May 2005. Simultaneously, it signed a concession agreement with the provincial authorities to mine ulexite in a nearby borax salt bed. The processing plant was reopened by the MTL and the PC in October 2005 and touted by Carlos Huerta as a major step forward.

The other large-scale MTL project, a workers' housing complex in the City of Buenos Aires, was totally financed by a loan from the city government. While the IMFC was instrumental in assisting the MTL in the creation of a construction cooperative and the subsequent management of the city funds, the award of the loan was facilitated by the political network and human resources of the PC. The MTL construction co-op Emetele obtained a 30-year loan for 13,600,000 pesos (approximately US$4,540,000) from the city's Housing Institute, some of whose officials had former ties to the PC (Carlos Huerta, interview, Buenos Aires, August 6, 2004). The Emetele cooperative nonetheless had to conform to the prerequisites of the city's Program for Self-Generating Housing in order to get what is the largest mortgage loan to date. This included the hiring of a technical team of engineers, architects, lawyers, accountants, and social workers to assist in the project (Limiroski, 2004). The MTL hired some of the most prestigious professionals to participate in the construction, among them the architectural firm Pfeifer and Zurdo, which has designed some of the signature landmarks of Buenos Aires (Limiroski, 2004). Carlos Huerta explained: "Basically the Institute [IMFC] is always next to us, always willing to assist us; but as we began to explore the world, the human resources were there. There is a great deal of technical expertise, a lot of experience, excluded from the labor market. The only thing that was missing was the political decision of managing a construction company and have these men contribute their experience" (Carlos Huerta, interview, Buenos Aires, August 6, 2004).

The 18,000-square-meter lot, purchased by the Co-op for 1,400,000 pesos, will include 334 family apartments, 10 commercial shops, a community center, a day care center, and a small clinic. The city and the MTL consider this housing venture a pilot project for similar undertakings in which popular organizations administer state resources. The project also has symbolic importance; the property where the Barrio Piquetero is being built used to be a paint factory belonging to the Argentine Bunge & Born Corporation, a close business ally of the Menem administration. During the 1990s, Bunge & Born tore down the paint factory and used the premises to operate a "dry port" where they stored containers of imported goods. When the housing project is completed, the MTL will reopen a street that had been closed off by Bunge & Born with a massive warehouse (*Newspaper Acción*, June 2004).

In order for the Emetele cooperative to continue receiving the city's disbursements, the approximately 300 construction workers employed in the complex must be Buenos Aires residents, must have received no past city loans, and may not be on any type of government assistance (Limiroski, 2004). A future MTL assembly will decide the financial-need qualifications that will permit 334 MTL families to become homeowners who will repay the city loan as mortgage payments, up to a maximum of 42,000 pesos (approximately US$14,000) per family (for the larger, three-bedroom apartments) (Limiroski, 2004). With approximately 30,000 MTL members nationwide, this particular venture will not have a dramatic impact on the living standards of unemployed piqueteros, but the MTL leadership believes that its success could lead to more cooperatives being administered by the movement and financed by the state.

Concluding Remarks

We began this analysis with two main questions: How did the coalition between the MTL and the PC emerge? And how is the MTL's radical mobilization sustained? We argue here that the MTL association with the PC offered an alternative to traditional patterns of government-labor relations. The MTL's ability to draw upon the PC's autonomy and institutional strength allowed it to adopt more radical methods by avoiding compromise and dependence on government. For social movements, autonomy from government is crucial to avoid co-optation.

This would seem to be an odd coalition, given the radically different structures of these two groups—on the one hand a horizontally organized social movement, on the other a hierarchically structured political party. Our research reveals that the coalition was the result of preexisting ties between the PC, the CTA, and unemployed workers, coupled with conditions of economic collapse and policy decentralization. Further, the portrayal by the PC of the

CTA as a conciliatory organization created an opportunity for the MTL to move away from the centrist position of larger piquetero blocs. Under these conditions, the coalition became attractive to both PC activists and unemployed workers. It served the MTL because the PC was willing to grant it organizational autonomy and provide financial support for its employment projects through the IMFC. The PC's agenda calls for creating, organizing, and financing cooperative projects. The coalition may, however, prove more beneficial for the MTL than for the PC. When asked if the MTL members would vote PC, Viktor Kot, the PC's undersecretary said (interview, Buenos Aires, August 2004), "Of course not. They vote Peronist." The electability of the PC (and other leftist parties) remains as limited as ever.

VII

TRANSNATIONAL DIMENSIONS OF SOCIAL MOVEMENTS

Foro Mesoamericano rally, San Salvador, El Salvador, July 2004. Photo courtesy of Rose J. Spalding.

P REVIOUSLY, SOCIAL MOVEMENTS were thought of as loose collections of individuals and groups organizing around issues of social change within a national society, acting outside the framework of that country's normal political conventions and institutions. The process of globalization has left that definition behind, as the social changes that affect people's lives are increasingly impacted by decision-making mechanisms above the level of the nation-state, such as transnational corporations (TNCs), international financial institutions (IFIs), or the instantaneous electronic transfer of vast quantities of money in the global currency markets. The spread of neoliberal ideology has facilitated this shift in the locus of power by deregulating the movement of capital and commodities (but not labor) around the world, while selling the idea that consumer "choice" is a substitute for democracy. In this altered environment engendered by globalization from above, grassroots movements for social justice are challenged to find new organizing sites and strategies to develop alternative forms of globalization from below.

The idea of globalizing grassroots movements sounds contradictory, but organizers are learning to move beyond nostalgic views of what it means to be an activist in their respective communities. In the examples considered in this section, indigenous peoples in Chiapas have built networks around a broadened "Zapatista" identity, while peasants and small farmers around the world have constructed an identity of a peasant international, and local groups opposing dam projects and sweatshops in southern Mexico and Central America have come together as a Mesoamerican movement against free trade agreements and mega-development projects. These newer transnational movements follow in the footsteps of earlier attempts to organize transnational human rights and social justice movements in Central America, the United States, and Western Europe in the 1980s. Whether the newer movements constitute loose "networks" or more fully integrated transnational social movements, there is clearly an emerging transnational dimension where issues are framed and movements strategize forms of resistance against the dominant model of globalization.

Alicia Swords focuses on the way the Zapatistas, rooted in indigenous communities in Chiapas, built "neo-Zapatista networks" of Mexican and international grassroots and nongovernmental supporters. Those networks, which sprang up immediately following the January 1994 rebellion, proved crucial in parrying the government's attempt to crush the Zapatistas and in breaking the information blockade. Swords analyzes the cultural politics of the networks, arguing that through a process of "networked learning" that is transforming politics well beyond the communities in Chiapas, these networks have begun to redefine social power by changing the way we think about such crucial concepts as democracy and development.

María Elena Martínez and Peter Rosset offer a detailed inside look at the emergence and consolidation of La Vía Campesina, a kind of peasant international that spread from Latin America to five continents. They suggest it may be one of the most important examples of a transnational social movement in the world. They situate this development in the context of the changing political economy and emerging collective consciousness among the region's rural poor 500 years after colonization. Highlighting the movement's accomplishments in forcing the concept of people's food sovereignty onto the global agenda, Martínez and Rosset attribute the success of Vía Campesina to its persistently combative forms of nonviolent direct action, its bottom-up structure, and its independence from governments and other hierarchical actors.

Rose Spalding's analysis of the Foro Mesoamericano coalition formed in 2001, which mobilized against Mexican President Vicente Fox's proposed Plan Puebla Panamá (PPP) and the Central America Free Trade Agreement (CAFTA), sounds a more cautionary note. Bypassing negotiations for fear of co-optation, the Foro's confrontational style was used as an excuse by national governments and international agencies to fast-track their free-trade schemes and evade accountability. The movement's transnational networking had some success in coordinating issue framing and consciousness raising, but the Foro was less effective in defending economic and social rights at the policy level.

The chapters in this section highlight the importance of strategic flexibility in building transnational movement alliances that can adapt to the changing forms and sites of globalization struggles. It should also be noted that the development of transnational organizing around the phenomena of migration and immigrant rights is another—though not well-studied—piece of the picture. As globalization reduces the relevance of geography and the regulatory significance of national borders, social movements are reimagining communities and redesigning organizing strategies accordingly. The transnationalization of social movements has had positive outcomes by reducing the isolation of some grassroots organizations, developing more sophisticated strategies, and, in several cases, halting repressive mechanisms of the state. Some outcomes, however, are less successful, as the grass roots can be co-opted by transnational nongovernmental organizations, develop dependency on them, or become overwhelmed with the dual pressures of maintaining their grassroots efforts while also engaging the global.

17

Neo-Zapatista Network Politics

Transforming Democracy and Development

Alicia C. S. Swords

SINCE THE INDIGENOUS ZAPATISTA UPRISING in 1994 in Chiapas, Mexico, Zapatista autonomous communities have inspired liberation-theology, campesino, women's, human rights, and indigenous organizations—even some that they oppose publicly—to support their demands. This chapter uses ethnographic evidence to examine the cultural politics (Alvarez, Dagnino, and Escobar, 1998a) by which three independent organizations learned practices of participation and autonomy to challenge hegemonic procedural democracy and neoliberal economic development. I first outline my research approach, the context, and the position of these organizations in neo-Zapatista networks (Leyva-Solano, 1999). I go on to describe how three of them learned to implement participatory democracy from observing elections, carrying out a popular referendum, and challenging the government's military strategy. Finally, I examine how they are beginning to create modes of autonomous development by opposing the Plan Puebla-Panamá infrastructure development project and rejecting government programs. Independent organizations influenced by the Zapatistas developed unique positions in challenging corporate pressures and state policies. Between 1994 and 2004, neo-Zapatista networks succeeded in strengthening demands for deeper democracy, and implementing networked modes of political participation and community-based survival projects. While calling for autonomy, they reembedded political and economic decision making in social values of respect, dignity, and community. This suggests that change agents in a network may include organizations that are not recognized

The original version of this essay appeared in *Latin American Perspectives* 34 (2), March 2007: 78–93.

or explicitly supported by the initial proponents of change. As lessons from the Zapatistas are adapted, political learning is diffused through civil-society networks as it constitutes new forms of network politics and extends the resistance to neoliberalism.

This research is based on ethnographic fieldwork conducted during 16 months from June 2002 to August 2004 in Chiapas, Mexico. The core of the project was a collaborative inquiry (Reason and McArdle, 2004) with popular educators from three neo-Zapatista organizations: the Coffee Initiative (a network of coffee producers in northern Chiapas), an indigenous women's collective from the frontier region, and the Alianza Cívica-Chiapas (Chiapas Civic Alliance—ACCh), a pro-democracy organization. (Names of all individuals, and of the first two organizations, have been changed, following participants' preferences.) I selected these organizations because of their support for the demands of the Ejército Zapatista de Liberación Nacional (Zapatista Army of National Liberation—EZLN) and their commitment to political education and interest in reflecting on political education strategies. These organizations are not "representative" of the network, but they give a sense of its diversity. The research involved meetings with popular educators and participant observation at several network meetings and at 16 two-to-three-day workshops and forums. I analyzed historical documents and organizational archives and conducted 35 interviews with workshop participants, as well as with government leaders, intellectuals, and journalists. Observing power relationships among participants and documenting changes in practices over time allowed me to examine the broader consequences of the neo-Zapatista networks for politics in Mexico and beyond.

The G8 nexus, or leaders of the top world economies (United States, Japan, Germany, France, Britain, Italy, Canada, and Russia), pressure states to reform their constitutions to facilitate capital expansion and constrain democracy (Gill, 1998) and to use military force to protect strategic resources (Ceceña, 2002). I examine the globalization project (McMichael, 2000) as a lived material process buttressed by an ideological formation—sets of discourses and practices in a contested field of power relationships. While democracy and development are potential organizing concepts for neoliberal governance, they are also taken up by those dispossessed by neoliberalism. Nongovernmental organizations (NGOs) and grassroots groups are a major terrain of struggle between elite neoliberal interests and their challengers.

This chapter focuses on the cultural politics of the neo-Zapatista networks— how these actors generate meanings and practices that "redefine social power" (Alvarez, Dagnino, and Escobar 1998b, 7). The Latin American social movement theorists Alvarez, Dagnino, and Escobar understand cultural politics as "the process enacted when sets of social actors shaped by, and embodying, different cultural meanings and practices come into conflict with each other." Such cultural politics are enacted when movements "deploy alternative conceptions of woman, nature, race, economy, democracy, or citizenship that unsettle dominant cultural meanings." I focus on the neo-Zapatista networks' challenge to the dominant meanings and practices of "democracy" and "development" as enacted specifically through neoliberal capitalist relations in southern Mexico. I argue that some NGOs and grassroots organizations, when confronted with the neoliberal notions of democracy and development, based on individualism and competition, choose to take lessons from the Zapatistas. Such choices are based on values of cooperation, community and solidarity, which have been taught through popular education, or informal consciousness-raising workshops led by civil society organizations (Swords, 2005). These organizations undermine the hegemonic practices (Gramsci, 1971) of state officials, the mainstream media, and international funders by implementing alternative modes of political action. For Gramsci, hegemonic practices are those that are accepted as part of popular common sense so as not to require physical force to be imposed. These organizations' innovative politics includes resisting government social programs and "rule by obeying" (*mandar obedeciendo*)—a concept used by the Zapatistas to refer to the creation of new relationships between leaders and society involving accountability and horizontal decision making.

Since the 1994 uprising in Chiapas, Zapatista support-base communities have moved toward autonomy from the Mexican state. To assert autonomy— the ability to make community decisions locally (see Burguete, 1999; Stahler-Sholk, 2005; Esteva, 2003)—and to distance themselves from organizations that accept government funding, Zapatista leaders established *Juntas de Buen Gobierno* (good-government councils) in August 2003. With the June 2005 Sixth Declaration of the Lacandón Jungle, the Zapatistas declared their commitment to building an anticapitalist movement, beginning with the "Other Campaign," an outreach effort to link nonpartisan organizations around the country. As political candidates carried out presidential speaking tours, the Zapatistas created what I call a "listening tour," emphasizing politics from the bottom up and inviting people to tell their stories and share experiences of their struggles.

I focus here on organizations that support the Zapatistas but that the Zapatistas do not recognize as part of their base of support. Following Leyva Solano, I use the term "neo-Zapatista networks" to refer to networks linking three kinds of organizations: (1) the Zapatista core (the rebel army and autonomous or support-base communities); (2) independent grassroots organizations; and (3) NGOs, which act as intermediaries between the grassroots organizations and funders, internationals, and others. Through meetings, workshops, conferences, discussions, and debates these organizations form power-laden webs of social relations that involve conflict and collaboration. The neo-Zapatista networks are not simply transnational advocacy networks (Keck and Sikkink, 1998); they go beyond advocacy to take diverse actions against multiple targets in a common struggle against neoliberalism. Their historical origins are in the campesino, indigenous, liberation-theology, and women's movements that emerged during the crisis of development in Chiapas (Swords, 2005). Their access to capital and resources varies, from grassroots organizations that rely on volunteers' labor to NGOs with national or international funders. Corporations, governments, and international institutions vie for their loyalties and commitments with programs and funds.

Through interviews and conversations, I learned that the social bases and interests of the neo-Zapatista networks vary. Racial, ethnic, gender, class, religious, generational, and educational differences are significant, as are alliances and political strategies. The indigenous women's collective gained limited funds from an international donor. Its participants grew up on plantations as the children of indentured workers and now live in a rural village. Today they see "being organized," running their corn mill and corner-store cooperative, and challenging violence in their community as matters of survival but also as part of their commitment to family and to their indigenous identity. In terms of socioeconomic position, communal history, and social ties, this collective is relatively close to the Zapatista support base.

The Coffee Initiative includes indigenous farmers of several ethnic groups (smallholders with less than two hectares), and mestizo university researchers and extension agents. Bridging rural and urban realities, workshops promote organic fair-trade coffee production with a grant from a U.S. foundation. While researchers advance their studies and commitment to ecological farming, farmers earn a better price for their coffee so they can survive as rural producers. Some members of the Coffee Initiative are with the Zapatista support base; others align themselves with other organizations, and still others oppose the movement.

The ACCh employs a small staff, mainly college-educated, mestizo urban residents who are motivated by solidarity with poor and indigenous people in Chiapas. They have supported the Zapatista communities ideologically and with resources and logistics. The organization receives grants from a variety of sources for leadership education for grassroots leaders and municipal authorities. As a chapter of a national organization, the ACCh has mobility and access to resources beyond the state.

Although these and other neo-Zapatista organizations express support for the Zapatistas' demands, their economic and social bases, alliances and strategies differ and may contradict the Zapatistas' efforts. NGOs and grassroots organizations sometimes compromise their principles to satisfy funders (see Benessaieh, 2004), seek government favors, or acquiesce in government strategies of demobilization (Hidalgo, 2006). Since 1994, Zapatista responses to organizations that offer solidarity have changed. By developing the Juntas, the Zapatistas more strictly regulate their support base. They control NGO activities in their territory so that outsiders cannot speak for them or set agendas (see, e.g., Earle and Simonelli, 2005). In November 2005 the EZLN dissolved the Frente Zapatista de Liberación Nacional (Marcos, 2005) and limited the roles of Enlace Civil and other intermediaries so that proximity to the EZLN could not be used for personal or group advantage. The focus here is on learning inspired by Zapatistas. Further study may consider Zapatista responses to neo-Zapatista practices.

Democracy

During the past 10 years the neo-Zapatista networks have pushed to deepen the definition of "democracy" and expand participation. Independent movements in Mexico began in the 1970s to demand and achieve democratic reforms (N. Harvey, 1998). There has been increasing consensus that democracy is central to development (Levy and Bruhn, 2001) as diverse sectors challenge concentration of power in the president (Garrido, 1989) and control by the Partido Revolucionario Institucional (Institutional Revolutionary Party—PRI), which governed for more than 70 years. In a formal sense democracy may mean free and fair elections, but popularly it came to mean removing the PRI. The Zapatistas forced the government to consider more far-reaching reforms than would have been considered prior to 1994. Their demands extend beyond procedural democracy, the current hegemonic form of politics in which voting is limited to certain spheres so that citizen participation does not constrain capital (Gill, 1998). They extend to rights to participation in all areas of social, economic, cultural, and political life (N. Harvey, 1998). Through interactions with Zapatista efforts, ACCh leaders came to see the removal of the PRI as insufficient and promoted practices based on respect and protection for indigenous peoples, peasants, and others marginalized by neoliberal and electoral politics. The experiences of ACCh electoral observers, organizers of the 1999 indigenous rights referendum, and those demanding demilitarization after the 2000 elections exemplify networked learning. Their testimonies demonstrate how a neo-Zapatista organization redefined democracy as a process that includes discussion, educating citizens and officials, and transforming power relations toward "rule by obeying" in their everyday work.

Observing Elections

Monitoring elections raised consciousness among ACCh volunteers about the possibilities for citizen participation in national decision making. Marta, a popular educator with ACCh, saw monitoring as a strategy for educating observers and other citizens (interview, San Cristóbal, 2004). Mario, another observer, described people's determination to vote in 1994 in the Zapatista support-base community Ejido Morelia (interview, San Cristóbal, 2004). A community group denounced the violation of their right to vote because the federal army had confiscated their electoral credentials after the Zapatista uprising. By ten o'clock on Election Day, ballots were running out, so the ejidal assembly approved the use of alternative ballots. People kept voting, although official procedures did not validate their votes. One family generously cooked for voters who came from far away. Mario said it was not the elections' results in Morelia but the people's desire to participate and enthusiasm for collective effort that motivated his leadership with the ACCh.

The election observers saw that people could organize to make decisions and began to feel that people's participation mattered, but Mario and Marta became frustrated with limited roles as observers. Witnessing the collective spirit for organization pushed them not only to challenge electoral corruption but also to build deeper democratic processes. Because they now saw possibilities for more inclusive decision-making, they pushed the ACCh to change its organizing focus. Mario explained that as their programs changed from "purely electoral work" to developing leaders, "the national office criticized us. They said, 'You and your little workshops!' because they only counted the political-electoral part. I said, 'Nooooo!' What's important is base organizing and local development which became our strength" (interview, San Cristóbal, 2004).

The 1999 Indigenous Rights Referendum

Popular referenda (*consultas*) were another way in which NGO and grassroots volunteers learned to challenge constrained democracy. In 1999, the EZLN and its civil base of support proposed a referendum on indigenous rights. They asked Mexicans to vote on including indigenous peoples in Mexico's national project, on recognizing indigenous rights and the 1996 San Andrés Accords (on indigenous rights and culture), on demilitarizing the country, and on permitting self-organization toward "rule by obeying." The ACCh received and counted the votes. To prepare for the referendum, EZLN delegates and thousands of civil-society volunteers organized educational forums with local organizations throughout Mexico. At least 851,858 people participated in organizing 4,811 working groups and assemblies around the country (Sámano Rentería, 2000). Five thousand Zapatista representatives, approximately half women and half men, traveled the country to raise awareness about indigenous rights. This process demonstrated the EZLN's capacity for political mobilization and embodied a networked popular education campaign (Swords, 2005). It was empowering for Zapatista delegates and other volunteers to develop leadership, visit parts of Mexico they had never seen, talk with sympathetic organizations, hear about the range of struggles in Mexico, and teach about rights and political participation. As Gustavo Castro of the Centro de Investigaciones Económicas y Políticas de Acción Comunitaria (Center for Economic and Political Research for Community Action—CIEPAC) stated, "as the largest volunteer mobilization in years, [the referendum] shows that the most oppressed have this capacity" (interview, San Cristóbal, 1999).

I traveled to Chiapas in March 1999 to observe the referendum. In Acteal, site of the paramilitary massacre in 1997, 16 Zapatista delegates arrived to raise awareness about the referendum. The elders of the civil organization Las Abejas offered the Zapatistas a ritual welcome. The Zapatistas explained the questions in the local indigenous language, Tzotzil, listened to the community's questions and concerns, and invited community members to vote. Their visit included celebratory dancing and music, and a collective remembrance of the victims of the massacre. A woman from Acteal told me, "Our hearts are sad today for the victims of Acteal, but happy and hopeful about the referendum." My observations and interviews suggest that, more than a voting procedure, the referendum was a relationship-building process that created linkages between Zapatistas and other organizations through recognition of their mutual struggles, losses, and possibilities for healing.

In the referendum, participants and leaders learned a process for discussing issues of collective concern. Citizens cast ballots after talking with Zapatista delegates about their struggles and learning about issues beyond their localities. With this process, the EZLN challenged the PRI's long-standing practices of electoral fraud, manipulation, and coercion. Volunteers and Zapatista delegates learned to listen to others' concerns and educate them about broader issues. This process strengthened the legitimacy and capacity of the independent organizations. The referendum's questions raised awareness about the inclusion of indigenous people in Mexico's national project, territorial and cultural rights, "rule by obeying," and an end to the military presence in Chiapas. Of those who voted, 95 percent voted yes on all four questions (Sámano Rentería, 2000). Although the media minimized the results, the referendum gathered knowledge about grassroots experiences, developed leadership, and transmitted practices of democracy as "rule by obeying."

In spite of their initial narrow mandate, in the process of organizing the referendum members of the ACCh staff began to see democracy as requiring deeper participation, including education and leadership development. As Marta said, "When you promote the referendum, you must explain what you're asking. . . . It's not the result that's important but the process of education and organizing." They also came to believe that enhancing democratic processes required education of both citizens and authorities. Marta explained,

> There's an educational component for the people *and* for the authorities, so that the authorities understand that citizens have the right to inform them, make proposals, and demand that they do their jobs. We used to believe that if the government said something, the people should just say, "Yes, Sir, Mr. President." . . . The issue is to seek adequate channels so that they don't disregard you so easily.

After the referendum, the ACCh began to organize workshops to educate municipal authorities about civic participation. As Marta explained, they aimed to shift power relationships and create "adequate channels" so that the authorities would learn from their constituents about how to govern. This, she said, was the real meaning of "rule by obeying" (interview, 2004).

From the referendum, some neo-Zapatista organizations learned to increase the everyday inclusion and participation of indigenous people and women and others traditionally left out of decision making. The ACCh began a series of workshops for grassroots leaders called the "Methodological School," which included a unit about democracy as a process of organizing, public meetings, collective debate, and popular education. Rosa of the indigenous women's collective said that the women used to cover their faces in shame, but after taking part in ACCh's workshops they now shared their opinions in meetings. They had begun rotating jobs in the cooperative, which they saw as part of the Zapatista philosophy of "rule by obeying" (Rosa, interview, Zona Fronteriza, 2004). Raúl of the Coffee Initiative noted that after taking part in the workshops, coffee farmers learned to expect more involvement in leading their local organizations. They began challenging traditional cacique (boss) leadership by questioning leaders (interview, San Cristóbal, 2004). In these ways, networks and organizations are transmitting and implementing practices learned in the referendum.

Democracy and Demilitarization

In 2000, opposition parties won the federal and Chiapas state elections, reflecting a long-term movement for democracy. Vicente Fox won the presidency in part due to strategic voting (*el voto útil*) by supporters of the center-left Partido de la Revolución Democrática (Revolutionary Democratic Party—PRD) (Camín, 2000), after Fox promised to resolve the Chiapas problem in 15 minutes (Fox, 2001), pass an indigenous rights law in accordance with the San Andrés Accords, and design regional development with indigenous participation (N. Harvey, 2004). The EZLN had advocated abstention, as Subcomandante Marcos (2000) declared, "Democracy is much more than an electoral contest or the alternation of power." In response to the elections, neo-Zapatista organizations including the ACCh, the indigenous women's collective and the Coffee Initiative insist that democracy means not only removing the PRI but also creating civil solutions to the Chiapas conflict based on values of peace and dignity.

When Vicente Fox assumed the presidency, he prioritized Chiapas on the national agenda and ordered the closure of 53 military checkpoints (Hidalgo, 2006), but military occupation continues (Gallardo et al., 2000). After months of silence, the Zapatistas recognized a new political opportunity and outlined conditions for reinitiating dialogue: upholding the San Andrés Accords, liberation of the Zapatista prisoners, and the closing of seven military bases in the Zapatista zone (SIPAZ, 2004). In December 2000 Fox sent a constitutional reform to Congress on indigenous rights and culture, but Congress passed a version of the Indigenous Law in August 2001 that did not consider the proposal that had resulted from the San Andrés dialogues. It relied on a limited concept of indigenous autonomy and violated the San Andrés Accords by not recognizing community and municipal forms of association and collective rights to territory and resources (SIPAZ, 2004). The EZLN and its supporting organizations denounced the law as a betrayal (Red de Defensores, 2001).

Pablo Salazar's victory in the Chiapas gubernatorial elections reflected pressures for indigenous rights, transparency and democracy, and a break with fraud, including the PRI's appointment of "elected" officials (see N. Harvey, 1998; Ross, 2000). Yet while the Salazar and Fox governments replaced the direct military strategy in Chiapas with co-optative measures and multiculturalist rhetoric, their political and economic strategies continued to exclude indigenous people (Hernández, Paz, and Sierra, 2004) and to co-opt and demobilize them using a military counterinsurgency strategy (Hidalgo, 2006). In this context, neo-Zapatista organizations from San Cristóbal convened a Hemispheric Conference against Militarization in San Cristóbal in May 2003. Workshops explained the international context of militarization in Chiapas, and the Mexican government's need to demonstrate harsh repression against the threat of a people's movement. The final declaration stated that militarization helped national and international elites gain access to oil, biodiversity, and water resources and undermine indigenous rights to territory (Castro,

2003). At workshops I observed as part of a Demilitarization Week in San Cristóbal in November 2003, participants denounced military attacks and human rights violations. Leaders explained that these undermined democracy. Rosa from the indigenous women's collective testified, "We felt so much humiliation and fear from soldiers, [PRI-ist] municipal authorities, and paramilitaries, but we are supposed to have freedom of organization." By hearing each other's testimony, participants learned that their experiences were not isolated but part of a statewide government-military plan. They concluded that the Fox and Salazar governments could not achieve democracy without fulfilling the San Andrés Accords.

In the pro-Zapatista forums in which I participated, leaders and participants frequently denounced the low-intensity warfare in Chiapas, a term that the San Cristóbal-based NGO SIPAZ (2006) defines as the "modality of counterinsurgency war against organized peoples" that uses psychological, military, religious, and informational tools to disarticulate movements that challenge the status quo and "destroy the support bases of the EZLN." Anthropologist López y Rivas (2004) and some human rights advocates use the term "war of attrition," to highlight that the war's intensity is not "low" for its victims. Terms for describing military policy in Chiapas are heavily politicized and debated. "Low-intensity warfare" usually refers to the use of death squads, assassinations, and other forms of overt violence, and it seems risky to extend the concept. Yet leaders and participants in NGO and grassroots-organization activities often extended the term's meaning to include government social programs aimed at breaking down the communal social fabric and isolating Zapatista supporters (López y Rivas, 2004; Hidalgo, 2006). Jorge Santiago of the San Cristóbal NGO Socio-Economic Development of Indigenous Mexicans (Desarrollo Económico Social de los Mexicanos Indígenas—DESMI) accused the Salazar government of continuing low-intensity warfare in a more "publicly acceptable way" through social programs (interview, San Cristóbal, 2004). Counterinsurgency-oriented social programs are complemented by direct violence of paramilitaries, whose links with the government have been documented by the Fray Bartolomé Human Rights Center, among others.

Low-intensity warfare and government programs were topics of roundtables at the Mesoamerican Forum for Biological and Cultural Diversity at Xela (Quetzaltenango, Guatemala) in June 2002 and the Forum against Neoliberalism at Huitiupan (Chiapas) in March 2004. Although government programs were not directly violent, some NGO and grassroots-organization leaders believed that they caused "community divisions," interethnic and intergroup conflicts, paralysis of independent organizations, and destruction of community life. In interviews (Zona Fronteriza, 2004), Francisca and Rosa of the indigenous women's collective described effects of low-intensity warfare, including harassment at military checkpoints, arguments with neighbors who belonged to the PRI, replacement of pro-Zapatista clergy, and attrition when members accept government programs. Raúl of the Coffee Initiative criticized the government's "counterinsurgency strategy" of co-opting cooperatives through "palliatives, paternalistic programs that limit people's voice and consciousness" (interview, San Cristóbal, 2004). After the 2000 elections, these leaders asserted that democracy could not be achieved in a context of war, in which government programs undermined independent social organization and divided communities.

Through election monitoring, the 1999 referendum, public forums, and daily organizational practices, the neo-Zapatista networks create deeper meanings of democracy not as procedure but as a collective educational process of expanding participation. For the ACCh, democracy is a collective process enacted with grassroots leadership training schools and education for elected officials. For the indigenous women's collective, it means staying organized and rotating jobs, and for the Coffee Initiative it means questioning leaders and increasing farmers' involvement. Beginning January 1, 2006, the Zapatistas traveled with the "Other Campaign" to meet with independent organizations across the country. These efforts may inspire a commitment on the part of the neo-Zapatista organizations to deepen democracy by including people and issues left out of national political debates.

Social Development

According to Marcos Mena, Director of Institutional Management in Planning of the Ministry of Social Development, after the Zapatista uprising federal efforts to address indigenous poverty increased (interview, Mexico City, 2004). Federal public spending in Chiapas has remained at about 3 percent of the national total since 1994, but targeted funds for poverty alleviation through the Oportunidades program increased from 3 percent in 1994 to 9.7 percent of the national total or $285 million (V. Fox, 2005). Development discourse appeared as the main analysis of the rebellion (Hernández, Paz, and Sierra, 2004). Social programs were first implemented by the army with Plan Cañadas and targeted non-Zapatista recipients (Ledesma, 2000). Since 1994 the EZLN and Zapatista support-base communities have been expected to reject government programs. They challenge dominant notions of social development by consolidating autonomy through a regional process of governance with the Juntas de Buen Gobierno (Stahler-Sholk, 2005, 2006). They disrupt the meanings and practices of development by insisting on respect for local autonomy and by organizing with other anticapitalist organizations nationally and internationally.

As the Zapatistas continue to build autonomy and networks of movements, neo-Zapatista networks take up their lessons with alternative development initiatives and attempts to live "in resistance."

The Campaign against Plan Puebla-Panamá

In 2002, a network of organizations across southern Mexico said a consistent no to the Plan Puebla-Panamá, a massive infrastructure and economic development program (see Spalding chapter in this volume). Along with the EZLN, NGOs and grassroots organizations alleged that the plan threatened indigenous rights to territory, resources, and autonomy with hydroelectric dams, gas and oil pipelines, biological corridors, and free-trade zones. Participating organizations expressed demands as campesinos, women, indigenous people, workers, students, and teachers, calling for alternative regional development with an explicit social agenda (Call, 2002). I observed network workshops that linked the plan with corporate pressures on the government to remove indigenous communities from ancestral lands, to privatize and commodify genetic, biological, and mineral resources, to militarize the region, and to open the area to free trade.

In 2002, my conversations with independent indigenous, campesino and women's organizations turned quickly to the plan. On October 12, 2002, tens of thousands marched to protest the plan throughout Mesoamerica in one of the first regionally coordinated actions (Pickard, 2003). Since 2000, Chiapan NGOs and grassroots groups had been forming networks to coordinate statewide and regional educational forums in which they taught each other skills for organizing. Two or three hundred organizations attended the forums in Tapachula, Chiapas (May 2001), Guatemala (November 2001), Nicaragua (July 2002), and Honduras (July 2003) (Call, 2002). In network meetings I observed, responsibilities were rotated to teach "newer" groups organizing skills. Activists visited each other's community and shared stories of successful resistance. Communities designated as sites for dams or highways shared experiences with those that had resisted these projects. At network events I attended, participants shared information on proposed projects, expressed consistent opposition, insisted on true participation in planning and implementation, resisted government-led planning events, and promoted alternative local development strategies (see also Call, 2002; N. Harvey, 2004).

Widespread grassroots protests and changing international capitalist pressures due to Mexico's economic stagnation and China's attraction as a labor source forced the Fox government to rethink the Plan Puebla-Panamá. By September 2002 Fox had failed to attract low-interest loans for the plan from the

Inter-American Development Bank and the World Bank. The federal budget for the plan was cut from US$750 million in 2002 to US$210 million in 2003 (Pickard, 2003). By 2003, the plan was hardly mentioned in the press, and analysts believed that it was frozen. Its general coordinating office admitted that the public relations campaign for the plan had failed (Pickard, 2003). In addition to financial failures, my observations suggest that the organizations were so diverse that the state could not easily co-opt their demands. The network demonstrated such resistance that the Mexican government could not push through the plan without seeking local legitimacy (Pickard, 2003; Call, 2003).

As the Plan Puebla-Panamá is removed from the public eye, its projects continue to be implemented separately. From 2002 to 2004 I observed many pro-Zapatista organizations that continued to oppose the plan. Networks of NGOs and grassroots organizations in San Cristóbal, southern Mexico and in Central America kept on gathering information and mobilizing to denounce the plan. Building on the EZLN's efforts toward autonomy, the campaign opposing the plan popularizes counterhegemonic practices of development that fit with its social values, including territorial autonomy, and popular control over land, work, resources, knowledge, and life forms. In this vein, Mario from the ACCh asserts that corporations can't control life: "What we need, is control, right? Control over what you eat, what you consume, what you produce, control over your seeds, your land, your water. The work to build alternatives is the work to gain control over your life" (interview, San Cristóbal, 2004).

Farmers from the Coffee Initiative participated in forums against the Plan Puebla-Panamá and against neoliberalism. Raúl explained that because of what they had learned at the forums, the Coffee Initiative had shifted from just seeking fair-trade markets for coffee to diversifying production and seeking food security: "We're working for a more equitable system to benefit campesino communities" (interview, San Cristóbal, 2004). A few communities began growing exotic fruits, honey, and eggs, which made it easier for people to feed their families.

In Resistance

From 2002 to 2004 I observed Mesoamerican forums of NGOs and grassroots organizations, interviewed participants, and observed the organizations' popular education activities. Organizers (see Red de Defensores, 2001; Castro, 2003, for lists of participating organizations) shifted the emphasis in popular education programs from opposing the Plan Puebla-Panamá to opposing government programs (Swords, 2005) such as Oportunidades and PROCEDE, which they saw as opposed to communal values and as a new strategy for dividing communities and controlling resources. The federal program Oportunidades (Opportunities) provides cash payments to poor women with school-age children if they attend workshops on public health, sanitation and family planning. PROCEDE (Program of Certification of Ejido Rights and Titling of Urban Parcels) is the federal land titling program that began after the 1992 reforms allowed the sale of ejido lands. At a forum against neoliberalism, Mercedes Olivera (2004), adviser to the Independent Women's Movement, explained that the Oportunidades program aimed to make women subordinate so that they would reproduce cheap labor.

Some Chiapan-led grassroots organizations followed the EZLN's call to reject government programs. Although the EZLN does not recognize it as support-base community, the indigenous women's collective declares it is "in resistance." Francisca (interview, Zona Fronteriza, 2004) explains,

> We say no more crumbs from the government. . . . The municipal president's office offered a sheep and chicken project. We thought the sheep would thrive, but most of them died. The chickens *all* died. Then [the municipal government representatives] said we had to pay for the sheep. (*Laughs*). We said, "We won't pay for them. They all died!" . . . How is it good for us if the animals all die? So [the collective] signed a declaration to no longer receive [government funding].

Up to 28 out of 35 women dropped out of the collective when they could not challenge their husbands' demands that they accept funds from Oportunidades rather than take part in the collective (Francisca, interview, Zona Fronteriza, 2004). But, Francisca insisted, it's "better to work with our two cooperatives" than accept government funding because the women who left the organization had no time to attend meetings. She felt their cooperative was a more secure alternative than government cash assistance programs because it allowed the women to stay organized. She distinguished between "independent" cooperatives like hers in which members benefited collectively, and "government programs" in which benefits targeted individuals:

> It's a disgrace. . . . Some [organizations] were with the EZLN, but when they received land grants, they negotiated with the government. They said, "we got what we wanted, so we'll leave the EZLN, even if the government screws us later." In my organization, I never negotiate with the government. I demand that they respect my rights. Then they can't control me, because I'm not getting anything from them. They offer projects to trick us, to cover our eyes so we can't tell whether they're complying with the [San Andrés] dialogues. For me a real project is a project of life, of respect.

For the collective's women, living "in resistance" goes beyond the struggle for economic survival; it means demanding respect, especially from their hus-

bands and fathers. Patricia's father, who was loyal to a government organization, challenged her participation. "He'd threaten me, 'Either you leave my
house or you leave the organization.' But I didn't obey him. . . . Now it's a little better. I say I'm going and he says, 'OK, take care'" (interview, Zona Fronteriza, 2003). Patricia's experience exemplifies how gaining leadership through
network activities has pushed women to demand respect in unequal household and intimate relationships.

Transforming Politics through Networked Learning

These ethnographic observations highlight innovative social-movement practices. Learning from the Zapatistas in election monitoring and the referendum,
participants in the ACCh, the indigenous women's collective and the Coffee Initiative have developed modes of participatory democracy shaped by community values that are challenging hegemonic practices of democracy. Through
network activities, they learn to implement "rule by obeying" by educating and
questioning leaders, rotating jobs, discussing issues, and challenging hierarchies.
Through analysis of Fox's and Salazar's military policies at network events, participants recognize patterns of human rights violations, reject government programs, and assert the right to organize. At forums opposing the Plan Puebla-
Panamá and government programs, NGO and grassroots-organization leaders
learn alternatives for challenging hegemonic concepts of development: cooperative production, diversification, and "control over life." From the Zapatistas' example and at network events, the women of the collective learn to reject government programs, strengthen cooperatives, rotate leadership, and challenge
men's authority. Coffee Initiative leaders learn to enhance indigenous farmer
participation, crop diversification and food security. The three organizations
challenge prescriptions for development and procedures for democracy as they
adapt lessons from the Zapatistas to local realities.

The neo-Zapatista networks enact learning processes that open spaces for
indigenous people and women to assert their right to make political and economic decisions. As these networks use cultural politics to confront procedural democracy and neoliberal development, they extend changes beyond
the Zapatista support base. Further research should examine how state and
transnational actors respond to organizational networks in Mexico and in
comparative contexts. As networks adapt lessons to local realities and broaden
participation beyond vanguard models, they achieve unique flexibility, but
they are not without tensions. To prevent their absorption or neutralization
by neoliberal policies, autonomous efforts must connect in broader movements. Neo-Zapatista network politics represents this potential.

18

La Vía Campesina

Transnationalizing Peasant Struggle and Hope

María Elena Martínez-Torres and Peter M. Rosset

A NALYSTS HAVE LONG PREDICTED the demise and disappearance of the peasantry as an inevitable result of the penetration of agriculture by capitalism (Kaustky, 1899; Hobsbawm, 1994). Nevertheless, Latin American peasant communities have not only refused to disappear, but in recent years have organized in a sophisticated, transnational way to respond to the neoliberal phase of late capitalism (Kearney, 1996). In the neoliberal era, supranational corporations and institutions dictating neoliberal policies have negatively affected most sectors of society, in such a way that class or cultural differences are no longer the barrier they once were for transnational collective action. In fact, Latin American rural organizations, together with peasantries around the world have globalized the struggle from below, by forming La Vía Campesina (literally, "the peasant way"; see www.viacampesina.org). In doing so, they have envisioned an "agrarian trajectory that would reintegrate food production and nature as an alternative culture of modernity" (McMichael, 2006: 416). Many consider Vía to be the most important transnational social movement in the world (Borras, 2004; McMichael, 2006; Patel, 2005, 2006; Edelman, 2005). It is arguably among the grassroots movements that are "the most innovative actors in setting agendas for political and social policies" (Yúdice, 1998: 353). No other sector has been able to build such a structured, representative, and legitimate movement, with a common identity, that links social struggles on five continents. It is present in many countries that share the same global problems even though they confront different local and national realities. It has been called a "real Farmers' International, a living example of a new relationship between North and South"

(Bové, 2001: 96), which has bridged the "global divide" between actors from northern and southern countries (J. Smith, 2002).

Vía today is the leading network of grassroots organizations with presence in the antiglobalization, or "*altermundista*" ("another world"), movement, as manifested in protests against the World Trade Organization (WTO) and Free Trade Area of the Americas (FTAA), in the World Social Forum (WSF) process, in its scathing critiques of World Bank land policies, and in its ability to force the novel concept of *food sovereignty* into common usage (Rosset, 2006a, 2006b; Vía Campesina, 2004; McMichael, 2006; Patel, 2005, 2006). Its member organizations have even helped topple national governments, as in Ecuador in 2000 and Bolivia in 2003 (Edelman, 2005: 337).

It can be thought of as "the international peasant movement," analogous to "the international environmental movement," or "the international women's movement," though Vía Campesina has a tighter, more formal coordination than either of those two examples. It is also an autonomous (independent from political parties, governments, religious institutions, or nongovernmental organizations [NGOs]) and pluralistic movement (Desmarais, 2002, 2003a, 2003b, 2003c, 2005).

In order to understand the rise of La Vía Campesina, we must first locate this process within the transformation of the state in Latin America (mirrored in other continents) and its role in rural areas. It is the changing nature of state intervention in recent decades that generated significant new challenges for rural peoples, and in coping with and confronting states, peasants formed a new generation of organizations that have moved toward the international stage. The neoliberal model forced a restructuring of state/society relations, and it was in this space that new forms of social movement organizing—more autonomous, horizontal, and more based on collective identities rather than just social class—began to flourish (Alvarez, Dagnino, and Escobar, 1998a).

As political parties and their domesticated organizations became increasingly irrelevant for rural peoples, a new generation of peasant organizations came to the fore. The older organizations either disappeared altogether, or became mere shells of their former selves, having leaders but few followers, or they mutated into the new style of organizations. These new organizations, either born from the older ones or founded virtually from scratch (sometimes with former members of armed guerrilla movements in their leadership), were typically founded on principles of *autonomy* from political parties, government offices, the church, and NGOs (see Foley, 1995, for example). To a greater or lesser extent these new organizations rejected the clientelism and corporatism of their forebears and refused to be subordinated to urban interests. They called for a mixture of restoring improved versions of the state services cut back by neoliberalism and making structural changes (such as agrarian reform and support for national markets), a policy mix that would combine to favor peasant agriculture. They were, and remain, much more radical than the earlier generation of corporatist organizations, though it would be an exaggeration to say that they have eradicated clientelistic behaviors and attitudes, which vary from country to country and organization to organization (Petras and Veltmeyer, 2002). But these organizations, born in the age of the minimalist state, soon found that national problems could not be solved by just appealing to, or pressuring, weak national governments (Desmarais, 2002, 2003a, 2003b, 2003c, 2005).

In the 1980s and 1990s, the greatest problem their members faced was the rapid decline of crop and livestock prices due to globalization felt through market opening under structural adjustment and free trade agreements like the GATT (General Agreement on Tariffs and Trade), WTO, and NAFTA (North American Free Trade Agreement), as well as through the budget cutting and free market conditionality forced on their governments by the World Bank and International Monetary Fund (Conroy, Murray, and Rosset, 1996; Lappé et al., 1998; Rosset, 2006a). The organizations rapidly developed a political analysis that identified transnational corporations and international finance capital as driving forces behind the WTO, World Bank, International Monetary Fund (IMF) and free trade agreements, and it therefore became imperative to organize themselves at a supra- or transnational level.

Reasoning that their real enemies were transnational, the Vía Campesina organizations began to formulate a counter-hegemonic discourse informed by the transnational communication networks they were developing. Seeing that organizations in different countries faced the same problems led these organizations to seek common causes and identify common enemies. This then is the contextual reason why La Vía Campesina was born as a transnational peasant movement.

From *500 Years of Resistance* to a Transnational Social Movement

The birth of La Vía Campesina as a global peasant movement was foreshadowed in Latin America by the founding, in the early 1990s, of one of its direct forebears, the *Coordinadora Latinoamericana de Organizaciones del Campo* (Latin American Coordination of Rural Organizations—CLOC) (CLOC, 1994). CLOC in part grew out of the *"500 Years of Indigenous, Afro-descendant, Peasant and Popular Resistance" Continental Campaign*, which was launched in Colombia in 1989 (Edelman, 2003). Drawing on the powerful symbolism of the quincentennial of the arrival of Columbus in the Americas, and in opposition to the big celebrations planned by governments, the Declaration of

Quito—written after a "500 Years of Indian Resistance" meeting in 1990—outlined the basis of what later became the transnational peasant movement. The participants expressed a collective concern for the destruction of nature, with what Stefano Varese (1996: 60) calls the "moral management of the cosmos" or "moral ecology": "We do not own nature . . . it is not a commodity . . . it is an integral part of our life; it is our past, present, and future."

According to Varese (1996: 62), the "ecological cosmology of rural communities, based essentially on the notion and practice of individual usufruct of collective property and the primacy of use value, resisted the intrusion of a cosmology based on exchange value that corresponded to the capitalist market economy." Harkening back to the "moral economy" of James Scott (1977), Varese argues that even while indigenous and peasant families participate in capitalist market relations that are external to their communities, they maintain and reproduce noncapitalist relations on the inside. In this moral economy, community economic relations are based on the logic of reciprocity (neighbors helping neighbors) and production for subsistence. In fact, Marc Edelman (2005) argues that the transnational peasant movement is bringing the "moral economy" directly into the global debate over the future of agriculture, counterposing it to the dominant "market economy" paradigm.

Denouncing the "domination and exploitation suffered by our continent since the arrival of the invaders" (CLOC, 1997: 30), the 500 Years Campaign brought together organizations of indigenous people, peasants, workers, students, youth, teachers, unions, academics, women, and popular urban sectors, who questioned "official" versions of Latin American history that virtually ignored resistance to the conquest. The campaign made a culturally and ethnically diverse Latin American identity visible and generated pride in the continued resistance of peoples to conquest. Many of the Latin American movements were involved in struggles to establish rights: rights to livelihood, to one's body, to land, and "rights to have human rights," even those individual rights already established as universal rights in government constitutions (Pasuk, 1999: 4–5). Movement struggles in Latin America have increasingly insisted that collective/social rights must be part of a revised citizenship compact.

It is common for movements of very poor and marginalized people to have as their first goal to "recover their dignity and status as citizens and even as human beings" (Alvarez, Dagnino, and Escobar, 1998b: 5). The 500 Years Campaign helped create a deep project of constructing new collective identities and unity on the basis of peoples' right to self-determination and strengthening oppressed peoples' trust in their own intellectual, moral, and political capacity to fight for and exercise this right. At the same time, the campaign affirmed the cultural validity of the point of view of "the oppressed," in contrast to the dominant or official viewpoints (Girardi, 1994). This view was also reinforced by the "preferential option for the poor" advanced by liberation theology throughout Latin America (see Issa, this volume). Latin American social movements were fighting for the democratization of society as a whole, and that was to include an assault on the cultural practices that 500 years had embodied in social relations of exclusion and inequality (Dagnino, 1998: 47). Rooted in Latin America, these social movements "confront authoritarian culture through a resignifying of notions as rights, public and private spaces, forms of sociability, ethics, equality and difference, and so on" (Alvarez, Dagnino, and Escobar, 1998b: 10).

One very important outcome of the efforts in the campaign to link different sectors at a continental level was the decision in 1991 and 1992 by Latin American rural organizations to coordinate struggles for land, and against the then-new neoliberal model, by founding the CLOC (Doula, 2000: 366). The broad and overwhelming nature of the challenge that neoliberalism presented to all rural sectors meant that the CLOC was able to bring together groups whose sometimes diverging interests at the local level had historically kept them apart—like landless people, farm workers, and farmers, or indigenous and nonindigenous peasants.

Forty-seven organizations (peasants, indigenous people, farm workers, and rural women) from nineteen countries founded this transnational alliance, structured in five regions (North, Central, Caribbean, Andean, and Southern Cone), with a collective leadership composed of two rotating representatives from each region, an International Secretariat, and an issue-based or "thematic" division of work (Doula, 2000: 367). Such collective and rotating leadership is a characteristic of major contemporary Latin American social movements, like the Landless Workers' Movement (MST) in Brazil, the Zapatistas in Mexico, indigenous people in Ecuador, and so forth, and likely contributes to their strength by reducing the individualistic, personalistic, and clientelistic leadership that had weakened earlier generations of peasant organizations, albeit perhaps at some cost to "efficiency" as prioritized by "old left" and neoliberal institutions alike. By opening a transnational space, the CLOC was strengthening Latin American movements (J. Fox, 1994), so they were able to gain political influence and legitimate their claims through the simultaneous mobilization of actors at local, national, and international levels (Perreault, 2003: 100).

While Latin Americans were building the CLOC, peasant and family farm organizations in India, Europe, and North America were also coming to the conclusion that transnational struggle was needed to confront neoliberalism. While 200,000 peasants from across India held the "Seed Satyagraha" rally in Delhi against the patenting of seeds by multinational corporations under

GATT (Shiva, 1993), 30,000 farmers from across Europe marched against the GATT ministerial in Brussels (Edelman, 2003: 203), even as North American family farm organizations began building international connections with farmer groups in other countries (Desmarais, 2007).

National movements against neoliberal policies were cresting as they reached national borders, and they overflowed into rapidly jelling transnational networks. In the early 1990s, La Vía Campesina emerged from Latin America's CLOC and from similar concerns of organizations on other continents, as the wave of peasant dissatisfaction and movements "crested" into the international sphere, and they hooked up with each other as a transnational social movement, or *globalization-from-below* (Edelman, 2001: 304). In 1992, peasant and family farmer organizations from Central America, the Caribbean, North America, and Europe met in Managua, Nicaragua, during the Second Congress of the *Unión Nacional de Agricultores y Ganaderos* (National Union of Farmers and Cattle Ranchers—UNAG). Parts of this process have been documented by Marc Edelman (1998) and Aurelie Desmarais (2002, 2003a, 2003b, 2003c, 2005, 2007).

Participants in this meeting analyzed and discussed the impact of neoliberal policies on agriculture and rural communities. Farmer and peasant leaders developed a "common frame of meaning" (Keck and Sikkink, 1998: 7) in which the brutal consequences of this model based on free trade, low prices, and industrial agriculture—greater impoverishment and marginalization in the countryside—were found to be totally unacceptable. They agreed that an alternative model was desperately needed, and peasants themselves, they felt, must be at the heart of developing the rural and food policies that invariably impact rural communities (see Desmarais, 2003a; McMichael, 2006; Patel, 2005, 2006; Webster, 2004).

As a follow-up to the Managua initiative, more than seventy peasant and farm leaders from around the world met in Mons, Belgium, in May of 1993. At this conference, peasant and farm organizations from around the world formally committed to work collectively to defend their rights in the context of trade liberalization, as producers of the world's food, and became the First International Conference of La Vía Campesina (Desmarais, 2002, 2003a, 2003b, 2003c, 2005). Participants agreed on a mission statement and organizational structure and defined a very general policy framework to protect the rights and interests of farming families, establishing an International Operative Secretariat (IOS) in Honduras (Desmarais, 2003a). La Vía Campesina essentially adopted the structure of the CLOC at a global level, with an International Coordinating Commission (ICC) made up of two regional coordinators (one man and one woman) from each of eight regions. The regions are Africa, East and Southeast Asia, South Asia, Europe, North America (includes Mexico), South America, Central America, and the Caribbean. A powerful "founder effect" can be noted in that Latin American presence is represented by four of the regions. This is not surprising since Latin America is the region of the world with the most unequal distribution of land and income, and the region that particularly experienced a sharp decline of living standards during the "lost decade" of the 1980s as neoliberal policies hit Latin America. Although Latin American member organizations offered to translate the name into each language—for example, to "The Farmer Way" or "The Peasant Way" in English—organizations from other continents insisted on keeping "La Vía Campesina," in part in tribute to the Latin American role and in part because they "liked the sound."

Peoples' Food Sovereignty: Coherent Proposal for an Alternative Modernity

La Vía Campesina works on many issues, but perhaps its central goal is to construct, propose, and defend an alternative model of agriculture and rural life—the "food sovereignty" paradigm (called *Peoples' Food Sovereignty* by La Vía Campesina). The concept of food sovereignty was brought to the public debate by La Vía Campesina during the World Food Summit in 1996, as an alternative paradigm to frame issues about food and agriculture. Since that time, the concept has gained tremendous popularity and echo in civil society sectors of nations both North and South, and has been developed into a holistic and internally coherent alternative framework (Vía Campesina et al., n.d.; Vía Campesina, 2003; Rosset, 2003; McMichael, 2004; Desmarais, 2002).

Dominant neoliberal viewpoints see food and farming as little more than producing interchangeable products for trade (Rosset, 2006a). In contrast, food sovereignty argues that food and farming are about much more than trade and that, from the perspectives of broad-based and inclusive local and national economic development, production for local and national markets is more important than production for export in terms of addressing poverty and hunger; preserving rural life, economies, and environments; and managing natural resources in a sustainable fashion.

Vía argues that every country and people must have the right and the ability to define their own food, farming, and agricultural policies, as well as the right to protect domestic markets and have public sector budgets for agriculture that may include subsidies that do not lead to greater production, exports, dumping, and damage to other countries. Vía believes that low prices are the worst force that farmers face everywhere in the world and, therefore, that we need to effectively ban dumping, apply antimonopoly rules nationally and globally, effectively regulate overproduction in the large agroexport countries, and eliminate the kinds of direct and indirect, open and hidden subsidies that enforce low prices and overproduction. In other words, Vía Campesina believes we need to move from mechanisms that enforce low prices to those that would promote fair prices for farmers and consumers alike. This alternative model also includes agrarian reform, with limits on maximum farm size and equitable local control over resources like seeds, land, water, and forests; the model is opposed to patenting seeds (Rosset, 2006a; Rosset and Martinez, 2007). Central pillars in the fight of La Vía Campesina for food sovereignty include its *Global Campaign for Agrarian Reform* (Borras, 2004; Monsalve Suárez, 2006; Vía Campesina, 2004) and its campaign *Seeds: Patrimony of Rural Peoples in the Service of Humanity* (Welch, 2005), both led by Latin American members (agrarian reform out of Honduras, and seeds out of Chile).

Century-long debates over the persistence of the peasantry have puzzled analysts of the agrarian question. The conception of the peasantry as essentially precapitalist (Bernstein, 2003; McLaughlin, 1998), and therefore all the associated attributes of "antiquated," "out of touch with the times," and so on, create a cognitive dissonance precisely when rural societies are proposing an alternative way of experiencing modernity (Patel, 2006; McMichael, 2006; Desmarais, 2002). The food sovereignty proposal embodies the construction of new rights and the transformation of society as a whole. Over the past twenty to thirty years in rural areas of the world, as neoliberal economic policies began cutting back and in many cases eliminating the institutions that supported peasant and family agriculture, the legitimacy of government policies, political parties, and international financial institutions was eroded in the eyes of peasants and family farmers. The assertion of rights and other demands for change by rural peoples, like the right to land, the right of rural peoples to produce, and the right to continue to exist as such, have been the points of unity of peasants in Latin America and the world.

Food sovereignty is a concept coined by actively appropriating and inventing language. On the one hand, "discussions over the use of words often seem like nit-picking, [and] language seems to be irrelevant to 'real' struggles. Yet the power to interpret, and the active appropriation and invention of language, are crucial tools for emergent movements seeking visibility and recognition for the views and actions" (Franco, 1998: 278). It has indeed had this effect, as the term has been picked up around the world. Food sovereignty offers a sophisticated attempt at developing a "grounded, localized and yet international humanism around the food system. The call is an active attempt to incite context-specific transformation within a context of universal (and defensibly humanist) principles of dignity, individual and community sovereignty, and self-determination" (Patel, 2005: 81). As Phillip McMichael (2006: 42) has written, this campesino politics "reasserts the right to farm as a social act of stewardship of the land and food redistribution against the destabilizing and exclusionary impacts of the neoliberal model."

A step forward in the construction of the food sovereignty model is the work in alliances to link peasant struggles to other sectors, such as workers; the urban informal sector; and environmental, women's, and indigenous rights movements. In February 2007 at the Nyeleni Forum for Food Sovereignty organized by La Vía Campesina in Mali, representatives of all these sectors participated.

Evolutionary Phases of a Transnational Movement

We identify three phases in the evolution of the Vía Campesina movement (Rosset and Martinez, 2005):

Phase One (1990s): Taking Their Place at the Table

Through La Vía Campesina, peasants "muscle" their way to the table wherever key debates or negotiations take place that affect the future of rural communities, whether at international summits, trade negotiations, civil society gatherings, and so forth. Pushing aside NGOs and others who had previously "spoken on behalf" of rural peoples, their message is clear: "We are here, and we can speak for ourselves."

Social movement is commonly understood to mean that the entity in question is grass roots based, is sometimes but not always membership based, and involves a large number of people fighting together on an issue or set of related issues. The accountability of leaders in a social movement is downward to the membership or base, and decisions are typically taken by consensus or at least democratically. Social movements have few staff relative to their membership base, which typically is huge. They most often have relatively little external funding compared to their size and impact. Perhaps their most important feature is that social movements have mobilization capacity: that is, they can put people in the streets for a protest, a march, or fill large halls for a convention or congress (Rosset and Martinez, 2005).

Because Vía Campesina is composed of "peer" groups, it has largely avoided the tension that occurs in many transnational networks where "old colonial patterns may be replicated in the relation between northern-dominated nongovernmental organizations (NGOs) and local grassroots organizations in the South," as the authors of the introductory chapter in this volume warn (see also J. Smith, 2002, and J. Fox and Brown, 1998, for discussion of this risk; Alvarez, 1998, for the case of the women's movement; and Incite! 2007, on the contradictions between the logic of NGOs and radical activism). Northern-country members are national family farmer or farm worker organizations, not NGOs, and Third World members have shown as much or more leadership within the movement (Rosset and Martínez, 2005).

At the First Conference, Vía Campesina defined itself as a *peasant movement* and as a *political space* for peasant organizations, chose its name, and made the critical decision to be *autonomous of the NGOs* that in the past had so often "managed" peasant organizations. During this phase, the dynamism and political significance of Vía were again demonstrated at the Second Conference in Tlaxcala, Mexico (April 1996), in which the organization ratified itself as a *movement*, not just a mere "coordination," consolidated its *regional structure*, identified the *gender* issue as critical to its internal functioning, and developed the seminal concept of *food sovereignty* (see also Rosset, 2003 and 2006a, 2006b).

Phase Two (2000–2003): Taking on a Leadership Role

This phase started with the Third Conference in Bangalore, India (September/October 2000). Vía launched a strategy of building *alliances* with other actors to pressure international institutions like the World Bank, WTO, IMF, and United Nations, especially its Food and Agriculture Organization (FAO). Following up on the gender issue, Vía adopted a rule requiring *gender parity* in representation at all levels, making Vía the only transnational rural movement with gender parity at the highest level.

As Vía's strength grew by leaps and bounds, actors ranging from the NGOs to the international financial institutions (IFIs), the United Nations, and governments, came to recognize their leadership on rural issues. Vía Campesina became stronger than most other civil society actors and began to build alliances from a position of leadership and strength. Perhaps the clearest example of this is the lead role it played in the civil society forums, lobbying, and protest that helped lead to the collapse of the WTO Ministerial in Cancún, Mexico, in September 2003 (Rosset, 2006a; see later in this section). In this phase, La Vía Campesina had to confront tactics by international organizations like the World Bank, trying to co-opt the movement by offering to fly in leaders to expensive dialogs that would achieve little. In response, Vía developed the position that with "clear enemies" like the World Bank and the WTO it would not dialog, just demonstrate resolute opposition. On the other hand, dialog was permitted with actors like the FAO of the United Nations, because these actors might conceivably be alternative spaces to the World Bank and the WTO for determining agricultural and trade policies.

World trade negotiations geared toward agreements and treaties for "trade liberalization" have been taking place continually since 1986, with the inauguration of the Uruguay round of negotiations in the framework of the GATT, which became the WTO in 1995. Together with the enactment of NAFTA in 1994 and the numerous bilateral and regional free trade agreements signed since, these negotiations constitute the framework for today's antipeasant "corporate food regime," characterized by low prices to farmers; the global homogenization of unhealthy food consumption patterns; emphasis on large-scale agroexport production to the detriment of peasant agriculture; widespread privatization; and the growing corporate control over all aspects of food production, processing, and marketing (McMichael, 2004).

"Dumping" is one of the most injurious aspects of this food regime. It is the export of products to third countries at prices below the cost of production. When foreign products enter a local market at prices below the cost of production, local farmers cannot compete and are driven off the land and into deepening poverty. Dumping is driving millions of peasants off the land throughout the Third World and into urban slums and international migratory streams. It causes the low crop prices that make earning a livelihood off the land increasingly impossible. Dumping is typically a product of agricultural policies in major food exporting countries (primarily the United States and the European Union) that drive down farm prices, with compensatory subsidies for larger, wealthier farmers, so that giant trading corporations like Cargill and Archer-Daniels-Midland can buy cheap, export to other countries, undercut local farmers there, and capture ever-growing market segments in those countries (Rosset, 2006a). In 2002, a typical year, the percentage that price lagged below cost of production for U.S.-exported wheat was 43 percent; for soybeans, 25 percent; maize, 13 percent; cotton, 61 percent; and rice, 35 percent (Ritchie, Murphy, and Lake, 2004), hurting farmers worldwide. Nor do U.S. or European family farmers benefit from their nations' low-price exports. Chronically low crop and livestock prices, coupled with subsidies that go to larger, corporate farms, leave family farmers in the North without either a price or a subsidy that can cover their living expenses and farm loans, leading to massive farmer bankruptcies. The fact that these policies hurt both farmers in the North and farmers in the South forms the objective basis for global collective action by La Vía Campesina and is the reason why family farmers from the North and peasants from the South came to the conclusion, in exchanges with each other, that they had common interests (Rosset, 2006a).

In human terms, dumping has meant the cultural and, in many cases, literal death of peasant farmers, as was dramatized in Cancún, Mexico, in 2003, at Vía's protests against WTO negotiations taking place in that city. On

September 10, 2003, Lee Kyung Hae climbed up on the police barricades surrounding the site of the WTO negotiations with a sign bearing the now-famous slogan: "WTO Kills Farmers." Mr. Lee was a peasant leader from South Korea, who came to Cancún to march side-by-side with Mexican peasants protesting the devastating impacts of trade liberalization. He made the supreme sacrifice that day by giving his life in protest, when he stabbed himself in the heart (Rosset, 2006a). Lee had founded a cooperative and a farmer's association in Korea, had been a state legislator, and had been recognized by the government of Korea and by the United Nations as an outstanding farmer. Yet he lost his land, as did millions of other Korean farmers, after his government signed the GATT in 1992. This trade liberalization agreement opened the Korean market to a flood of very cheap food imports. Korean farmers' income plunged, and many committed suicide when they realized that due to low crop prices that could not cover the payments on their crop loans, they would be the first in their family history to lose the farm inherited from their ancestors. They could not live with that shame (Rosset, 2006a).

Korea is not the only country to be faced with a rash of farmer suicides, which have in fact reached epidemic proportions in recent years among peasants and family farmers around the world, from Iowa to India to Mexico (*New York Times*, January 14, 1986, and September 19, 2006; *Cuarto Poder* [Mexico], July 29, 2005; Rosset, 2006a). Death is in fact a recurring theme and reality of the peasant struggle in Latin America and the world, deaths from both hunger-related illnesses in impoverished rural areas and the ongoing criminalization and repression of peasant struggles. Whether it is the murder of organized indigenous peoples, peasants, and farm workers in Honduras in 2003 (COCOCH-CNTC, 2003; Weinberg, 2003), or the 1996 massacre of MST members in El Dorado de Carajás, Brazil, the killing of peasant activists further underscores the life and death nature of struggle and paradoxically gives greater strength and determination to the struggle.

Phase Three (Contemporary): Deepening and Internal Strengthening

Vía realized that the external political space it had occupied at the international level was disproportionately large compared to its own degree of internal political and organizational development. Thus, the decision was made to focus on catching up internally, giving extra effort to internal training for member organizations, strengthening operational mechanisms, and building regional secretariats to ensure sustained regional and local engagement. This was a critical challenge, as some organizations were much weaker than others.

The structure is defined in a participatory and democratic way during Vía Campesina International Conferences. The International Conference is the highest decision-making entity, where representatives of the member organizations engage in collective analysis and policy development. The International Conference takes place every three or four years and defines the political direction and strategies of Vía, as well as the internal functioning of the movement (Rosset and Martínez, 2005). The International Coordinating Committee (ICC) meets two times a year to evaluate and analyze compliance with the International Conference agreements in the individual regions. In addition, the ICC engages in a collective analysis of what is occurring in agriculture at the global level and defines plans for joint action and advocacy at the international level. The International Operative Secretariat, which is currently based in Jakarta, Indonesia, is in charge of coordinating actions and implementing the agreements reached at the conference and at the ICC meetings (Rosset and Martínez, 2005).

Vía Campesina currently has over 140 member organizations in more than fifty-five countries (Desmarais, 2005), including twenty-one countries from Latin America and the Caribbean, with a substantial number of additional organizations in the "getting-to-know-you" stage prior to becoming formal members. It would be fair to say the La Vía Campesina organizations represent some 300 million rural families worldwide. The members come from the ranks of organizations of peasant farmers, family farmers, rural workers, the landless, indigenous people, artisan fisher folk, and rural women and youth. It is a transnational social movement with a high degree of density and cohesion (J. Fox, 2000), made up of national or regional peasant organizations in which each member organization has its own social base or constituency that participates in its internal decisions and actions, and to whom that organization is accountable.

The decision-making process of La Vía Campesina is by consultation and consensus, which is very respectful of the autonomy of member organizations. Positions are created by articulating the concerns of the base within each national organization, bringing them to table in La Vía Campesina, and having a dialog to reach common positions (Rosset and Martínez, 2005). This is a slow process, especially since peasant organizations, in contrast to NGOs, do not respond quickly, yet time has shown that this method builds the strong basis of trust that is so important for collective action (Rosset and Martínez, 2005; Desmarais, 2005). By taking the time to build consensus among members, who interact as equals, La Vía Campesina has avoided the internal splits that have crippled many other transnational political alliances and coalitions (see J. Fox and Brown, 1998, for examples).

At the Fourth Conference held near São Paulo, Brazil, in June 2004, additional emphasis was placed on working on the internal mechanisms of the movement, and on strengthening its member organizations. Many new members were added, especially from Asia, but also notably from Africa. Other actions included the further consolidation of the ICC, the decision to rotate the IOS from Honduras to Indonesia, the integration of *mística* (see Issa, this volume) as a sort of social glue inside Vía, and emphasizing internal political and leadership training to strengthen member organizations.

Special emphasis was made toward gender parity at all levels, by working through the formation of an international women's commission in all regions and all countries. The fact that the ICC has a man and a woman representative from each region, as do other commissions, led some member organizations, like the MST in Brazil, to make similar changes to their internal structure (see Desmarais, 2003b; Vía Campesina, 2006; and Monsalve Suárez, 2006, for discussion of gender in La Vía Campesina).

Transnational Collective *Campesino* Identity and the Politics of Representation

The attempt to (re)create, maintain, and strengthen a peasant, or *campesino*, identity is a key cultural "glue" that helps hold La Vía Campesina together. There is a conscious sense of building "campesino pride," or "farmer pride." In speeches at meetings, it is common to hear statements like "Being a *farmer* is one of the most important professions in any society, at least as important as doctors and far more important than lawyers." Or, "A country could survive without lawyers, but how could it survive without farmers? What would people eat?" Or, "Survival of peasant farmers is not something that just concerns rural areas; it is a matter that concerns all of society." There is a strong feeling that peasants are "for humanity" (Patel, 2005, 2006), yet have long been excluded from the cultural projects of most countries (D. Davis, 1999: 617). All Vía meetings begin with a *mística* using powerful imagery and symbols—typically seeds, soil, water, fire—to create a strong sense of collective belonging and commitment.

La Vía Campesina is at least partially responding to a politics of representation that all too often excluded peasant voices. The privatization mania of neoliberalism in the 1980s affected foreign assistance and funding policies of international donors, who increasingly cut aid to governments and passed it instead to NGOs (see Conroy, Murray, and Rosset, 1996). Donors thus "encouraged the growth of organizations that were able to make claims to represent a constituency in the Global South. . . . The ability of these organizations to deliver 'the peasantry' in order to comply with the structures of 'accountability,' 'transparency' and 'participation' that have emerged in response to the criticisms received by these international financial institutions, is the key to the survival of these NGOs" (Patel, 2006: 78–79). This tendency of NGOs to speak "on behalf of peasants" led one Vía Campesina leader to state that "to date, in all global debates on agrarian policy, the peasant movement has been absent: we have not had a voice. The main reason for the very existence of the Vía Campesina is to be that voice and to speak out for the creation of a more just society" (Paul Nicholson, 1996, cited in Desmarais, 2002: 96).

Thus, from the very beginning Vía clearly staked out its differences from NGOs and would not include organizations that were not truly grassroots and peasant based. It also staked out its differences from foundations and aid agencies, refusing to accept resources that come with conditions attached nor permitting any kind of external interference in its internal decisions, thus guaranteeing the independence and autonomy that are so critical (Rosset and Martínez, 2005).

The political style of La Vía Campesina is that of a poor peoples' movement: people who have been pushed to the edge of extinction by dominant power in their countries and in the world; people who have usually not been taken into account, who have been "fooled too many times" by smooth-talking politicians and NGOs; people who were never invited to sit at the table and had to "elbow their way" into the seat they now occupy. Like the individuals involved in most social movements, these people have a deep distrust, based on bitter experience, of methods that channel and "calm" dissent: that is, of "conflict resolution," "stakeholder dialog," World Bank "consultations" and "participation," and so forth (Rosset and Martínez, 2005).

The political tactics are more "outside" than "inside" and more protest than lobby, though Vía does sometimes engage in coordinated inside-outside strategies with its allies and does sometimes lobby. When it addresses an issue or "takes on" an institution like FAO, Vía typically occupies and defends political space and then rapidly moves the debate out of the merely "technical" realm and onto moral terrain. This has proven to be an effective strategy for shifting the terms of the debate on many of the issues that Vía addresses (Rosset and Martínez, 2005).

The typical story in the typical country is that when rural people reach a certain level of anger, protest, and mass mobilization, the authorities offer to negotiate, form joint study commissions, and, in general, engage in other forms of conflict resolution. The usual result is that the moment of mobilization passes, the momentum is lost, and the demands are never met nor the promises kept. Piven and Cloward (1978) found, in general, that poor peoples' organizations are most effective at achieving their demands when they are most confrontational and least effective when they take more conciliatory positions and invest their energies in dialogue. Thus, it should come as no surprise that La Vía Campesina tends to be more confrontational than other international actors on rural issues and tends to engage in protest and aggressive debate. This is most clearly demonstrated by its militant opposition to the WTO. To date, a combination of La Vía Campesina–led street protests and the stubborn refusal of many governments to give in to the United States and European Union has kept the WTO stymied.

Conclusion: A Peasant Internationalism

Vía Campesina is an international alliance of peasant and family farmer organizations from the Americas (North, Central, and South America, and the Caribbean), Asia (Southeast and South), Europe, and Africa. It groups nationally or regionally based organizations to struggle together on common issues at the international level, yet the autonomy of these member organizations is carefully respected. La Vía Campesina is also a transnational social movement, with roots in Latin America, that has been able to create an international peasant discourse and identity in tune with the times, without trying to build a political party structure. Today, the organization is an international reference point for rural issues and problems, for social movements, and for the construction of proposals, mediated by the legitimacy and trust forged through its years of struggle.

Vía, built from the bottom up, is independent of governments, funders, political parties, NGOs, and nonpeasant special interests. The agenda of La Vía Campesina is defined by La Vía Campesina and no one else. It has built up and shown its strength in mobilizations and nonviolent but radical direct actions, opposing the real powers in the world as an alternative, democratic, and mass-based peasant power base. It is a movement that takes positions of collective defiance (Piven and Cloward, 1978) toward the WTO and World Bank, while also putting forth consistent and coherent alternative proposals that result from peasant reality and are shared by organizations from the great variety of situations in which peasants from different countries find themselves. More than simply a North-South discourse, these proposals have created a true peasant internationalism.

19

Neoliberal Regionalism and Resistance in Mesoamerica

Foro Mesoamericano Opposition to Plan Puebla-Panamá and CAFTA

Rose J. Spalding

Transnational Resistance Networks

A T THE BEGINNING OF THE TWENTY-FIRST CENTURY, the Mesoamerican region became a focal point for neoliberal globalization. With a long history of dictatorships, war, and revolution, intermittently devastated by earthquakes, flooding, and hurricanes, southern Mexico and Central America contained some of the poorest areas in Latin America. Its low-cost labor pool, largely undeveloped tourism prospects, extensive natural resources (petroleum, hydroelectric, biological) and increasing connections to the United States attracted the attention of international investors. Two initiatives, Plan Puebla-Panamá (PPP) and the Central American Free Trade Agreement (CAFTA), emerged as twin strategies to integrate this region more deeply into the global economy.

As economic globalization initiatives advanced across the region, so too did resistance. This chapter explores one innovative resistance network—the Foro Mesoamericano—which developed in response to neoliberal regionalism in Mexico and Central America. Beginning in southern Mexico in 2001, this coalition initially focused on challenging PPP, a regional development plan advanced by Mexican president Vicente Fox (2000–2006) to construct infrastructural linkages through southern Mexico and into Central America. As plans for CAFTA, a free trade agreement (FTA) between Central America and the United States, advanced the following year (with the Dominican Republic added in 2004), this resistance network expanded to confront free trade negotiation. Rotating throughout the region in a series of annual meetings, the

Foro Mesoamericano drew hundreds of activists and organizations into a regional opposition network.

Social activists resisting economic globalization often develop rich cross-national linkages (Keck and Sikkink, 1998; Tarrow, 2005; della Porta and Tarrow, 2005; Hertel, 2006). Transnational activism increases as participants draw the physical and conceptual connections between processes occurring in multiple national sites. These linkages are particularly visible under conditions of what might be termed *neoliberal regionalism*—that is, the market restructuring across a whole region that emerges from integration agreements, regional development projects, and multilateral trade accords. Unlike structural adjustment initiatives introduced by individual governments, which may be perceived primarily as national processes, or particular infrastructural development projects, which may be perceived largely in local terms, regional development projects and trade agreements are by definition cross-national. The transparency of these multination interconnections facilitates an "upward scale shift" (Tarrow, 2005: 121–124) in which activist resources are combined and protest strategies coordinated across national boundaries to better confront transnationalized decision centers far removed from daily contact.

Social movements commonly employ "condensing symbols" (Tarrow, 2005: 73) to link a cluster of issues and draw various opposition groups together. PPP and CAFTA functioned as such integrative devices in the Mesoamerican region. Concerns about the detrimental consequences of these projects fostered linkages among preexisting organizations that focused on such diverse issues as indigenous rights, cultural survival, labor rights, environmental protection, democratization, social equality, women's rights, and social development. These heterogeneous movements connected across national boundaries through shared rejection of integrated regional market schemes that threatened their displacement.

Neoliberal Regionalism in Mesoamerica

Mexico's poor, rural south had come increasingly into focus following the 1994 uprising of the *Ejército Zapatista de Liberación Nacional* (Zapatista Army of National Liberation—EZLN). Propelled by a new sense of urgency about southern poverty, a group of Mexican policy makers in the Zedillo administration (1994–2000) turned their attention to reforming national development policy. Santiago Levy, a U.S.-trained economist and undersecretary of *Hacienda y Crédito Público* (Treasury and Finance) during the Zedillo administration, coauthored a plan to address economic marginality of the south through infrastructural development and private sector job creation (Dávila,

Kessel and Levy, 2000). Some critics locate conceptual antecedents in controversial proposals dating from the López Portillo and de la Madrid administrations (Sandoval, 2003: 25–33). Newly elected president Vicente Fox, putting together a non–Partido Revolucionario Institucional (Institutional Revolutionary Party) controlled government for the first time in seventy years and short on both technical staff and concrete policy ideas, took up this proposal (and Levy himself, who became director of the Mexican Social Security Institute). Facing the prospect of ongoing turbulence in Mexico's southern states and having promised during the campaign to solve the Chiapas problem quickly ("in fifteen minutes"), the Fox administration embraced the plan and added its own stamp.

As it was reconceptualized, PPP leapt the border and became a regional proposal that extended through Mexico to Panama (with Colombia added in 2006). This cross-national recasting may have been influenced by a warm reception at the Inter-American Development Bank (IDB), which had an established interest in integrating regional infrastructure. The plan involved building and refurbishing a highway system that would extend from the central Mexican state of Puebla through Central America to Panama. Priming the pump for increased foreign investment, the plan layered in a network of air and seaports and an electricity production/distribution system extending through the Mesoamerican region (Presidencia de la República, 2001a, 2001b). Designed to promote deeper integration into the global production and distribution processes, the plan was also advertised abroad as a tool to reduce migration and enhance regional security (Bartra, 2004: 31–38).

Announced by Fox in Guatemala City almost three months before his inauguration, PPP allowed the new administration to not only address its own structural economic problems in the Mexican south-southeast but also assume leadership of its seven adjoining neighbors to the south, prompting criticism of Mexico's role as a "sub-imperial satellite" by columnist Carlos Fazio (*La Jornada* [Mexico], May 28, 2001: 11). Central American leaders met with Fox shortly after his inauguration; their support was formalized in a June 2001 summit meeting hosted by Salvadoran president Francisco Flores.

Perhaps one reason for the quick embrace by Central American leaders was the familiarity of core components. The neoliberal vision of development, which emphasized privatization, trade liberalization, and increased foreign investment in the *maquila* and tourism sectors, had consolidated throughout the region in the postrevolutionary 1990s (Robinson, 2003). Pieces of the proposed highway infrastructure had already been approved and financing secured from multilateral lenders and bilateral sources; "new" initiatives, like an integrated electrical transmission network, had long been under discussion. What PPP offered was a conceptual umbrella (Barreda, 2004) that tied together preexisting project commitments in the region and added important cross-regional connections. PPP's new promise for Central American leaders was the ability to connect more fully with the United States and Mexico and to position the region for large-scale international funding.

Following immediately on the heels of the PPP announcements, Central American countries advanced toward an FTA with the United States. Over the previous two decades, Central American exports to the United States had grown and extended into nontraditional products as a result of U.S. trade openings provided by the Caribbean Basin Initiative (CBI). This nonreciprocal arrangement was only temporary, however, and conversation about a permanent Central American FTA had begun in the early 1990s, inspired by concerns about market diversion under NAFTA (North American Free Trade Agreement) (A. González, 2005: 8). Discussion deepened in 2001 as the termination date for Caribbean Basin preferences came into sight. Some Central American presidents, like Francisco Flores, an enthusiastic market reformer who had recently dollarized the Salvadoran economy, eagerly pursued a new trade and investment agreement with the United States.

As negotiation of a hemisphere-wide Free Trade Area of the Americas (FTAA) met with rising resistance, the U.S. Trade Representative Robert Zoellick linked up with Central American leaders to advance formal discussion of a subregional FTA. Unable to bring Latin America as a whole into a trade agreement, the Bush administration pursued this agenda piecemeal. The U.S. Congress granted Bush the requisite Trade Promotion Authority in the wake of September 11, accepting a restricted role in the process (a yes/no vote without the possibility of amending the text) and placing negotiations into the hands of a technocratic team of trade specialists. CAFTA drafting proceeded through nine quick rounds between January and December 2003, with Costa Rica signing in January 2004 and the Dominican Republic joining in August 2004.

The twin PPP and CAFTA processes generated a long list of concerns in activist circles around the region. Large-scale infrastructural projects raised questions about environmental damage and the land and cultural rights of indigenous communities in the isthmus. Trade liberalization triggered concern about the debilitating impact on precarious economic sectors such as small- and medium-sized and peasant producers, and poor working conditions in the *maquila* (export manufacturing assembly plant) sector. Additional protections for foreign investors and further reductions in state regulatory powers raised concerns about the erosion of sovereignty and lack of democratic control.

To confront the challenges posed by these new forms of neoliberal regionalism, sectors of Mesoamerican civil society began to organize across national boundaries. The forms of mobilization were far from uniform; organizational, ideological, and strategic variations unfolded. In El Salvador, for example, the anti-CAFTA camp divided into two competing coalitions—"critical negotiators," who attempted, without success, to modify the text of the agreement by participating in negotiation rounds, and "transgressive resisters," who rejected negotiation in favor of resistance (Spalding, 2007; see also W. Smith and Korzeniewicz, 2007, and Hertel, 2006). Activists most averse to corporate-led globalization and least convinced of the utility of negotiation were drawn to a resistance network organized around the Foro Mesoamericano.

Foro Mesoamericano

From the time PPP was announced, highly visible elements of civil society mobilized against it. Early leadership of the opposition was provided by Zapatista spokesperson Subcomandante Marcos. During his historic "march to the North" less than three months after Fox's inauguration, Marcos decried the plan as yet another neoliberal assault on native peoples. Calling for PPP to be renamed, "Plan Guatemala-Panamá," Marcos concluded, "There will no longer be any plan or project that doesn't take us into account—not Plan Puebla-Panamá, nor a trans-isthmus megaproject, nor anything that means the sale or destruction of the home of the indigenous people, which, do not forget, is part of the home of all Mexicans" (as quoted in *Reforma* [Mexico], February 26, 2001).

Concern about PPP galvanized and connected regional opposition forces. Inspired by the EZLN's international solidarity process, described in more detail in Alicia Swords's chapter in this volume, Foro organizers called for mobilization across Mesoamerica. Even before the presidents' meeting to officially launch PPP, activists from the region gathered in Tapachula, Chiapas, to denounce it. The May 2001 "Declaration of Tapachula," issued by representatives of 132 organizations (Foro Mesoamericano, 2001b), concluded,

> Considering that any development plan should be derived from a democratic, not an authoritarian, process, we firmly rejected the so-called Plan Puebla-Panamá (PPP) as another savage colonization project for south-southeast Mexico and Central American countries, announcing the arrival of big capital, transnationals and the oligarchies. This plan will deepen the impoverishment of the *pueblos*, the destruction of our cultures and of nature.

From its origins in Tapachula, the Foro Mesoamericano emerged as a transnational resistance network that gathered antineoliberal organizations and activists across the region for information sharing, reflection, and strategic planning. Although many other gatherings of activists took place in the region during this time, often focusing on particular sectors or issues, the Foro

Mesoamericano was distinct in its transnational reach, conceptual scope, commitment to action, and recurrent character. Its organizational "design code" emphasized permanent, decentered campaigns organized through polycentric structures, an approach characteristic of newer forms of transnational activism (Bennett, 2005). Unlike the World Social Forum, which initially met only in its inaugural setting (Porto Alegre, Brazil), the Foro Mesoamericano was envisioned from the outset as a rotating gathering. According to Nicaraguan Foro organizer Alejandro Bendaña (director, Centro de Estudios Internacionales— CEI, interview, Managua, July 18, 2003; correspondence, March 18, 2007), a constantly changing locale allowed the network to strengthen local affiliates sequentially and to distribute the burden and rewards of organizing among a short list of those equipped for this undertaking.

The meeting agendas, designed largely by the local coordinators with varying degrees of input from regional partners, contained both fixed and fluid elements. The central critique of neoliberal economic transition was an invariant, defining feature, but particular subthemes emerged in response to prevailing issues of the moment and the organizational missions of an expanding pool of participants. Over time, the core forum became encased in a series of pre- and postconference gatherings on additional and overlapping themes. The 2004 Foro Mesoamericano in San Salvador, for example, included eight formal companion Foros on women, peasants, young people, biodiversity, dams, labor unions, popular education, and community.

To build a network that could confront neoliberal regionalism, Foro activists called for persistent effort and recurring gatherings. The inaugural critique of PPP gave rise to a second, held six months later in Xelajú (Quetzaltenango, Guatemala); the Third Foro Mesoamericano followed in Managua, Nicaragua (July 2002). The fourth, fifth, and sixth meetings, which took place during the CAFTA negotiation and ratification processes, rotated to Tegucigalpa, Honduras (July 2003); San Salvador, El Salvador (July 2004); and San José, Costa Rica (December 2005).

As the process became better consolidated and communications within the antineoliberalism movement moved beyond insider networks, the visibility of the Foro increased and attendance grew. The inaugural Foro began with an estimated 250 individual participants in May 2001 (Foro Mesoamericano, 2001b). Reported attendance climbed to around 800 at the Guatemala meeting six months later and rose further to 1,000 (864 registered) the following year in Managua (Foro Mesoamericano, 2001a; Foro Mesoamericano, 2002a, 2002b: appendix). Boosted by the high-profile CAFTA negotiations underway at that time, registration increased a remarkable 73 percent to 1,495 at the 2003 gathering in Tegucigalpa (Foro Mesoamericano, Comité Organizador, 2004: 125). When the Foro rotated to San Salvador in July 2004, registration climbed again, to 1,747 (Foro Mesoamericano, 2004b).

Attentive to issues of gender equality, the Salvadoran organizers proudly announced that 43.5 percent of participants in 2004 were women, up from 34 percent in 2003 (Foro Mesoamericano, 2004b; Foro Mesoamericano, Comité Organizador, 2004: 215). Cross-regional participation also improved over time. Whereas 81 percent of the organizations represented at the first gathering in Chiapas were Mexican, by the time of the 2003 gathering in Honduras, host country organizations represented only 31 percent of the total. Organizations from only four of the PPP countries were present at the first Foro gathering; by 2003, all eight countries were represented. Lead organizations in each country recruited participants and raised funds from international NGOs (nongovernmental organizations) to cover meeting costs (interview with coordinator of MPR12, San Salvador, July 26, 2004).

Transnational activist networks commonly have internal tensions and divisions produced by variations in their resources, locations, and priorities (Hertel, 2006). These differences challenge resistance activists to maintain an ongoing process of dialogue and norm construction. The brokerage function played by the annual Foro assemblage became more critical as the Foro constituency expanded. In a process defined as a "frame alignment" by Snow and Benford (1988), organizers worked to bridge the national and sectoral components of the movement through participatory workshops and summative declarations. The Foro gathering functioned as an integrating mechanism, allowing this embryonic movement to pursue a role as a "signifying agent" (198) and assist in the negotiations over differences and the production of shared meanings. Value alignment was promoted in part through the use of a preexisting resistance framework. The celebration of indigenous dress and dance in opening ceremonies and evening retreats implicitly attached the Foro movement to this cultural lodestone of anticolonial resistance and shared history. The symbolic potency of the frequently used image of *maíz* (corn) or the waving of machetes during culminating protest marches blended the regional movement with emotion-laden themes of peasant and indigenous identity.

The Foro Mesoamericano process brought together resistance networks with varying characteristics. It linked organizations that represented heterogeneous social subjects having different kinds of structures and resources. To illustrate the point, let us look at the two Salvadoran coalitions responsible for organizing the 2004 gathering—the *Movimiento Popular de Resistencia-12 de Octubre* (October 12 Popular Resistance Movement—MPR12) and the *Red Sinti Techán* (Sinti Techán Network—RST). The MPR12 drew together several mass membership organizations. It connected umbrella coalitions like the *Foro de la Sociedad Civil* (Civil Society Forum—FSC), forged to mobilize civil society in the wake of 1998 Hurricane Mitch, and a number of Salvador's larger rural organizations such as the *Confederación de Federaciones de la Reforma Agraria Salvadoreña* (Confederation of Salvadoran Agrarian Reform

Federations—CONFRAS), composed of agrarian reform cooperatives emerging from the Salvadoran civil war. Since headcount affects a movement's credibility claims, the MPR12's organizational reach provided an important element in the Foro bid for recognition.

The RST, in contrast, networked an urban cluster of well-organized, professional NGOs. Its affiliates included feminist (Las Dignas), environmental (Unidad Ecológica Salvadoreña), and consumer rights (Centro para la Defensa del Consumidor) organizations (interview with coordinator, RST, San Salvador, August 2, 2004). Although the RST could not claim a broad membership base, it provided rich links to the international "*altermundista*" movement (promoting "another world" distinct from the corporate-dominated model of globalization). These ties reinforced the principles, guidelines, and discipline emerging within the main hemispheric resistance network, the *Alianza Social Continental* (Hemispheric Social Alliance—ASC). RST coordinator Raúl Moreno was an active participant in the ASC, which sponsored his research and publications (see Moreno, 2003; Bloque Popular Centroamericano, Alliance for Responsible Trade, and Alianza Social Continental, 2004). Connections between lead Foro organizers and resistance networks operating at the hemispheric level helped integrate the Mesoamerican process into the larger regional and global effort. Although such connections can diminish local movement autonomy by imposing the discipline of a region-wide framework, they also infuse local processes with continent-wide learning, helping to build more coherent transnational processes.

The Foro Mesoamericano was launched in the same year as the World Social Forum, and it pursued many of the same objectives. Workshops offered space for the articulation of decentered and egalitarian visions of globalization and helped develop stimulating materials for use in popular education campaigns. Mutual learning, the sharing of experiences, interpersonal networking, and informational updating on local and global processes were central goals. Although not always successful, organizers promoted horizontal processes in workshop discussions and declaration drafting, seeking inclusive and democratic engagement.

Unlike the World Social Forum, however, the Foro Mesoamericano was also designed as an action front. Concerned that the Foro would be only an episodic exercise disconnected from the ongoing resistance activities of participants, organizers encouraged attendees to define a common action agenda and plan simultaneous cross-national protests. Although Foro organizers did not achieve a high degree of ongoing coordination between meetings, they were able to orchestrate several follow-up protests. The action agenda for the 2002 Managua Foro, for example, called for simultaneous protest marches across the region on October 12, the Día de la Raza, a day resonant with anticolonial resistance.

Road blockages in Guatemala that year closed the Pan-American Highway, a key symbol of regional integration; protesters closed four border crossings in El Salvador; in Mexico, Zapatista supporters blocked the entrance to a Chiapas military base, and protesters halted highway traffic in Oaxaca (*Reuters*, October 15, 2002; *El Diario de Hoy* [El Salvador], October 13, 2002; H. Rodríguez, 2003; Weinberg, 2007: 15–16). A "network of networks," the MPR12 was itself a product of this process, created in 2002 by the network of organizations implementing the Managua Foro action agenda in El Salvador.

These resistance networks attempted to disentangle their agenda from the work of political parties. Activists viewed electoral candidates and postrevolutionary parties as opportunists who often negotiated away core principles. Resisters emphasized street-level opposition rather than electoral coalitions or legislative strategies. Defending social mobilization as an effective strategy, Foro organizers celebrated recent victories in the water privatization "war" in Bolivia, the opposition to privatization of telecommunications and electricity in Costa Rica, the campaign against the privatization of health care and social security in El Salvador, and the halt to construction of an airport mega-project on peasant land in San Salvador Atenco, México (Moreno, 2003: 90). These successful confrontations demonstrated that neoliberalism could be stopped, it was argued—but only with forceful and sustained mobilization.

Challenges to Resistance

The central goal of the Foro was "to strengthen the resistance processes for the Mesoamerican peoples of an anticapitalist, antipatriarchal and multicultural character" (Foro Mesoamericano, 2004c). Calling the Mesoamericano region an "Area of Humanitarian Disaster," the 2004 final declaration pledged collective opposition to CAFTA, the FTAA, PPP, and other forms of "institutionalized violence expressed in feminicides, ethnocides, genocides and violence against young people" (Foro Mesoamericano, 2004a).

Immediate achievement of these material objectives proved elusive. In spite of the resistance mobilizations, government officials pushed ahead with their development plans. New tactics, such as decentralization of project administration and the repackaging of programs, allowed plan architects to move some sensitive projects under the radar. In other cases, like CAFTA, where officials had less latitude, a public relations campaign quickly moved the process toward ratification and implementation.

In Mexico, where the PPP's official author, Vicente Fox, distanced himself, the project temporarily faded. In the face of spreading and interlinked civil society opposition to PPP, especially in Chiapas and Oaxaca, and confounded by executive-legislative gridlock and economic stagnation, the Fox administration stepped back from the plan. Inability to secure low-interest IDB loans and ambivalence of Central American economic elites who feared Mexican competition may have also been factors (Pickard, 2004). Although Fox performed public relations visits in Central America on behalf of the plan, Mexican government financing for its PPP office was cut sharply in 2003 and coordination was reassigned to mid-level staffers. Pieces of PPP projects still moved forward, however, without the damaged PPP brand name (McElhinney and Nickinson, 2004; Pickard, 2004). Road building and highway renovation projects progressed, relabeled as conventional federal or state public works programs.

In Central America, in what McElhinney and Nickinson (2004: 35) labeled an "accountability shell game," sensitive PPP projects such as the Anillo Periférico bypass around San Salvador were taken on by the *Banco Centroamericano de Integración Económica* (Central American Bank for Economic Integration—BCIE), a Central American regional development bank headquartered in Honduras. With disclosure standards and environmental regulations weaker than those of the IDB, BCIE control raised new concerns. Fragmentation of the PPP projects, shifts in the execution mechanisms, and the substantially lowered public profile obfuscated the target and slowed the momentum of the regional resistance campaign.

The CAFTA process also eluded challenge, in spite of resistance efforts by Foro affiliates. Outside of Costa Rica, where legislative ratification stalled and debate prompted an unprecedented national referendum, CAFTA approval advanced in sync with political developments in the United States. Once George Bush's 2004 reelection was secured, Salvadoran president "Tony" Saca launched his legislative ratification process. Attempting to head off a rubber-stamping of the agreement, MPR12 staged a takeover of the legislative assembly on December 16, 2004. Arriving early in the morning, protesters occupied the chamber seats, preventing the convening of the session until they were forcibly removed. Alarmed pro-CAFTA legislators moved to immediate approval. Officially presented to the legislature only fifteen days before and not yet even on the official legislative agenda, the agreement was introduced and approved precipitously on December 17, following a marathon overnight session lasting eighteen hours. By a vote of forty-nine to thirty-five, the Salvadoran legislature became the first to ratify the agreement (Asamblea Legislativa de la República de El Salvador, 2004; Portillo, 2004; Spalding, 2006). The Salvadoran *Procuradora para la Defensa de los Derechos Humanos* (Human Rights Defenders Office) denounced the proceedings as a violation of previously agreed-upon legislative processes and an end-run around legislative review and deliberation (Alamanni de Carrillo, 2005).

Three months later, the Bloque Popular, a leading Foro Mesoamericano affiliate, organized protests and attempted a similar legislative intervention in

Honduras. Forcing legislators to retreat to a closed chamber in order to call the vote, demonstrators took over the vacated seats and ran their own mock session (*La Prensa* [Honduras], March 4, 2005). In spite of these protests, CAFTA was approved in Honduras on March 3, 2005. In the midst of escalating protests, the CAFTA agreement was also approved in Guatemala only a week after the Honduras vote, triggering five days of protest that left one dead and ten wounded (*Prensa Libre* [Guatemala], March 16, 2005).

Ratification by the U.S. Congress (July 2005) followed forceful lobbying by the Bush administration. U.S. labor and environmental activists joined forces with Central American opponents of different stripes to challenge the Bush administration claims about benevolent outcomes and sweeping Central American support for the measure (Bloque Popular Centroamericano, Alliance for Responsible Trade, and Alianza Social Continental, 2004). In spite of U.S. activist efforts, CAFTA was approved easily in the Senate and, again in late-night voting, by a two-vote margin (217–215) in the House. Once U.S. ratification was secured, approval soon followed in the Dominican Republic (September 2005) and, with feeble opposition from the Sandinista National Liberation Front, Nicaragua (October 2005).

The Foro Mesoamericano continued to challenge CAFTA, rotating in 2005 to Costa Rica, where the CAFTA fight was still underway. With ratification already completed in the other countries, however, opposition movements began to lose traction in the rest of the region. The VI Foro gathering in Costa Rica was delayed until December of that year, and attendance dropped. From the peak registration of 1,747 at the Foro in 2004, participation was reported at "more than 1300 representatives" at the Foro in 2005 (Foro Mesoamericano, 2005). No meeting took place in 2006 or 2007.

As the regional opposition movement faltered, PPP planning was reenergized. Felipe Calderón, Vicente Fox's successor, embraced the project and, with his hair's-breadth victory in July 2006, PPP regained momentum. Colombia was officially added as a member in 2006, and Ecuador and the Dominican Republic requested observer status (*Declaración Conjunta*, 2007). In April 2007, all PPP member-state presidents except Nicaragua's Daniel Ortega—who objected to the inclusion of Colombia due to a dispute with that country over maritime borders and oil exploration rights (Weinberg, 2007: 5–8)—launched a new phase in PPP expansion.

Reflections on Transnational Resistance

PPP, announced with so much fanfare in 2000, became a catchword among opponents for the ills associated with neoliberal deepening in Mesoamerica. The rise of a resistance movement, building off a residue of anti-NAFTA organizing, resurgent indigenous movements, fading revolutionary movements, and new forms of social activism, transformed PPP into a regional plebiscite on globalization. The movement soon expanded to confront the CAFTA process, focusing attention on the disruptive regional consequences of that advancing trade and investment pact. The economic restructuring envisioned under PPP and CAFTA foreshadowed dislocations that moved organizations to action. Sharing information, consulting on strategies, and working to counter the information deficit, protesters built a network across national boundaries.

In spite of these efforts, neoliberal regionalism advanced. This momentum highlights the distinct difficulties faced by resistance coalitions, particularly those attempting to frame discontent and mobilize cross-nationally. Many success stories in the resistance canon are, as the introductory chapter to this volume indicates, descriptions of how participants confronted immediate threats to their villages and neighborhoods. A transnational project, where the threat may be physically distant or emerge piecemeal, may not muster the sense of urgency needed to sustain high levels of mobilization across a long period of time. Recognizing these challenges, leading social movement theorists question the common claim that cross-border activism has given rise to transnational social movements. Keck and Sikkink (1998) and Tarrow (1998:184–195) suggest that these actors may be better understood as "transnational advocacy networks," that is, collectivities that cobble together local movements but lack the requisite integration of these domestic social networks to be called social movements. Tarrow (2005) argues that activists with cross-border agendas might be best understood as "rooted cosmopolitans" who are primarily identified with their domestic struggles but who periodically develop organizational linkages and vision that embrace a regional or transnational understanding.

Transnational organizing through far-flung networks confronts particular financial and logistical obstacles. New styles of transnational activism tend to emphasize participatory and polycentric structures (Bennett, 2005: 215). More inclusive and elastic than their predecessors, these networks may face special problems of coordination and collective decision making. Foro Mesoamericano processes attempted to structure collaboration, but they were often weakly institutionalized—witness the 2006 breakdown in the annual Foro gathering routine when CAFTA's passage in much of the region removed the immediate catalyst for action. Faced with these difficulties, transnational coalitions may lack the capacity to either maintain consistent pressure or adapt to continually changing opportunities. In spite of real efforts to mobilize sustained street-level protests and pursue transformative visions, transnational activists may achieve only episodic expression, posing little immediate threat to dominant powers.

Resistance movements often become reactive, confined to the exhausting task of trying to halt dislocation. The "fetishism of autonomy," described by Hellman (1992), leads organizers to eschew electoral campaigns and dismiss conventional tactics like legislative strategizing and lobbying. Rejecting mainstream politics, resisters may develop a limited repertoire, characterized by repetitive actions. Resistance coalitions may lack the agility to adapt when the executive agency shifts or the process enters a new stage. Identification of new strategies when the immediate locus of decision shifts from the IDB to the BCIE, for example, or from U.S. trade negotiators to the local legislature, poses a particular challenge for cross-national resistance coalitions.

Under the best of circumstances, economic globalization processes are difficult to confront. Analysts of transnational advocacy networks have noted the usefulness of organizational tactics like "boomerangs" and "insider/outsider coalitions." These tactics allow activists who are unable to influence their own governments to align with international organizations that then pressure these governments to fulfill commitments made under international agreements. These mechanisms, which allow activists to use international forums to press for domestic reforms, have proven effective in producing national policy change (Keck and Sikkink, 1998). The potential for such success, however, is greater when organizers are advancing political or civil rights claims, where international human rights norms are relatively well established. Social and economic rights claims, which involve challenges to the dominant economic model, are more difficult to assert effectively as powerful "outsider" resources have been scarce (della Porta and Tarrow, 2005: 6).

In spite of these difficulties, transnational resistance coalitions represent a critical political development. Movement success should not be defined simply in terms of policy victories and material changes; a more sophisticated rendering of the concept of success identifies various places and ways in which a transnational network can leave an imprint. Social movement theorists Keck and Sikkink (1998: 25), for example, have assessed influence in terms of a five-stage hierarchy, beginning with relatively modest achievements like "issue creation" and the construction of "discursive positions"—changes that simply reflect growing awareness of the problem. As momentum builds, the movement may be able to secure additional changes, including new institutional procedures, formal policy shifts, and even changes in state behaviors. Along the same lines, Jonathan Fox (2002: 386–387) has developed a multilayered framework that explores impacts of organizing on both the target and the campaign itself. His analysis calls us to reflect on the interplay of material versus discursive concessions and intended versus unintended consequences associated with transnational advocacy. These complex assessment schemes identify changes related to movement work that fall short of an immediate rollback of neoliberal regionalism, but that nonetheless reflect achievement.

In Mesoamerica, Foro networks have helped to motivate and enrich local processes, alert vulnerable populations to larger trends, and promote cross-border mobilizations. Connections forged in deliberations over PPP facilitated rapid response to CAFTA; as Central America moved toward subsequent trade negotiations with the European Union, regional activists built on prior learning and cross-border ties to begin planning their response. The VII Foro Mesoamericano gathering planned for Panama in 2008 could allow regional activists to support Panamanian organizers challenging the new U.S.-Panama FTA and the extension of PPP infrastructure south through the Darién into Colombia.

The material results of this struggle may emerge only over time, as the costs of corporate globalization become clearer. Already we see signs of growing skepticism about the advantages of neoliberal regionalism in Mesoamerica. Long-term polling by the Instituto Universitario de Opinión Pública (IUDOP, 2003: 31, 2006: 8) in El Salvador, for example, reveals erosion in public support for CAFTA. In 2006, 50 percent of Salvadoran respondents concluded that CAFTA would generate more poverty, up from only 28 percent who held that view about FTAs in 2003. Evidence of rising opposition may also be found in both Costa Rica and Mexico, where the 2006 presidential candidates most closely identified with FTAs and corporate-based development strategies—Oscar Arias and Felipe Calderón—failed to achieve majority support and won election by knife-thin margins.

Although poll results and voting patterns only weakly reflect larger beliefs and values, these developments suggest deepening concerns about the course of neoliberal globalization in this region. Resistance movements, which have begun to link activists across the region, highlight the costs of this form of development and call people to mobilize in opposition. Episodic and little institutionalized, these gatherings have been unable to halt the advance of hegemonic globalization. Resisters, however, remain actively engaged in the struggle in their local settings. As Tarrow (2005: 219) notes, "Transnational activism does not resemble a swelling tide of history but is more like a series of waves that lap on an international beach, retreating repeatedly into domestic seas but leaving incremental changes on the shore."

20

Challenges Ahead for
Latin America's Social Movements

*Glen David Kuecker, Richard Stahler-Sholk,
and Harry E. Vanden*

L IKE OTHERS WHO HAVE TRIED to come to terms with the extraordinary development of new social movements in Latin America, David Slater, in his
1994 article, examined the emergence of new subjective identities and noted
their capacity to drive change (Slater, 1994a; Dagnino, 1998). Slater's original
Latin American Perspectives article and those accompanying it in the 1994
issue anticipated what was to come in the following years, as multiple subjects
spawned a proliferation of movements. He also highlighted the exciting potential for multiple paths of emancipation from social injustice and embraced
the political imaginary emerging from the rich diversity of the movements
themselves (Slater, 1994b, 1994c). Slater and the other authors of that 1994
issue identified a future horizon of challenges to power. This would include
challenging conventional definitions of politics and power, with a shift in the
locus of contestation from the state to society. The cases examined in this volume largely confirm many of the movement dynamics that these authors anticipated. After fourteen years, we have a much richer range of movements
(Broad, 2002; Mertes, 2003) and can better begin to assess their impact.

The social actors examined in these pages share an ability to frustrate, if not
defeat, the neoliberal project in Latin America. A noteworthy change in the regional context since the 1994 compilation is that the "Washington Consensus"
on free-market reform has in fact broken down. Considering the inequality of
power relationships between transnational corporations, international financial
institutions, and elite dominated national institutions, and some of the poor
and marginalized people in Latin America, it is very remarkable that the subjects that formed these movements proved capable of confronting neoliberalism

to the extent they have. As noted in several cases, the struggle against neoliberalism is not necessarily a struggle against capitalism, which many still identify as the underlying cause of social and economic injustice. Radical change in Latin America, by definition, is not compatible with the continuation of capitalism in its present form. Yet the reformist tendencies in many of these social movements may prove their undoing if, in fact, those advocating neoliberalism regroup to effectively reshape the ideological packaging and political strategies of the project, and devise new ways to suppress, confuse, fragment, and co-opt opposition (Veltmeyer, 2007). The emergence of multiple new identity-based social subjects carries the danger that it could fracture class solidarity (Foweraker, 1995). The challenge for social movements is to mobilize around the diverse subjective experiences of oppression, while unifying those at the bottom in struggle against the common structures that oppress them.

These social movements are closely correlated with the historically significant regional shift to governments of the political left. However, this may be a case of correlation rather than causation, as there are multiple factors giving rise to the region's new movements and left-of-center regimes. The United States' imperial fiasco in Iraq and its problematical intervention in Afghanistan have opened some space for the Left in Latin America (see Vanden, forthcoming). However, the "Global War on Terror" (which seems to have replaced cold war anticommunism) is a club that could easily be wielded against popular movements in Latin America. Social movements and their ability to mobilize are also key components of the support base for the radical regimes in Venezuela, Bolivia, and Ecuador, as well as the less radical yet progressive regimes in Argentina, Nicaragua, and Uruguay. In several cases, the interjection of new, more subjectively based movements made it impossible for the political right to continue governing. Indeed, their demise was caused by the constellation of new movements engaged in multiple and diverse forms of opposition. The social movements played key roles in displacing neoliberalism and supporting leftist political alternatives (Hershberg and Rosen, 2006; Prashad and Ballvé, 2006). The radical and progressive regimes must take the social movements seriously, and in the process they will find a countervailing force to oppose old powerbrokers such as the World Bank, International Monetary Fund, or multinational oil companies.

The growing history and long-term survival of many of the "new" movements highlights the importance of their maturity as significant players in the political, economic, social, and cultural arenas. They are no longer the emergent phenomena that scholars like Slater (1994a) and Alvarez, Dagnino, and Escobar (1998a) identified in the nineties. With ten, twenty, even thirty years of struggle, the movements have accumulated a repertoire of knowledge—a praxis—that can only be gained from direct experience. Further, this knowledge is being passed on to a new generation of organizers, organic intellectuals, and activists. Their historical trajectories provide the movements with an important societal sedimentation, permanence, and presence that make them fixtures and points of reference for the body politic. The maturity that many movements have achieved means they have a history of tactics and strategies applied in battles won and lost. This historical memory makes them a force to contend with in politics, society, the economy, and culture, because it enhances their ability to navigate crisis, see pitfalls and traps, and better wage the Gramscian war of position. Social movement maturity also generates important societal spin-offs, as other sectors learn from the lessons of the new formulations, thus altering the terrain from which other struggles spring. One important lesson is that an exclusive preoccupation with seizing state power, whether by revolutionary or electoral means, neglects the slow but essential work of social and ideological transformation that is essential for lasting change.

Another success for social movements is the creation and implementation of an enhanced political imagination. The multiple emancipations of the region-wide struggle generate inspirational models that provide optimism and hope within an often bitter if not brutal reality. The ability to envision a plan for creating a more just community might be a success in and of itself, but to implement the imaginary is remarkable, especially given the paucity of material resources, the limits of human capital, and the hostile and often repressive structures of power. Taken as a whole, the essays in this volume capture the remarkably diverse manifestations of the acts of resistance that extend the possibilities of human emancipation and that broaden the horizon of alternatives to the status quo and the misery it engenders.

Success is often measured by positive changes in people's lives. The multiple points of struggle in Latin America have generated countless individual victories in countless communities. While not amounting to macro-level revolutionary change, these victories carry real meaning for those caught up in struggles from below, because they change lives. Perhaps the biggest aspect to everyday quality of the successes is the ways struggle alters power relations within families, especially in terms of gender, and within communities. More and more of Latin America's marginalized have become subjects of their own history, agents in defining the world in which they live (Zibechi, 2005). Ultimately, social movements have dramatically altered the most basic power issue facing humanity—who has the power to decide—by claiming the right to have rights. Indeed, they may well change how politics are conceived and practiced in Latin America.

Having far greater voice in decision making, the social movements constitute a serious challenge, if not threat, to authoritarian decision making and the system of power in Latin America. History suggests that those people and institutions that concentrate power and decision making seldom, if ever, give up that power willingly. Rather, it has to be taken from them through contestation, which, in Latin America (with its elitist, rigid, vertical political structures and entrenched oligarchy/military/U.S.-allied elite) has resulted in deep levels of violent conflict. While violent repression persists in Latin America, an important success of the social movements is their ability to contest power without provoking waves of extreme violence such as that which characterized the "dirty wars" and the brutal military regimes in the 1970s and 1980s. Although repressive structures and the problem of impunity persist, today's social movements have not been entirely eradicated by the military, death squads, paramilitaries, or police forces, and the "recovery of historical memory" has figured prominently in the agenda of many movements (Jelin, 2005). The ability to survive one's resistance indicates that the nexus of power in Latin America has altered dramatically, and the social movements have played a key part in this change. It has forced the masters of power into strategic retreats and has required them to engage in new tactics and strategies of domination, oppression, and repression, which often necessitate their expropriation of tactics and strategies of the social movements, as well as their discourses, in formulating the new nexus of power.

Latin American social movements have also made a significant contribution to social science thinking. The sophistication of their struggles has challenged scholars to rethink old categories, push debates deeper, and advance new ideas for understanding the social realities analyzed. Social movements can lay legitimate claim to much of the resultant knowledge generated in academia, especially as scholars attempt to better comprehend the politics of everyday life. The South's contribution to the production of knowledge results in pushing the horizon of alternatives available to those in struggle. This contribution generates new and often difficult positions for scholars, as academic activism often runs into conflict with the more conservative role of the university in capitalist society—that of legitimizing the system and reproducing the dominant ideology.

Slater's 1994 essay uses Peterson to caution us about being overly optimistic about the alternative horizons produced by Latin America's social movements. Peterson (1989) reminds us that social movements often have a functional place in capitalist society, one that allows the system to reproduce itself by ensuring that more radical challenges to it do not come forward. This critique is important in considering whether there has been a "transcendental" shift in "power" relations as a consequence of the proliferation of social movements. In looking to future horizons, Peterson and Slater's caveats invite us to consider the many challenges ahead.

While movement maturity provides positives, it also carries limitations. Some movements may undergo significant burn-out due to many years, even decades, of daily struggle. The toll on the human spirit, material resources, and human capital is extensive, and over time attrition can set in, weakening the grassroots foundations of movements. Maturity also can distance a movement from its grassroots origins, whereby it loses its core identity, objectives, and strategies. Time's generational shift can reinvigorate movements, but it also carries the threat of leadership loss. As they mature, movements tend to become institutionalized, which can undermine the creative, fluid, and diverse dynamics that made them important actors to begin with. We must ask how long each of the movements can sustain struggle and how well they will navigate the perils of the maturity process.

Latin America's radical regimes face the problem of delivering benefits to their base of support. With multiple identity groups composing civil society, we need to be aware of how leftist regimes attend to their constituents. In the hierarchy of need distribution that defines the substance of politics, which social movements will be rewarded, and on what terms and at what cost will those rewards come? Likewise, what happens to those new social subjects if they descend in the radical pecking order and become subordinated to interests of state or to tactical alliances? Do they wait in line, submissively, in hopes of getting a piece of the alternative future being constructed? While the political context is much more favorable to the social movements, they still operate in a political world, one full of contestation, competition, and the negotiations that define power. A movement's "power to" can still be severely constrained by a radical regime's "power over." Even worse, if a movement falls out of favor or simply cannot compromise, where does it turn? As has been said for too long in Latin America, "*la lucha sigue*," "the struggle continues." These concerns raise the substantive theoretical question of whether the new movements, by definition, are in a state of perpetual struggle. This question is not unique to social movement dynamics but has also been faced by revolutionary movements at various moments.

Latin America, along with the rest of the world, faces immense challenges in the decades ahead. Many scholars are identifying these challenges as a global resource crisis, imperial breakdown, or even catastrophic systemic collapse. As the essays in this volume show, we now know that social movements play a critical role in community sustainability in the face of the brutalities of neoliberal globalization, especially as states are less and less able to address fundamental human problems. This volume assembles recent analyses of a variety of cases and dimensions of Latin American social movements. The contributions shed light on the *origins* of these movements, their evolving *strategies* and dynamics, and their *outcomes* and prospects for achieving fundamental social change. One observable pattern is that the upsurge in popular mobilization in the last quarter-century reflects broad dissatisfaction with the impact of global free-market economic policies and with the empty promises of procedural democracy in which formal equality of individual rights is undercut by massive social and economic inequalities. The new social movements have challenged this atomization of society, defining new collective identities and communities, and demanding that these be recognized as part of a broad reconceptualization of citizenship rights.

Social movement strategies have diversified to include a wide "repertoire of contention" (Tilly, 1978; Tilly and Tarrow, 2006), adapting to the changing context that gave rise to the movements. Contributors to this volume have highlighted the creative ways in which seemingly marginalized social actors have nurtured solidarity and consciousness in a variety of spaces in their everyday lives. At the same time, the movements face ongoing dilemmas in connecting these particular subjectively experienced struggles to broader networks: Will ethnic/racial, gender, and other identities be subsumed under the Left's traditional class-based organizing or under the agendas of parties or governments claiming to represent popular interests? Are identity-based movements capable of avoiding dead-end fragmentation and of building alliances without losing their autonomy? Can social movements go transnational, building a countervailing power to global capital, without getting recolonized from the North?

The outcomes of social movements are difficult to assess and, in any case, never final. Many of the chapters in this compilation point to successes in broadening the range of actors and actions, changing political configurations (and even toppling governments), generating lasting consciousness within movements, and transforming discourse and politics in the wider societies. At the same time, political elites have adapted their strategies of co-optation and modified the neoliberal discourse to mimic the language of participatory democracy. Some of the studies in this volume question whether local victories are merely "not-in-my-backyard" displacements of global problems, as transnational capital and regulatory elites readjust their strategies of accumulation and hegemony.

In other eras, the conventional wisdom may have been that it was unrealistic to think that the seemingly disempowered could overturn the powerful, that slavery could be abolished or women could gain the vote, or that authoritarian regimes serving the empire could be toppled. It is our hope that this collection will stimulate critical thinking among scholars and students of social movements and among those who are engaged in various parts of the struggle to make a better world possible.

References

Ackelsberg, Martha A. 1988. "Communities, resistance, and women's activism: Some implications for a democratic polity." Pp. 297–313 in Ann Bookman and Sandra Morgen (eds.), *Women and the politics of empowerment*. Philadelphia: Temple University Press.

Adler, Judith. 1970. "The politics of land reform in Mexico." Master of Philosphy thesis, London School of Economics.

Adriance, Madeleine Cousineau. 1996. *Terra prometida: As comunidades eclesiais de base e os conflitos rurais*. São Paulo: Paulinas.

Alamanni de Carrillo, Beatrice. 2005. *Posición de la procuradora para la defensa de los derechos humanos de El Salvador sobre el Tratado de Libre Comercio entre Estados Unidos, Centroamérica y República Dominicana*. March 15. www.pddh.gob.sv/docs/DR-CAFTA.pdf (accessed November 20, 2005).

Albro, Robert. 2005. "The water is ours, carajo! Deep citizenship in Bolivia's water war." Pp. 249–271 in June C. Nash (ed.), *Social movements: A reader*. Malden, MA: Basic Blackwell.

Almeida, Lucio Flávio de, and Felix Ruiz Sanchez. 2000. "The landless movement and social struggles against neoliberalism." *Latin American Perspectives* 27(5): 11–32.

Altimir, Oscar, and Luis Beccaria. 1999. *El mercado de trabajo bajo el nuevo régimen económico en Argentina*. CEPAL Serie Reformas Económicas 28.

Alvarez, Sonia E. 1990. *Engendering democracy in Brazil: Women's movements in transition politics*. Princeton, NJ: Princeton University Press.

———. 1998. "Latin American feminisms 'go global': Trends of the 1990s and challenges for the new millennium." Pp. 293–324 in Sonia Alvarez, Evelina Dagnino, and Arturo Escobar (eds.), *Cultures of politics, politics of cultures: Re-visioning Latin American social movements*. Boulder, CO: Westview Press.

Alvarez, Sonia E., Evelina Dagnino, and Arturo Escobar (eds.). 1998a. *Culture of politics, politics of cultures: Re-visioning Latin American social movements.* Boulder, CO: Westview Press.

———. 1998b. "Introduction: The cultural and the political in Latin American social movements." Pp. 1–29 in Sonia E. Alvarez, Evelina Dagnino, and Arturo Escobar (eds.), *Cultures of politics, politics of cultures: Re-visioning Latin American social movements.* Boulder, CO: Westview Press.

Alvarez, Sonia E., and Arturo Escobar. 1991. "New social movements in Latin America: Identity, strategy and democracy." Panel Proposal, Latin American Studies Association Meeting, Washington, DC.

Amnesty International. 2007. "Ecuadorian community activists are facing death threats and attacks for being against copper mining operations." AI Index: AMR 28/002/2007 (July 25).

Andean Group Report (AGR). 2003a. "Are indigenous uprisings the latest domino theory?" November 4: 7–9.

———. 2003b. "Ecuadorean coalition looks fragile as Pachakutik row escalates." July 29: 1.

Andolina, Robert. 2003. "The sovereign and its shadow: Constituent Assembly and indigenous movement in Ecuador." *Journal of Latin American Studies* 35(4): 721–750.

Andrade, Susana. 2003. "Gobiernos locales indígenas en el Ecuador." *Revista Andina* 37: 115–135.

Andrews, George Reid. 1991. *Blacks & whites in São Paulo, Brazil, 1888–1988.* Madison, WI: University of Wisconsin Press.

———. 2004. *Afro-Latin America: 1800–2000.* New York: Oxford University Press.

Angelo, Gloria. 1987. *Pero ellas son imprescindibles.* Santiago, Chile: Biblioteca de la Mujer/Centro de Estudios de la Mujer.

APDHB/ASOFAMD/CBDHDD/DIAKONA/FUNSOLON/RED-ADA. 2004. *Para que no se olvide 12–13 de febrero 2003.* La Paz, Bolivia: Plural Editores.

Arditi, Benjamin, and José Carlos Rodríguez. 1987. *La sociedad a pesar del estado: Movimientos sociales y recuperación democrática en el Paraguay.* Asunción, Paraguay: EI Lector.

Arenhart, Deise. 2003. *A educação da infância no MST: O olhar das crianças sobre uma pedagogia em movimento.* Florianópolis, Brazil: Universidade Federal de Santa Catarina.

Arze, Carlos, and Thomas Kruse. 2004. "The consequences of neoliberal reform." *NACLA Report on the Americas* 38(3): 23–28.

Asamblea Legislativa de la República de El Salvador. 2004. *Acta No. 84. Sesión Plenaria Ordinaria del 16 de diciembre del año 2004.* Versión taquigráfica.

Assies, Willem. 1994. "Urban social movements in Brazil: A debate and its dynamics." *Latin American Perspectives* 21(2): 81–105.

———. 2003. "David versus Goliath in Cochabamba: Water rights, neoliberalism, and the revival of social protest in Bolivia." *Latin American Perspectives* 30(3): 14–36.

Associação Amigos de Gegê dos Moradores da Gamboa de Baixo, Associação dos Moradores do Nordeste de Amaralina, Conselho de Moradores do Bairro da Paz, Grupo de Mulheres do Alto das Pombas. 2001. "Carta aberta dos(as) moradores(as) das comunidades populares de Salvador." *Cadernos do CEAS* 194: 91–94. Salvador: Centro de Estudos e Ação Social.

Auyero, Javier. 2000. *Poor People's Politics: Peronist Survival Networks and the Legacy of Evita*. Durham: Duke University Press.

———. 2001a. "Glocal riots." *International Sociology* 16(1): 33–54.

———. 2001b. "Life in the picket line: Biography and protest in the global South." Sociology Department, State University of New York at Stony Brook, mimeo handout.

———. 2001c. *Poor people's politics: Peronist survival networks and the legacy of Evita*. Durham, NC: Duke University Press.

———. 2003. *Contentious lives: Two Argentine women, two protests, and the quest for recognition*. Durham, NC: Duke University Press.

Azuela, Mariano. 2002. *The underdogs [Los de abajo]*. Trans. E. Munguía, Jr. New York: Modern Library.

Báez Rivera, Sara, and Víctor Bretón Solo de Zaldivar. 2006. "El enigma del voto étnico o las tribulaciones del movimiento indígena: Reflexiones sobre los resultados de la primera vuelta electoral (2006) en las provincias de la sierra." *Ecuador Debate* (December): 19–36.

Baierle, Sérgio Gregório. 1998. "The explosion of experience: The emergence of a new ethical-political principle in popular movements in Porto Alegre, Brazil." Pp. 118–138 in Sonia E. Alvarez, Evelina Dagnino, and Arturo Escobar (eds.), *Cultures of politics, politics of cultures: Re-visioning Latin American social movements*. Boulder, CO: Westview Press.

Baiocchi, Gianpaolo. 2005. *Militants and citizens: The politics of participatory democracy in Porto Alegre*. Stanford, CA: Stanford University Press.

Ballvé, Teo. 2004. "A tale of two Bolivias: Behind the ongoing gas wars, a geographic rift between rich and poor." *Narco News Bulletin* (34). http://www.narconews.com/Issue34/article1056.html (accessed December 13, 2007).

———. 2005. "¡Bolivia de Pie!" *NACLA Report on the Americas* 39(2): 40–44.

Banford, Sue, and Oriel Glock. 1985. *The last frontier: Fighting over land in the Amazon*. London: Zed Books.

Barreda, Andrés. 2004. "The Dangers of Plan Puebla Panama." Pp. 131–208 in Armando Bartra (coordinador), *Profound rivers of Mesoamerica: Alternatives to Plan Puebla Panama*. Translation by irlandesa and Tom Hansen. México: Instituto Maya, El Atajo and Mexico Solidarity Network.

Barrett, Michelle. 1988. *Women's oppression today: The Marxist/feminist encounter*. London: Verso.

Barrig, Maruja. 1991. "The difficult equilibrium between bread and roses: Women's organizations and the transition from dictatorship to democracy in Peru." Pp. 114–148 in Jane Jacquette (ed.), *The women's movement in Latin America*. Boulder, CO: Westview Press.

Barros, Ruben. 1986. "The left and democracy: Recent debates in Latin America." *Telos* 68 (Summer): 49–70.

Bartra, Armando. 2004. "The South: Mega-Plans and Utopias in Mesoamerica." Pp. 13–130 in Armando Bartra (coordinador), *Profound rivers of Mesoamerica: Alterna-*

tives to Plan Puebla Panama. Translation by irlandesa and Tom Hansen. México: Instituto Maya, El Atajo and Mexico Solidarity Network.

Barthes, Roland. 1957. *Mythologies.* Paris: Editions du Seuill.

Beck, Scott H., and Kenneth J. Mijeski. 2006. "The indigenous vote in Ecuador's 2002 presidential election." *Latin American and Caribbean Ethnic Studies* 1 (September 2006): 165–184.

Becker, Marc. Forthcoming. *Indians and leftists in the making of Ecuador's modern indigenous movements.* Durham, NC: Duke University Press.

Beneria, Lourdes, and Martha Roldan. 1987. *The crossroads of class and gender.* Chicago: University of Chicago Press.

Beneria, Lourdes, and Gita Sen. 1981. "Accumulation, reproduction, and women's role in economic development: Boserup revisited." *Signs* 7: 279–298.

Benessaieh, Afef. 2004. "¿Civilizando la sociedad civil? La cooperación internacional en Chiapas durante los años noventa." Pp. 33–51 in Daniel Mato (ed.), *Políticas de ciudadanía y sociedad civil en tiempos de globalización.* Caracas: Universidad Central de Venezuela.

Benhabib, Seyla, and Drucilla Cornell. 1987. "Beyond the politics of gender." Pp. 1–15 in Seyla Benhabib and Drucilla Cornell (eds.), *Feminism as critique.* Minneapolis: University of Minnesota Press.

Bennett, W. Lance. 2005. "Social movements beyond borders: Understanding two eras of transnational activism." Pp. 203–226 in Donatella della Porta and Sidney Tarrow (eds.), *Transnational protest and global activism.* Lanham, MD: Rowman & Littlefield.

Bernstein, Henry. 2003. "Farewell to the peasantry." *Transformation* 52: 1–19.

Betto, Frei. 1994. "Teologia da libertação e espiritualidade popular." Pp. 44–45 in Leonardo Boff and Frei Betto (eds.), *Mística e espiritualidade.* Rio de Janeiro: Rocco.

———. 2001a. *Dez conselhos para os militantes de esquerda.* São Paulo: MST.

———. 2001b. "Valores da mística da militância política." Pp. 51–62 in *Mística da militância: Encontro nacional de fé e política.* Goiás, Brazil: Editora Rede.

Big Noise Films. 1998. *Zapatista!* (videocassette). New York. http://www.bignoisefilms.com.

Bloque Popular Centroamericano, Alliance for Responsible Trade, and Alianza Social Continental. 2004. *Por qué decimos no al TLC: Análisis crítico del texto oficial.* San Salvador, El Salvador: Editorial Maya.

Bobbio, Norberto. 1989. *Democracy and dictatorship.* Minneapolis: University of Minnesota Press.

Boff, Leonardo. 1993. "Alimentar nossa mística." Pp. 7–25 in *Cadernos fé e política.* Petrópolis, Brazil: Movimento Fé e Política.

———. 1994a. "Mística e cultos africanos." Pp. 93–95 in Leonardo Boff and Frei Betto (eds.), *Mística e espiritualidade.* Rio de Janeiro: Rocco.

———. 1994b. "Que é mística?" Pp. 12–13 in Leonardo Boff and Frei Betto (eds.), *Mística e espiritualidade.* Rio de Janeiro: Rocco.

Bogo, Ademar. 1999. *Lições da luta pela terra.* Salvador: Memorial das Letras.

———. 2002. *O vigor da mística.* São Paulo: MST.

Bonfil Batalla, Guillermo. 1990. *México profundo: Una civilización negada.* Mexico, DF: Grijalbo: Consejo Nacional para la Cultura y las Artes.

Borras, Saturnino. 2004. "La Vía Campesina: An evolving transnational social movement." Transnational Institute, TNI Briefing Series No. 2004/6.

Bové, José. 2001. "A farmers' international?" *New Left Review* 12: 89–101.

Bowles, Samuel, and Herbert Gintis. 1986. *Democracy and capitalism.* New York: Basic Books.

Bradford, Sue, and Jan Rocha. 2002. *Cutting the wire: The story of the landless movement in Brazil.* London: Latin American Bureau.

Brazilian Institute of Statistics. 2001. Statistical Report 2001, as cited from "Pais termina anos 90 tão desigual como começou," *Folha de São Paulo* (April 5, 2001). In Tom Lewis, "Brazil: The struggle against neoliberalism," *International Socialist Review* (June/July) (accessed December 13, 2007).

Brecher, Jeremy, Tim Costello, and Brendan Smith. 2000. *Globalization from below: The power of solidarity.* Cambridge, MA: South End Press.

Broad, Robin (ed.). 2002. *Global backlash: Citizen initiatives for a just world economy.* Lanham, MD: Rowman & Littlefield.

Brusco, Valeria, Marcelo Nazareno, and Susan Stokes. 2004. "Vote buying in Argentina." *Latin American Research Review* 39(2): 66–88.

Brysk, Alison. 2000. *From tribal village to global village: Indian rights and international relations in Latin America.* Stanford, CA: Stanford University Press.

Budds, Jessica, and Gordon McGranahan. 2003. "Are the debates on water privatization missing the point? Experiences from Africa, Asia and Latin America." *Environment and Urbanization* 15(2): 87–113.

Burdman, Julio. 2002. "Origen y evolución de la 'piqueteros.'" http://www.nuevamayoria .com/invest/sociedad/cso180302.htm (accessed December 13, 2007).

Burguete Cal y Mayor, Araceli (ed.). 1999. *Mexico: Experiencias de autonomía indígena.* Copenhagen: IWGIA.

———. 2003. "The de facto autonomous process: New jurisdictions and parallel governments in rebellion." Pp. 191–218 in Jan Rus, Rosalva Aída Hernández Castillo, and Shannan L. Mattiace (eds.), *Mayan lives, Mayan utopias: The indigenous peoples of Chiapas and the Zapatista rebellion.* Lanham, MD: Rowman & Littlefield.

Bustamante, Jaime. 1985. "Algunos antecedentes estadísticos sobre las O.E.P. según catastro de 1985." Pp. 157–174 in Luis Razeto et al. (eds.), *Las organizaciones económicas populares* (2nd edition). Santiago, Chile: PET.

Butler, Kim D. 1998. *Freedoms given, freedoms won: Afro-Brazilians in post-abolition, São Paulo and Salvador.* New Brunswick, NJ: Rutgers University Press.

Cabral, Amilcar. 1979. *Unity and struggle: The speeches and writings of Amilcar Cabral.* New York: Monthly Review Press.

Caldart, Roseli Salete. 2000. *Pedagogia do Movimento Sem Terra.* Petrópolis, Brazil: Editora Vozes.

Caldeira, Teresa Pires de Rio. 1990. "Women, daily life and politics." Pp. 47–114 in Elizabeth Jelin (ed.), *Women and social change in Latin America.* London and Geneva: Zed/UNRISD.

Caldwell, Kia Lilly. 2007. *Negras in Brazil: Re-envisioning black women, citizenship, and the politics of identity.* New Brunswick, NJ: Rutgers University Press.

Call, Wendy. 2002. "Resisting the Plan Puebla-Panama." Silver City, NM: Interhemispheric Resource Center.

————. 2003. "PPP focus moves south as Mexican backing loses momentum." *PPP Spotlight #1*. Silver City, NM: Interhemispheric Resource Center.

Calvo, Ernesto, and Marcelo Escolar. 2005. *La nueva política de partidos en la Argentina: Crisis política, realineamientos partidarios y reforma electoral*. Buenos Aires: Prometeo.

Calvo, Ernesto F., and Maria Victoria Murillo. 2005. "Who delivers? Partisan clientelism in the Argentine electoral market." *American Journal of Political Science* 48(4): 742–757.

Camín, Héctor Aguilar. 2000. "El voto útil: Elecciones y el proceso electoral en México." *Proceso* (April 16): 41.

Campero, Guillermo. 1987. *Entre la sobrevivencia y la acción política: Las olganizaciones de pobladores*. Santiago, Chile: ILET.

Carbajal Ríos, Carola. 1988. "Una experiencia de participación de las campesinas en el movimiento popular." Pp. 424–430 in Josefina Aranda Bezaury (ed.), *Las mujeres en el campo*. Oaxaca, Mexico: Instituto de Investigaciones Sociológicas de la Universidad Autónoma Benito Juárez de Oaxaca.

Cardoso, Ruth Corrêa Leite. 1992. "Popular movements in the context of the consolidation of democracy in Brazil." Pp. 291–302 in Arturo Escobar and Sonia A. Alvarez (eds.), *The making of social movements in Latin America: Identity, strategy, and democracy*. Boulder, CO: Westview Press.

Carrillo, Teresa. 1990. "Women and independent unionism in the garment industry." Pp. 213–233 in Joe Foweraker and Ann L. Craig (eds.), *Popular movements and political change in Mexico*. Boulder, CO: Lynne Rienner Publishers.

Castañeda, Jorge G. 1994. *Utopia unarmed: The Latin American left after the cold war*. New York: Vintage Press.

Castañeda, Jorge G., Marta Harnecker, James Petras, and Steve Ellner. 2005. "Left strategy in Latin America: A symposium." *Science & Society* 69: 137–190.

Castells, Manuel. 1984. *The city and the grassroots*. Berkeley: University of California Press.

Castoriadis, Cornelius. 1987. *The imaginary institution of society*. Oxford: Polity Press.

Castro, Gustavo. 2003. "I encuentro hemisférico frente a la militarización." *Chiapas al Día* (CIEPAC). http://www.ciepac.org/bulletins (accessed May 12, 2003).

Ceceña, Ana Esther. 2002. "La batalla de Afganistan." Pp. 167–188 in Ana Esther Ceceña and Emir Sader (eds.), *La guerra infinita: Hegemonía y terror mundial*. Buenos Aires: CLACSO.

————. 2004. "El agua, la vida y los nuevos discursos de la resistencia." Pp. 6–28 in Ana Esther Ceceña (ed.), *La guerra por la agua y por la vida*. Cochabamba, Bolivia: Coordinadora de Defensa del Agua y de la Vida.

Central del Partido Comunista [Argentina]. 2004. "Documento político aprobado por el comité." http://www.pca.org.ar.

Centro de Estudios de la Mujer (ed.). 1988. *Mundo de mujer*. Santiago, Chile: Centro de Estudios de la Mujer.

Centro de Estudios Legales y Sociales [Argentina] (CELS). 2003. "Reporte sobre Plan Jefe y Jefas: Derecho social o beneficio sin derechos." Buenos Aires.

Cheyre, H., and E. Ogrodnick. 1982. "El programa de empleo mínimo: Análisis de una encuesta." *Revista de Economia* No. 7 (November). Santiago: Universidad de Chile.

Cholango, Humberto. 2006. "Entrevista." *Renovación* 4 (November/December): 34.

Chomsky, Noam. 1989. *Necessary illusions: Thought control in democratic societies.* London: Pluto Press.

Cleary, Eda. 1988. *Frauen in der politik chiles.* Aachen, Germany: Alano Verlag.

Colley, Peter. 2001. "The political economy of mining." Pp. 19–36 in Geoff Evans, James Goodman, and Nina Lansbury (eds.), *Moving mountains: Communities confront mining and globalization.* Sydney: Otford Press.

Collier, George A. 1994. "The new politics of exclusion: Antecedents to the rebellion in Mexico." *Dialectical Anthropology* 19(1): 1–44.

Collins, Jennifer. 2004. "Linking movement and electoral politics: Ecuador's indigenous movement and the rise of Pachakutik." Pp. 38–57 in Jo-Marie Burt and Philip Mauceri (eds.), *Politics in the Andes: Identity, conflict, reform.* Pittsburgh: University of Pittsburgh Press.

Collins, Patricia Hill. 1998. *Fighting words: Black women and the search for justice.* Minneapolis: University of Minnesota Press.

———. 2000. *Black feminist thought: Knowledge, consciousness, and the politics of empowerment.* New York: Routledge.

———. 2001. "Like one of the family: Race, ethnicity, and the paradox of U.S. national identity." *Ethnic and Racial Studies* 24: 3–28.

Colloredo-Mansfeld, Rudi. 2002. "Autonomy and interdependence in native movements: Towards a pragmatic politics in the Ecuadorian Andes." *Identities: Global Studies in Culture and Power* 9(2): 173–195.

Comissão Pastoral da Terra. 1998. *Trabalho escravo nas fazendas, Pará e Amapá 1980–1997.* Belém, Brazil: Comissão Pastoral da Terra.

Confederación de Nacionalidades Indígenas del Ecuador (CONAIE). 1989. *Las nacionalidades indígenas en el Ecuador: Nuestro proceso organizativo.* Quito: Ediciones Tincui-Abya-Yala.

Connolly, William E. 1991. *Identity/difference: Democratic negotiations of political paradox.* Ithaca, NY: Cornell University Press.

Conroy, Michael E., Douglas L. Murray, and Peter M. Rosset. 1996. *A cautionary tale: Failed U.S. development policy in Central America.* Boulder, CO: Lynne Rienner Publishers.

Coordinadora Latinoamericana de Organizaciones del Campo (CLOC). 1994. *Ier Congreso de la Coordinadora Latinoamericana de Organizaciones del Campo.* Quito, Ecuador: ALAI.

———. 1997. *II Congreso de la Coordinadora Latinoamericana de Organizaciones del Campo.* Brasilia: Peres Editores.

Consejo Coordinador de Organizaciones Campesinas de Honduras-Central Nacional de Trabajadores del Campo (COCOCH-CNTC). 2003. "Peasant assassinated in Honduras." Declaration and press release from the Central Nacional de Trabajadores del Campo and the Consejo Coordinador de Organizaciones Campesinas de Honduras, July 21.

Corcoran-Nantes, Yvonne. 1990. "Women and popular urban social movements in São Paulo, Brazil." *Bulletin of Latin American Research* 9(2): 249–264.

Cowie, Jefferson. 1999. *Capital moves: RCA's 70-year quest for cheap labor.* Ithaca, NY, and London: Cornell University Press.

Crespo Flores, Carlos. 2000. "La guerra del agua en Cochabamba: Movimientos sociales y crisis de dispositivos de poder." *Ecología Política* 20: 59–70.

———. 2002. "Water privatization policies and conflicts in Bolivia: The water war in Cochabamba (1999–2000)." PhD diss., Oxford Brookes University.

Crespo Flores, Carlos, Omar Fernández Quiroga, and Carmen Peredo. 2004. *Los regantes de Cochabamba en la guerra del agua*. Cochabamba, Bolivia: CESU-UMSS.

Dagnino, Evelina. 1998. "Culture, citizenship, and democracy: Changing discourses and practices of the Latin American left." Pp. 33–63 in Sonia E. Alvarez, Evelina Dagnino, and Arturo Escobar (eds.), *Cultures of Politics, Politics of Cultures: Revisioning Latin American social movements*. Boulder, CO: Westview Press.

———. 2006. "Meanings of citizenship in Latin America." *Canadian Journal of Latin American and Caribbean Studies* 31(62): 15–52.

Dangl, Benjamin. 2007. *The price of fire: Resource wars and social movements in Bolivia*. Oakland, CA: AK Press.

Dávalos, Pablo. 2003a. "Ecuador: Entre el neoliberalismo y la participación social." *América Latina en Movimiento* (February 11): 4.

———. 2003b. "Pachakutik: Crónica de una traición anunciada." *Tintají* (primera quincena de septiembre): 5.

Dávila, Enrique, Georgina Kessel, and Santiago Levy. 2000. *El sur también existe: un ensayo sobre el desarrollo regional mexicano*. México: Secretaría de Hacienda, mimeo.

Davis, Diane. 1999. "The power of distance: Re-theorizing social movements in Latin America." *Theory and Society* 28(4): 585–638.

Davis, Helen. 2004. *Understanding Stuart Hall*. Thousand Oaks, CA: Sage Publications.

Declaración Conjunta Cumbre de Mandatarios Para el Fortalecimiento del Plan Puebla Panamá. 2007. April 10. http://www.planpuebla-panama.org/documentos/Declaracion%20PPP%20Campeche.pdf (accessed June 6, 2007).

De Friedemann, Nina. 1993. *Presencia Africana en Colombia: La saga del Negro*. Santa Fe de Bogotá: Instituto de Ciencia Humana/Facultad de Medicina, Pontifica Universidad Javeriana.

De Friedemann, Nina, and Jaime Arocha. 1995. "Colombia." Pp. 47–76 in Minority Rights Group (ed.), *No longer invisible: Afro-Latin Americans today*. London: Minority Rights Publications.

de la Cadena, Marisol. 2000. *Indigenous mestizos: The politics of race and culture in Cuzco, Peru, 1919–1991*. Durham, NC: Duke University Press.

de la Cruz, Pedro. 2006. "Enfrentar a Noboa y construir la unidad de los Pueblos." *Renovación* 4 (November/December): 56–60.

De la Cruz, Rafael. 1989. "Nuevos movimientos sociales en Venezuela." In D. Camacho and R. Menjívar (eds.), *Los movimientos populares en America Latina*. Mexico City: Siglo Veintiuno.

Delamata, Gabriela. 2004. "The organization of unemployed workers in greater Buenos Aires." Working Paper No. 8. Center for Latin American Studies. University of California, Berkeley.

De La Vega, Pablo. 2004. Opening comments at Social Forum, Quito, Ecuador (August).

della Porta, Donatella, and Sidney Tarrow (eds.). 2005. *Transnational protest and global activism*. Lanham, MD: Rowman & Littlefield.

Desmarais, Annette Aurelie. 2002. "The Vía Campesina: Consolidating an international peasant and farm movement." *Journal of Peasant Studies* 29(2): 91–124.

———. 2003a. "The Vía Campesina: Peasants resisting globalization." PhD diss., Department of Geography, University of Calgary.

———. 2003b. "The Vía Campesina: Peasant women on the frontiers of food sovereignty." *Canadian Woman Studies/les cahiers de la femme* 23(1): 140–145.

———. 2003c. "The WTO . . . will meet somewhere, sometime. And we will be there." Essay prepared for *Voices: The Rise of Nongovernmental Voices in Multilateral Organizations.* Ottawa, Canada: The North-South Institute (accessed December 13, 2007).

———. 2005. "United in La Vía Campesina." *Food First Backgrounder* 11(4): 1–4.

———. 2007. *La Vía Campesina: Globalization and the power of peasants.* Halifax: Fernwood Publishers.

De Vos, Jan. 2002. *Una tierra para sembrar sueños: Historia reciente de la Selva Lacandona, 1950–2000.* Mexico City: CIESAS/Fondo de Cultura Económica.

Díaz-Polanco, Héctor, and Consuelo Sánchez. 2002. *México diverso: El debate por la autonomía.* Mexico City: Siglo XXI.

Dietz, Mary G. 1987. "Context is all: Feminism and theories of citizenship." Pp. 1–24 in Jill K. Conway, Susan C. Bourque, and Joan W. Scott (eds.), *Learning about women: Gender, politics, and power.* Ann Arbor: University of Michigan Press.

Dixon, David. 1994–2000. "Black social movements and human rights in Latin America." Field Research notes, Ecuador, Colombia, and Brazil.

———. 2002. "Democracy and black social movements in Afro-Latin America: The Case of Colombia." Pp. 79–93 in Gonzalo Sichar Moreno et al. (eds.), *La semilla democrática: Experiencias de democracia participativa en América Latina.* Madrid: CIDEAL.

Doula, Sheila Maria. 2000. "Redes de movimientos campesinos en la América Latina contemporánea: Identidad en la lucha." *Universum* 15: 365–376.

Dzidzienyo, Anani, and Suzanne Oboler. 2005. *Neither enemies nor friends: Latinos, blacks, Afro-Latinos.* New York: Palgrave Macmillan.

Earle, Duncan, and Jeanne Simonelli. 2005. *Uprising of hope: Sharing the Zapatista journey to alternative development.* Lanham, MD: AltaMira Press.

Eber, Christine. 2003. "Buscando una nueva vida: Liberation through autonomy in San Pedro Chenalhó, 1970–1998." Pp. 135–159 in Jan Rus, Rosalva Aída Hernández Castillo, and Shannan L. Mattiace (eds.), *Mayan lives, Mayan utopias.* Lanham, MD: Rowman & Littlefield.

Eckstein, Susan. 2004. "Globalization and mobilization in the neoliberal era in Latin America." International Institute of Social History: Labour Again. http://www.iisg.nl/labouragain/documents/eckstein.pdf.

Eckstein, Susan E., and Sonia E. Alvarez (eds.). 1992. *The making of social movements in Latin America: Identity, strategy, and democracy.* Boulder, CO: Westview Press.

Eckstein, Susan, and Timothy P. Wickham-Crowley (eds.). 2003. *Struggles for social rights in Latin America.* New York: Routledge.

Ecuarunari. 2006. "Ecuador empezó su revolución." *Boletín/2006,* November 26.

Edelman, Marc. 1998. "Transnational peasant politics in Central America." *Latin American Research Review* 33(3): 49–86.

———. 2001. "Social movements: changing paradigms and forms of politics." *Annual Review of Anthropology* 30: 285–317.

———. 2003. "Transnational peasant and farmer movements and networks." Pp. 185–220 in Mary Kaldor, Helmut Anheier, and Marlies Glasius (eds.), *Global civil society yearbook 2003*. London: Centre for the Study of Global Governance.

———. 2005. "Bringing the moral economy back in . . . to the study of 21st-century transnational peasant movements." *American Anthropologist* 107(3): 331–345.

Ejército Zapatista de Liberación Nacional (EZLN). 2005. "Sixth Declaration of Lacandon Jungle." June 30.

Ellner, Steve. 2004. "Leftist goals and the debate over anti-neoliberal strategy in Latin America." *Science & Society* 68: 10–32.

———. 2006. "The defensive strategy on the left in Latin America: Objective and subjective conditions in the age of globalization." *Science & Society* 79: 397–410.

Ellner, Steve, and Miguel Tinker-Salas. 2005. "Venezuela: New perspectives on politics and society." *Latin American Perspectives* 32(3): 3–7.

Epstein, Edward C. 2006. "The piquetero movement in greater Buenos Aires: Political protests by the unemployed poor during the crisis." Pp. 95–115 in Edward C. Epstein and David Pion-Berlin (eds.), *Broken promises? The Argentine crisis and Argentine democracy*. Lanham, MD: Lexington Books.

Escobar de Pabón, Silvia. 2003. "Demandas ignoradas, políticas anti-campesinas: ajuste y liberalización, las causas del conflicto social." *OSAL* 4(12): 47–55.

Escudé, Carlos. 2005. *Los Piqueteros: Prebenda y extorsión de los estratos marginales de un estado parasitario*. Universidad del CEMA Serie de Documentos de Trabajo 287.

Esteva, Gustavo. 2003. "The meaning and scope of the struggle for autonomy." Pp. 243–269 in Jan Rus, Rosalva Aída Hernández Castillo, and Shannan L. Mattiace (eds.), *Mayan lives, Mayan utopias: The indigenous people of Chiapas and the Zapatista rebellion*. Lanham, MD: Rowman & Littlefield.

Evans, Geoff, James Goodman, and Nina Lansbury. 2001. "Introduction: Globalization: Threats and opportunities." Pp. xi–xxiii in Geoff Evans, James Goodman, and Nina Lansbury (eds.), *Moving mountains: Communities confront mining and globalization*. Sydney: Otford Press.

Evers, Tilman. 1985. "Identity: The hidden side of new social movements in Latin America." Pp. 43–71 in David Slater (ed.), *New Social Movements and the State in Latin America*. Cinnaminson, NJ: Foris/CEDLA.

Eyerman, Ron, and Andrew Jamison. 1991. *Social movements: A cognitive approach*. Oxford: Polity Press.

Fabregas, Andrés. 2005. "La interculturalidad en el mundo contemporáneo." *Gaceta*, órgano de difusión de la Universidad Intercultural de Chiapas, Octubre.

Falleti, Tulia G. 2005. "A sequential theory of decentralization: Latin American cases in comparative perspective." *American Political Science Review* 99: 327–346.

Farinetti, Marina. 1999. "Que queda del 'movimiento obrero'? Las formas del reclamo laboral en la nueva democracia argentina." *Trabajo y Sociedad* 1(1). http://www .geocities.com/trabajoysociedad/Zmarina.htm (accessed December 13, 2007).

Fernandes, Bernardo Mançano. 1996. *MST: Formação e territorialização em São Paulo*. São Paulo: Editora Hucitec.

———. 2000. *A formação do MST no Brasil.* Petrópolis, Brazil: Editora Vozes.

———. 2001. *Questão agrária, pesquisa e MST.* São Paulo: Editora Cortez.

———. 2005. "The MST and the land question." Paper presented at the conference "New Social Movements and Democracy in Latin America," University of South Florida, Tampa, Florida, March 20–21.

Fieweger, Mary Ellen. 1998. *Es un monstruo y pisa fuerte: La mineria en el Ecuador.* Quito, Ecuador: Abya Yara.

Flax, Jane. 1991. *Thinking fragments: Psychoanalysis, feminism, and postmodernism in the contemporary west.* Berkeley: University of California Press.

Foley, Michael W. 1995. "Privatizing the countryside: The Mexican peasant movement and neoliberal reform." *Latin American Perspectives* 22(1): 59–76.

Foran, John (ed.). 2003. *The future of revolutions: Rethinking political and social change in the age of globalization.* London: Zed Books.

Foro Mesoamericano. Comité Organizador del IV Foro Mesoamericano por la Autodeterminación y Resistencia de los Pueblos. 2004. Memoria, IV Foro Mesoamericano por la Autodeterminación y Resistencia de los Pueblos. Tegucigalpa: Guaymuras.

Foro Mesoamericano por la Autodeterminación y Resistencia de los Pueblos. 2001a. Declaración del Foro. Xelajú, Guatemala. November. www.lasolidarity.org/noppp/declarations.htm (accessed October 11, 2007).

———. 2001b. Declaración del Foro de Información, Análisis y Propuestas, El pueblo es primero frente a la globalización. Tapachula, Chiapas, May 12. www.lasolidarity.org/noppp/declarations.htm (accessed October 11, 2007).

———. 2002a. Declaración Política del III Foro Mesoamericano Managua, July 18. www.lasolidarity.org/noppp/declarations.htm (accessed October 11, 2007).

———. 2002b. Memoria, III Foro Mesoamericano. Frente al Plan Puebla Panamá: El Movimiento Mesoamericano por la Integración Popular. Managua, n.p.

———. 2004a. Declaración del V Foro Mesoamericano. San Salvador, July 21. www.lasolidarity.org/noppp/declarations.htm (accessed October 11, 2007).

———. 2004b. V Foro Closing Session. Author notes. San Salvador, July 21.

———. 2004c. Information packet. V Foro Mesoamericano. San Salvador, July 19–21.

———. 2005. Declaración Final. San José, Costa Rica. December 16. www.encuentropopular.org/documentos/foro_mesoamericano/declarcion5.htm (accessed February 19, 2007).

Foucault, Michel. 1980a. *The history of sexuality.* Vol. 1. *An introduction.* New York: Vintage Books.

———. 1980b. "Truth and power." Pp. 109–133 in Colin Gordon (ed.), *Power/knowledge: Selected interviews and other writings.* New York: Pantheon Books.

———. 1982. "The subject and power." Pp. 208–226 in Hubert L. Dreyfus and Paul Rabinow, *Michel Foucault: Beyond structuralism and hermeneutics.* Chicago: University of Chicago Press.

———. 1986. "The subject and power: An afterword." Pp. 208–226 in Hubert L. Dreyfus and Paul Rabinow, *Michel Foucault: Beyond structuralism and hermeneutics.* Brighton: Harvester Press.

———. 1988. "The ethic of care for the self as a practice of freedom." Pp. 1–20 in James Bernauer and David Rasmussen (eds.), *The final Foucault.* Cambridge, MA: MIT Press.

Foweraker, Joe. 1990. "Popular movements and political change in Mexico." Pp. 3–20 in Joe Foweraker and Ann L. Craig (eds.), *Popular movements and political change in Mexico*. London and Boulder, CO: Lynne Rienner Publishers.

———. 1995. *Theorizing social movements: Critical studies of Latin America*. London: Pluto Press.

———. 2005. "Toward a political sociology of social mobilization in Latin America." Pp. 115–135 in Charles H. Wood and Bryan R. Roberts (eds.), *Rethinking development in Latin America*. University Park: Pennsylvania State University Press.

Foweraker, Joe, and Ann L. Craig (eds.). 1990. *Popular movements and political change in Mexico*. London and Boulder, CO: Lynne Rienner Publishers.

Fox, Jonathan. 1992. "The difficult transition from clientelism to citizenship: Lessons from Mexico." Paper presented at the Latin American Studies Association meetings, Los Angeles.

———. 1994. "The difficult transition from clientelism to citizenship: Lessons from Mexico." *World Politics* 46(2): 151–184.

———. 1997. "The difficult transition from clientelism to citizenship: Lessons from Mexico." Pp. 391–420 in Douglas A. Chalmers et al. (eds.), *The new politics of inequality in Latin America: Rethinking participation and representation*. New York: Oxford University Press.

———. 2000. "Assessing binational civil society coalitions: Lessons from the Mexico-U.S. experience." Chican/Latino Research Center Working Paper No. 26, University of California, Santa Cruz.

———. 2002. "Lessons from Mexico-U.S. civil society coalitions." Pp. 386–87 in David Brooks and Jonathan Fox (eds.), *Cross border dialogues: U.S.-Mexico social movement networking*. La Jolla, CA: Center for US-Mexican Studies, University of California, San Diego.

Fox, Jonathan A., and L. David Brown. 1998. *The struggle for accountability: The World Bank, NGOs, and grassroots movements*. Boston: MIT Press.

Fox, Peter, William Onorato, and John Strongman. 1998. "World Bank group assistance for minerals sector development and reform in member countries." World Bank Technical Paper No. 405, Washington, DC.

Fox, Vicente. 2001. *Entrevista a Vicente Fox en el Rancho San Cristóbal*. Presidencia de la República (accessed December 14, 2007).

———. 2005. "Quinto Informe de Gobierno." Mexico City: Presidency of the Republic. http://quinto.informe.presidencia.gob.mx/index.php (accessed April 22, 2006).

Franco, Jean. 1998. "Defrocking the Vatican: Feminism's secular project." Pp. 278–289 in Sonia E. Alvarez, Evelina Dagnino, and Arturo Escobar (eds.), *Cultures of politics, politics of cultures: Re-visioning Latin American social movements*. Boulder, CO: Westview Press.

Franko, Patrice. 2003. *The puzzle of Latin American economic development*. Lanham, MD: Rowman & Littlefield.

Freire, Paulo. 1967. *A pedagogia do oprimido*. Rio de Janeiro: Paz e Terra.

Fuentes, Marta, and André Gunder Frank. 1989. "Ten theses on social movements." *World Development* 17: 179–191.

Fuss, Diana. 1989. *Essentially speaking: Feminism, nature, and difference*. London: Routledge.

Gallardo, José Francisco, et al. (eds.). 2000. *Always near, always far: The armed forces in Mexico*. San Francisco and Chiapas, Mexico: Global Exchange/Mexico Department, Centro de Investigaciones Económicas y Políticas de Acción Comunitaria AC (CIEPAC), and Centro Nacional de Comunicación Social (CENCOS).

Galtung, Johan. 1980. *The true worlds: A transnational perspective*. New York: The Free Press.

García Linera, Alvaro. 2004. "La crisis del estado y las sublevaciones indígeno-plebeyas." Pp. 27–86 in Luis Tapia Mealla, Alvaro García Linera, and Raúl Prada (eds.), *Memorias de octubre*. La Paz, Bolivia: Muela del Diablo.

García Linera, Alvaro, Raquel Gutiérrez, Raúl Prada, and Luis Tapia. 2001. *Tiempos de rebelión*. La Paz, Bolivia: Muela del Diablo.

García Orellana, Alberto, Fernando García Yapur, and Luz Quitón Herbas. 2003. *La crisis política: La "guerra del agua" en Cochabamba*. La Paz, Bolivia: PIEB.

Garretón, Manuel Antonio. 1989. "Popular mobilization and the military regime in Chile: The complexities of the invisible transition." Pp. 259–277 in Susan Eckstein (ed.), *Power and popular protest*. Berkeley: University of California Press.

Garrido, Luis Javier. 1989. "The crisis of presidencialismo." Pp. 417–434 in Wayne A. Cornelius et al. (eds.), *Mexico's alternative political futures*. La Jolla, CA: Center for U.S.-Mexican Studies.

Gedicks, Al. 2001. *Resource rebels: Native challenges to mining and oil corporations*. Cambridge, MA: South End Press.

———. 2007. "Challenging Canadian mining companies: Imposing mining projects on communities of resistance." *Z Magazine* 20(6): 50–55.

Gele-Hanhanzo, Maurice. 1995. United Nations Special Rapporteur on Racism and Racial Discrimination, Xenophobia and Other Forms of Racial Intolerance: Brazilian Mission, 1995. United Nations Economic and Social Council: The Commission on Human Rights, 52 Session, e/cn.4/1996/72 /Add. Geneva, January 23.

———. 1997. The United Nations Social and Economic Council: The Commission on Human Rights, 53rd Session, e/cn.41997/Add. Geneva, January 13.

Gerchunoff, Pablo, and Juan Carlos Torre. 1996. "La política de liberalización económica en la administración de Menem." *Desarrollo Económico* 36(143): 733–767.

Gerlach, Allen. 2003. *Indians, oil, and politics: A recent history of Ecuador*. Wilmington, DE: Scholarly Resources, Inc.

Giarraca, Norma. 2001. *La protesta social en la Argentina. Transformaciones económicas y crisis social en el interior del país*. Madrid/Buenos Aires: Alianza Editorial.

Gill, Stephen. 1998. "New constitutionalism and the reconstitution of capital." Paper presented at the Globalisation, State and Violence conference, University of Sussex, Brighton, UK, April 15–18.

Gills, Barry. 2000a. "American power, neo-liberal economic globalization, and low-intensity democracy: An unstable trinity." Pp. 326–344 in Michael Cox, G. John Ikenberry, and Takashi Inoguchi (eds.), *American democracy promotion: Impulses, strategies, and impacts*. Oxford: Oxford University Press.

——— (ed.). 2000b. *Globalization and the politics of resistance*. London: Macmillan.

———. 2000c. "Introduction." Pp. 3–11 in Barry K Gills (ed.), *Globalization and the politics of resistance*. New York: Palgrave.

Girardi, Giulio. 1994. *Os Excluídos construirão a nova história?* São Paulo: Ática.

Godio, Julio. 1990. *El movimiento obrero Argentino (1943–1955): Hegemonía nacional-ista-laborista*. Buenos Aires: Editorial Legasa.

———. 1991. *El movimiento obreroArgentino (1955–1990): De la resistencia a la encru-cijada menemista*. Buenos Aires: Editorial Legasa.

———. 1998. *¿La incertidumbre del trabajo: Que se esconde detrás del debate por la es-tabilidad en Argentina?* Buenos Aires: Corregidor.

———. 2004. "La recuperación de empresas por los trabajadores en Argentina." *Revista Pistas* No. 11 (March 14). http://www.rebanadasderealidad.com.ar/godio-10.htm (accessed December 18, 2007).

———. 2005. "Pobreza, conflictos laborales y sociales." *Sociedad*, Regional Latinoamer-icana de la Unión Internacional de Trabajadores de la Alimentación y la Agricultura.

Gómez, Luis. 2004. *El alto de pie: Una insurrección aymara en Bolivia*. La Paz, Bolivia: HdP/Indymedia/La Comuna.

Gómez-Peña, Guillermo. 1996. *The new world border: Prophecies, poems & locuras for the end of the century*. San Francisco: City Lights Books.

Gómez Tagle, Silvia. 1987. "Democracy and power in Mexico: The meaning of conflict in the 1979, 1982, and 1985 federal elections." Pp. 208–210 in Judith Gentleman, (ed.), *Mexican politics in transition*. Boulder, CO: Westview Press.

———. 1989. "La demanda democrática del 6 de julio." Paper prepared for the XV In-ternational Congress of the Latin American Studies Association, Miami, Florida.

González, Anabel. 2005. *El proceso de negociación de un tratado de libre comercio con Estados Unidos: La experiencia del Tratado de Libre Comercio entre Centroamérica, Estados Unidos y República Dominicana*. Unpublished manuscript.

González, Lélia. 1987. "Por un feminismo afrolatinoamericano." *ISIS International* 9 (June): 133–141.

González, Mario. 1996. "A la caza del voto indígena." June 13. http://ecuador.nativeweb .org/96elect/caza.html.

González, Roosbelinda Cárdenas. 2004. "Black bodies, (in)visible hands: Black *domes-ticas'* struggle in Salvador, Bahia." M.A. Thesis, Department of Anthropology. Austin: University of Texas.

Goodwin, Jeff, and James M. Jasper. 2004. *The social movements reader: Cases and con-cepts*. Cornwall, UK: Blackwell Publishing.

Görgen, Frei Sergio. 1997. "Religiosidade e fé na luta pela terra." Pp. 279–292 in João Pedro Stedile (ed.), *A reforma agrária e a luta do MST*. Petrópolis, Brazil: Editora Vozes.

Gramsci, Antonio. 1971 [1929–1935]. *Selections from the prison notebooks*. Trans. Quintin Hoare and Geoffrey Nowell Smith. New York: International Publishers.

Green, Duncan. 2003. *Silent revolution: The rise and crisis of market economics in Latin America*, 2nd edition. London: Latin American Books.

Grupo Documental 1° de Mayo. 2001. *Matanza*. Scripts. Buenos Aires.

Gutiérrez Aguilar, Raquel. 2001. "La coordinadora de defensa del agua y de la vida: Un año de la guerra del agua." Pp. 193–211 in Alvaro García Linera, Raquel Gutiérrez Aguilar, Raúl Prada, Felipe Quispe, and Luis Tapia Mealla (eds.), *Tiempos de rebe-lión*. La Paz, Bolivia: Muela del Diablo.

Haber, Paul Lawrence. 1990. "Cárdenas, Salinas and urban popular movements in Mexico: The case of El Comité de Defensa Popular, General Francisco Villa de Du-rango." Unpublished manuscript.

Hale, Charles A. 1989. *The transformation of liberalism in late nineteenth-century Mexico.* Princeton, NJ: Princeton University Press.

Hale, Charles R. 2002. "Does multiculturalism menace? Governance, cultural rights, and the politics of identity in Guatemala." *Journal of Latin American Studies* 34(3): 485–524.

———. 2004. "Rethinking indigenous politics in the era of the 'indio permitido.'" *NACLA Report on the Americas* 38(2):16–21.

Hanchard, Michael George. 1994. *Orpheus and power: The movimento negro of Rio de Janeiro and São Paulo, Brazil, 1945–1988.* Princeton, NJ: Princeton University Press.

Hardt, Michael, and Antonio Negri. 2000. *Empire.* Cambridge, MA: Harvard University Press.

Hardy, Clarisa. 1987. *Organizarse para vivir: Pobreza urbana y organización popular.* Santiago, Chile: PET.

Hardy, Clarisa, and Luis Razeto. 1984. "Los nuevos actores y practicas populares: Desafios a la concertación." Documento de Trabajo No. 47, CED, Santiago, Chile.

Harnecker, Marta. 2003. *Landless people: Building a social movement.* São Paulo: Expressão Popular.

Harvey, David. 1989. *The condition of postmodernity: An inquiry into the origins of cultural change.* Cambridge, UK: Blackwell.

———. 2003. *The new imperialism.* New York: Oxford University Press.

Harvey, Neil. 1998. *The Chiapas rebellion: The struggle for land and democracy.* Durham, NC: Duke University Press.

———. 2004. "Disputando el desarrollo: El Plan Puebla-Panamá y los derechos indígenas." Pp. 115–136 in Rosalva Aída Hernández, Sarela Paz, and María Teresa Sierra (eds.), *El estado y los indígenas en tiempos del PAN: Neoindigenismo, legalidad e identidad.* Mexico City: CIESAS.

———. 2005. "Inclusion through autonomy: Zapatistas and dissent." *NACLA Report on the Americas* 39(2): 12–17.

Held, David. 1991. "Democracy, the nation-state, and the global system." Pp. 197–235 in David Held (ed.), *Political theory today.* Oxford: Polity Press.

Heller, Carlos. n.d. "Formación de bancos cooperativos a partir de la fusión de cooperativas de ahorro y crédito: el caso de la Argentina." IMFC Internal Document.

Hellman, Judith Adler. 1978. *Mexico in crisis,* 1st edition. New York: Holmes & Meier.

———. 1980. "Social control in Mexico." *Comparative Politics* 12(2): 225–242.

———. 1981. "Capitalist agriculture and rural protest." *LABOUR Capital and Society* 14(2), November: 30–46.

———. 1983. "The role of ideology in peasant movements: Peasant mobilization and demobilization in the Laguna region." *Journal of Interamerican Studies and World Affairs* 25(1), Februrary: 3–29.

———. 1988. *Mexico in crisis,* 2nd edition. New York: Holmes & Meier.

———. 1992. "The study of new social movements in Latin America and the question of autonomy," Pp. 52–61 in Arturo Escobar and Sonia E. Alvarez (eds.), *New Social Movements in Latin America: Identity, Strategy and Democracy.* Boulder, Colorado: Westview Press.

———. 1994. "Mexican popular movements, clientelism, and the process of democratization." *Latin American Perspectives* 81(2): 124–142.

———. 1995. "The riddle of new social movements: Who they are and what they do." Pp. 165–183 in Sandor Halebsky and Richard L. Harris (eds.), *Capital, power, and inequality in Latin America.* Boulder, CO: Westview Press.

Helmke, Gretchen, and Steven Levitsky. 2003. "Informal institutions and comparative politics: A research agenda." Paper presented at the Informal Institutions in Latin America conference, University of Notre Dame, South Bend, Indiana, April 23–24.

Henriques, Julian, et al. (eds.). 1984. *Changing the subject.* London and New York: Methuen.

Hernández, Rosalva Aída, Sarela Paz, and María Teresa Sierra (eds.). 2004. *El estado y los indígenas en tiempos del PAN: Neoindigenismo, legalidad e identidad.* Mexico City: CIESAS.

Hershberg, Eric, and Fred Rosen (eds.). 2006. *Latin America after neoliberalism: Turning the tide in the 21st century?* New York: The New Press/NACLA.

Hertel, Shareen. 2006. *Unexpected power: Conflict and change among transnational activists.* Ithaca, NY: Cornell University Press.

Heymann, Daniel. 2000. *Políticas de reforma y comportamiento macroeconómico: La Argentina de los noventa.* CEPAL Serie Reformas Económicas 61.

Hidalgo, Onésimo. 2006. "Análisis de la estrategia actual de la contrainsurgencia y la militarización en Chiapas." *Chiapas al Día* (CIEPAC). http://www.ciepac.org/bulletins (accessed June 5, 2006).

Hobsbawm, Eric J. 1994. *The age of the extremes: The short twentieth century 1914–1991.* London: Abacus.

Holloway, John. 2002. *Change the world without taking power: The meaning of revolution today.* London: Pluto Press.

Hooker, Juliet. 2005. "Indigenous inclusion/black exclusion: Race, ethnicity and multicultural citizenship in Latin America." *Journal of Latin American Studies* 37: 285–310.

Howard, Dick. 1988. *The Marxian legacy.* Basingstoke: Macmillan.

Huizer, Gerrit. 1968. *The role of peasant organizations in the process of agrarian reform in Latin America.* Washington, DC: Comité Interamericano de Desarrollo Agrícola.

Huntington, Samuel. 1984. "Will more countries become democratic?" *Political Science Quarterly* 99 (Summer): 193–218.

Hylton, Forrest. 2003. "People's insurrection in Bolivia." *New Socialist* (44): 24–27.

Hylton, Forrest, and Sinclair Thomson. 2004. "The roots of rebellion: Insurgent Bolivia." *NACLA Report on the Americas* 38(3): 15–19.

Ibarra, Alberto "Beto." 2002. "Hablan las organizaciones sociales: Movimiento Territorial de Liberación." Segundo Enfoque. http://www.segundoenfoque.com.ar/ horg_mtliberacion.htm (accessed December 13, 2007).

INCITE! 2007. *The revolution will not be funded: Beyond the non-profit industrial complex.* Cambridge, MA: South End Press.

Instituto Brasileiro de Geografia e Estatística (IBGE). 2004. "Pesquisa Mensal De Emprego, Março 2004: Características Da População Em Idade Ativa Segundo a Cor Ou Raça Nas Seis Regiões Metropolitanas."

Instituto Nacional de Estadística [Bolivia] (INE). 2001. *Anuario estadístico, 2000.* La Paz.

Instituto Universitario de Opinión Pública (IUDOP). 2003. "Encuesta de evaluación del año 2003: Consulta de opinión pública de Noviembre–Diciembre de 2003." *Serie de Informes* No. 102, December.

———. 2006. "Evaluación del país a finales del 2006 y perspectivas para 2007," *Boletín de prensa*, Año XXI, No. 3. San Salvador.

Intag Solidarity Network (ISN). 2006. "Report of the Intag Solidarity Network denouncing the activities of Ascendant Copper in Intag region, Ecuador." June 12.

Intag Solidarity Network (ISN). 2007. "The Upsidedown World of Ascendant Copper." Unpublished report.

Inter Press Service and Latin American Data Base (IPS/LADB). 2003. "Allies No More." *Latinamerica Press* 35 (August 13, 2003): 2–3.

———. 2006. "Evaluación del país a finales del 2006 y perspectivas para 2007," *Boletín de prensa*, 21(3): XX.

Jacquette, Jane (ed.). 1991. *The feminist movement in Latin America*. Boulder, CO: Westview Press.

Janis, Irving. 1972. *Victims of groupthink*. Boston: Houghton Mifflin.

Japan International Cooperation Agency/Metal Mining Agency of Japan. 1996. "Informe final sobre la exploración mineral de cooperación técnica en las áreas de cooperación técnica de Ecuador." Environmental impact study.

Jelin, Elizabeth. 1990. "Citizenship and identity: Final reflections." Pp. 184–207 in Elizabeth Jelin (ed.), *Women and social change in Latin America*. London: Zed Books.

———. 1994. "The politics of memory: The human rights movements and the construction of democracy in Argentina." *Latin American Perspectivas* 21(2), Spring: 38–58.

———. 2005. "Human rights and the memory of political violence and repression: Constructing a new field in social science." Pp. 183–201 in Charles H. Wood and Bryan R. Roberts (eds.), *Rethinking development in Latin America*. University Park: Pennsylvania State University Press.

Johnson III, Ollie A. 1998. "Racial representation and Brazilian politics: Black members of the National Congress, 1983–1999." *Journal of Interamerican Studies and World Affairs* 40(4), Winter: 97–118.

Johnston, Hank. 1995. "A methodology for frame analysis." Pp. 217–246 in Hank Johnston and Bert Klandermans (eds.), *Social movements and culture*. Minneapolis: University of Minnesota Press.

Johnston, Hank, and Paul Almeida (eds.). 2006. *Latin American social movements: Globalization, democratization, and transnational networks*. Lanham, MD: Rowman & Littlefield.

Johnston, Hank, and Bert Klandermans (eds.). 1995. *Social movements and culture*. Minneapolis: University of Minnesota Press.

Julien, Isaac, and Kobena Mercer. 1988. "Introduction: de margin and de centre." *Screen* (Autumn): 2–10.

Karakras, Ampan. 1985. "CONACNIE." Pp. 47–48 in Agencia Latinoamericana de Información (ALAI) (ed.), *Forjando la unidad: El movimiento popular en Ecuador*. Quito, Ecuador: Communicare.

Kautsky, Karl. 1899 [1988 reprint]. *On the agrarian question*. Winchester, MA: Zwan Publications.

Kearney, Michael. 1996. *Reconceptualizing the peasantry: Anthropology in global perspective*. Boulder, CO: Westview Press.

Keck, Margaret, and Kathryn Sikkink. 1998. *Activists beyond borders: Advocacy networks in international politics*. Ithaca, NY: Cornell University Press.

Kelley, Robin D. G. 1993. "'We are not what we seem': Rethinking black working-class opposition in the Jim Crow South." *Journal of American History* 80(1): 75–112.

Kharas, Homi. 2005. "Lifting all boats." *Foreign Policy* 146 (January/February): 54–56.

Kohan, Anibal. 2002. *A las calles! Una historia de los movimientos piqueteros y caceroleros de los '90 al 2002.* Buenos Aires: Ediciones Colihue.

Kohl, Benjamin. 2003. "Restructuring citizenship in Bolivia: El Plan de Todos." *International Journal of Urban and Regional Research* 27: 337–351.

———. 2004. "Privatization Bolivian style: A cautionary tale." *International Journal of Urban and Regional Research* 28: 893–908.

Korten, David. 1999. *The post-corporate world: Life after capitalism.* West Hartford, CT: Kumarian Press.

Kuecker, Glen. 2004. "Latin American resistance movements in the time of the posts." *History Compass* 2(LA126): 1–23.

Laclau, Ernesto. 1989. "Politics and the limits of modernity." Pp. 63–82 in Andrew Ross (ed.), *Universal abandon? The politics of postmodernism.* Edinburgh: Edinburgh University Press.

——— (ed.). 1990. *New reflections on the revolution of our time.* London: Verso.

Laclau, Ernesto, and Chantal Mouffe. 1985. *Hegemony and socialist strategy: Towards a radical democratic politics.* London: Verso.

Landsberger, Henry, and Cynthia N. Hewitt. 1970. "Ten sources of weakness and cleavage in Latin American peasant organizations." Pp. 559–583 in Rodolfo Stavenhagen (ed.), *Agrarian problems and peasant movements in Latin America.* Garden City, NY: Doubleday.

Lappé, Frances Moore, Joseph Collins, and Peter Rosset, with Luis Esparza. 1998. *World hunger: Twelve myths,* 2nd edition. New York: Grove Press.

Lara Junior, Nadir. 2005a. "A mística no cotidiano do MST: A interface entre a religiosidade popular e a política." Master's thesis, Pontifícia Universidade Católica de São Paulo.

———. 2005b. "As manifestações artísticas no processo de formação identitária do Sem Terra." *Revista Psicologia Argumento* (43): 69–79. http://www.pucpr.br/template.php?codredir=550&&codigo=423.

Latin American Weekly Report (*LAWR*). 2002. "Two indigenous candidates in the race." March 12: 129.

Laufer, Rubén, and Claudio Spiguel. 1999. "Las 'puebladas' argentinas a partir del 'santiagueñazo' de 1993. Tradición histórica y nuevas formas de lucha." Pp. 15–44 in M. Lopez Amaya (ed.), *Lucha Popular, democracia, neoliberalismo: Protesta popular en América Latina en los años del ajuste.* Caracas, Venezuela: Nueva Sociedad.

Laurie, Nina. 2005. "Establishing development orthodoxy: negotiating masculinities in the water sector." *Development and Change* 36: 527–549.

Laurie, Nina, Robert Andolina, and Sarah Radcliffe. 2002. "The excluded 'Indigenous'? The implications of multi-ethnic policies for water reform in Bolivia." Pp. 252–276 in Rachel Sieder (ed.), *Multiculturalism in Latin America: Indigenous rights, diversity, and democracy.* Basingstoke, Hampshire, UK, and New York: Palgrave Macmillan.

Lechner, Norbert. 1991. "La democratización en el contexto de la cultura posmoderna." *Revista Foro,* no. 14 (April): 63–70.

Ledesma Arronte, Ernesto, et al. (eds). 2000. *Always near, always far: The armed forces in Mexico.* San Francisco: Global Exchange.

Levine, Daniel H., and Scott Mainwaring. 1989. "Religion and popular protest in Latin America: Contrasting experiences." Pp. 203–240 in Susan Eckstein (ed.), *Power and popular protest.* Berkeley: University of California Press.

Levitsky, Steven. 2003. *Transforming labor-based parties in Latin America: Argentine peronism in comparative perspective.* New York: Cambridge University Press.

Levy, Daniel C., and Kathleen Bruhn. 2001. *Mexico: The struggle for democratic development.* Berkeley: University of California Press.

Leyva Solano, Xóchitl. 1999. "De Las Cañadas a Europa: Niveles, actores y discursos del nuevo movimiento zapatista (NMZ) (1994–1997)." *Revista Destacatos* 1: 56–87.

———. 2003. "Regional, communal and organizational transformations in Las Cañadas." Pp. 161–184 in Jan Rus, Rosalva Aída Hernández Castillo, and Shannan L. Mattiace (eds.), *Mayan lives, Mayan utopias.* Lanham, MD: Rowman & Littlefield.

Limiroski, Sergio. 2004. "Como sera el barrio piquetero porteño." *La Prensa Digital,* January 26. www.laprensa.com.ar/secciones/nota.asp?ed=1258&tp=11&no=41420 (accessed December 13, 2007).

Lindblom, Charles. 1982. "The market as prison." *Journal of Politics* 44: 325–36.

Lockwood, David. 1981. "The weakest link in the chain: some comments on the Marxist theory of action." *Research in the Sociology of Work* 1: 435–481.

Lodola, German. 2003. "Popular mobilization and geographic distributive paths: The case of Argentine Plan Trabajar." Paper delivered at the LACEA-PEG Cartagena de las Indias, Colombia.

López y Rivas, Gilberto. 2004. *Autonomías: Democracia o contrainsurgencia.* Mexico City: Ediciones Era.

Löwy, Michael. 2001. "The socio-religious origins of Brazil's Landless Rural Workers Movement." *Monthly Review* 53(2): 32–40.

Lucas, Kintto. 2000. *We will not dance on our grandparents' tombs: Indigenous uprisings in Ecuador.* London: Catholic Institute for International Relations.

———. 2003. *El movimiento indigena y las acrobacias del coronel.* Quito, Ecuador: La Pulga.

———. 2006. "No hay cama pa' tanta gente." *Tintají* (segunda quincena de enero): B1.

Luccisano, Luisa. 2005. "Mexico's Progresa: An example of neoliberal poverty alleviation programs concerned with gender, human capital development, responsibility and choice." Pp. 31–57 in Keith M. Kilty and Elizabeth A. Segal (eds.), *Poverty and inequality in the Latin American-U.S. borderlands: Implications of U.S. interventions.* Binghamton, NY: Haworth Press.

Lucero, José Antonio. 2006. "Representing 'real Indians': The challenges of indigenous authenticity and strategic constructivism in Ecuador and Bolivia." *Latin American Research Review* 41(2): 31–56.

Macas, Luis. 2006. "Quieren boicotear la candidatura de Macas." http://www.luismacas .org/2006/08/quieren-boicotear-la-candidatura-de.html (accessed August 4, 2006).

Mamani Ramírez, Pablo. 2004a. *El rugir de la multitudes: La fuerza de los levantamientos indígenas en Bolivia-Qollasuyu.* La Paz, Bolivia: Aruwiyiri and Yachaywasi.

———. 2004b. "Territoria y estructuras de acción colectiva: microgobiernos barriales en El Alto." *Barataria* 1(1): 29–32.

Marcos, Subcomandante. 2000. "Sobre el próximo proceso electoral (19 de Junio 2000)." http://palabra.ezln.org.mx/ (accessed April 12, 2006).
———. 2003. "Chiapas: La treceava estela." July. http://www.ezln.org/documentos/1995/199501xx.en.htm.
———. 2005. "EZLN anuncia disolución del Frente Zapatista (20 de Noviembre de 2005)." http://palabra.ezln.org.mx/ (accessed April 12, 2006).
Martínez Saldeña, Tomás. 1980. *El costo social de un exito político.* Chapingo, Mexico: Colegio de Postgraduados.
Martins, José de Souza. 1997. "A questão agrária brasileira e o papel do MST." Pp. 11–76 in João Pedro Stedile (ed.), *A reforma agrária e a luta do MST.* Petrópolis, Brazil: Editora Vozes.
Marx, Karl. 1959 [1844]. *Economic and philosophical manuscripts of 1844.* Moscow: Progress Publishers.
Mattiace, Shannan. 2003. *To see with two eyes: Peasant activism and Indian autonomy in Chiapas, Mexico.* Albuquerque: University of New Mexico Press.
McAdam, Doug, John D. McCarthy, and Mayer Zald. 1996. *Comparative perspectives on social movements: Political opportunities, mobilizing structures, and cultural framings.* New York: Cambridge University Press.
McAdam, Doug, Sidney Tarrow, and Charles Tilly. 2001. *Dynamics of contention.* New York: Cambridge University Press.
McElhinney, Vince. 2004. *Update on PPP Energy Integration Initiative (SIEPAC).* March 12. www.interaction.org/idb/ppp.htm (accessed March 22, 2004).
McElhinney, Vince, and Seth Nickinson. 2004. "Plan Puebla-Panamá: Recipe for Development or Disaster." Paper presented at the XXV International Meeting of the Latin American Studies Association, Las Vegas, Nevada, October 6–9.
McLaughlin, Paul. 1998. "Rethinking the agrarian question: The limits of essentialism and the promise of evolutionism." *Human Ecology Review* 5(2): 25–39.
McMichael, Philip. 2000. "Globalisation: Trend or project?" Pp. 100–114 in Ronen Palan (ed.), *Global political economy: Contemporary theories.* London and New York: Routledge.
———. 2004. "Global development and the corporate food regime." Paper prepared for Symposium on New Directions in the Sociology of Global Development, XI World Congress of Rural Sociology, Trondheim, Norway.
———. 2006. "Peasant prospects in the neoliberal age." *New Political Economy* 11(3): 407–418.
Melucci, Alberto. 1977. *Sistema politico, partiti e movimenti sociali.* Milano: Feltrinelli.
———. 1980. "The new social movements: a theoretical approach." *Social Science Information* 19(2): 199–226.
———. 1989. *Nomads of the present.* London: Hutchinson.
———. 1992. "Liberation or meaning: Social movements, culture, and democracy." Pp. 43–77 in Jan Nederveen Pieterse (ed.), *Emancipations, modern and postmodern.* London: Sage.
Mercer, Kobena. 1990. "Welcome to the jungle: Identity and diversity in postmodern politics." Pp. 43–71 in Jonathan Rutherford (ed.), *Identity: Community, culture, difference.* London: Lawrence and Wishart.

Merino, Gerardo. 2005. *Abril, bombas mil: La represión desde el poder.* Quito, Ecuador: Abya-Yala, CEDHU.

Mertes, Tom (ed.). 2004. *A Movement of Movements: Is Another World Really Possible?* London: Verso.

Meyer, David. 2002. "Opportunities and identities: Bridge-building in the study of social movements." Pp. 3–21 in David Meyer, Nancy Whittier, and Belinda Robnett (eds.), *Social movements: Identity, culture, and the state.* Oxford: Oxford University Press.

Meyer, David, Nancy Whittier, and Belinda Robnett (eds.). 2002. *Social movements: Identity, culture, and the state.* Oxford: Oxford University Press.

Michaels, Walter Benn. 2006. *The trouble with diversity: How we learned to love identity and ignore inequality.* New York: Metropolitan Books.

Middlebrook, Kevin. 1986. "Political liberalization in an authoritarian regime: The case of Mexico." Pp. 123–147 in Guillermo O'Donnell, Philippe C. Schmitter, and Laurence Whitehead (eds.), *Transitions from authoritarian rule: Latin America.* Baltimore: Johns Hopkins University Press.

Milani, Brian. 2000. *Designing the green economy: The postindustrial alternative to corporate globalization.* Lanham, MD: Rowman & Littlefield.

Ministerio de Economía [Argentina]. n.d. "Serie histórica." http://www.indec.mecon .gov.ar.

Ministerio de Trabajo [Argentina]. 2004. "Planes de Jefas y Jefes de Hogares." Buenos Aires.

Ministry of Energy and Mining [Ecuador]. 2001a. "Andean opportunities await evaluation." Promotional supplement. *Mining Journal* (November).

———. 2001b. "The PRODEMINCA Project." Promotional supplement. *Mining Journal* (November).

Minority Rights Group (ed.). 1995. *No longer invisible: Afro-Latin Americans today.* London: Minority Rights Publications.

Miranda Pacheco, Carlos. 1999. "Del descubrimiento petrolífero a la explosión del gas." Pp. 241–267 in Fernando Campero Prudencio (ed.), *Bolivia en el siglo XX: La formación de la Bolivia contemporánea.* La Paz, Bolivia: Harvard Club de La Paz.

Mohanty, Chandra. 1988. "Under Western eyes: Feminist scholarship and colonial discourses." *Feminist Review* 30 (Autumn): 61–88.

Moisés, José. 1991. "Democracy threatened: The Latin American paradox." *Alternatives* 16 (Spring): 141–159.

Moltmann, Jurgen. 1997. *The source of life.* Philadelphia: Fortress Press.

Monsalve Suárez, Sofia. 2006. "Gender and land." Pp. 192–207 in Peter Rosset, Raj Patel, and Michael Courville (eds.), *Promised land: Competing visions of agrarian reform.* Oakland, CA: Food First Books.

Moody, Roger. 2001. "Foreword." Pp. vi–viii in Al Gedicks, *Resource rebels: Native challenges to mining and oil corporations.* Cambridge, MA: South End Press.

Moreno, Raúl. 2003. *The Free Trade Agreement Between the United States and Central America: Economic and Social Impact.* http://www.afsc.org/latinamerica/PDF/Raul morenoenglish.pdf (accessed August 4, 2004).

Mouffe, Chantal. 1988. "Hegemony and new political subjects: Toward a new concept of democracy." Pp. 89–101 in Cary Nelson and Lawrence Grossberg (eds.), *Marxism and the Interpretation of Culture*. Champaign-Urbana: University of Illinois Press.

Movimento dos Trabalhadores Rurais Sem Terra (MST). 2000. *O MST e a Cultura*. Cuadernos de Formacão No. 34. São Paulo: Ademar Bogo.

——. 2001a. "Fundamental principles for the social and economic transformation of rural Brazil." Translated by Wilder Robles. *Journal of Peasant Studies* 28(2): 146–152.

——. 2001b. *O Brasil Precisa de um Projecto Popular*. São Paulo: MST Secretariat of Popular Consultation.

Movimiento Territorial de Liberación [Argentina] (MTL). n.d. "Nuestra Propuesta." Internal Document.

Munck, Geraldo L. 1990. "Identity and ambiguity in democratic struggles." Pp. 23–42 in Joe Foweraker and Ann L. Craig (eds.), *Popular Movements and Political Change in Mexico*. Boulder, CO: Lynne Rienner Publishers.

Murillo, Victoria. 1997. "La adaptación del sindicalismo argentino a las reformas de mercado en la primera presidencia de Menem." *Desarrollo Económico* 37 (147): 419–446.

Nash, June C. 1992. "Interpreting social movements: Bolivian resistance to economic conditions imposed by the International Monetary Fund." *American Ethnologist* 19: 275–293.

——. 2001. *Mayan visions: The quest for autonomy in an age of globalization*. New York: Routledge.

——. 2003. "Indigenous development alternatives." *Urban Anthropology and Studies of Cultural Systems and World Economic Development* 32(1): 57–98.

Navarro, Zander. 2002. "Mobilização sem emancipação: As lutas sociais dos Sem-Terra no Brasil." Pp. 1–28 in Boaventura de Sousa Santos (ed.), *Produzir para viver*. Rio de Janeiro: Civilização Brasileira.

Nef, Jorge. 1988. "Review: The trend toward democratization and redemocratization in Latin America: Shadow and substance." *Latin American Research Review* 23(3): 131–153.

Nickson, Andrew, and Claudia Vargas. 2002. "The limitations of water regulation: The failure of the Cochabamba concession in Bolivia." *Bulletin of Latin American Research* 21(1): 99–120.

Nueva Mayoría. 2001. "Agosto fue el mes récord en cantidad de cortes de rutas desde 1997." http://www.nuevamayoria.com/ (accessed September 5, 2001).

——. 2002a. "Argentina es el país del mundo en el cual el fenómeno del trueque tiene mayor dimensión social." May 8, 2002. http://www.nuevamayoria.com/.

——. 2002b. "Desde marzo, las asambleas barriales se han incrementado un 21%." http://www.nuevamayoria.com/ (accessed September 6, 2001).

——. 2004a. "2004 prácticamente duplicaría la conflictividad de 2003." http://www.nuevamayoria.com/ (accessed December 10, 2004).

——. 2004b. "Está reapareciendo el cacerolazo como expresión de protesta de la clase media" http://www.nuevamayoria.com/ (accessed February 6, 2004).

——. 2005. "El 2005 está mostrando el mayor nivel mensual de cortes de rutas y vías públicas desde 2002." July 11. http://www.nuevamayoria.com/.

Nun, José. 1991. "Democracy and modernization, thirty years after." Paper presented at the plenary session "Democratic Theory Today: Empirical and Theoretical Issues," 15th World Congress of the International Political Science Association, Buenos Aires, July 21–26.

Oakley, Peter. 2001. "Social exclusion and Afro-Latinos: A contemporary review." Working Paper, Inter-American Development Bank, Washington, DC.

O'Donnell, Guillermo. 1997. *Contrapuntos: Ensayos escogidos sobre autoritarismo y democratización.* Buenos Aires: Paidós.

Oliveira, Sidney de Paula. 2000. "Exaltaçao a negra mulher guerreira." *Cadernos Negros: Poemas Afro-Brasileiros.* São Paulo.

Olivera, Mercedes. 2004. "Las mujeres y la política actual en Chiapas." Paper presented at the Forum against Neoliberalism, Huitiupan, Chiapas, March.

Olivera, Oscar, and Tom Lewis. 2004. *¡Cochabamba! Water war in Bolivia.* Cambridge, MA: South End Press.

Ollman, Bertell. 1971. *Alienation.* Cambridge: Cambridge University Press.

Oporto, Henry. 1991. *La revolución democrática: Una nueva manera de pensar Bolivia.* La Paz, Bolivia: Los Amigos del Libro.

Otero, Gerardo (ed.). 2004. *Mexico in transition: Neoliberal globalism, the state and civil society.* London: Zed Books.

Otto Wolf, Frits. 1986. "Eco-socialist transition on the threshold of the 21st century." *New Left Review* 158 (July/August): 32–42.

Oviedo, Luis. 2001. *Una historia del movimiento piquetero: De las primeras Coordinadoras a las Asambleas Nacionales.* Buenos Aires: Ediciones Rumbo.

Oxhorn, Philip. 1991. "The popular sector response to an authoritarian regime: Shantytown organizations since the military coup." *Latin American Perspectives* 18 (Winter): 86–91.

Pacheco, Mariano. 2004. "Del piquete al movimiento. Pt. 1. De los orígenes al 20 de diciembre de 2001." *Cuadernos de la Fundación de Investigaciones Sociales y Políticas* 11 (January): 17.

Pasuk, Phongpaichit. 1999. *Theories of social movements and their relevance for Thailand.* Position paper for the Thailand Research Fund Project on Social Movements in Thailand, Chulalongkorn University, Bangkok.

Patel, Rajeev. 2005. "Global fascism, revolutionary humanism and the ethics of food sovereignty." *Development* 48(2): 79–83.

———. 2006. "International agrarian restructuring and the practical ethics of peasant movement solidarity." *Journal of Asian and African Studies* 41(1/2): 71–93.

Pateman, Carole. 1970. *Participation and democratic theory.* Cambridge: Cambridge University Press.

———. 1988. *The disorder of women: Democracy, feminism, and political theory.* Stanford, CA: Stanford University Press.

Patton, Paul. 1989. "Taylor and Foucault on power and freedom." *Political Studies* 37 (June): 260–281.

Peloso, Ranulfo. 1994. *A força que anima a militância.* São Paulo: MST.

Peña, Devon G. 1997. *The terror of the machine: Technology, work, gender & ecology on the U.S.-Mexico Border.* Austin, TX: CMAS.

Pérez Ruiz, Maya Lorena (ed.). 2004. *Tejiendo historias: Tierra, género y poder en Chiapas*. Mexico City: INAH.

Perreault, Thomas. 2003. "Making space: Community organizations, agrarian change, and the politics of scale in the Ecuadorian Amazon." *Latin American Perspectives* 30(1): 96–121.

———. 2006. "From the Guerra del Agua to the Guerra del Gas: Resource governance, neoliberalism and popular protest in Bolivia." *Antipode* 38: 150–172.

Peterson, Abby. 1989. "Social movement theory." *Acta Sociológica* 32(4): 419–426.

Petras, James. 1997. "Alternatives to neoliberalism in Latin America." *Latin American Perspectives* 24(1): 80–91.

———. 2000. "The Rural Landless Workers Movement." *Z Magazine*, March: 32–36.

Petras, James, and Fernando Ignacio Leiva. 1986. "Chile's poor in the struggle for democracy." *Latin American Perspectives* 13 (Fall): 5–25.

Petras, James, and Morris Morley. 1992. *Latin America in the time of cholera: Electoral politics, market economics, and permanent crisis*. New York: Routledge.

Petras, James, and Henry Veltmeyer. 2002. "The peasantry and the state in Latin America: A troubled past, an uncertain future." *Journal of Peasant Studies* 29(3, 4): 41–82.

———. 2005. *Social movements and state power: Argentina, Brazil, Bolivia, Ecuador*. London and Ann Arbor, MI: Pluto Press.

Pickard, Miguel. 2003. "Grassroots protests force the Mexican government to search for a new PPP Strategy." *Chiapas al Día* (CIEPAC). http://www.ciepac.org/bulletins (accessed January 22, 2003).

———. 2004. "The Plan Puebla-Panama revived: Looking back to see what's ahead." *Americas Policy Report*. Silver City, NM: Americas Program, Interhemispheric Resource Center. June. http://americas.irc-online.org/reports/2004/0406ppp.html (accessed November 25, 2007).

———. 2005. "In the crossfire: Mesoamerican migrants journey north." Special report, Americas Program, Silver City, New Mexico, March 18. http://americas.irc-online.org/reports/2004/0406ppp.html (accessed December 14, 2007).

Pinheiro, Eloísa Petti. 2002. *Europa, França e Bahia: Difusão e adaptação de modelos urbanos (Paris, Rio e Salvador)*. Salvador: Editora da UFBA.

Piven, Frances Fox, and Richard Cloward. 1978. *Poor people's movements: Why they succeed, how they fail*. New York: Vintage Books.

Portillo, Edith. 2004. "Asamblea ratifica TLC con Estados Unidos sin ni siquiera leerlo." Elfaro.net [El Salvador], December 13–20. www.elfaro.net (accessed November 9, 2005).

Postero, Nancy. 2005. "Indigenous responses to neoliberalism." *PoLAR: Political and Legal Anthropology Review* 28(1): 73–92.

Pozo, Erick Fajardo. 2005. "Una evaluación de la experiencia cochabambina: La guerra del agua." *El Juguete Rabioso* 5(127): 12–13.

Prashad, Vijay, and Teo Ballvé (eds.). 2006. *Dispatches from Latin America: On the frontlines against neoliberalism*. Cambridge, MA: South End Press.

Presidencia de la República [México]. 2001a. *Plan Puebla-Panamá: Diagnóstico Centroamérica*. Mexico: Presidencia de la República.

———. 2001b. *Plan Puebla-Panamá: Documento Base, Capítulo México*. Mexico: Presidencia de la República.

Public Citizen. 2004. *Will the World Bank back down? Water privatization in a climate of global protest.* Washington, DC: Public Citizen Water for All Campaign.

Ramírez Saiz, Juan Manuel. 1986. *El movimiento urbano popular en México.* México, D.F.: Siglo Veintiuno.

——. 1990. "Urban struggles and their political consequences." Pp. 234–246 in Joe Foweraker and Ann L. Craig (eds.), *Popular movements and political change in Mexico.* Boulder, CO: Lynne Rienner Publishers.

Reason, Peter, and Kate Louise McArdle. 2004. "Brief notes on the theory and practice of action research." Pp. 114–119 in Saul and Alan Bryman Becker (eds.), *Understanding research methods for social policy and practice.* Bristol: Policy Press.

Red de Defensores, et al. 2001. "Boletín de prensa conjunto de las organizaciones civiles de San Cristóbal sobre la Ley Indígena." http://www.laneta.apc.org/sclc/opinion/010505cdh.htm (accessed April 5, 2006).

Reygadas, Luis. 2006. "Latin America: Persistent inequality and recent transformation." Pp. 120–143 in Eric Hershberg and Fred Rosen (eds.), *Latin America after Neoliberalism: Turning the Tide in the 21st Century?* New York: The New Press/NACLA.

Rich, Bruce. 1994. *Mortgaging the earth: The World Bank, environmental impoverishment, and the crisis of development.* Boston: Beacon Press.

Richards, Howard, and Joanna Swanger. 2006. *The dilemmas of social democracies: Overcoming obstacles to a more just world.* Lanham, MD: Lexington Books.

Rikcharishun. 2002a. "Alianza Pachakutik Sociedad Patriótica." *Rikcharishun* 19 (December): 4.

——. 2002b. "Pachakutik con más respaldo popular." *Rikcharishun* 19 (December): 3.

——. 2006. "He sentido la solidaridad y la fraternidad de la gente." *Rikcharishun* 34 (September): 3.

Riley, Denise. 1988. *"Am I that name?" Feminism and the category of "women" in history.* Minneapolis: University of Minnesota Press.

Ritchie, Mark, Sophia Murphy, and Mary Beth Lake. 2004. "United States dumping on world agricultural markets. February 2004 update." Cancun Series Paper no. 1. Minneapolis: Institute for Agriculture and Trade Policy.

Roberts, Bryan, and Alejandro Portes. 2005. "Coping with the free market city: Collective action in six Latin American cities at the end of the twentieth century." Working Paper Series No. 05-06, the Center for Migration and Development, Princeton University.

Robinson, William I. 1996. *Promoting polyarchy: Globalization, U.S. intervention, and hegemony.* Cambridge: Cambridge University Press.

——. 2003. *Transnational conflicts: Central America, social change and globalization.* London: Verso.

——. 2004. *A theory of global capitalism: Production, class, and state in a transnational world.* Baltimore: Johns Hopkins University Press.

Robnett, Belinda. 1997. *How long? How long? African-American women in the struggle for civil rights.* New York: Oxford University Press.

Rodrigues Brandão, Carlos. 2001. *Historia do menino que lia o mundo.* Fazendo Historia No. 7. Veranópolis: ITERRA.

Rodríguez Garavito, César A., Patrick S. Barrett, and Daniel Chavez (eds.). 2005. *La nueva izquierda en América Latina.* Bogotá: Grupo Editorial Norma.

Rodríguez, Hector [interview with Diego Murcia]. 2003. "Movimiento Popular de Resistencia 12 de octubre, no somos apéndice del FMLN." [El Salvador]. www.elfaro.net (accessed November 9, 2005).

Rodríguez, Olga R. 2005. "Verdicts in Juárez slayings raise ire." *Austin-American Statesman.* January 9.

Rose, Nicolas. 1999. *Powers of freedom: Reframing political thought.* Cambridge: Cambridge University Press.

Rose, Nicolas, and Andrew Barry. 1996. *Foucault and political reason: Liberalism neoliberalism and rationalities of government.* Chicago: University of Chicago Press.

Rosen, Fred, and Deidre McFadyen (eds.). 1995. *Free trade and economic restructuring in Latin America.* New York: Monthly Review Press.

Ross, John. 2000. *The war against oblivion: The Zapatista chronicles.* Monroe, ME: Common Courage Press.

Rosset, Peter M. 2003. "Food sovereignty: Global rally cry of farmer movements." *Food First Backgrounder* 9(4): 1–4.

———. 2006a. *Food is different: Why we must get the WTO out of agriculture.* London: Zed Books.

———. 2006b. "Moving forward: Agrarian reform as part of food sovereignty." Pp. 301–321 in Peter Rosset, Raj Patel, and Michael Courville (eds.), *Promised land: Competing visions of agrarian reform.* Oakland, CA: Food First Books.

Rosset, Peter M., and María Elena Martínez. 2005. *Participatory evaluation of La Vía Campesina: Public version.* Oslo: The Norwegian Development Fund and La Vía Campesina.

———. 2007. "Soberanía alimentaria: propuesta de las organizaciones campesinas del mundo." *América Latina en Movimiento* 419: 7–9.

Rother, Larry. 2003. "Bolivia's poor proclaim abiding distrust of globalization." *New York Times,* October 17.

Rowe, William, and Vivian Schelling. 1991. *Memory and modernity: Popular culture in Latin America.* London: Verso.

Rus, Jan. 1995. "Local adaptation to global change: The reordering of native society in highland Chiapas, Mexico 1974–1994." *European Review of Latin American and Caribbean Studies* 58 (June): 71–89.

Rus, Jan, and Miguel Tinker-Salas (eds). 2006. "The Mexican presidency, 2006–2012: Neoliberalism, social movements, and electoral politics." *Latin American Perspectives* 33(2).

Saavedra, Luis Angel. 2002. "Indigenous candidates aim for Congress." *Latinamerica Press* 34 (October 21): 6–7.

———. 2003. "Turn to the right." *Latinamerica Press* 35 (August 27): 1–2.

———. 2004a. "Gutiérrez on the tightrope?" *Latinamerica Press* 36 (June 16): 4–5.

———. 2004b. "A survivor in power." *Latinamerica Press* 36 (December 1): 1–2.

Sacks, Karen. 1988. *Caring by the hour.* Chicago: University of Illinois Press.

Safa, Helen. 1998. "Race and national identity in the Americas." *Latin American Perspectives* 25 (3): 3–20.

Sámano Rentería, Miguel Ángel. 2000. "La consulta nacional zapatista en el marco del convenio 169 de la OIT." Pp. 175–187 in José Emilio Rolando Ordóñez Cifuentes (ed.), *Análisis interdisciplinario del convenio 169 de la OIT.* Mexico City: UNAM.

Sampat, Payal. 2003. "Scrapping mining dependence." Pp. 110–129 in Linda Starke (ed.), *State of the World 2003*. New York: W. W. Norton.

Sánchez Gómez, Luis. 2004. "Directing SEMAPA: An interview with Luis Sánchez-Gómez." Pp. 87–94 in Oscar Olivera and Tom Lewis (eds.), *¡Cochabamba! Water war in Bolivia*. Cambridge, MA: South End Press.

Sánchez Gómez, Luis, and Philipp Terhorst. 2005. "Cochabamba, Bolivia: Public-collective partnership after the water war." Pp. 121–130 in Belén Balanyá, Brid Brennan, Olivier Hoedeman, Satoko Kishimoto, and Philipp Terhorst (eds.), *Reclaiming public water: Achievements, struggles, and visions from around the world*. Porto Alegre, Brazil: Transnational Institute and Corporate Observatory Europe.

Sandoval Ballesteros, Irma Eréndira. 2003. "Una visión crítica del 'Plan Puebla-Panamá.'" Paper presented at the XXIV International Meeting of the Latin American Studies Association, Dallas, Texas, March 27–29.

Saporta Sternbach, Nancy, et al. 1992. "Feminisms in Latin America: From Bogotá to San Bernardo." *Signs* 17 (Winter): 393–434.

Savoia, Claudia, Pablo Calvo, and Alberto Amato. 2004. "Jaque a los piqueteros: El desafío de la convivencia social." *Clarín*, August 8: 30–31.

Schild, Verónica. 1994. "Recasting 'popular' movements: Gender and political learning in neighborhood organizations in Chile." *Latin American Perspectives* 21(2): 59–80.

Schkolnik, Mariana, and Berta Teitelboim. 1988. *Pobreza y desempleo en poblaciones: La otra cara del modelo neoliberal*. Santiago, Chile: Programa de Economía del Trabajo.

Schneider, Cathy. 1991. "Mobilization at the grassroots: Shantytown and resistance in authoritarian Chile." *Latin American Perspectives* 18(1): 92–112.

Schumpeter, Joseph A. 1987 (1943). *Capitalism, socialism, and democracy*. London: Unwin Paperbacks.

Scott, James C. 1977. *The moral economy of the peasant: Rebellion and subsistence in Southeast Asia*. New Haven, CT: Yale University Press.

Scribano, Adrián. 1999. "Argentina 'cortada': cortes de ruta y visibilidad social en el contexto del ajuste." Pp. 45–72 in Margarita Lopez Amaya (ed.), *Lucha Popular, democracia, neoliberalismo: Protesta popular en América Latina en los años del ajuste*. Caracas, Venezuela: Nueva Sociedad.

Selbin, Eric. 1998. *Modern Latin American revolutions*, 2nd edition. Boulder, CO: Westview Press.

Selby, Jan. 2005. "Oil and water: The contrasting antinomies of resource conflicts." *Government and Opposition* 40: 200–224.

Serrano, Claudia. 1988. "Pobladores: Lecciones a partir de sus organizaciones." Apuntes CIEPLAN No. 70, CIEPLAN, Santiago, Chile.

Serulnikov, Sergio. 1994. "When looting became a right: Urban poverty and food riots in Argentina." *Latin American Perspectives* 21 (Summer): 69–89.

Servicio Internacional para la Paz (SIPAZ). 2004. "Proceso de paz, proceso de guerra: Breve síntesis de la historia del conflicto en Chiapas: 1994–2003." http://www.sipaz.org/fini_esp.htm (accessed December 3, 2004).

———. 2006. "Glosario." http://www.sipaz.org/glosario/glosesp.htm (accessed March 31, 2006).

Shapira, Yoram. 1977. "Mexico: The impact of the 1968 student protest on Echeverría's reformism." *Journal of Interamerican Studies and World Affairs* 19(4): 557–580.

Sheehan, Molly O'Meara. 2003. "Uniting divided cities." Pp. 130–151 in Linda Starke (ed.), *State of the world 2003*. New York: W. W. Norton.

Shifter, Michael. 2003. "Latin America's new political leaders: Walking on a wire." *Current History* 102 (February): 51–57.

Shiva, Vandana. 1993. "Indian farmers rally against Dunkel Draft and MNCs." *South North Development Monitor* [Geneva], March 5. http://www.chasque.net/frontpage/suns/trade/areas/agricult/03051093.htm (accessed December 13, 2007).

Shultz, Jim. 2003. "Bolivia: The water war widens." *NACLA Report on the Americas* 36 (January/February): 34–37.

———. 2005. *Deadly consequences: The International Monetary Fund and Bolivia's "black February."* San Francisco and Cochabamba: The Democracy Center.

Silva, Benedita da. 1997. *Benedita da Silva: An Afro-Brazilian woman's story of politics and love [as told to Medea Benjamin and Maisa Mendonça]*. Oakland, CA: Institute for Food and Development Policy.

———. 1999. "The black movement and political parties: A challenging alliance." Pp. 179–187 in Michael Hanchard (ed.), *Racial politics in contemporary Brazil*. Durham, NC: Duke University Press.

Sistema de Información, Monitoreo y Evaluación de Programas Sociales (SIEMPRO). 1997. "Evaluación Programa Trabajar I." Buenos Aires: Sistema de Información, Monitoreo y Evaluación de Programas Sociales.

———. 1998. "Evaluación Programa Trabajar II." Buenos Aires: Sistema de Información, Monitoreo y Evaluación de Programas Sociales.

Sklair, Leslie. 2000. *The transnational capitalist class*. New York: Blackwell.

Slater, David (ed.). 1985. *New social movements and the state in Latin America*. Amsterdam: CEDLA.

———. 1991a. "Towards the regionalization of state power: Peru, 1985–1990." *Regional Politics and Policy* 1 (Autumn): 210–222.

———. 1991b. "New social movements and old political questions: Rethinking state-society relations in Latin American development." *International Journal of Political Economy* 21 (Spring): 32–65.

———. 1992. "On the borders of social theory: Learning from other regions." *Environment and Planning D: Society and Space* 10: 307–327.

———. 1994a. "Power and social movements in the other Occident." *Latin American Perspectives* 21(2): 11–37.

——— (ed.). 1994b. *Social Movements and Political Change in Latin America 1. Latin American Perspectives* 21(2).

——— (ed.). 1994c. *Social Movements and Political Change in Latin America 2. Latin American Perspectives* 21(3).

Smith, Jackie. 2002. "Bridging global divides? Strategic framing and solidarity in transnational social movement organizations." *International Sociology* 17(4): 505–528.

Smith, Jackie, Ron Pagnucco, and Charles Chatfield. 1997. "Social movements and world politics: A theoretical framework." Pp. 59–80 in Jackie Smith, Charles Chatfield, and Ron Pagnucco (eds.), *Transnational social movements and global politics: Solidarity beyond the state*. Syracuse, NY: Syracuse University Press.

Smith, William C., and Roberto Patricio Korzeniewicz. 2007. "'Insiders,' 'outsiders' and the transnational politics of civil society in the Americas." Pp. 151–172 in Gordon

Mace, Jean-Philippe Thérien, and Paul Haslam (eds.), *Governing the Americas: Regional institutions at the crossroads.* Boulder, CO: Lynne Rienner Publishers.

Snow, David, and Robert Benford. 1988. "Ideology, frame resonance, and participant mobilization." Pp. 197–217 in Bert Klandermans, Hanspeter Kriesi, and Sidney Tarrow (eds.), *From structure to action: Social movement participation across cultures.* Greenwich, CT: JAI.

——. 1992. "Master frames and cycles of protest." Pp. 133–155 in Aldon D. Morris and Carol M. Mueller (eds.), *Frontiers in social movement theory.* New Haven, CT: Yale University Press.

Spalding, Rose J. 2006. "Free trade and democratic processes: A comparative analysis of CAFTA negotiation and ratification in El Salvador and Costa Rica." Paper presented at XXVI International Congress of the Latin American Studies Association, San Juan, Puerto Rico, March 15–18.

——. 2007. "Civil society engagement in trade negotiations: CAFTA opposition movements in El Salvador." *Latin American Politics and Society* 49(4), Winter: 85–114.

Speed, Shannon, and Jane F. Collier. 2000. "Limiting indigenous autonomy in Chiapas, Mexico: The state government's use of human rights." *Human Rights Quarterly* 22(4): 877–905.

Speed, Shannon, R. Aída Hernández Castillo, and Lynn M. Stephen (eds.). 2006. *Dissident women: Gender and cultural politics in Chiapas.* Austin: University of Texas Press.

Spelman, Elizabeth V. 1988. *Inessential woman: Problems of exclusion in feminist thought.* Boston: Beacon Press.

Spronk, Susan, and Jeff Webber. 2005. "The two Bolivias square off." *Canadian Dimension* 39 (May–June): 17–19.

Stahler-Sholk, Richard. 1998. "Massacre in Chiapas." *Latin American Perspectives* 25(4): 63–75.

——. 2001a. "Globalization and social movement resistance: The Zapatista rebellion in Chiapas, Mexico." *New Political Science* 23(4): 493–516.

——. 2001b. "Revolution." Pp. 13299–13302 in Neil J. Smelser and Paul B. Baltes (eds.), *International encyclopedia of the social and behavioral sciences,* vol. 26. Oxford: Pergamon.

——. 2005. "Time of the snails: Autonomy and resistance in Chiapas." *NACLA Report on the Americas* 38 (5): 34–40.

——. 2006. "Autonomy and social movement strategies in the neoliberal era: The Zapatista movement in Chiapas, Mexico." Paper presented at the 26th Congress of the Latin American Studies Association, San Juan, Puerto Rico, March 15–18.

Stahler-Sholk, Richard, Harry E. Vanden, and Glen Kuecker (eds.). 2007. "Globalizing resistance: The new politics of social movements in Latin America." *Latin American Perspectives* 34(2): 5–16.

Starn, Orin. 1991. *Reflexiones sobre rondas campesinas: Protesta rural y nuevas movimientos sociales.* Lima: IEP.

Stedile, João Pedro, and Bernardo Mançano Fernandes. 1999. *Brava gente: A trajetória do MST e a luta pela terra no Brasil.* São Paulo: Fundação Perseu Abramo.

Stephen, Lynn. 1992. "Women in Mexico's popular movements: Survival strategies against ecological and economic impoverishment." *Latin American Perspectives* 19(1): 73–96.

———. 1997. "Pro-Zapatista and Pro-PRI: Resolving the contradictions of Zapatismo in rural Oaxaca." *Latin American Research Review* 32(2): 41–70.

Stokes, Susan. 2003. "Do informal institutions make democracy work? Accounting for accountability in Argentina." Paper presented at the conference "Informal Institutions in Latin America," University of Notre Dame, South Bend, Indiana, April 23–24.

———. 2005. "Perverse accountability." *American Political Science Review* 99(3): 315–325.

Sunkel, Osvaldo. 2005. "The unbearable lightness of neoliberalism." Pp. 55–78 in Charles H. Wood and Bryan R. Roberts (eds.), *Rethinking development in Latin America.* University Park: Pennsylvania State University Press.

Sutton, Alison. 1994. *Slavery in Brazil: A link in the chain of modernization, the case of Amazônia.* London: Anti-Slavery International.

Svampa, Maristella, and Sebastián Pereyra. 2003. *Entre la ruta y el barrio: La experiencia de las organizaciones piqueteras.* Buenos Aires: Biblos.

Swords, Alicia. 2005. "The power of networks: Popular political education among Neo-Zapatista organizations in Chiapas, Mexico." PhD thesis, Cornell University.

Szwarcberg, Mariela L. Forthcoming. "Feeding loyalties: An analysis of clientelism, the case of the manzaneras." PhD diss., Department of Political Science, University of Chicago.

Tajbakhsh, Kian. 2001. *The promise of the city: Space, identity, and politics in contemporary social thought.* Berkeley: University of California Press.

Tamayo G., Eduardo. 2006. "Contundente movilización indígena contra TLC en Ecuador." *América Latina en Movimiento* (March 29): 1–2, 6.

Tarrow, Sidney. 1985. "Struggling to reform: Social movements and policy change during cycles of protest." Western Societies Program Occasional Paper # 15, Center for International Studies, Cornell University.

———. 1998. *Power in movement: Social movements and contentious politics.* Cambridge: Cambridge University Press.

———. 2005. *The new transnational activism.* Cambridge: Cambridge University Press.

Taylor, Verta, and Nancy Whittier. 1995. "Analytical approaches to social movement culture: The culture of the women's movement." Pp. 163–187 in Hank Johnston and Bert Klandermans (eds.), *Social movements and culture.* Minneapolis: University of Minnesota Press.

Terán, Pablo. 2001. Interview. "Explore Ecuador." Supplement, *Northern Miner* (November 5): 1, 3, and 7.

Thomson, Sinclair, and Forrest Hylton. 2005. "The chequered rainbow." *New Left Review* (35): 19–64.

Tilly, Charles. 1978. *From mobilization to revolution.* Reading, MA: Addison-Wesley.

Tilly, Charles, and Sidney Tarrow. 2006. *Contentious politics.* Boulder, CO: Paradigm Publishers.

Tirado Jimenez, Ramón. 1990. *Asamblea de barrios: Nuestra batalla.* Mexico City: Editorial Nuestro Tiempo.

Tironi, Eugenio. 1987. "Marginalidad, movimientos sociales y democracia." *Proposiciones* 14.

———. 1990. *Autoritarismo, modernización y marginalidad: El caso de Chile 1973–1989.* Santiago, Chile: SUR.

Torre, Juan Carlos. 1980. "Sindicatos y trabajadores en la Argentina: 1955–1976." El país de los argentinos 186, Primera Historia Integral Argentina 58.

———. 1997. *El proceso político de las reformas económicas en América Latina.* Buenos Aires: Instituto Torcuato Di Tella, mimeo handout.

Touraine, Alain. 1975. "Les nouveaux conflits sociaux." *Sociologie du Travail,* 1: XX.

———. 1989. "La crisis y las transformaciones del sistema político en America Latina." Pp. 17–44 in Fernando Calderón (ed.), *Socialismo, autoritarismo y democracia.* Lima: IEP.

Twine, Frances Winddance. 1998. *Racism in a racial democracy: The maintenance of white supremacy in Brazil.* New Brunswick, NJ: Rutgers University Press.

United Nations Development Programme (UNDP). 1999. *Human development report 1999.* New York: Oxford University Press.

———. 2002. *Human development report, 2002: Deepening democracy in a fragmented world.* New York: Oxford University Press.

———. 2004. *Human development report, 2004: Cultural liberty in today's diverse world.* New York: United Nations Development Programme.

U.S. Office on Colombia. 2003. "Afro-Colombians under fire." Understanding Colombia Series. Washington, DC: U.S. Office on Colombia.

Valdes, Teresa.1987. "El movimiento de pobladores 1973–1985: La recomposición de las solidaridades sociales." Pp. 263–319 in Jordi Bolja (ed.), *Descentralización del estado: Movimiento social y gestión local.* Santiago: FLACSO.

Valdes, Teresa, Marisa Weinstein, and A. Maria Malinarich. 1988. "Las coordinadoras de organizaciones populares: Cinco experiencias." *Documento de Trabajo* 382. Santiago: FLACSO.

Valenzuela, Maria Elena. 1987. *La mujer en el Chile militar: Todas ibamos a ser reinas.* Santiago: Ediciones Chile America/CESOC/ACHIP.

Vales, Laura. 2002. "Plan Jefes y Jefas de Hogar: Pro y contra de un seguro." *Pagina 12* Web, May 12.

———. 2005. "Los piqueteros compraron una mina y la reactivaron." *Página 12* Web, October 12.

Vanden, Harry E. 2003. "Globalization in a time of neoliberalism: Politicized social movements and the Latin American response." *Journal of Developing Societies* 19(2–3): 308–333.

———. 2004. "New political movements, governance and the breakdown of traditional politics in Latin America." *International Journal of Public Administration* 27: 1129–1149.

———. 2005. "Brazil's landless hold their ground." *NACLA Report on the Americas* 38 (March/April): 21–27.

———. 2006. "Social movements, hegemony, and resistance." In Gary Prevost and Carlos Oliva (eds.), *The Bush doctrine and Latin America.* New York: Palgrave.

———. 2007. "Epilogue: The fable of the shark and the piranhas."In Jorge Nef and Harry E. Vanden (eds.), *Inter-American relations in an era of globalization: Beyond unilateralism?* Whitby, Ontario: de Sitter Publications.

Vanden, Harry E., and Gary Prevost. 1993. *Democracy and socialism in Sandinista Nicaragua.* Boulder, CO: Lynne Rienner Publishers.

Varese, Stefano. 1996. "The ethnopolitics of Indian resistance in Latin America." *Latin American Perspectives* 23(2): 58–71.

Vasconcelos, José. 1961. *La raza cósmica: Misión de la raza iberoamericana.* Mexico City: Aguilar S. A. Ediciones.

Veltmeyer, Henry. 2007. *On the move: The politics of social change in Latin America.* Peterborough, Ontario: Broadview Press.

Veltmeyer, Henry, and James Petras. 2002. "The social dynamics of Brazil's Rural Landless Workers' Movement: Ten hypotheses on successful leadership." *Canadian Review of Sociology and Anthropology* 39(1): 79–96.

Vía Campesina. 2003. "What is food sovereignty?" (accessed December 14, 2007).

———. 2004. "Campaña Global por la Reforma Agraria. Memoria de la Reunión del Grupo Facilitador." Honduras, Marzo 24–25.

———. 2006. "Seminario sobre el Feminismo de las Mujeres de Vía Campesina 18–21 de octubre 2006." Galicia. (accessed December 14, 2007).

Vía Campesina, et al. n.d. "Statement on People's Food Sovereignty: OUR WORLD IS NOT FOR SALE, Priority to Peoples' Food Sovereignty" (accessed December 14, 2007).

Vila, Pablo. 2000. *Crossing borders, reinforcing borders: Social categories, metaphors, and narrative identities on the U.S.-Mexico frontier.* Austin: University of Texas Press.

Vilas, Carlos. 1996. "Neoliberal social policy: Managing poverty (somehow)." *NACLA Report on the Americas* 29(6): 16–25.

———. 1997. "Participation, inequality, and the whereabouts of democracy." Pp. 3–42 in Douglas A. Chalmers et al. (eds.), *The new politics of inequality in Latin America: Rethinking participation and representation.* New York: Oxford University Press.

Villalón, Roberta. 2002. "Piquetes, cacerolazos y asambleas vecinales: Social protests in Argentina, 1993–2002." Master's thesis, University of Texas at Austin. http://www.utexas.edu/cola/depts/llilas/content/claspo/PDF/dissertations/Villalon.pdf.

Villegas Quiroga, Carlos. 2004. *Privatización de la industria petrolera en Bolivia: Trayectoria y efectos tributarios,* 3rd edition. La Paz, Bolivia: FOBOMADE/CIDES-UMSA/Diakona/CEDLA.

Wade, Peter. 1993. *Blackness and racial mixture: Dynamics of racial identity in Colombia.* Baltimore: Johns Hopkins University Press.

———. 1997. *Race and ethnicity in Latin America.* London: Pluto Press.

———. 2000. *Law 70* (Law of the Black Communities). Chicago: Northwestern University; the Institute of Diasporic Studies.

Ward, Kathryn (ed.). 1990. *Women workers and global restructuring.* Ithaca, NY: ILR Press.

Warren, Jonathan W. 2001. *Racial revolutions: Antiracism and Indian resurgence in Brazil.* Durham, NC, and London: Duke University Press.

Watson, Alan (ed.). 1985. *The digest of justinian.* Philadelphia: University of Pennsylvania Press.

———. 1995. *The spirit of Roman law.* Athens: University of Georgia Press.

Webber, Jeffery R. 2005. "'Agenda de Octubre' or 'Agenda de Enero'? The regionalization of class struggle and popular indigenous rebellion in Bolivia." *Against the Current #116* 20(2): 13–15.

Webster, Neal. 2004. "Understanding the evolving diversities and originalities in rural social movements in the age of globalization." United Nations Research Institute for Social Development, Civil Society and Social Movements Programme Paper 7: 1–39.

Weedon, Chris. 1987. *Feminist practice and poststructuralist theory*. Oxford: Blackwell.

Weffort, Francisco C. 1991. "La América errada." *Revista Foro*, no. 15 (September): 90–108.

Weinberg, Bill. 2003. "News from the south: Focus on Honduras." *Indian Country Today* (August 13). http://www.indiancountry.com/content.cfm?id=1060799505 (accessed December 13, 2007).

———. 2007. "The Return of Plan Puebla-Panama," World War 4 Report. 1 May. www.ww4report.com/node/3751 (accessed June 6, 2007).

Welch, Cliff. 1999. *The São Paulo roots of Brazil's rural labor movement, 1924–1964*. University Park: Penn State University Press.

———. 2001. *Grass war, peasant struggle in Brazil* [video]. New York: Cinema Guild.

———. 2005. "Estratégias de resistência do movimento camponês brasileiro em frente das novas táticas de controle do agronegócio transnacional." *Revista NERA* 8(6): 35–45.

———. 2006. "Movement histories: A preliminary historiography of Brazil's Landless Laborers' Movement (MST)." *Latin American Research Review* 41(1): 198–210.

Wilpert, Greg. 2007. *Changing Venezuela by taking power: The history and policies of the Chavez government*. London: Verso.

Wieacker, Franz. 1995. *A history of private law in Europe*. Oxford: Clarendon Press.

Williams, Heather L. 2001. *Social movements and economic transition: Markets and distributive conflict in Mexico*. New York: Cambridge University Press.

Winn, Peter. 1986. *Weavers of revolution: The Yarur workers and Chile's road to socialism*. Oxford: Oxford University Press.

World Bank. 1993. "Water resources management: Policy paper." Washington, DC.

———. 1994. "Ecuador—structural adjustment loan." Report No. PIC1551. December 13.

———. 1999. "Bolivia: Public expenditure review." Washington, DC.

———. 2000. "Ecuador—structural adjustment loan." Report No. PID9029. June 13.

———. 2003. "Evaluation of the World Bank group's activities in the extractive industries." Background Paper, Ecuador Country Case Study, Operations Evaluation Department. January 5.

———. 2004. "Ecuador poverty assessment." Report No. 27061-EC. April.

———. 2005. "World development indicators database." Washington, DC.

World Bank Inspection Panel. 2001. "Investigation report on Ecuador mining development and Environmental Control Technical Assistance Project." Report No. 21870. Loan Number 3655-EC. February 23.

Wright, Agnus, and Wendy Wolford. 2003. *To inherit the Earth: The landless movement and the struggle for a new Brazil*. Oakland, CA: Food First Books.

Wright, Melissa. 1998. "Maquiladora mestizas and a feminist border politics: Revisiting Anzaldúa." *Hypatia* 13(3): 114–31.

———. 2001. "Feminine villains, masculine heroes, and the reproduction of Ciudad Juárez." *Social Text* 19(4), Winter: 93–113.

Yashar, Deborah. 2005. *Contesting citizenship in Latin America: The rise of indigenous movements and the postliberal challenge*. Cambridge: Cambridge University Press.

Young, Gerardo, Lucas Guagnini, and Alberto Amato. 2002. "Piqueteros: La cara oculta del fenómeno que nació y crece con el desempleo." *Clarín*, September 26.

Young, Iris Marion. 1989. "Polity and group difference: A critique of the ideal of universal citizenship." *Ethics* 99 (January): 250–274.

Yúdice, George. 1998. "The globalization of culture and the new civil society." Pp. 353–379 in Sonia Alvarez, Evelina Dagnino, and Arturo Escobar (eds.), *Cultures of politics, politics of cultures: Re-visioning Latin American social movements*. Boulder, CO: Westview Press.

Zamosc, Leon. 2004. "The Indian movement in Ecuador: From politics of influence to politics of power." Pp. 131–57 in Nancy Grey Postero and León Zamosc (eds.), *The struggle for indigenous rights in Latin America*. Brighton, England: Sussex Academic Press.

Zermeño, Sergio. 1989. "El regreso del líder: crisis, neoliberalismo y desorden." *Revista Mexicana de Socología* 101 (October/December): 115–150.

Zibechi, Raúl. 2005. "Subterranean echos: Resistance and politics 'desde el sótano.'" *Socialism and Democracy* 19 (November): 13–39.

———. 2006. "Indigenous movements: Between neoliberalism and leftist governments." IRC Americas Program. Silver City, NM: International Relations Center.

Žižek, Slavoj. 1990. "Beyond discourse-analysis." Pp. 249–260 in Ernesto Laclau (ed.), *New reflections on the revolution of our time*. London: Verso.

Zorrilla, Carlos. 2006. "The police raid on my house." *Counterpunch* (October 26). http://www.counterpunch.org/zorrilla10262006.html (accessed 31 July 2007).

Index

About the Contributors

Isabella Alcañiz is assistant professor of political science at the University of Houston, Texas.

Marc Becker is associate professor of Latin American history at Truman State University, Kirksville, Missouri.

Kwame Dixon is assistant professor in the Department of African-American Studies at Syracuse University, Syracuse, New York.

Judith Adler Hellman is professor of social and political science at York University, Toronto, Canada.

Daniela Issa is a Ph.D. candidate in sociology at the Ecole des Hautes Etudes en Sciences Sociales (EHESS) in Paris.

Glen David Kuecker is associate professor of Latin American history at DePauw University, Greencastle, Indiana.

María Elena Martínez-Torres is professor and researcher at the Center for Research and Graduate Education on Social Anthropology-Southeast Campus (CIESAS-Sureste), San Cristóbal de las Casas, Chiapas, Mexico.

Mariana Mora is a PhD candidate in anthropology at the University of Texas at Austin.

Keisha-Khan Y. Perry is assistant professor of Africana studies and anthropology at Brown University, Providence, Rhode Island.

Peter M. Rosset is a researcher at the Center for the Study of Rural Change in Mexico (CECCAM), and co-coordinator, Land Research Action Network (www.landaction.org).

Melissa Scheier is assistant professor of political science at Georgetown College, Georgetown, Kentucky.

Verónica Schild is associate professor of political science at the University of Western Ontario, London, Canada.

David Slater is professor of social and political geography at Loughborough University, Loughborough, United Kindgom.

Rose J. Spalding is professor of political science at DePaul University, Chicago, Illinois.

Susan Spronk is a postdoctoral fellow in industrial and labor relations at Cornell University, Ithaca, New York.

Richard Stahler-Sholk is associate professor of political science at Eastern Michigan University, Ypsilanti.

Joanna Swanger is assistant professor and director of the Peace and Global Studies Program at Earlham College, Richmond, Indiana.

Alicia C. S. Swords is assistant professor of sociology at Ithaca College, Ithaca, New York.

Harry E. Vanden is professor of government and international affairs at the University of South Florida, Tampa.

Roberta Villalón is assistant professor of sociology at St. John's University, New York City.

Jeffery R. Webber is a PhD candidate of political science at the University of Toronto, Toronto, Canada.